The Punishment Response

The Punishment Response

Graeme Newman

Second Edition

With a new introduction by the author

Transaction Publishers

New Brunswick (U.S.A.) and London (U.K.)

New material this edition copyright © 2008 by Transaction Publishers, New Brunswick, New Jersey. Copyright © 1985 by Graeme Newman.

This book is printed on acid-free paper that meets the American National Standard for Permanence of Paper for Printed Library Materials.

Library of Congress Catalog Number: 2008019276
ISBN: 978-1-4128-0784-5
Printed in the United States of America

Library of Congress Cataloging-in-Publication Data
Newman, Graeme R.
  The punishment response / Graeme Newman ; with a new introduction by the author. -- 2nd ed.
       p. cm.
  Originally published: 2nd ed. Albany, N.Y. : Harrow and Heston, c1985.
  Includes bibliographical references and index.
  ISBN 978-1-4128-0784-5
    1. Punishment. I. Title.

HV8688.N495 2008
364.6—dc22
                                                                    2008019276

To the Memory of
Two Mothers,
Maisie and Elsie

Contents

Preface

Although much of this book is lightly historical and descriptive, it was written with a definite purpose: to search for a morality in this relativistic age. It has been a very painful process, and it is not until the last chapter, when I try to fly out of the pleasant mist of historical and scientific detail, that my pursuit becomes truly serious. Of course, one cannot find morality in one little book. But one can set the groundwork for the search, and it seemed to me that punishment was a good place to start.

The final chapter represents the bare conclusions at which I have arrived. I am aware of the highly schematic, speculative nature of the argument that I have outlined and that many of the views are, perhaps, shocking to some. I have tried to follow Norman Brown's example, to have the courage to pursue ideas to their logical, even if apparently outrageous, conclusions. In this regard, I am pleased to thank my former professor, Philip Rieff, for having helped me rediscover Freud's writings on culture. And among the many works I have used, Sir Leon Radzinowicz's *History of English Criminal Law* stands out as an indispensible source.

Once again, I thank my colleagues at the Graduate School of Criminal Justice and Deans Vincent O'Leary and Donald Newman, the University at Albany, for providing near perfect conditions for scholarly endeavor. Jack Kress, Ernest van den Haag, Bob Meier, and Joan Newman assiduously reviewed the manuscript, and I have benefited greatly from their helpful criticisms. My students also have had considerable input in the sharpening of my ideas. I thank them all.

The editing process has been made painless under the easy hand of Dick Heffron and the excellent copy editing of Dorothy Hoffman. Jo Anne DeSilva has typed and retyped the manuscript with an ease that I take too much for granted. I thank her deeply.

GRAEME NEWMAN
Albany, August 1977

Preface to the Second Edition

Foucault's challenging classic *Discipline and Punish* appeared in English only just as *The Punishment Response* was published. However, when I wrote this book, I was strongly influenced by Foucault's other writings, especially *Madness and Civilization*. In my view, Foucault remains the most challenging writer on punishment.

There are points of agreement and of divergence between *Discipline and Punish* and *The Punishment Response*. We agree as to the political and moral functions that punishment has fulfilled throughout history, especially the tendency more and more to its abstraction and symbolic representation. However, the full import of Foucault's position has not been properly understood because of his less than forthright exposition. The sensational opening description of the drawing and quartering of Damiens seduces the gullible reader into believing that what we have today *has to be better than that*. My reading of Foucault suggests that he was not at all that certain. He argues, using a metaphor derived from Bentham's Panopticon, that punishment has overflowed its banks, reaching out to all people in a "Panoptic" society. Punishment, through its transformation into discipline has produced a society in which all people are highly disciplined, and in which prisons are the mere reflection of this state of surveillance.

The thesis that readers of Foucault have subsequently ignored is that *the total amount of punishment in society today may be far, far greater than it was during the periods of public punishments like that of Damiens*. While it may be said that we find bodily punishments more repulsive, and more intense as punishments, the inescapable thesis in Foucault is that it is not altogether a good thing that we have developed this "disciplined" society; that we have paid a high price for this "progress."

I now think that I did not fully understand this point when I wrote *The Punishment Response*. Indeed, in a couple of places, I remarked with some confidence, that we had indeed made progress in our treatment of criminals. Although I was aware of the difficulty of the word "progress" when applied

xii   *The Punishment Response*

to civilization, I did not fully realize the import of this assumption in regard to punishment. Having read *Discipline and Punish* I looked further into this problem, and I began to pursue the implications of taking the opposite position—that is, that no progress had been made at all. I came up with some startling conclusions which were spelled out in *Just and Painful: A Case for the Corporal Punishment of Criminals*.

A point on which I was criticized in the first edition was my ambiguity concerning the principle of deterrence. My equivocation on this issue arose from two sources. First, there is ambiguity within the notion of retribution. Ernest van den Haag has argued that all punishment, including retribution, is essentially deterrence, and I think that when it's all boiled down, this is probably right. However, there are degrees of coercion (another word for deterrence) and some justifications of punishment allow for more than do others. Certain simple forms of retribution allow for very little (''old retribution'' as I have called it in *Just and Painful*), whereas others (preventive detention on the basis of predicted dangerousness; use of the death penalty as a deterrent; use of severe punishments such as prison terms for hitherto less serious offences, such as mandatory sentences for handgun possession) allow for considerably more coercion.

Second, ambiguity may have arisen from my advocacy of harsh treatments for some criminals. This was interpreted as *de facto* deterrence, since all treatment models appear to assume a utilitarian logic, and can be seen as a sub-type of deterrence. The error here was that I should have attended more closely to the specifics of the kinds of offenders who *deserve* such treatment, and those who do not. I confronted this question in *Just and Painful* and tried to answer it there. The solution lies in a clear and drastic differentiation between those offenders who should be locked up, and those who should not.

Certainly, any discussion about policies of punishment or the application of punishment makes absolutely no sense without an assessment as to the seriousness of offences, the kinds of offences, kinds of offenders, and their matching to the quality and severity of punishments.

A major point I learned from writing this book was the significance historically of the quality of punishments and their qualitative matching to crimes. The majority of corrections texts today do not recognize this at all. Nor do the courts in their sentencing practices—although some judges have begun to show more creativity in their approach to sentencing than have academic penologists.

What now? It is my view that if penology (better than the misnomer ''corrections'') is to take a new direction, closer attention needs to be given to the question of the quality of punishments. We need to develop a taxonomy of punishments; to encourage creativity in the matching of punishments to crimes. If *The Punishment Response* does nothing else, it reminds us that not too long ago, society had available to it a fantastic range of punishments. There was a "feeling" for the quality of punishments which we seem to have lost. Today, this feeling has been translated into one dimension: that of prison.

We have learned that punishment is almost entirely symbolic, abstract and unreal—although its "unintended" outcomes are tragically real. I have little doubt that historians of the 21st century will look back on prisons as one of the major tragedies of our time, just as we, with such smugness look back in horror at the punishment of Damiens. Hopefully, since punishment has become so abstract, we will be able to think our way out of it. But I doubt it. The symbolic force of punishment will ensure that any rational solution is put to other uses.

GRAEME NEWMAN
Albany, May 1985

Introduction to the Transaction Edition

Marvin Wolfgang (who had been the chair of my dissertation committee), was quite taken aback when I mentioned that I had written a book on punishment. I did not tell him that I had written this book partly because of a book he had co-edited, *The Sociology of Punishment and Corrections* (Johnston et al. 1970), in which I could find no chapter at all on what I thought of as punishment—that is, the intentional infliction of pain or other consequences commonly considered unpleasant on an offender. It seemed to me then, and still does, that the enormous institutional contraptions that have arisen to deal with those who have broken the law are driven at their core by the need or necessity to punish.

Of course, there were various textbooks that reviewed the history of punishment, cataloging in sequential fashion the change in punishment forms from violent to non-violent (Barnes 1972). But none of them addressed the institutional and cultural factors that seemed to me intertwined with punishment, such as why punishment changed its forms at particular times in history and why it changed its administrative structure. Foucault's *Discipline and Punish* had appeared in French a little before *The Punishment Response*, and when I read his book I was greatly impressed by his having addressed many of the issues that I thought were lacking in contemporary scholarship on punishment. In my book, I had muddled ahead, overwhelmed by the detail of punishments of bygone days, trying to understand why people did such terrible things to others. I was startled and felt considerably exonerated (not sure from what, though one of my colleagues when I was being considered for promotion labeled my book as "esoteric") by Foucault's opening the book with the now-acclaimed description of the drawing and quartering of Damiens. It was those punishments that had attracted my scholarly attention from the very beginning of *The Punishment Response*. I spent much time pondering over their cultural and societal significance. Foucault seemed to put his finger on the institutional significance of the changes in punishment's functioning in society, and what pleased me most was that he placed punishment at the center, rather than at the periphery of the study of society or culture. So, in my preface to the second edition of this book, I embarrassingly echoed the culture of adoration that had rapidly arisen in response to Foucault's poetically coined prose. He had moved the attention of social theorists, especially sociologists, on to punishment as a central institution worthy of study in itself, making it no longer possible for such theorists to assume that punishment was simply a product of class relations. Punishment was now either independent of, or anterior to, such standard sociological concepts. Yet this view of punishment did not gain weight among criminologists until Garland's (1993) *Punishment and Modern Society* gave a kind of official academic countenance to the study of punishment in society as a legitimate field of study, no longer a topic of fringe interests, or of curiosity.

Much has been written about punishment in society since *The Punishment Response*, too much for me to review in this brief introduction. However, I do not think that the basic questions I raise in this book have been addressed by criminologists or penologists. Perhaps this is the fault of my writing, since much of the argument of the book was hidden behind the historical details of punishment and embedded in an explicit Freudian framework. I came under considerable pressure from my publisher and reviewers of the manuscript to drop the Freudian theory, particularly the last chapter, but I stubbornly clung to it. I did this because it was as far as I could see the only theory that addressed adequately the basic questions of where punishment came from and why it was so intimately linked to violence. In retrospect, I think that the theory overshadowed what was the equally important idea of reciprocity, which I also thought then, and still do, was the necessary foundation for just about everything in human affairs. Reciprocity is wired into our brains (Cory 1999; Dawkins 1999; King-Casas et al.), and is probably mathematically necessary for maintenance of social life (by which I mean social order). This idea was overshadowed by Freud's assumption that violence (his proxy for libido in his later writings) is also wired into our brains. In fact, if I were to write this book over, I would replace the Freudian context with neo-Darwinian theory, which largely parallels or even supports Freud's explanation of punishment (Badcock 1995; Plotkin 1997; Sulloway 1992), without the overbearing preoccupation with sex and violence. In what follows,

I will illuminate further the role of reciprocity and force (my word for violence which has too many other meanings) in the explanation of punishment. Hopefully, this will make much of the book clearer to the reader.

Reciprocity as the Core of Social Affairs

Reciprocity in everyday life appears in many forms and lies hidden behind much if not all social interaction. For example, gift giving is expected to be reciprocated; even though we moralize that one should not give a gift in order to receive one. And rightly so: the giving of gifts should be "thoughtless" that is, the ingrained, submerged assumption of social interaction. If someone holds open a door for me, I respond "thank you." If I do not, I may be upbraided for rudeness.

Why does this principle of reciprocity exist? Without reciprocity, the basic necessity that all exchanges with others produce balanced ("fair" or "just") outcomes would collapse into violence and tyranny, since the brute force of individuals so endowed would win out. Societies with tyrannical and deceptive types of social arrangements have much shorter lives. This idea has been extensively investigated by biologists and ethologists, and simulated in the computer lab (Dawkins 1989; Ridley 1996; Axelrod 2006). There is now persuasive evidence that in contexts in which there is more than one individual of the same (sometimes even different) species certain patterns of interaction arise. The most dominant and persistent is one in which each individual returns a response that is the same as that which he receives. Thus, if A is hit by B, B hits back. There are many variations of this model (known as "Tit for Tat"), but they all demonstrate one important and basic element of all social groups: the reciprocal form of cooperation/competition is as essential as time and space to understand not only individual behavior, but also the behavior of groups. It is the foundation of all economic discourse: an economic exchange between two strangers depends entirely on the assumption that if I provide an article that you want, you will give me something in return (money, or barter). Without such reciprocity—the value term for it is "trust" (Cory 1999; Phelps 1975) or the legal term for it is "contract"—societies die.[1] Adam Smith (1776) marveled at the trust required in the market place when strangers exchanged goods and services even though each person was motivated by self interest.

Punishment and Reciprocity

Punishment expresses reciprocity in five different, though often intermingled ways.

1. Reflection

Reflection is the pure form of reciprocity in punishment. The idea of returning like for like is embedded in Judeo Christian culture (Chapter 3). The bible is full of such exhortations as "an eye for an eye." The principle of turning the offender's crime against himself as a punishment is embedded in everyday life. It is so basic that we take it for granted. For example, in the USA in 2002 there was a television commercial that promoted milk as a necessary companion to eating cookies. The scenario went as follows: A young man is eating a cookie at the zoo. He offers the cookie to a monkey through the bars of its cage, but snatches it away before the monkey can grab it. His crime is that he teases and torments the monkey. Then we see the man trying to purchase milk to go with his cookie. The vendor immediately pulls down a barrier over the counter, then proffers the milk to the man, pulling it away before he can grab it. The punishment, now, parallels the suffering of the monkey. We can see in this commercial that the offender, who teases and "tortures" the poor chimp is subjected to exactly the same offence, only this time we all enjoy seeing him "get what he deserved." There is little doubt that his punishment is a close reproduction of his own crime. Why does it make us feel so good? Why do we enjoy seeing the offender "taste his own medicine?" It is because of the elemental expression of reciprocity. His crime is exactly matched with his punishment. The advertisement has effectively used concepts (or more precisely sentiments) that are deeply embedded in our brains.

2. Specificity

In the 17th century, highly specific punishments were available for particular crimes (Chapter 6). For example, the scold's bridle was a contraption reserved for women who talked too much and spread gossip. The basic design of these bridles was to pin or constrict the offender's tongue so that she could not talk. This was a specific punishment for a specific crime. The modern counterpart to this practice of matching a specific punishment to a specifically identified part of the body held responsible for the crime is operant conditioning. In the movie *A Clockwork Orange* (based on the book by William Burgess) the violent murderer receives painful stimuli applied to him each time he looks at the kind of violence he himself had committed. While the crime itself is not exactly matched, it is nevertheless used as the reference point for the punishment/treatment. The ultimate design of this punishment is the same as the scold's bridle: to incapacitate the specific offending part of the body. This process is different from the symbolic substitution discussed below. There, a body part is substituted for the crime. In the current case, the body "part" (the biologically driven desire to do violence) is identified as the seat or cause of the crime. Obviously, castration of rapists, still legally permissible in parts of the United States, is another apt example.

3. Symbolic Substitution

In the realm of formal criminal law it is difficult to turn an offender's crime back on to him as the punishment. There are various reasons for this, not the least of which is that if a rapist were sentenced to be raped by law, it would be difficult to distinguish between the crime and the punishment. The way around this literal matching problem is to transform the elements of the crime into something else so that the punishment represents the basic elements of the crime in particular ways. This transformation is usually achieved through symbolic substitution. Socially or culturally acceptable substitutes may be made for basic elements of the crime, so that the punishment is able to achieve a level of justification or morality superior to that of the crime. For example, the practice of burning heretics at the stake during the Holy Inquisition was a punishment that transformed their crime of heresy (mere words after all, and not violent in themselves) into a violation against God and Heaven, so that the most appropriate punishment was to visit the heretics with Hell on Earth: to be consumed by fire (Chapter 3). A similar secular example occurred in the punishment of sailors at sea in the 18th century and, very likely, of boys who were caned in boarding schools. Disobedience was deemed "dishonorable." So the offender was whipped on his "dishonorable part" (the buttocks) to match the dishonorable act of disobedience.

4. Rational Abstraction

Closer to the realm of philosophy is the abstract idea that philosophers have proposed since the time of Aristotle at least, that a crime disturbs a mystical balance, perhaps of nature or of society. The belief in the balance of nature is entrenched in many societies, and probably forms the basis of the modern ecological movement. Whatever its basis, the idea that crime throws something out of balance which must then be corrected is truly ancient. Another view of balance, more prosaic (indeed Darwinian), is the assumption that the offender achieves an advantage over those who do not offend. Thus, the assessment of his advantage, usually expressed in terms of the seriousness of his offense is weighed against a punishment that is deemed to be of equal disadvantage for the offender (see the utilitarian theories of Bentham and others, Chapter 8). This balance has been achieved in punishment through two basic concepts: space and time.

Space. Perhaps the most primitive way of recreating the balance of nature when disturbed by a crime was to attend to the geography of the crime. Crimes and punishments occur in particular locations. In medieval England, it was common to identify the place in which the crime was committed. Then, the offender would be punished in that exact location. Or, if that were not possible, the offender, once executed, would be hung in chains or irons on the site of the crime. Another use of space in punishment has been the idea of confinement. The earliest uses of confinement were those of simple stocks, in which offenders were clamped or chained for specified periods. These confining punishments were later transformed into punishments in their own right, using space as the major element of the punishment itself: situated in the village square in full public view, used for crimes that seemed to invite the contribution of public sentiment to the punishment. The public was invited to enter into discourse by either adding more punishment to the offender (pelting him with stones or garbage) or to mitigate the punishment, by attaching notes of encouragement for an offender they considered inappropriately punished (See Chapter 6). These are examples of an interactive reciprocity, in which the punishers (i.e., the onlookers) engage in a dialog or discourse with the offender.

Time. Embedded in this abstract idea of recovering the balance disturbed by the crime is the assumption of measurement: the scales of justice demonstrate this beautifully. Thus, it is not too difficult to conclude that if we can assess the gravity or seriousness of the crime we can then match it with a punishment that is equal in seriousness, thus restoring the balance, and canceling out the crime.[2] Perhaps this is the single most important insight into the relationship between punishment and crime that has occurred throughout its history: the idea of quantifying punishment. An offender receives a particular number of strokes of the lash for his infraction. The number of strokes, of course, would depend on the abstract assessment of the seriousness of the offence. One can see that this requires the transformation of a concrete crime into an abstract crime whose measure of gravity is the quantification (that is, abstraction) of a concrete punishment (number of lashes).[3] This punishment is composed of the two basic elements of punishment: duration and frequency.

Let us look at these more closely. The lash is a form of punishment that lends itself to the application of many short pains, so its severity can most simply be adjusted according to the number of lashes administered (frequency). The duration of the punishment can be adjusted by regulating the time between each lash. (The intensity with which the lash is applied is also an important variable, but this element properly lies with the force of punishment which will be discussed below). However, the punishment that uses duration to great effect is, of course, prison. It is also a major user of space as confinement. Prison has become the modern solution to matching punishments to crimes. Its success in solving this problem is demonstrated by the universal use of prison throughout the world, in all kinds of societies, and all kinds of cultures (Newman, 1999).

Once we have made the step of transforming the concrete details of a crime into an abstraction of seriousness or gravity, there is no end to the logical punishments that can be constructed to match this transformed crime. The main punishment that has ensued from this process of abstraction (some would call it a civilizing process) is prison, whose abstraction hides the kinds of pain and suffering concretely experienced. The pains of imprisonment vary tremendously, many of them highlighted in popular movies, almost since the beginning of cinema. Examples include, *Cool Hand Luke, The Wild Ones, Shawshank Redemption, Bird Man of Alcatraz,* and many others. Yet we continue to pretend that the punishment is only that of time spent in "deprivation of liberty" when in actual fact many other pains are suffered. We will return to this issue again when we examine force in punishment.

5. Satisfaction

Satisfaction refers to the emotional satisfaction felt by the punisher or punishers, whether a third party or the victim, upon seeing the punishment carried out. Here, the close matching of the punishment to the crime is essential for satisfaction. At the simplest level, if there is no clear matching of punishment to crime, a sense that justice has been denied results. For example, a case occurred in Manhattan—and similar cases occur almost on a weekly basis—in which a young man was shot to death in Central Park because he would not turn down his radio (Newman, 1983). The 17-year-old offender was convicted of murder, and received three years' probation. The mother of the victim cried "There's no justice! He snuffed out my son's life for no reason. Why shouldn't he be made to suffer?" Clearly, there was no satisfaction here. We may observe also that given the restraints today on the lengths to which punishment may be taken, some crimes are impossible to match with satisfaction. Take for example, the execution of Timothy McVeigh for the Oklahoma City bombing, in which 168 people were killed. How could just one painless death (or even tortured death) match this horrendous crime?

Satisfaction may be obtained through several mechanisms that contribute to the validation of the punishment by demonstrating to the punisher and to onlookers that the punishment has had an effect, usually the desired effect. In their different ways these forms of punishment produce a special kind of satisfaction: the righteousness of the punishers and their supporters. But all of them are tied in some way to the crime itself. Let us look at some examples of each.

Sweet Revenge. "Revenge is sweet," so the saying goes. Sweet revenge is usually achieved by individuals acting alone, who get back at offenders by the use of cunning pranks, sometimes even referred to as "jokes." Their results bring about much personal satisfaction. There are several web pages devoted to personal revenge. The main one is *Revenge Unlimited.* This home page informs us:

> Welcome to Revenge Unlimited. Have you been wronged, mistreated, annoyed or ignored? Is someone tormenting you beyond what you can bare? Are you ready for some PAYBACK?! Do you feel that a good prank is an ART FORM? (http://revengeunlimited.com/default.asp).

There are also sites that view the revenge as a magical process. Take a look at the site that offers a divine voodoo spiritual spell casting service.

> Problem: My husband/wife/boyfriend/girlfriend/lover (gay or straight) left me for someone else:…you may want to use a spell kit such as Go Away Man or Go Away Woman, a Voodoo Revenge Doll, or perhaps even The Ultimate Revenge Kit (see warnings about using The Ultimate Revenge Kit), depending on your situation and the seriousness of the affair (http://www.spellmaker.com/).

One of the more interesting aspects of personal revenge is the personal satisfaction of accomplishing the revenge. In one of the many cases described in George Hayduke's *Up Yours* (1982) an individual got back at a bully who bullied him in College. He waited until the bully took a couple of days off and cut classes. He then called up the University Administration pretending to be the undertaker from the bully's home town, and informed the university that the bully had died, and to remove his name from all the class lists. To round this off he called the bully's parents and informed them that their son had died as a result of a party prank. What is significant about this and many other cases of sweet revenge is that they occur in secrecy, and even the victim (i.e., the person got back at) does not know who played the prank.

Violent Revenge. Popular culture is heavily devoted to this theme and variations of it. The entire justification for the crime fighting lives of Batman and The Lone Avenger are based on the apocryphal event of a dreadful injustice occurring to them or their family during childhood (Newman 1993). Batman (Pearson and Urrichio 1991; Miller 1986) especially is portrayed as a kind of vigilante. Of course, the quintessential movie that exploited this notion of revenge was that of *Death Wish*, where the urge for revenge, though quenched, eventually became uncontrollable. This movie, and the many that followed it, demonstrates how deep and forceful is the feeling for revenge. The hero of *Death Wish* carefully plans his revenge, and when confronted with the first opportunity to kill, his emotions almost get the better of him. But he carries out the act, performing his first kill in response to the rape and killing of his wife and daughter. He finds, though, that the satisfaction from this vengeful killing is so great, that he seeks out more "deserving" criminals upon whom he can vent his vengeful rage. Revenge, whether sweet or violent, is always done in the name of justice. Furthermore in these vigilante movies, there is often a tacit, if not open approval by the formal law enforcement authorities. *Death Wish* ends with the detective telling the vigilante to "get out of town by sundown," an approving nod to Wild West movies that use violence to obtain justice.

Affirmation of the Accused. The punisher, in order to achieve satisfaction from the punishment, must see that the accused has been affected by the punishment in some way. This is usually achieved through an affirmation of the accused that he or she has understood the connection between the punishment (or threatened punishment) and the offence. Of course, there is almost always a question of the sincerity of a confession (or, its counterpart, an apology). How does the punisher or participants in the punishment (i.e., onlookers or victims of the crime) become convinced that the offender has truly felt and understood the punishment, particularly its connection to the offence? There is only one sure way: by clear visibility of pain and suffering. In violent revenge, of course, the suffering of the offender is a foregone conclusion. But with lesser punishments, the suffering is not necessarily all that convincing. For example, in the scandal that surrounded President Clinton's behavior with an intern in the White House, President Clinton made a number of unsuccessful (unconvincing) attempts to confess his wrongdoing. The president finally managed to convince his supporters by at least displaying in public the personal pain and anguish his deeds had caused him. However, confession is often only the beginning of satisfaction as far as the observer or victim are concerned.

Credible Contrition. By far the master of the relationship between contrition and punishment is Dante, who dreamed up an amazing variety of punishments that he imagined would occur in Hell and Purgatory as a deserved payment for sins while on earth. He also specialized in matching punishments exquisitely to the offence, or at least the underlying human weakness that gave rise to the sin. To give just one example, the blasphemers in Hell were subject to an eternity of flames of fire rained down on them because in life their blaspheming talk was inflammatory...

> O'er all the sand-waste, with a gradual fall,
> Were raining down dilated flakes of fire
> (Inferno XIV, 28,29)

Who could doubt that these souls were truly suffering the punishment applied to them, and how could they escape the connection between their sin and the punishment? In sum, we see throughout the satisfaction that the punishers seek by way of the validation of the offender's suffering through confession, contrition and revenge. However, while satisfaction is reciprocally linked to the details of the crime, there is something more going on here in regard to the punisher's satisfaction. Clearly, the punishers have deep needs of their own to punish, which may go beyond matching the punishment to the crime. Indeed, in the case of *Death Wish*, the need to avenge a crime became uncontrollable, and the urge to commit violence eventually overtook the original justification of the punishment, and became, essentially, violence. Thus, we see a clear link here between reciprocity and force, to which we now turn as the second of the primary processes that contribute to punishment.

Punishment and Force

The opposing model to reciprocity that I identified in this book was that of obedience. However, at the time I wrote the book I do not think that I had quite grasped just how profound is the connection between violence and punishment. I now think that "force" comes closer to what I mean, where obedience is only one of several services that depend on force for their effectiveness. Force is also a better word than "violence" (which as we have seen also occurs in reciprocity), because it captures more the element of coercion which may or may not be part of violence. Reciprocity is concerned with keeping a balance, getting equal. Force is concerned with coercion, gaining advantage. Indeed, the essential element of force is to demand more punishment, as much as possible, without regard in many cases, to the amount of force reflected in the crime. There are four factors that produce this tendency of force to over play or exaggerate punishment.

1. Need Satisfaction

Consider some of the punishments I have so far described, such as the lash. In the 18th century, the average number of lashes for an infraction on regular navy ships was around 30, and in convict colonies in Australia, closer to 50 (Chapter 4). Or take vigilante revenge in *Death Wish*: The hero killed many more offenders than the mere two who raped and killed his family. Or, consider the revengeful killings in the *Godfather* epics, in which payback for offences against the family were paid with violence that far exceeded the offenses committed against them. There are many prints from the 16th to 18th centuries that depict punishments, all of them very violent (Kunzle, 1973; Hughes, 1968; Edgerton, 1985) and some are reproduced in this book. The inescapable conclusion is that there is a powerful force operating that sees to it that the punishments in many, if not all cases, exceed the offences to which they are applied. It is a force that overtakes reciprocity, a force which ensures that the "payback" will not be purely "tit for tat" but "tit for tat plus a little more," often a lot more. The "need"—if we can call it that, perhaps "urge" is a better word—is that of violence. One may argue that we are civilized and do not go to such violent measures today. The universal and excessive use of prison does not support this view. The violence (including AIDS) that occurs in prisons is well known. The difference today is that the violent urge in punishment is submerged, hidden from view.

2. Rule Affirmation: Obedience Is Supreme

Underlying the justification to punish, particularly when done on behalf of an authority (the accurate definition of punishment, after all, see Chapter 1), is the necessity to reassert, sometimes at horrendous cost, the affirmation by all people of the sanctity of rules and law. The Roman general Manlius ordered the execution of his own son for disobeying his order not to attack the enemy. Even though the son actually engaged the enemy and won the battle, his offense of disobeying an order could not be forgiven, and indeed more than that; his defiance of the rule was countered by excessive force (in terms of the reciprocity model): clearly an example to others. This story is vividly depicted in a 17th-century Dutch painting displayed in the Rijksmuseum in Amsterdam. The general is portrayed sitting on a throne, and his son before him with his head lopped off. Punishment constitutes not only the important opportunity to affirm the law, but also to issue a serious threat to other would-be offenders that dire consequences await them if they break the law. The reader will recognize this as the utilitarian postulate of deterrence (Chapter 10 and see below on functions of punishment).

3. Delivery

Force plays a great part in the selection or mode of delivery of the punishment. Will it be applied using a tool of some kind? Will the environment or nature be allowed to apply the punishments, as occurred to the Vestal Virgins when they were buried alive? If threats are part of violence, what kind of dreadful violence will frighten would-be offenders? How much of a role will the visibility of punishment play, given that visibility does not always play a part in the matching of punishment to crime in regard to reciprocity? And how intense will the punishment be? That is to say, how acutely painful will it be? Let us answer these questions in turn.

Visibility. Public punishments allow for the direct participation of individuals in applying the punishment. In this case the punishers act as surrogate third parties, representatives of the authority under which they serve. This type of punishment serves two main purposes: it allows public participation in the punishment, but at the same time it provides for the anonymity of the group. This is important because of the striking similarities between crime and punishment, not the least of which are that they often reflect each other's violence; they often claim the high moral ground, justifying their violence on the basis of pursuit of justice. Perhaps the most significant and obvious instance of this tension between crime and punishment is the death penalty when it is used for murder. Those who defend such punishments, the third parties, who may be either representatives of the state, or other political group, or may simply be members of a group that applies a punishment claiming its own authority (a lynch mob, for example) take certain actions in order to avoid responsibility for this doubtful enterprise of applying a punishment that looks uneasily like the crime that it so punishes! There are some interesting historical examples of this process, by which it becomes possible to shift responsibility for punishing from an individual to a group of unknown composition. Executioners have traditionally been masked, their identities protected. Firing squads supposedly include one rifle with blanks, so that it is unknown who exactly killed the offender. There are many other examples on record described in this book.

A special example is the ancient practice of stoning to death. As Jesus said, "Let he who is without sin cast the first stone." This punishment is widely viewed as a punishment in which individuals, through the anonymity of the group, unload their own guilt onto the offender by throwing stones. This form of punishment has certainly not disappeared from modern life. As recently as May, 2001, a case of stoning to death was carried out in Iran and made available on the Internet (http://www.iran-e-azad.org/stoning/video.html). These punishments continue throughout various countries of the Middle East. The public nature of these punishments does at least allow, in theory, the identification of those who participate in the punishment. This sets them apart from other kinds of punishments that allow avoidance of responsibility for the punishment. The form of punishment that allows avoidance for responsibility for the punishment is, however, the non-public punishment of prison. One could argue in fact that public punishments are morally superior to prison, because of the public and therefore accountable nature of the punishment. In contrast, prison is a silent and secretive punishment, that allows most people to applaud the punishment, but never have to face up to the details of the punishment that is applied (Newman 1983).

Intensity. Intensity, the concentration of pain and suffering put upon the offender is at the heart of punishment. It directly expresses the emotional basis of punishment, which may be described in various words as aggression, coercion, and violence. These are human attributes of which we are not especially proud, but which are probably unavoidable, and perhaps necessary, parts of social life. In terms of force, we can separate punishments into those that are acute and chronic (Newman, 1983). Acute punishments are those that apply great intensity for a short amount of time—the lash for example. Chronic punishments are those that apply a less intense amount of pain and suffering steadily over a longer period of time. Prison fits this category. Of course, it is possible to combine the two, and apply extremely acute pain and suffering intermittently over an extended period. Various forms of torture use this technique. So also does the popular punishment of "shock incarceration" which attempts to apply a form of incarceration of highly intense suffering such as personal humiliation, strict enforcement of rules etc.

4. Rationality

The rational use of force in punishment is conditioned by two factors: technology and organization. On first impression, it seems as though rationality has no place in the process of force in punishment, because we so far have viewed force as close to the emotional aspect of human behavior and therefore irrational. A moment's reflection reveals this view to be too simple. For it has been the rational use of violence in history that has probably been the most effective in achieving results. Wars, perhaps the epitome of violence, while they draw on emotions of the soldiers and fighters, nevertheless rely on the careful planning and implementing of battle plans. Thus, the roles of technology and organization are primary in the rational use of force in punishment. Often, it seems, it is the planning ahead that gives most pleasure to the avenger. The features that make force so powerful, therefore, are technology and organization.

Technology. The rationalization of punishment has, of course, been well described and critiqued by Foucault (1977). Punishments have evolved and benefited greatly from technological developments. The rough and messy executions of two or more centuries ago, requiring the hacking off of the head with a sword or axe, were improved upon by the guillotine. The invention of the drop and trap door, improved the method of hanging. And now, there is death by lethal injection, which takes technology to the ultimate in a "humane" way of applying a punishment that traditionally has been saved as the most severe and painful punishment of all. However, opponents of the death penalty now seek to demonstrate that even death by injection inflicts cruel and unusual punishment to the offender. In this case it might be concluded that technology works against the matching of punishment to the crime. The horror in the use of punishment technology has been captured in many great movies, by far the most effective being the 1958 movie, *I Want to Live*, starring Susan Hayward, which tells the story of the last woman executed in California in the gas chamber.

Prison, however, remains the ultimate solution to punishment of serious crimes. It transforms force into a bureaucratic process, and one that depends entirely on technology for is survival. There are now over two million individuals in US jails and prisons. World wide the imprisonment rate has doubled in the last ten years. Prison is a universal solution to punishment. No nation is without it. It is in fact demonstrably a product of the modern nation state, with its large bureaucracies and social services. The building and maintenance of prisons requires extensive planning and organization. Individuals have to be fed, clothed, entertained, made to suffer, made to work, and some even rehabilitated. At the same time, the inmates must be kept secure, and, because they outnumber the guards by a huge factor, must be kept in a submissive state to prevent them rising up in rebellion. The architecture of prisons is thus dictated by all these needs. The result has been a wide variety of artistic forms of prisons, in which organization, technology and art have combined to produce many prisons with imposing and menacing forms, both inside and out (Johnston 2000). The idea of prisons themselves, their isolated, secretive aura has fired the imagination of many. The most famous artworks of such inspirations are those of the Italian artist, Giovanni Battista Piranesi in his *Carceri*, etchings published in Italy in 1761. Prisons represent a crossover from technology to punitive organization.

Organization. The rational organization of criminal punishment means that the punishment, now called the "sentence" emerges after a long and often complex procedure. The judge tries to balance the two often opposing processes of reciprocity and force, which by this time is almost impossible, because he has so little to choose from. He must cope with the unreal and abstract circumstances in which the final pronouncement of the sentence (including a vague statement of the punishment) are announced in a situation that is far divorced from the original crime, maybe not even for the crime that was committed (because of plea bargaining). The rational organization of the modern criminal justice system has brought with it some important benefits, such as separation of the process of finding guilt from the infliction of punishment, which was clearly not the case in earlier times, such as with the Holy Inquisition. A great advantage here also, some would say, is that, with the delay in administering the punishment, the punishment may be decided upon with a cool head, and without the danger of over punishing. The assumption here is, though, that rational planned punishment will be more tailored to a balance with the seriousness of the offence. This is highly questionable. One need only look at the many sentences (and actual time served) applied in American criminal justice of long prison terms (two-plus years) for minor drug offences, and even one famous case of an offender sentenced to life in prison for stealing less than $100 (Newman 1983). The highly rationalized nature of criminal punishment today has in fact added to the difficulty in matching the punishment to the crime, because of the abstract nature of the punishment, and because it is not possible in many cases for the judge to specify in detail the actual punishment, and how it may match the crime. Rather, the only discretion the judge has in most serious crimes is to announce a prison term of whatever length, and even that may be mandatory. The actual punishments that the offender receives (that is, the actual pain and suffering experienced) will depend on a huge number of factors that predominate such as the kind of prison the offender is sent to, the other inmates, the architecture of the prison, the guards, the program of daily life imposed in the prison, etc. In sum, the rational organization of criminal punishment, which is largely reminiscent of the bureaucratic organization described by Max Weber (1978) and later by Foucault (1977), finally produces the sentence. It has little to do with the original crime committed. It has only a slight relationship to the final actual punishment of the offender.

The Paradoxical Relationship between Crime and Punishment

The opposition between force and reciprocity not surprisingly produces considerable puzzlement concerning the relationship between crime and punishment. For this seeming dyad—symbiotic couplet even—suggests that one cannot utter one of these words without implying the other. Or at least, one cannot utter "crime" without conjuring up its "punishment." It is through punishment that acts are essentially defined as crime; but paradoxically the crime also defines the punishment. Let me explain.

Punishment Defines Crime

First, punishment provides the essential ingredient of prohibitions: the infliction of pain and suffering for an infraction. Thus, criminal laws are essentially defined by the punishments attached to them. Without punishments, criminal laws would be useless, and would not really be criminal laws at all, because they are by definition prohibitions. Simply to enact a prohibition without a concomitant punishment, would be an "empty threat" and a useless criminal law. To see this more clearly, imagine enacting a criminal law that offered a reward, rather than a punishment, for contravening the law. This would be nonsensical.[4]

Second, criminal laws, once written down as criminal codes, legislation, or even traditional or customary law, anticipate that they will be broken. What would be the point of enacting a prohibition against some behavior if one did not expect that behavior to occur? Thus, criminal laws are not only threats but they are also *promises* to inflict pain or suffering on the offender. They create the possibility for punishment where no possibility existed before by defining an act as criminal. It also follows that we have a "right" to see it happen. After all, how does one justify breaking a promise? In sum, enacting crimes makes little sense without the prior existence or possibility of punishment. Punishment makes crime possible, but so also does crime make punishment possible by invoking it when a criminal law is enacted. That is, criminal law transforms force into punishment. Read on.

Crime Defines Punishment

First, punishment is a response. It relies on the act or acts of another for its inception. It cannot be spontaneously expressed or applied unless there is a proscribed act to which it should be applied. The relationship between the crime and the punishment that responds to it is a reciprocal relationship. The crime, therefore, is the primary reference point for the punishment. In choosing the punishment, one must begin with the crime itself. Its essential elements, its severity, its social and cultural context, will contribute heavily to the punishment that it invokes. It is, however only a starting point.

Second, if there is no crime (or other wrong committed upon an individual or group) that provides the "justification" for a matched response, there can be no punishment. The essential distinction therefore is that the punishment must occur after the crime in order to be a punishment.[5] If it occurs without a crime in many circumstances it may itself be a crime, and not a punishment. As the detective in *Death Wish* observed in regard to Kersey's vengeance: "Murder is not the answer to crime in this city."

Third, force is often a major element of criminal acts, especially those of violence and theft. In some, perhaps many, violent encounters, the participants in violence invoke justifications for their acts, which they see as justified on the basis of the perceived or actual wrong that the other commits. Such acts may or may not fit within the realm of punishment in an objective sense, and in such encounters punishment may be indistinguishable from violence. From the point of view of the person who is provoked, actions in response to provocation are often seen as applying "punishment." The work of Donald Black on crime as social control (Black, 1983) is especially relevant here, as is the analysis of "senseless murders" by Jack Katz (1988). Both these authors show that a sense of injustice motivates many acts of crime. The justifications for violence among feuding societies are also based on perceptions of injustice and the concomitant need for punishment (Newman and Marongiu, 1995). It is when such acts fall within the purview of a third party that represents an authority of some kind (whether as parent, teacher, priest or reverend, law enforcement officer, military commander, judge or jailer, or professor) that we feel more confident to term such a response a "punishment." For the moment, though, it is sufficient to observe that the overlap between punishment and force strongly suggests that both categories of action may have some common characteristics.

In sum, punishment is a response and crime is its reference point. If there is no crime, there can be no punishment. Force is their common element. So the paradox is that crime and punishment define each other reciprocally and involve a common element of force, which can make them at times virtually indistinguishable.

The Morality of Punishment in Society

The writings of Foucault (1977) and others before (Rusche and Kirkheimer 1939) and after him (Edgerton 2004; Savelsberg 1994) have reduced punishment to little more than power used in the service of tyranny. The mistake that these writers have made is to think that by uncovering the power basis of punishment they have also eradicated the idea of morality itself (Nietzsche was perhaps the first clearly to make this argument). It is certainly a reasonable observation that the forms of punishment have changed from physical forms to those of discipline as Foucault argues. But this does not mean that what we now have is a punishment process (Foucault calls it discipline, radical leftists call it structural oppression) that is intrinsically immoral or "power and nothing else" simply because it sits on a long history of what seem to us today to be disproportionate, violent punishments.

The neo-Darwinian thinkers of the past fifteen years have shown this to be a very superficial view of both the origins of tyranny (force) and of morality. On first impression, the biological and evolutionary origins of reciprocity and force would appear to be barren of moral implications, since their origins have been objectively described by biological and behavioral scientists. But "oughtness" is clearly implied in the descriptions of the behavioral processes of both reciprocity and force (Ridley 1996). Reciprocity demands a response. My act in the presence of others (actual or virtual) expects, indeed depends on you, to respond; it requires that it be reciprocal, that is an "equal" response that does not take advantage. If you open the door for me and I do not say "thank you" you rightly call me rude and self-centered. But force—that is, my (or my DNA's) drive to take advantage over others—demands that you reciprocate from a point of weakness, that is, that you obey me. The struggle between equality and dominance therefore is played out at every level of human endeavor—indeed, even in many animal species. But humans, unlike animals are able to add meaning—consciousness—to these attributes and to argue about them. So reciprocity and force are not just physical attributes tied to power, but are attributes to which are attached moral meaning. There is an embedded "rightness" in the idea that I should respond in kind to another. And if I use too much force (try to gain advantage) so the other may respond in kind by also trying to gain advantage. Thus, the escalating competition in human interaction evolves. If left without control such societies collapse since escalation ordains that inevitably one side completely destroys the other. This process occurs in real life in feuding societies, though in some of these societies ways have been worked out to head off the escalation, usually with unwritten codes of law (Newman and Marongiu 1995). Though even here, such societies constantly live on the edge of violent mutual destruction.

So while the first element of morality is composed of *expectations* of individuals to respond in kind, its second element is that of *prohibitions* in anticipation of attempts by others to gain advantage. There are clear moral exhortations in the Judeao-Christian tradition that exemplify these two basic elements of morality. "Do unto others as you would have them do unto you" is the moral exhortation of reciprocity. "Thou shalt not kill" is the moral exhortation that expresses the prohibition of force, or of gaining advantage.

In sum, the moral and the political are inextricably woven into the language of punishment so that it is close to impossible either to describe its processes or to understand its purposes in an objective manner. Thus, to attempt an analysis of the functions of punishment in society (that is, what or whose purposes does it serve?) unavoidably oversimplifies or exaggerates the roles of reciprocity or force, depending on the functions identified. This is why much of this book is taken up with descriptions of punishments in various contexts, largely free of formal analysis. In what follows, I recount the basic functions of punishment in society, all of which one may find embedded in the descriptions of punishment throughout the book. These functions may be divided into two kinds, following Merton's classic distinction between manifest and latent functions; though what is manifest and what is latent may depend on one's point of view.

Manifest Functions of Punishment

All of these functions focus on the effects of punishment on the offender. These are functions that are widely used to justify morally and politically the use of punishment in society. The link between the punishment and the individual being punished is direct and its effect on the individual is assumed to be its logical outcome. None of these acknowledge the negative effects of punishment such as creating resentment in the offender such that the punishment may be seen by the offender as nothing more than an act of violence.

1. *Obedience.* While the existence of punishment is inevitable because of the demands of reciprocity, punishment (in fact or threat) in all societies is also the lynchpin of obedience and thus to authority. To be sure, different kinds of social organization employ different kinds of punishments, often hidden from view, but they are nevertheless there as the reservoir from which those giving the orders may draw. The message of the punishment is: "Do what I tell you." And when well integrated into the authority structure of a social organization, the message is: "Do what I want you to without my having to make you." The presence or possibility of punishment is enough to ensure obedience. The ultimate aim, of course, is "Do what I want you to because you want to, not because I want you to." Here authority reaches perfection. In its less elegant but more

extreme form it tries to ape the comforting culture of authority by offering protection against unspecified future damage or injury in return for unquestioning obedience: "If you obey me, I will protect you"—the promise of protection racketeers.

2. *Deterrence.* The threat of punishment serves to deter one who would break the rules. Its aim is a little different from that of obedience. The message is, "Don't do what you want to do. If you do, I'll make you pay for it." In its extreme form it justifies punishing any individual, regardless of whether he or she has committed a crime or not. Thus, for example, the famous story of *The Lottery* by Shirley Jackson depicts a society in which individuals are randomly chosen for execution. The possibility that anyone could be punished regardless of what they have done is also closely aligned to the protection model of punishment noted above.

3. *Prevention.* There are two ways in which it is assumed that punishment will prevent crime. The first is by deterrence as described above. The threat of punishment is forward looking—aiming to prevent criminal acts in the future. These are acts that individuals contemplate, but do not carry out because of the threat of punishment. A second way in which particular types of punishment prevent crime is through those kinds of punishments that incapacitate individuals in certain ways. Prison (a form of incapacitation) of course is the obvious method of incapacitating offenders, although it ignores the new opportunities for crime that inmates may commit on each other. Other punishments such as cutting off the hand of a thief, branding or labeling offenders in ways that single them out as offenders, thus denying them anonymity, serve to incapacitate or restrict their activities.

4. *Justice.* Those who support the retributive justification most often assume that the equal punishment of an offender for his crime restores a balance, though it is often unclear exactly what is balanced. The scales of justice that commonly adorn court rooms reflect this idea. Certainly it is the affirmation that an offender may not reap the rewards of his deed, that is, he should gain no advantage by breaking the law. Others argue that it is a moral imbalance that has been disturbed by the crime. However, it is difficult to reconcile the punishment (intentional infliction of pain and suffering on an offender) as being itself a morally superior act, when it justifies itself by pointing to what it deigns to be a morally inferior act, the crime which often comprises the intentional infliction of pain and suffering on the victim.

5. *Moral education.* The fact that particular crimes are punished, usually in a public or at least formal way, teaches offenders and onlookers to the punishment, what is right and what is wrong, what is criminal and what is not. It is through punishment that individuals learn about the costs of breaking the law and about behaviors that are acceptable or prohibited. This process, traditionally used in homes, schools and churches, serves to shape whole personalities and to produce in every individual a sense of guilt, the key to obedience and to the acceptance of punishment when it is administered, indeed as psychoanalysts have argued, to offenders' need to be punished, and the identification of some offenders who commit crimes in order to be punished. In sum, guilt cuts short any plans an individual has to carry out a crime or break any rule. The individual has effectively internalized the punishment.

Latent Functions of Punishment

These functions mostly assume that punishment serves important functions for those who do the punishing and vicariously those who are onlookers to the punishment. While psychoanalysts argue that offenders need to be punished, they also say that we all have a strong need to punish them. This hidden social arrangement takes on various forms.

1. *Scapegoating.* Criminals who are infamous for their deeds often argue that they are scapegoats, used by the hypocritical masses to satisfy their own guilt at having also broken the law some time in their past and who perhaps even envy the offender's recklessness in carrying out the crime. Charles Manson is perhaps the most well known to have made this claim, though others such as Jean Genet the convict French playwright is no doubt the prototype. The most well known and eloquent encapsulation of this view of punishment is that proclaimed by Jesus, as noted above, when he said to those who were about to stone to death a woman for the crime of adultery: "Let he who is without sin cast the first stone." Each stone is a missile of guilt transferred from the onlooker or punisher to the offender (Roazen 1968:138-141; Freud 1946).
2. *Boundary definition.* Criminals are separated from the rest of us by an elaborate process that is both symbolic and functional. The

strong publicity that surrounds dreadful crimes in the present age, and the horrendous punishments administered in public in times gone by, serve an important purpose to let us tell ourselves: "We are not criminals, but they are. They must be awful criminals, otherwise they would not be receiving such terrible punishment." Thus the psychological and social distance of criminals from us is clearly established. The witch trials at Salem are a good example of boundary definition through punishment (Erickson 2004). Today, prison physically extends this separation between Us and Them and serves other important functions as well. Prisons do us much more service than public punishments, since they hide away the recipients of our punishments so we can easily forget about them. We do not even have to acknowledge what happens to offenders when they go to prison, and we can be satisfied that they are not in the prison system, but in a corrections system where they will be rehabilitated. Thus we can feel content that we are doing good when we send criminals to prison as punishment, even though it is well known by researchers and those who have spent any time inside a prison that they are horrendous places to spend a week in, let alone years.

3. *Catharsis.* The basis of this essentially Freudian theory is that aggression is an instinct that demands expression, and if not released builds up until there is terrible explosion. Thus, society has devised various ways for release of this aggression, such as through violent sports, and other legitimate channels such as criminal punishment. Crime, therefore, is necessary for society's mental health (Dollard et al. 1939: 28-35; Berkowitz 1969: 595; Miller 1941). As Nietzsche (1960:199) said: "The object of punishment is to improve him who punishes."

4. *Social solidarity.* The setting of boundaries, the identification of criminals as "them" as opposed to "us," and the urge to punish (inflict violence) produce a feeling of solidarity among those who are doing the punishing. Depending on social structure and cultural context, this feeling of solidarity is expressed as moral indignation against those who would dare to break the law (Ranulf 1938; Durkheim 1964).

5. *Reaffirmation of the social order.* A swimming pool needs regular shots of chlorine or some other sanitizer to keep it free of algae. So too does the social order which depends for its legitimacy upon the regular punishment of wrongdoers. Furthermore, the distribution

of punishment throughout the social order (that is, according to the various components of the social structure such as social class or subcultural components) affirms that structure: Since lower classes receive more punishment for the traditional crimes that they more often commit, their location in the social structure is affirmed. The rare but highly publicized punishments of those offenders from the upper echelons of society affirms the "fairness" of the distribution of the punishment. In other words, as radical criminologists would argue, punishment serves the masters of society as an effective and "legitimate" tool to keep the lowers classes in their place (Reiman 2001). While there may be some truth in this observation, it risks ignoring the equally important function of punishment in affirming the social order which is that, in distributing the punishments in tandem with the social structure (whatever it may be), it also serves to keep upper as well as the lower classes in order, though admittedly at the greater expense of the lower classes. Punishment functions to keep all members of society in order, regardless of the class structure (Durkheim 1964).

Punishment as a Result, Not a Cause

The last latent function, affirmation of the social order, leads us to a different way of explaining punishment, probably the most popular way expounded by criminologists and penologists in the 20th century. This is that punishment is not the product of basic elements of human nature, or even the interaction of basic human characteristics with historical or environmental factors, but that it is entirely manufactured by errors (as argued in part by Beccaria in the 18th century) of societal organization. These errors of human relationships are reflected in the unequal distribution of wealth and property, consequentially the exploitation of the weak by the strong (viz. of the working classes by the owners of production) which results in a biased administration of justice. Hence, there is no subconscious or even hidden function of punishment here: it is a blatant and purposeful misuse of power to keep others in suppression. In this type of theory punishment is seen not so much as a function that produces certain results (i.e., class structure), but as an *expression* of those results (Reiman 2001). Differential punishments according to class will therefore disappear once the class system is abolished. In this case punishment is an end result of faulty social arrangements. It is an effect of class structure, not its cause. That there is something wrong with this theory is quite obvious: punishment exists in all societies no matter what their structure. It is universal. Even after violent revolutions that eradicate social classes, punishment quickly assumes a central place in the administration of justice. This is why I gave rather little attention in this book to the views of radical criminologists (who were just developing their ideological theories at the time). It seemed to me that they had mixed up cause and effect.

However, there is a sense in which the idea of punishment as an expression rather than as a primary cause may be correct, which is in the explanation of the different forms of punishment, and in speculating on reasons why such changes in punishment have occurred throughout its history. There are several views of why such changes have occurred which I briefly summarize as follows:

1. *Religion.* From primitive religions to modern religions, punishment has taken an important place, whether formalized or not. In chapters 1 and 2 I suggest that the symbolic and ritual aspects of punishment can be found buried in the distant practices of primitive religion. I demonstrate why particular kinds of punishments (plowing off the head for example, reflecting the sin or crime in the punishment by extracting certain body parts) were the preferred forms of punishment in primitive times. These were times in history when prison, for example, did not exist as a punishment (though incapacitation did, such as the use of the stocks).
2. *Politics.* Kings, Queens, generals and even parliaments have used the public nature of cruel punishments to inspire awe in their subjects. So also have revolutionaries such as in the French revolution when the guillotine was used with great effect. These punishments were the primary means by which the rulers could establish an intimacy with their subjects (Foucault 1977). They could only work because the subjects themselves understood punishment in a biological sense. The rulers simply exploited a human characteristic that already existed. They did not invent it.
3. *Science.* Drawing and quartering of criminals was a messy and drawn out affair. The execution of Damiens, for example, took many hours because when it came to the stage where his limbs should be torn from his body by horses pulling each arm and leg in different directions they would not come apart, and a local butcher was enjoined

to finish the job. So too was the beheading with an axe famously botched in the case of Anne Boleyn, Henry VIII's second wife. These methods of inflicting punishment depended on the skill of the punisher. In the case of the lash, the punishers could be bribed to do either a quick or light job or to make the lashes wrap round the torso thereby inflicting greater pain. And hanging was also a ghastly affair subject to interference by onlookers who would pull down on to the dangling legs to try to hasten the death, since it typically took up to twenty minutes to die. The invention of the guillotine for beheading and the trap door for hanging made these forms of punishment much more efficient. Today, these refinements have continued with the firing squad, the application of electric shock and lethal gas in the 20th century, followed by lethal injection. Bentham invented a whipping machine (never built), and his Panopticon heralded the modern view of prisons to be designed with efficiency and security in mind as well as to inspire the awe of a fortress-like construction, so well illustrated by Piranesi.

4. *Economics.* Orthodox Marxists and others have long argued that the economic basis of society, especially capitalism, is the cause of differential punishments, especially its distribution. These days, this explanation, though it has accumulated much evidence in its favor, seems rather quaint, given that some of the most extensive punishment systems, especially prisons, have been produced by countries devoted to some form of Marxism (the prison archipelago in the old Soviet Union—which still persists now under the Sovietized form of capitalism; and the forced labor and indoctrination camps and prisons of China). The forms of punishment in the Middle East that conform to the Koran also do not seem amenable to this kind of explanation, except that they do occur in countries that are not democracies per se. So it may be that Foucault was closer to the truth: that it is raw power (tyranny) regardless of the political or ideological system that produces the amount and intensity of punishments. This explanation however also does not quite fit America's very high levels of punishment, especially its use of prison, for the USA is hardly a tyranny (unless it is of the majority as de Toqueville observed long ago). However, the most persuasive argument for the influence of economics on punishment forms is the history of the transition to prisons from the transportation of offenders to Australia and other places in England of the 18th century. The prison hulks were a blight on English pride. They

were emptied into ships not much better equipped and sent to Australia. For a while, this saved both pride and money. But eventually, transportation became far too expensive. The punishment of transportation was therefore in a matter of twenty years or less, given up in favor of a much cheaper and easier to hide system of prisons (Hughes 1987).

5. *Taste.* Good manners or tastes are part of our everyday lives. Elias (2000) has argued that manners have become refined over many generations, and that this refinement begins in the educated or upper classes and gradually trickles down to the lower or uneducated masses (the state plays a part too). His argument is essentially Freudian, such as for example, the use of the knife and fork at the table was not possible until aggression had been repressed by the civilizing process (in Freudian terms essentially the psychological sophistication arising from the emergence of the superego among the upper classes and the sublimation of the libido into art and science). The theory of change here is essentially evolutionary from a primitive state to one of complexity. Punishment, so the argument goes, has changed its forms in response to this evolution in manners, though its primary impetus (aggression, libido, etc.) nevertheless remains submerged into the societal unconscious. This is essentially Durkheim's view as expounded in his *Division of Labor* (1964, 83-87), where he argues that vengeance remains at the bottom of punishment, performing rough and ready services in the primitive society of "mechanical solidarity" and becoming more refined and precise in application when society becomes more complex in organization. Yet the idea that our discontinuance of the drawing and quartering of criminals in public is the result of the same process that made us discontinue defecating in public seems to trivialize the horrendous nature of such punishments. Worse, it seems to ignore the now obvious fact that there are still societies that do administer violent punishments in public. From which we are forced to conclude according to this theory, that such societies are primitive. Yet the simple observation that fashions come and go, carries a lot of weight, whatever the theory, when one considers such dramatic changes such as the incredible change in public behavior in countries where cigarette smoking has been banned. In my classes when I was writing this book, students routinely brought their cigarettes along with them, and ashtrays were freely available in the classroom. Today, my students bring along their bottles of

water. The idea that a student or professor could light up a cigarette in class is inconceivable. These changes in public behavior appear like viruses, they come and go so rapidly—historically speaking. The neo Darwinian, Richard Dawkins argues that these rapid changes are the cultural equivalent to DNA replication (Dawkins 1989, 1999. See also: Brodie 1996; Blackmore 1999; Lynch 1996).

What Now?

One word: *globalization*. When I wrote this book, I noted that Bentham had nightmares after reading *Lives of the Saints*, a catalogue of all the most dreadful tortures administered to the Saints over the ages. When I read of the violent punishments of criminals throughout the ages I could not have known that some of these violent punishments—the beheading of captives, for example as occurred in Iraq and elsewhere, or the stoning to death for adultery—would be available for everyone to see on the Internet and even in mainstream mass media. Although globalization of sorts has been going on for a very long time on this planet, it has not been widely acknowledged as a world changing process until the last decade, roughly coinciding with the incredible technological innovations that have produced global transportation and especially the information revolution that has ensured that the global media, including the Internet have been able to convey images and text to even the most remote corners of the world. Terrible punishments, therefore, have not gone away, and cannot be said to be effectively sublimated. Furthermore, the graphic portrayals of punishments (through violence though often now indistinguishable from punishment) in film and video games militates strongly against the idea that sublimation can keep the ever present urge for revenge in check. It is too early to say where this will lead us in the forms of punishment that will be acceptable in the future. We do know that one aspect of punishment has become universally exported around the world not only as a result of the colonial legacy but also as a result of the global trade in goods and services; and this is prison. Prisons are without doubt the universal expression of criminal punishment in every country of the world regardless of its cultural, economic or social history. Its emergence as a popular punishment has been well researched in particular countries (Botsman 2005). For example, Ignatieff (1980) says it was the industrial revolution that did it, and Rothman (1971, 1980) various matters of economic and political convenience. But these confined attempts to explain the emergence of prison as a punishment in recent years do not explain its current universality. Of course its use varies considerably in extent and intensity. Why this is so would be the subject of another book, perhaps many books. Why it is a *universal* solution to punishment, though, I explain in my book *Just and Painful* (Newman 1983).

Perhaps we can take some consolation in the re-emergence of Darwinian theory to explain not only individual but group behavior in humans. It is steadily replacing the "homo homini lupus" view of human nature, invented by the Romans, and popularized by Thomas Hobbes. I am persuaded that certain patterns of behavior are "wired" into human brains. They include reciprocity, getting even, dominance and submission, individual and group behavior that maximizes replication of DNA, cultural processes that seem to mimic biological processes, to mention just some examples. While there is much to learn, it is apparent that the dark side of human nature—violence—is just one small part of many other attributes wired into human behavior. We have not been around long on earth, but it is a fair conclusion to make at this stage that punishment has arisen for some evolutionary reason. What that reason or reasons are remain to be discovered, though some very promising beginnings have been made (Gottschalk 2001). We can already manipulate DNA, albeit in an elementary manner. If punishment plays a part in the replication of certain aspects of culture, perhaps its mechanism of replication can be accessed and changed. That is, if we have the courage to do so.

Notes

1. The study of artificial life is a new area of scientific endeavor. There is much activity on the Web, and there are many variations of the principle outlined here. To experience these artificial societies see: http://gral.ip.rm.cnr.it/luigi/alg_sci. htm.
2. It should be noted, however, that quantification itself does not guarantee balance. It is only a mechanism for doing so. Bentham introduced quantification into punishment, but he argued that the pain of the punishment should be sufficient to overtake the pleasure derived from the offence. Thus, he does not seek to exactly match the crime, but to exceed it (Chapter 8).
3. Possibly one of the early instances of the quantification of punishment was conducted in the 15th and 16th centuries during the period in which indulgences were sold by the Roman Catholic Church. The matching of the indulgences to the sins committed or to buy loved ones out of purgatory was unsystematic, however, and seemed to be related more to the "market" (a monopoly market

suitably supplemented by a "black market" in reliquaries) of how much money could be extracted rather than matching the indulgences to the gravity or number of sins. For an account of how these indulgences worked, see the excellent biography of Martin Luther (Banton, 1950) who attacked this system in his 95 theses.

4.   There are, of course, many laws that are not enforced. These are not, however, "empty laws" but laws that nevertheless offer the threat of punishment. They provide the ever present possibility that an authority may return to them and use them to affirm rules. As a general point, we may observe that it is much easier for legislators to make new laws, and much more difficult to repeal old laws. The Rockefeller Drug Laws in New York State are a prime example. Attempts to repeal or even slightly revise these harsh laws have not succeeded in thirty years. See for example http://www.prdi.org/rocklawfact.html for a brief history of attempts to change these laws.

5.   This statement is admittedly an oversimplification because it ignores the utilitarian school of punishment. The utilitarians argue for the use of punishment in order to deter others from committing crime (general deterrence). The idea of the punishment following the crime is not entirely lost here. Rather, the punishment *is* the crime in the present instance, but looking forward, it is a punishment for a crime that will occur in the future. It is a kind of "back to the future" justification of the use of punishment. See chapters 9 and 10.

References

Axelrod, Robert. (2006). *The Evolution of Cooperation*. Revised edition. New York: Perseus Books Group.

Badcock, Christopher (1995). *Psycho-Darwinism: The New Synthesis of Darwin and Freud*. New York: Harper Collins.

Banton, Roland H. 1950. *Here I Stand: A Life of Martin Luther*. New York: Mentor.

Barnes, Harry Elmer. (1972). *The Story of Punishment*. 2d ed., revised. Montclair, N.J.: Patterson Smith.

Berkowitz, (1969). The Expression and Reduction of Hostility. In Henry Clay Lindgren (ed.) *Contemporary Research in Social Psychology*. New York: John Wiley & Sons.

Black, D. (1983). Crime as social control, *American Sociological Review*, 48: 34-45r.

Blackmore, Susan (1999). *The Meme Machine*. New York: Oxford University Press.

Botsman, Daniel V. (2005). *Punishment and Power in the Making of Modern Japan*. Princeton: Princeton University Press.

Brodie, Richard (1996). *Virus of the Mind*. Seattle: Integral Press.

Cory, Gerald A. Jr. (1999). *The Reciprocal Modular Brain in Economics and Politics: Shaping the Rational and Moral Basis Organization, Exchange, and Choice*. New York: Kluwer/Plenum.

Dawkins, Richard. (1989). *The Selfish Gene*. 2d ed. New York: Oxford University Press.

Dawkins, Richard. (1999). The Extended Phenotype: The Long Reach of the Gene. New York: Oxford.

Dollard, John, Leonard W. Doob, Neal E. Miller, O. H. Mowrer, and Robert R. Sears. (1939). *Frustration and Aggression*. New Haven, CT: Yale University Press.

Durkheim, Emile (1964)[1933]. *The Division of Labor in Society.* New York: Free Press.

Edgerton, Keith (2004). *Montana Justice: Power, Punishment, & the Penitentiary.* Seattle, WA: University of Washington Press.

Edgerton, Samuel Y., Jr. (c1985). *Pictures and Punishment: Art and Criminal Prosecution during the Florentine Renaissance.* Ithaca, NY: Cornell University Press.

Elias, N. (2000). *The Civilizing Process: Sociogenetic and Psychogenetic Investigations.* London: Blackwell. Originally published 1982 in 2 volumes.

Erikson, Kai T. (2004). *Wayward Puritans: A Study in the Sociology of Deviance,* 2d. ed. New York: Allyn and Bacon.

Foucault, M. (1977). *Discipline and Punish.* New York: Pantheon.

Freud, Sigmund (1946). *Totem and Taboo.* Trans. A. A. Brill. New York: Random House.

Garland, David (1993). *Punishment and Modern Society: A Study in Social Theory.* London: Oxford University Press.

Gottschalk, Martin. (2001). *Punishment and Evolution.* Doctoral Dissertation. University at Albany.

Hayduke, George. (1982). *Up Yours! A Guide to Advanced Revenge Techniques.* Boulder, CO: Paladin Press.

Hughes, Robert. (1987). *The Fatal Shore.* New York: Knopf.

Hughes, Robert. (1968). *Heaven and Hell in Western Art.* New York: Stein and Day.

Ignatieff, Michael (1980). *A Just Measure of Pain: The Penitentiary in the Industrial Revolution,* 1750-1850. New York: Columbia University Press.

Jackson, Shirley. (1974). In Douglas Angus (ed.) *The Best Stories of the Modern Age* New York: Ballantyne.

Johnston, Norman, Leonard Savitz and Marvin E. Wolfgang (eds.) (1970). *The Sociology of Punishment and Corrections.* New York: Wiley.

Johnston, Norman. (c2000). *Forms of Constraint: A History of Prison Architecture.* Urbana and Chicago: University of Illinois Press.

Katz, Jack. (1988). *Seductions of Crime : Moral and Sensual Attractions in Doing Evil.* New York: Basic Books.

King-Casas, Brooks, Damon Tomlin, Cedric Anen, Colin F. Camerer, Steven R. Quartz, P. Read Montague (2005). Getting to Know You: Reputation and Trust in a Two-Person Economic Exchange. *Science Magazine.* April 1, Vol. 308. no. 5718, pp. 78–83.

Kunzle, D. (1973). *History of the Comic strip.* Vol. 1. Berkeley, CA: University of California Press.

Lansing, Stephen J. (2002). Artificial Societies and the Social Sciences. *Artificial Life.* Summer, Vol. 8, No. 3, pp. 279-292.

Lynch, Aaron (1996). *Thought Contagion: How Beliefs Spread Through Society.* New York: Basic Books.

Miller, Frank. (1986). *The Dark Knight Returns.* New York: Warner and DC Comics.

Miller, Neal E. (1941). The Frustration-Aggression Hypothesis. *Psychological Review,* 48.

Morris, Norval, and Rothman, David J. (eds.) (1995). *The Oxford History of the Prison: The Practice of Punishment in Western Society.* New York: Oxford University Press.

Newman, Graeme and Pietro Marongiu. (1995). *Vendetta.* Florence: Giuffre.

Newman, Graeme. (1983). *Just and Painful A Case for the Corporal Punishment of Criminals*. New York: Macmillan.

Newman, Graeme. (1993). "Batman and Justice: the True Story" *Humanity and Society*, August.

Newman, Graeme. (1999). *Global Report on Crime and Justice*. United Nations, New York: Oxford University Press.

Nietzsche, F. W. (1960). *Joyful Wisdom*. New York: Ungar.

Pearson, R. and W. Urrichio (1991). *The Many Lives of the Batman*. New York: Routledge.

Phelps, Edmund S. (ed.) (1975). *Altruism, Morality, and Economic Theory*. New York: Russell Sage Foundation.

Plotkin, Henry (1997). *Evolution in Mind*. Cambridge, MA: Harvard University Press.

Ranulf, Svend (1938). *Moral Indignation and Middle Class Psychology: A Sociological Study*. Levin & Munksgaard.

Reiman, Jeffrey (2001). *The Rich get Richer, the Poor get Prison*. Needham Heights, MA: Allyn and Bacon.

Ridley, Matt (1996). *The Origins of Virtue*. London and New York: Penguin.

Roazen, Paul (1968). *Freud: Political and Social Thought*. New York: Alfred A. Knopf.

Rothman, David J. (1971). *The Discovery of the Asylum: Social Order and Disorder in the New Republic*. Boston: Little, Brown.

Rothman, David J. (1980). *Conscience and Convenience: The Asylum and Its Alternatives in Progressive America*. Boston: Little, Brown,

Rusche, G. and O. Kirchheimer (1939). *Punishment and Social Structure*. New York: Columbia University Press.

Savelsberg, Joachim J. (1994). "Knowledge, Domination, and Criminal Punishment." *American Journal of Sociology*, Vol. 99, No. 4, pp. 911-943.

Smith, Adam. (1976) [1776]. *An Inquiry into the Nature and Causes of the Wealth of Nations*. Ed. R. H. Campbell and A.S. Skinner. Oxford: Clarendon.

Sulloway, Frank J. (1992). *Freud: Biologist of the Mind*. Cambridge, MA: Harvard University Press.

Vowell, Sarah. (2001). American Squirm: Crime and Punishment. *Salon Magazine*. http://www.salon.com/ent/music/vowe/1999/03/24vowe.html.

Weber, M. (1978). *Economy and Society*. Vols. 1 and 2, G. Roth and C. Wittich (eds.). Los Angeles: University of California Press.

Acknowledgments

Permission to quote from copyright works has been obtained from the following authors and publishers:

Olive W. Burt and Oxford University Press for *American Murder Ballads and Their Stories*, by Olive W. Burt. John Wiley and Sons for *Learning Theory and Behavior*, by O. H. Mowrer. A. S. Barnes and Co. for *The Fatal Gallows Tree*, by J. D. Potter. Grove Press, Inc., for *The Wretched of the Earth*, by Frantz Fanon, copyright by Presena Afriraine. Citadel Press for *A History of Capital Punishment*, by J. Lawrence. W. W. Norton for *Civilization and Its Discontents*, by Sigmund Freud. T. Werner Laurie, Ltd., for *The History of Corporal Punishment*, by George Ryley Scott. Athlone Press for *An Introduction to the Principles of Morals and Legislation*, by Jeremy Bentham in *Collected Works*, edited by J. H. Burns and H. L. A. Hart. Mrs. Marianne Rodker and The Hogarth Press for *Malleus Maleficarum*, by H. Dramer and J. Sprenger, translated by Montague Summers. Patterson Smith for *Punishment: Its Origin, Purpose and Psychology*, by H. Von Hentig. Pantheon Books, A Division of Random House, for *The Making of the English Working Class*, by E. P. Thompson. Russell and Russell, Inc., for *The Works of Jeremy Bentham*, edited by John Bowring. Random House and Alfred A. Knopf, Inc., for *Centuries of Childhood*, by Philippe Aries. Ross D. Parke and Academic Press for *Early Experiences and the Process of Socialization*, edited by R. A. Hoppe. Macmillan Publishing Co., Inc., and Routledge and Kegan Paul, Ltd., for *The Moral Judgment of the Child*, by J. Piaget. Harcourt, Brace and Jovanovich, Inc., A. M. Heath and Co., and Mrs. Sonia Brownell Orwell for *Such, Such Were the Joys*, by George Orwell. Charles Skilton, Inc., for *Under the Lash: A History of Corporal Punishment in the British Army*, by S. Claver. Eyre and Spottiswoode, Ltd., for *The Inquisition of the Middle Ages*, by H. C. Lea. Harper and Row, Inc., for *Cannibalism: Human Aggression and Cultural Form*, by E. Sagan, and *Cradel of Life: The Story of One Man's Beginnings*, by Louis Adamic, copyright 1936 by Louis Adamic.

Cover illustration: Cartoon by Jossot from *L'Assiette au Beurre,* 1901, "Gentlemen of the jury. . . ."

Facing Chapter 1: Woodcut by Erhard Schoen, from *Brandenburgische Halsgerichtsordnung, Nurberg,* Jobst Gutknecht, 1516, XI. Compliments, Prints Division, New York Public Library, Astor, Lenox and Tilden Foundations.

Facing Chapter 2: Woodcut by Lucas Cranach the Elder, *"Old and New Testament,"* c. 1529 (only the "Old Testament" detail reproduced). Compliments, Prints Division, New York Public Library, Astor, Lenox and Tilden Foundations.

Facing Chapter 3: Woodcut by Wolf Traut, from *Bambergische Halgerichtsordung, Bamberg,* H. Pfeil, 1507. Compliments, Prints Division, New York Public Library, Astor, Lenox and Tilden Foundations.

Facing Chapter 4: Etching by L. Hermitte, from *The Criminal Prosecution and Capital Punishment of Animals,* by E. P. Evans, 1906.

Facing Chapter 5: Engraving by Jan Luyken, *"E'ulampia neffens haaren broeder in die gekook."* Plate 25 from *Tafereelen der eerste Christenen,* 1722. Compliments, Prints Division, New York Public Library, Astor, Lenox and Tilden Foundations.

Facing Chapter 6: Engraving (artist unknown) from W. Andrews, *Bygone Punishments,* 1899. Probably c. 1700.

Facing Chapter 7: Engraving by William Hogarth, *"The Idle 'Prentice Executed at Tyburn."* Compliments, Prints Division, New York Public Library, Astor, Lenox and Tilden Foundations.

Facing Chapter 8: From J. Bentham, *Panopticon; or, The Inspection House.* London: T. Payne, 1791.

Facing Chapter 9: Etching by Giovani Battista Piranesi, *Carceri,* Plate II.

Facing Chapter 10: Engraving by James Gillray, *"Ahithophel in the Dumps,"* 1785, from *The Works of James Gillray with the Addition of Many Subjects Not before Collected.* London: H. G. Bohn and C. Whiting, 1849.

Facing Chapter 11: Etching by George Cruikshank, *"The Automation Police Office, and Real Offenders."* An illustration for "The Mudfog Papers," by Charles Dickens, published July 1838 in *Bentley's Miscellany.*

Facing Chapter 12: Engraving by Albrecht Dürer, *"The Scourging of Christ,"* 1512. Compliments, Prints Division, New York Public Library, Astor, Lenox and Tilden Foundations.

Facing Chapter 13: Engraving by James Gillray, *"The Blood of the Murdered Crying for Vengeance,"* 1793, from *The Works of James Gillray with the Addition of Many Subjects Not before Collected.* London: H. G. Bohn and C. Whiting, 1849.

1

Introduction:
The Problem of Punishment

1

Punishment occupies a central place in our lives and, I venture to say, our minds. We suffer a profound ambivalence about it. Persons who have been punished or are liable to be punished have long objected to the legitimacy of punishment. "Who has the right?"

We are all the objects of punishment, yet we are also its users. Our ambivalence is so profound that not only do we punish others, but we punish ourselves as well. Not only do we view those who submit too willingly to punishment as "obedient" verging on the groveling coward, but we also view the resister to punishment as "disobedient," a rebel.

Some argue that punishment promotes discrimination and divisiveness in society. Others argue that it is through punishment that order and legitimacy are upheld. It is important that we understand that punishment is neither one nor the other; it is both. This point, simple though it seems, we have never come to grips with. This is why we wax and wane in our uses of punishment; why our punishing institutions are clogged by bureaucracy; why the death penalty comes and goes like the tide.

A recent report, *Doing Justice*,[2] the results of several years' work by a very prestigious panel of lawyers, social scientists, educators, philosophers, and theologians, concluded that the most "just" principle for the punishment of criminals is that of retribution, which in its simplest form means, "If you break a rule, you deserve to be punished in proportion to your offense, and that's the end of it." It is the law of "just deserts." But what is "just" about deserts? One of the members of that panel, Professor Leslie Wilkins, stated in an appended comment that although he supported generally the principles laid down by the committee, it was really because all other alternatives appeared worse, not because he affirmed the principle of retribution itself. Professor Wilkins lamented that the committee embarrassingly had rediscovered sin.

Is punishment that old? It was this question that propelled me to starting this book and to adopting a strong sociohistorical perspective. The more one reads of modern writings on punishment—predominantly legalistic in orientation—the more one comes to the conclusion that the concept of punishment has been cut off from its history, cut off from culture. My aim in writing this book has been to rescue the idea of punishment from this realm of abstraction.

Although I shall in later chapters focus mainly on criminal punishment, I wish to emphasize that punishment is first a cultural process and secondly a mechanism of particular institutions, of which criminal law is but one. Furthermore, because academic discussions of punishment have been confined to legalistic preoccupations, much of the policy and justification of punishment have been based on discussions of extreme cases. The use of punishment in the sphere of crime, after all, is an extreme case in itself, since crime is a very minor aspect of daily life. The uses of punishment (and the moral justifications for punishment) within the family and school have rarely been considered, certainly not to the exhaustive extent that criminal law has been. Yet punishment in such areas forms the backdrop to a great deal of punishment justifications advanced today.

Criminology textbooks typically begin their "history" of criminal punishment with a few paragraphs on Beccaria and Bentham of the eighteenth century. It is not recognized that these great thinkers had also been children and subject to punishments common to the period. Bentham, for example, was raised on the frightening stories of punishment told to him from Fox's macabre *Book of Martyrs,* which describes in gory detail the most horrendous of punishments. His contemporary, criminal law reformer Sir Samuel Romilly, had recurrent nightmares about this book. We shall get a taste of this later.

The point to be recognized is that there is continuity between the idea and the practice of punishment. Ideas do not exist unto themselves. They are produced by people, and people live in a social world that has a very ancient history. The ideas are transmitted along with the social experience of each individual. Therefore, they cannot be properly understood unless seen within the context of the history of culture.

I have undertaken this rescue of the concept of punishment with a vengeance—perhaps too much so in trying to trace punishment from its origin at the beginning of time to the present in just a small book. It was necessary to take this broad swipe at history to convey a moving picture of the "progress" of punishment. One senses an element of despair in Professor Wilkins's lamentation, as though we have perhaps turned back the clock of justice. Have we reached a deadend? Has the "progress" been merely circular, or even superficial?

The modern temptation is to say that we have made no progress in our use of punishment. At least the academic penologist is apt to make such a claim. It is easy enough to show (as I will in this book) that the effects and methods of punishment used today are much less severe than in the seventeenth and eighteenth centuries when violent punishments were at their height. The popular argument against this observation is that we continue to punish just as much, but the forms of punishment have changed from physical to more "psychological," especially in the use of prison. This claim is wrong, of course. It assumes that because the typical forms of punishment during the middle ages were physical, there was virtually no "social" or "psychological" punishment. In fact both were used extensively, as we shall see, especially in Chapters 5 and 6. Furthermore, it is a misconception that prison as a large-scale penal measure is a "modern" phenomenon. It is as ancient as many other forms of punishment, probably reaching its height during the Spanish Inquisition.

A more serious misconception may arise from a superficial awareness of the violent punishments of the past. This is the belief that there is something inherently bad in punishment itself. In fact, it is this overwhelming preoccupation that has dominated the twentieth-century thinking and research on punishment, to the extent that the majority of twentieth-century legal and philosophical work has been concerned with justifications for its use, not with comprehending it. Although this is understandable for legal theorists whose work is largely concerned with justifications, it certainly is not defensible for philosophers. Even scientists were befuddled by the preconception of the inherent evil of punishment, as shown by their constant misinterpretation of research data on the effectiveness of punishment to the point of even ignoring significant research findings which supported its effectiveness. This we shall see in Chapter 11. The idea of the inherent evil of punishment was first introduced by the utilitarians, especially Jeremy Bentham in the eighteenth century. For this reason, I will examine his work in some detail (Chapter 8), for it represents a crucial turning point in the history of the idea of punishment. I will also examine closely the practices of punishment during that period and the social conditions that surrounded them. Prior to that time, punishment was taken for granted as a natural part of everyday life.

It was, and still is. And in that sense its actual use does not have to be justified. The only aspect of punishment that needs justification is its distribution. For is it fair that some be punished more than others? We cannot answer this question until our survey of punishment is completed. The final chapter will address this question.

What do I mean by punishment being "natural"? We shall see in Chapter 2 that punishment is natural in the sense that it is unavoidable. Man is (and always has been) punished by his physical environment, an environment that is harsh, that man has devoted most of his civilization to conquering, that is never quite predictable, that brings us droughts, floods, ice, famines, plagues. When punishment began, how did primitive man deal with such painful problems? Of course, he dealt with them religiously, just as we tend to do today when all else has failed. Primitive man imputed a character to his physical environment and adopted many rituals and rites to deal with the pains that the environment brought him. Yet primitive man was also a part of nature, so he easily blamed himself when things went wrong. The seeds of punishment were sewn in this climate, as Chapter 2 will show.

Death has also played a part. To primitive man the world of the dead was just as "alive" as the world of the living. Killing and dying have always been central features of Western civilization. People, both innocent and guilty, have been sacrificed to various gods, and sometimes these sacrifices have appeared in the form of punishment. In Chapter 3 we will see that special kinds of punishments, especially methods of applying the death penalty, have essentially ritualistic origins, whether to ward off the spirit of the slain, act out sacred or divine feelings of honor, "reflect" a crime by a punishment similar to it, give vent to collective religious sentiment, such as stoning to death, or, perhaps most significant for today, avoid responsibility for actually administering the punishment by leaving the offender to be "killed by nature" or by "persons unknown" (the firing squad).

As we follow the evolution of punishment from its primitive origins, we must also follow the evolution of religion, for various forms of religion have been champions of punishment throughout the ages. We shall see in Chapter 5 how the Italian Inquisition developed an incredibly sophisticated system of punishment and how the sacred aspects of punishment were blended into politics with great precision. Yet we shall also see that Protestantism played its part in furthering the use of punishment on a more decentralized plane, especially in England. During the seventeenth and eighteenth centuries in England, religion played a key role in the promotion and expression of punishments and helps explain the behavior of the masses, especially the ribald and hysterical behavior of the mob under London's Tyburn Tree gallows. These were terrible years, to which we would not want to return. Chapter 7 analyzes this period.

There is also an "institutional" or, perhaps more accurately, a "political" side to punishment, both in its origins and its modern application. Although punishment has natural origins, it was also of central importance in the birth of civilization, which, if one accepts the significance of the mythical reconstruction of the birth of society, was a political act. According to Freud, the day a band of brothers ganged up to kill the leader who ruled by raw power (physical force), civilization was born. This single act created the central elements of society: a collective sentiment; guilt at having killed the "father"; fear of another uprising, leading to the development of strict rules concerning the social order (in the primitive sense, social order meant who could sleep with whom). Thus, the incest taboo was born, out of which developed the highly structured, totalitarian family, kinship systems, clan organizations, and so on. The idea of *obedience* was born, carrying with it the three central elements of obedience: rules, punishment, and submission. The oldest social function of punishment was therefore punishment in the service of obedience. This I have termed the "obedience" model of punishment, and we shall, in Chapters 4, 5, and 6, see how punishment was put to the service of the evolving social institutions that required obedience. Those surveyed in these chapters are the social institutions of the family, school, slavery, the military, religion, and criminal justice. We shall see that the obedience model has remained the oldest and predominant function of punishment throughout history, except for a few brief periods when another model of punishment, which I term the "reciprocity" model, held sway.

The reciprocity function of punishment is also very ancient, originating as a secondary function to the early clan system. Although punishment for obedience predominated within clans, when it came to regulation between clans, conflict arose. Punishment between clans, therefore, took on a different form in ancient history, since it was ostensibly punishment between equals. Thus, the feud is the prototype of reciprocal punishment, where two opposing factions return one wrong for another. We shall see in Chapter 6 that this feuding form of punishment existed very early, at least since Homer's time.

The reciprocal form of punishment is the purest form of what we call retribution today. However, we can see that it cannot exist today in pure form, since society is not divided into groups of "equals." Therefore, punishment used in the name of retribution is a special kind of retribution; it is retribution in the service of the state. It is really the obedience model, which forms the basis for what is now known as deterrence. These and other modern models of punishment we will discuss in Chapter 10. But we can see already that the popular belief today that retribution is some kind of "opposite" or "alternative" to deterrence is false. They serve essentially a similar political function.

The Definition of Punishment

The definition of punishment has been a major obsession with the English linguistic philosophers of this century, and the results of their labors have been taken over and extended by legal theorists. They have produced an often repeated "standard definition" of punishment, which I will reproduce below, with some changes.[3] Professor H. L. A. Hart[4] distinguishes the primary definition of punishment from its secondary part. Since Professor Hart is a legal theorist, it is understandable that he should consider those aspects of punishment relating to the law as the "primary part." However, we are not so constrained, and, indeed, it is a thesis of this book that "nonlegal" punishment preceded "legal" punishment by a long time. As I present his definition, I shall add any additional elements that I consider necessary, in order to make it a *comprehensive* definition of punishment.

1. "It must involve pain or other consequences normally considered unpleasant."[5] On the surface, this seems quite straightforward until one asks, what does "pain" mean: physical or psychological pain? Professor Anthony Flew in his 1954 definition had purposely avoided the use of the word pain, one suspects because of its very complex philosophical and physiological meaning. If one accepts Professor Thomas Szasz's definition of pain, for example, the definition of punishment is very difficult: "Pain is a subjective and personal experience—actively created and fashioned by the self, rather than a sensation passively undergone and endured."[6] Professor Szasz reduces all physical pain to mental pain. This is, of course, pain seen from a clinical point of view.

Even the English commission on whipping in the military in the early nineteenth century observed that whipping, though applied with precision to each offender, was nevertheless reacted to differently by each. That same commission recognized the great difficulty in standardizing the pain of prison (see Chapter 5). In any event, if a criminal insisted that he "felt" no pain as a result of being imprisoned, would it still be a punishment? Our answer, of course, would have to be "yes." And this is why Professor Hart utilizes his escape clause, "normally considered unpleasant." It is an appeal to a collective judgment.

We shall also see in Chapter 11 that scientists have offered a similar solution, in their experiments to measure the effects of punishment. By using certain intensities of electric shock related to observations of discomfort in the subject, the inference is made that punishment has occurred, and the question of whether the subject actually felt pain or not is treated as irrelevant. That is, it is sufficient to observe response to what is considered a painful stimulus (electric shock) and leave it at that.[7]

Perhaps the best we can do is to rely on the intentions of the punishers. For punishment to be punishment, it must at least be intended by the punishing agent that some kind of pain, deprivation, or suffering affect the person punished. If it is difficult to be more specific, perhaps the meaning is made more clear when we look at the other side: it would be a ridiculous contradiction if a punisher intended that his punishment would reward or be pleasurable to the person punished. We shall have more to say about intentionality in punishment under point 4.

2. It must be for an offense against a rule. There are many kinds of rules—legal rules, school rules, military rules, religious rules, and so on. All of these are established and enforced by the basic institutions of our society. The establishment of a rule also implies, as part of its definition, (a) that there is a propensity for it to be broken and (b) punishment serves as a signifier of the rule, i.e., it signifies to the actor and audience that there is a rule and it has been broken. In Franz Kafka's brilliant allegory of punishment, "In the Penal Colony," the officer says, "Our sentence does not sound severe. Whatever commandment the prisoner has disobeyed, is written upon his body by the Harrow. This prisoner, for instance—the officer indicated the man—will have written on his body: HONOR THY SUPERIORS!"[8] In other words, the sentence is the commandment, and the commandment is the punishment. An inherent part of the definition of a commandment or rule is the punishment that goes with it.

3. "It must be for an actual or supposed offender for his offense." In the initial chapters of this book, I have gone a little beyond this delimitation of punishment to "actual offenders or supposed offend-

ers." Punishment of nonoffenders would be sacrificial punishment—the punishment of innocents. Some of the ancient instances of this practice I have surveyed in Chapter 3, since the forms of sacrificial punishments may have preceded, or at least influenced, other forms of punishments for the specific breaking of rules. Perhaps we should also distinguish between sacrifice and persecution. In ancient times, those sacrificed were mostly seen as innocents (although there were some exceptions). Persecution refers to the punishment of individuals who at the time of punishment were seen by the punishing agents as offenders but today are seen as "innocent." Examples of these are the Christians under Nero or women and Jews during the Holy Inquisition.

4. "It must be intentionally administered by human beings other than the offender." In the initial chapters of the book, it was necessary for me to go beyond "human beings" to include the "supernatural"—the forces of nature and spirits that have been perceived by primitive man as intentionally punishing him. It is entirely possible, of course, that many of these natural disasters are, objectively speaking, "accidents." But what is important is that man has historically perceived them as intentional and still tends to today. Therefore, such occurrences may quite reasonably be considered intentional punishments. Of course, that man may perceive himself as punished by God needs no elucidation.

The phrase "other than the offender" shelters a very difficult problem related to the inherent subjectivity of punishment, to which I referred earlier. Even before Freud, it was apparent that there were some people and some classes of people that punished themselves. Indeed, the traditional Christian conscience is a kind of psychological societal punishment, in which the individual perceives ahead of time the threat of punishment and the threat itself becomes the punishment. The complicated dynamics of this mechanism we shall review in Chapter 11. But apart from the mechanisms of psychological self-punishment, we must also be aware that, at least according to Freud, we are all to some degree (greater or smaller depending on each individual) masochists. We live in a culture of sadomasochism that fluctuates from one to the other. The cultural origins of this emotional state have been traced by Freud back to the ancient myth of the first great crime of killing the "father." Chapters 2 and 13 review the cultural and political significance of this myth. An intangible sense of guilt was created by that ancient act. As Kafka's officer noted,

"Guilt is never to be doubted." The need for punishment follows naturally.

5. "It must be imposed and administered by an authority constituted by a legal system against which the offense is committed." Applied to an historical analysis of punishment, this definition is much too narrow and difficult to apply. For example, what one would term a "legal system" at various periods during the middle ages is a matter of conjecture, especially in feuding situations where punishment was meted out among equals. On the other hand, there has always been a tradition in punishment: an accepted way that "wrongs" should be "righted," whether by the feud, legal trial, or religious inquisition. In other words, punishment has always been a central feature of moral regulation. Although this role of punishment was quite clear up to the nineteenth century, today it is often called into question. Certainly modern attempts to secularize criminal law try to minimize its role as a moral regulator.[9] The general point to note is that punishment comes down to us from a great tradition which says that punishment is the way to deal with wrongs. The inherent authority of any punishment, therefore, is its history: over 2,000 years of it.

All punishment must have an object. The object may be either human or animal—it seems entirely arbitrary to exclude animals since historically, as we shall see in Chapter 5, animals have played an important role as defendants in criminal and ecclesiastical prosecutions. Today, domestic animals, especially, are often subject to discipline and punishment by their owners, to say nothing of the extensive use of animals in the psychology laboratory experiments on punishment. Since the "criminal" is popularly seen as bearing the brunt of society's frustrations, it seems appropriate to review how man has treated his animals, since traditionally he has been known to take out his frustrations on them also.

Mass punishment, that is the punishment of a group of individuals for the offense of one of its members, should also be considered, although I have not uncovered many instances of this practice other than the well-known example of Hitler's Gestapo and a few cases of decimation in the military. This type of punishment would appear to be more commonly a military punishment, however analogues of it have been used on school children, such as the punishment of a whole class for one pupil's misbehavior.

Armed with our very broad delineation of punishment—perhaps

one could call it the "general case" of punishment—we may now try to comprehend both the concept and the practice as it unfolds with the story of Western civilization. It is essentially a story of the search for order and order's justification.

2

When Punishment Began

Throughout history punishment, in its severest physical forms, has been present in all major civilizations. But we should not assume that because of this universality punishment originated with society or that it is entirely social in nature. In fact, punishment preceded society. It originated in the natural condition of man in relation to the physical world as well as the social world. Man's juxtaposition in this external world has made punishment a necessary and unavoidable part of life. To understand this point, we must understand the primitive origins of man and his world.

Many philosophers and social theorists have tried to reconstruct the primitive origins of man's social, psychological, and material life, especially those of the nineteenth and early twentieth centuries, such as Spencer, Durkheim, Marx, Freud, and more recently Fromm and Montagu. There has been much argument as to the accuracy of their reconstructions, most of which have a kind of bedtime story quality.

It is precisely because of this quality that we must address ourselves to the same question concerning punishment. The earliest periods in the history of our civilization are shrouded in the silence of the ages. Archaeologists try to piece together tiny fragments of information. We are able to reconstruct an *idea* of what the dawning of civilization may have been like. But this is an image and not the "real thing." It is mythical. But this does not mean that because these reconstructions are mythical they are therefore false. Cultures revolve around myth.

Many of the themes of these reconstructions of primitive life may be traced forward through hundreds of years.

The Natural Origins of Punishment

There are three natural (and closely related) sources of punishment. The first is the presence of a harsh environment with which man has to deal. The second is the occurrence of natural disasters, which is really a variation of the first. The third is religion.

Herbert Spencer was perhaps the first social theorist to see clearly the importance of the harsh environment for the development of man. Indeed, he saw man's intelligence as a product of having to cope with the harsh environment.[1] It is also apparent that other aspects of the harsh environment have influenced man's political and economic practices. Marx has noted that primitive society developed out of competition for scarce resources, and this state of affairs wa⸗ responsible for man's early and deep alienation from the world. Man must fight the world to gain supremacy. It was a simple step from fighting the environment to fighting other men. Competition is often seen as the basis of primitive society.

Enter Freud. We no doubt owe much of our confusion and many of our insights to Freud's mythology of family life. Yet he, more than any other social theorist, highlights the importance and power of myth—the fantastic capacity of man to symbolize, to fictionalize his past. Freud suggests that civilization began with a heinous crime: a band of "brothers" ganged up on their leader to kill him. In *Totem and Taboo* Freud tried to show how the original crime occurred. He assumed the "leader," in the most primitive form, would be defined as the most physically powerful individual (the father, probably) who held all others in *individual* subjection (not submission). The "sons" discovered that by banding together they could *as a group* overpower the leader. The bond of "society" was formed as a means to obtain freedom (in the simplest, most primitive form this means sexual freedom), but the price paid for this goal was a heinous crime: the basis of our guilt culture. In recompense for this crime the sons created a new leader, but this time they remained in submission—to a great extent voluntarily. Rigid rules were developed, and those who broke the rules were punished. Sexual taboos, such as the incest taboo, were born. Now, ironically, because of the incest taboo, sexual freedom was not attained.

Of course, as far as Freud is concerned, both history and desire will never go away, so the memory and the urge to kill the leader (now the father) remains in the unconscious, and still does today in the form of the Oedipus complex. But that is another story.

Suffice it to say that Freud's mythology of the origin of punishment transforms the simple relationship of man in competition for scarce resources into a big psychological problem.[2] It was through this original crime that the possibility was created for an enduring social order not based on physical violence. Freud's reconstruction of the heinous crime is an attempt to explain where rituals and taboos come from. We shall return to this model of the origin of taboos and their punishments many times throughout this book.

Erich Fromm's book, *The Anatomy of Human Destructiveness*, attempts to document evidence that the primal horde was not, as Freud portrays it, an unruly "savage" band competing for scarce resources.[3] He quotes evidence from a number of anthropologists and archaeologists[4] who argue that the prehistoric period was a period of plenty and the idea of scarce resources is a myth. There are two difficulties with this argument. First, even if the construction of the primitive life of man by various social theorists is mythical, it does not make too much difference, for we know that myths are probably a great, even the greatest, moving force in history. They are the stuff of culture. The primal horde may or may not have been competitive. It may or may not have been driven by the continuing desires of sex and aggression. The original murder of the father by his sons may or may not have happened. We will probably never know.

The second shortcoming is that Fromm's argument concerning scarcity is incomplete. If his theory that prehistoric times were a period of plenty is correct, one is forced to ask, why did it change? Why did civilization begin; why did it take on the course it did? Fromm points the finger at civilization, with its particular social structure of haves and have-nots causing the enormous levels of aggression displayed throughout history. But he has mistaken a symptom for its cause. If the tribe of prehistory existed in benign repose both with nature and interpersonally, then one must ask how did a much maligned civilization grow out of such beginnings? If one presumes a prehistory of scarcity and war of all against all, then the civilizations we have today are more easily explainable. The crucial logical flaw in Fromm's theory is that he places society out of sequence with history. He tries to show that society, not man, produced aggression.[5]

It is my concern to show that punishment moves out of the natural order of a physical environment which both includes and excludes man. Man is not completely separate from nature, he is part of it—part of the natural order of things. The "tension" arises in man's ability to conceive of himself as separate from nature. This is why civilizations and societies are created and developed. In contrast to the animal kingdom, where animal "societies" function instinctively as a part of the natural order, man creates his societies not only as a part of the natural order, but also *against* it. This is why societies and civilizations tend to achieve a life and structure of their own above and beyond nature.

Fortunately, the resolution of the arguments over the origins of civilization is not essential to our quest for the primitive source of punishment. Although all major civilizations have bloody histories of the use of punishment, they do not all display "guilt culture" in the way that Western civilization does. There must, then, be other reasons besides those of guilt culture. Perhaps the guilt origin of punishment in Western civilizations will explain the *forms* of punishment which have arisen. But it is certainly not enough to explain why punishment exists at all. We are returned to our original propositions: that punishment must be a natural part of the life process (used in its broadest sense) and that it arises from man's interaction with the external environment.

If one does not accept the conceptualization of the environment as harsh because of scarcity of resources, perhaps my second point, really an extension of the first, will make the view more convincing. I refer to the occurrence of natural disasters and the more regular, though equally devastating to man, changeability of the physical environment. In most parts of the world, where the major civilizations now predominate, the seasons of the year change dramatically. Where there are long, cold winters, this has meant that man, the hunter, must become man, the planner—he must store food for the winter. Fables such as the *Ant and the Grasshopper* are clear examples of this natural problem. In addition, man must adapt over the ages. If there are sudden changes (that is, during his lifetime), he will be seriously affected. If it becomes too cold, he must keep warm either from fires, shelter, or clothing. If it is too hot, he becomes lethargic. However, the seasons are sufficiently regular that man learns to expect them and plan for them. It is a disaster if something goes wrong, and as we know from many historical sources, things have gone wrong for as long as we can remember. The Bible is full of famines, droughts, floods, and disease. This especially applied to the period when man became an agriculturalist as well as a hunter. For the seed to grow, the seasons had to be predictable. If they did not keep to their regular schedule, the seeds would be rendered infertile and the people would starve. It is small wonder that so many examples of sexual fertility rites should be tied up with rituals relating to the seasons. Scores of examples of such rituals in many different cultures are catalogued in James Frazer's *New Golden Bough.*[6] The evidence is so great that we can easily accept the idea of a natural "punitiveness" of the seasons and physical environment.

I have substituted "punitiveness" for "harshness" of the environment at this stage quite intentionally. It is an important step in our analysis, because it suggests that the only interpretation primitive man could make of the world when something went wrong—either the seasons did not perform to schedule or there was a natural disaster—was that he himself had done something wrong to cause it. That is, primitive man could not accept such disasters as "natural." He must view *himself* as the object of the disaster, and it is in this sense that we are able to speak of "punishment."

One may ask, since primitive man has by definition a simple mind, why does he insist on drawing the relationship between himself and the disasters of nature? The answer is simple. In his primitive state man *is* a part of nature. He lives in a one-to-one relationship with the physical environment. Therefore if something goes wrong with the environment, something also has gone wrong with him.

There is another important attribute about man that at the same time separates him from the physical environment: he thinks, and more importantly he thinks *teleologically.* That is, he must, and has, learned to plan ahead, to perform tasks for the future. One might at first be tempted to observe that birds, animals, and even insects in preparing for the seasons in advance do not think intentionally, but rather instinctively. And since primitive man has a simple mind, why not instinctual too? The observation which mitigates against this view is that of the intricate and wide range of rituals which cultures have developed in relation to the seasons and other important facets of nature. True, elaborate rituals have been observed among birds and animals. But these rituals are not related to the seasons as such, but to mating. Man developed mating rituals, but these were *consciously* extended into the fertility rituals in relation to the seasons. We must now add a further dimension to man's primitive teleological thought. It means that not only did he think ahead and learn to plan and expect nature to behave in a certain way, but he was also able to think backwards and interpret the past.

Here we have found the crucial explanation of man as the punished object. Since he is at the same time both a part of nature and its teleological interpreter, it follows that when primitive man observes that "something is wrong with nature" he must come to two cataclysmic conclusions: (1) that "something is wrong with me" and (2) "I have done something wrong."

Why does he not also impute intentionality to nature? Of course, he does. And it is here that we must consider briefly the primitive origins of religion, since as those of us in Western civilization well know, punishment and religion have enjoyed a long and lasting friendship over the ages. In fact, punishment and religion are probably closely related in all civilizations and all cultures. Its excessive use, we will see in Chapter 4, has undoubtedly accompanied religious fervor at various historical periods. It is also significant that modern criminal law, though becoming increasingly secularized, is nevertheless based on early religious themes and prohibitions. An examination of the primitive origins of religion may help us to unearth the basic elements of punishment, in terms of both the motivation to punish and the forms that punishment has taken over the ages.

Punishment and Primitive Religion

Emile Durkheim refers to the two most common theories of primitive religion as naturism and animism. Naturism refers to the association by the primitive of sacred and special rites to the "great cosmic forces of nature" such as the sun, planets, moon, stars, animals, and rocks. Animism refers to the attachment of sacred significance to "nonexistent" spiritual beings or souls, demons, divinities which are not ordinarily visible to human eyes. This is a religion of the spirit.[7]

Durkheim rejects both of these theories as inadequate to explain primitive religion because both are also substantial aspects of modern or "civilized" religion. However, if one takes the Freudian view, Durkheim's criticisms are undercut, for it is precisely because these aspects of religion *are* primitive that they should also remain as the substrata of modern culture.

I have earlier suggested that primitive man sets himself apart from nature by interpreting nature's order. By so doing, man offers himself as the object of nature because he separates himself from the natural order.[8] But the work on naturism and animism shows that man, far from being separate from nature, lies extremely close to nature, because—and this is the crucial point—the primitive makes no distinction between animate and inanimate. Reality for the primitive is totally animate (which, by the way, is similar to the view of young children).

We must again be careful of our time sequence. Prehistoric man cannot always have indulged in animism, since one assumes that originally, during the millions of years over which he evolved, he was a part of nature, which has no psychological intention or purpose. It is only as primitive man developed his intellect, the ability to think teleologically, that he gradually began to separate himself from nature. Yet after millions of years as part of nature, it is not at all surprising that in an intermediate stage man, in his attempt to stay close to nature, has reinterpreted it as more like him, imputing to nature specific intentions and thought processes. Matter becomes animate.[9]

There are other reasons. As Claude Levi-Strauss and others have pointed out, animals and birds have abilities different from man's. Birds can leave the ground, primitive man could not. It is not surprising that primitive man should be prepared to impute thought processes and special powers to such creatures, to say nothing of the greater cosmic forces of the sun, moon, stars, thunder, and lightning. All of these natural phenomena fill modern-day man with a sense of awe and wonder; why should they not be sufficient to excite spiritual ideas in a primitive man who is not sure whether he is a part of or separate from the forces of nature?

Taking all these factors into account, it seems reasonable that primitive man should assume, when a famine occurs, not only that he has done something wrong, but also that nature is intentionally punishing him because of that wrong. The Bible is full of examples of such reasoning.

One feature of animism is worth considering, since it may be related to the primitive forms that punishment has taken: the worship of the dead, sometimes referred to as the "cult of the ancestors." E. B. Tylor has noted that "the first rites were funeral rites, the first sacrifices were food offerings to satisfy the needs of the departed, and the first altars were tombs."[10] The primitive conception of death, it is commonly argued, easily accepts a life after death. The reason given for this is that the primitive leads "two lives": one awake and one asleep. However, when the primitive dreams, for example, that he has visited his relative in a distant village, he believes that he really did pay the visit. Thus, the primitive believes that he has a "soul" or "spirit" which can leave his body and lead a life of its own. It is a simple step of logic for the primitive to believe next that, because death is so similar to sleep, the souls of the dead continue to live. Hence the attempts to offer food at the altars of the dead.

But if the life of spirits is accepted by the savage as simply another side of his everyday life, why should he make such a big deal out of worshiping them? Especially in the face of clear evidence that dead men decay, why should not the savage conclude that, since the "soul" has its home in the body, when the body dies the soul does too? An immediate answer to this is that, in fact, dead bodies actually last a long time in the form of skeletons. They do not, therefore, easily disappear. The soul was believed to reside in, or even be a part of, the physical shape of the corpse, especially the bones. A common practice of primitive peoples has been to break up the bones of the dead, especially where some wrongdoing was involved, as we shall see in Chapter 3. All of this means that punishment *after* death may be just as significant to the primitive as punishment in life. And as we shall see in following chapters, it was a very common practice to administer punishment after death well into the eighteenth century.

In sum, there are two sources of religious punishment for the primitive. Nature may intentionally do him harm for a wrong that he presumes he has committed, and souls or spirits may intentionally punish him for wrongs he assumes he has committed either directly against the spirits of the dead or against persons who subsequently die, releasing their spirits to punish him.

The Primitive Origins of Order

A third basic element of punishment may now be postulated. I have argued that punishment occurs naturally as a result of man's perception of the physical environment (i.e., harm does not "occur," rather nature does him harm) and the supernatural environment (i.e., spirits may also do him harm). His primitive response to these teleological interpretations of his own making is to develop rites of appeasement, to sanctify objects, animals, particular geographic areas, and special kinds of behavior. The essential negative element of this sanctification process is that of *taboo*. The positive element is that of *worship.* Because punishment is our main concern, it is the negative element of taboo that interests us.

One may well ask, why taboos at all? It seems simple enough that if primitive man blames himself for what goes wrong with nature and "supernature," then the rites that he develops in relation to these objects will incorporate prescriptions of what to do and what not to do. Indeed, there is probably no culture which does not espouse some kind of ethic distinguishing between behavior that is "right" and behavior that is "wrong." It is next to impossible to imagine a society which is all "positive"—that is, all worship. Logic impels us to presume that hallowed ground requires a specific set of behaviors relating to it. For example, it may be prohibited to walk on it. The creation of "the sacred" logically implies both positive and negative sanctions. In other words, in primitive cultures rites are rules which imply prohibitions. And once they are stated in the form of prohibitions, punishment is a necessary outcome.[11]

There are, of course, other forms of prohibition not necessarily connected with rites. These prohibitions, which one might call *functional prohibitions,* are necessary for the economic well-being of the tribe. Bronislaw Malinowski's work demonstrates this very clearly in his study of the Trobriand islanders. Each native had his particular task and role to perform as part of the total economic activity of the culture. However, the operation of punishment in this area was very rare, simply because each individual was so well socialized that the situation of someone not fulfilling his economic role of reciprocity never arose. Economically, man was not separate from the culture—he was part of it. In contrast, when punishments did arise (and of course these were mostly self-administered), they were in relation to noneconomic activities in the realm of taboos.

What were the first taboos? And is it important that we know? It is indeed, for the answers to these questions may lead us to yet another vital ingredient of punishment and an important evolutionary step: the identification of classes of phenomena which are taboo, with the concomitant identification of classes of people and behaviors that are taboo. Punishment, after all, is not applied to persons by chance as in a lottery. Particular classes of persons are punished. And a highly complex system has been developed for deciding what classes of behavior should be punished (the criminal law).

This requires one final digression into the controversial question of totemism, one of the most primitive forms of social organization and social order. It is a crucial area of inquiry since it is often argued that punishment is necessary to maintain the social institutions of society, and totemic systems, it may be argued, are the primitive forms of social institutions. Indeed, as we saw in Chapter 1, the supposition that punishment must be administered by a recognized institution of authority has been put forward as part of the definition of punishment.

For many years totemism was viewed as a basic element of primitive religion. Frazer's monumental *Totemism and Exogamy* attempted to catalogue all known facts about totemism, but these facts were based on three preconceived assumptions about its nature. It was assumed that totemism was made up of three kinds of phenomena: an organization into clans, the attribution of animals and plants to the class as insignia, and a belief in a relation between clan and animal. Evidence was collected to show that all primitive societies were organized into some kind of clan system, exogamy was a basic law of all cultures, and violations of this law were punished. A further assumption, later given considerable credence by Durkheim,[12] was that the essential element of totemism was religious sentiment: members of a clan were bound together by a strong cohesive force, the totem was treated as sacred, and the worship of the "cult of ancestors" was predominant. It was then a simple step for Durkheim to argue that punishment, therefore, reinforced the solidarity of the group.

Unfortunately, as Levi-Strauss[13] points out in his penetrating critique of totemic theory, the universality of these observations, let alone the presumed religious sentiment as the binding force of these three elements, is nowhere near as great as Durkheim supposed. Levi-Strauss observes, for example, that the Thompson River Indians had totems but no clans; the Iroquois had clans named after animals that were not totems; the Australian aborigines had many totems that were not plants or animals but aspects of the larger cosmic order (sun, stars, wind, etc.) and even kinds of behavior (e.g., laughing). How could these inconsistencies be reconciled?

Durkheim reduces the explanation of the totemic system to the totem or insignia itself, in which is invested the moral sentiment of the clan. But did the sentiment produce the totem or vice versa? And why did the sentiment produce the clan system? Durkheim confuses us by presuming that the totem is both a product and a cause of sentiment. But he is unable to go beyond this to explain why such sentiment is expressed as a clan system. That is, surely a strong social sentiment would bind the whole of the tribe rather than separate it into classes.

Freud provided a possible explanation for this problem when he observed: "sexual need does not unite men; it separates them."[14] Building on Darwin's picture of the presocietal horde of men, Freud speculated that the most powerful of the men possessed more wives. The rest of the story I have already told. The primal father was killed and eaten:

> The totem feast, which is perhaps mankind's first celebration, would be the repetition and commemoration of this memorable, criminal act with which so many things began, social organization, moral restrictions and religion.[15]

The social organization which ensued was that of the totemic system—the displacement of ambivalent feelings of love and hate for the father onto animals, a process so often reported by psychoanalysts in their observations of children. Since the animal world is clearly organized into classes and species, human social organization developed as a kind of mirror of the animal kingdom. The moral restrictions that resulted were generally of two kinds. The incest taboo or exogamy, which required that sexual intercourse must not occur within the clan. Thus the clan will be kept united, and the possibility of another uprising to kill the father is avoided. The other type of taboo is related to the sacred worship of the totem: if it is an animal, it must not be eaten (except on special ritual occasions), or one must not touch it. And the formulation of religion, of course, is bound up in both these aspects, in addition to the predominant sense of guilt among the sons.

Levi-Strauss dismisses all of this as totally unsubstantiated, and in addition insists that the sentiments or affectivity are not the cause of the totemic system, but its consequence. His analysis of totemism at this point is at once crucial and challenging, driving us into the very center of the problem of punishment—as it was then and is today.

Levi-Strauss points out that the Australian aborigine totem arranges animal species in pairs of opposites. He then makes what is an astounding yet obvious observation: when two primitives declare that they are two different species of animals (that is, from two different clans), he insists that it is not the *animality* that is so significant to the primitive, but rather the *duality*. It is a special kind of duality: an intellectual principle consisting of the union of opposites. This principle can be seen in all languages and cultures: male/female, summer/winter, day/night, Yang and Yin. Thus, totemism fulfills an important intellectual function for man: it allows him to integrate the world. It is a form of comprehension. "[N]atural species are chosen not because they are 'good to eat' but because they are 'good to think.' "[16]

The totem, for Levi-Strauss, becomes metaphor: a rational, intelligent interpretation of the world. In contrast, for Freud, the totem becomes a symbol: a symbol of man's repression of his most horrible desires, a symbol of his guilt. And for Durkheim, the totem becomes the mere external insignia to which is attached social sentiment. But the "stuff" of social sentiment is unknown, or at least indefinable.

And now we are at the root of it all and can discern the significance of all this for punishment. Both Freud and Levi-Strauss reduce the question of social order to psychology. Levi-Strauss arbitrarily dismisses the primal importance of instinctual or emotional drives, but allows that they occur as consequences of the totemic system: "Emotion is indeed aroused, but when the custom, in itself indifferent, is violated."[17] In contrast, Freud sees the emotion or, more precisely, the consummation of aggression followed by its repression as the cause of custom and the whole range of the totemic system. For both theorists, then, man creates the social order, but with a different basis and, it must be said, different implications concerning the extent that nature is involved.

The problem for anthropology, as Rousseau has suggested, is to explain the passage from nature to culture. Both Freud and Levi-Strauss see that the passage is that of the human psyche. But Freud's view must lead to a greater and perhaps more abrupt separation of man from nature since the social order he creates is almost entirely the product of instincts within himself without regard for an interpretation of nature itself. In other words, man and his incipient civilization is thrust headlong into nature, and he is left there, mainly with his intellect, to try to patch up the pieces. For Levi-Strauss, the passage from nature to culture is much more studied. Man is not driven by passions, but rather by a speculative and observant intellect. He studies nature, and not only observes its order, but also interprets it metaphorically regarding the way he relates socially to other men. Thus, although man creates his social order, he is not driven to do so, but does it reflectively based on his observations of nature, social life, and himself.

The implications for punishment in these two views of social order are of great importance. We are forced to face up to the question of whether punishment is a product of guilt and repressed emotion, whose use must constantly be monitored lest it get out of control. Or is it a product of a rational contemplative process in society? The major formal works on punishment, as we shall see in Chapter 8 have been oriented toward the latter view. Most theories of punishment are rationalistic attempts to justify its use. Yet, at the same time, many of these theories make the same assumption as Freud and Durkheim did: the need for punishment to reinforce the social order and prevent the ever-present threat of the war of all against all.

One final point needs to be considered concerning punishment and social order. The simplest form of social order is the direct obedience of a group of equals to its sole leader. Even here, however, a measure of differentiation is necessary to employ the word "order." Once differentiation within a culture occurs (that is a totemic system in which cultures are divided into classes where exogamy is the requirement), social order becomes a much more complex phenomenon. Not only is obedience to leaders necessary, but also obedience to custom. In addition, the complexity of relationships among an enormous variety of exclusive groups requires considerable regulation. Thus, regardless of how the totemic system arose Durkheim's main point should not be overlooked: that society, once created, makes considerable demands upon its members. Society develops a "life of its own," as it were, in much the same way that spirits, because of the "omnipotence" of man's thought, develop a life of their own. Spirits and gods, as Durkheim observed, make demands on their worshipers, mainly because they were created by men as a means of going beyond nature. Men are taxed beyond themselves by the spirits they create. They are forced to forgo certain pleasures, to abide by certain taboos and interdictions, with the result that most religions develop some form of asceticism as a way of life.

Similarly, society, once created, makes constant demands upon men. Interdictions, once made, says Durkheim, must be enforced. Punishment, the bane of man's existence, becomes the natural food for the beautiful monster he has created: society.

3

The Sacred Forms of Punishment

We have seen, very briefly, why punishment was a necessary and natural part of primitive life. We know in very general terms where both the urge and the necessity to punish come from.

Because man has the capacity to interpret nature, he reproduces the natural order in the form of societies and various social relationships which comprise culture. Eventually, two domains of culture are produced by this interpretive and metaphorical process: the sacred, in the form of rituals and rites such as those of fertility, worship and taboo, totemism, animism and naturism; and the institutional, in the form of social institutions such as the family, slavery, the school, the criminal law, and the military. In this chapter we will consider the sacred forms of punishment, and subsequent chapters will investigate the institutional forms. One should be aware that this division is in no way meant to classify types of punishment. Most punishments may be interpreted as a function of both rituals and institutions.

We saw in Chapter 2 that death has played an important role in the origin of religious (or sacred) prohibition, so it comes as no surprise that the largest source of material on the sacred forms of punishment concerns the use of the death penalty. In addition, death, probably the most ancient of all forms of formal punishment, has been the pivotal criminal punishment in Western society from ancient times until the nineteenth century. For these reasons, I will deal in this chapter mainly with the sacred forms of the death penalty and

27

reserve discussion of most tortures and corporal punishments until later, since they have more often been used in an institutional setting and for institutional purposes, such as extracting confessions. I shall discuss tortures and mutilations only as they relate to the various forms of executing death.

The Sacred Origins of Vengeance

One historian of capital punishment has noted that the "taking of life was the primitive and supreme satisfying of personal vengeance."[1] We have seen that death (whether inflicted by others or not) raises serious psychological problems concerning man's relationship with the world around him and also inevitably leads to the construction of a fantastic world, where, among other things, the dead go on living.

The intentional killing of another, therefore, does not necessarily leave the killer in a position of complete security and domination. For by killing the physical form, he has unleashed the victim's spiritual form. In primitive life the lives of the dead tend to be (though not universally) tied into a family cult system. By killing one person, in ancient times, one not only killed a part of the physical family, but also added to its spiritual part. This was a "fact" even if the killing of the other was entirely justified or accidental. Very often in Greek myths "offenders" were punished by the gods for the objective acts of killing and other misdeeds, without circumstance or intention being taken into account.[2] In any event, one can see that an important aspect of vengeance was that it could not be an isolated act. Whole families quite naturally became involved in the process.

Vengeance was also an intensely individual obligation, an absolute duty on the part of the Homeric man, and certainly was not done for the sake of the family alone.[3] It was a process that had to be followed through to the end. "Blood is drunk up by the nourishing earth, but is ineffaceable and cries for vengeance," wrote Aeschylus.[4]

Most writers have argued that because of the inherent societal self-destruction of the vengeance and feuding process, either "civic justice" intervened to administer punishment or interventions of the monarchy were necessary.[5] Some, however, have argued that both private (vengeance) and public justice have always existed side by side. There is, unfortunately, insufficient information to settle this debate. My own view is that, for public justice to intervene, some minimally sophisticated form of public governance or social structure would be necessary to administer it. Therefore, since vengeance requires (a) an absolute individual sacred obligation followed by (b) the sacred institution of the family (i.e., cult of the dead), it is probably more primitive than and preceeds public punishment. Public justice may, of course, have evolved to satisfy other needs, such as the control of economic life, but it seems reasonable to consider that it also helped hinder the social process of feuding.[6]

Mosaic law is especially full of laws of vengeance, where it is specified what acts may be avenged and what cannot. In general,[7] unintentional and accidental killings were clearly among those acts which should be avenged. However, three conditions were necessary to invoke blood killing: that the deed be a product of enmity or hatred; the situation of the killing be one such as ambush; and the presumption of guilt be based on the type of instrument used for killing. But in its most primitive form, vengeance saw a crime in every injury.[8] In Mosaic law, the blood feud was also a divine duty, and in some situations the act of vengeance could be dealt against the head of the offender's family. Moses specifically countenanced this type of punishment.[9]

Moses must also have recognized the dangers of vengeance unleashed, because his solution was to establish "cities of refuge," designated cities where an offender could seek refuge and have his case "tried."[10] Here, the first recognition of "intent" was taken. If the village councils decided that the offender had killed with malicious intent or with a murderous weapon, he had to be delivered up to the avenger. If unintentional, the avenger had to wait until the slayer stepped outside the city. Flight by the slayer into the city of refuge was perhaps one of the earliest forms of voluntary exile, later adopted by both Greeks and Romans.

There has been a tendency to equate blood feud with the primitive notion of *lex talionis*—"an eye-for-an-eye"—and although this principle is deeply embedded in Mosaic law, it is only partly related. Many offenses which did not result in the death of the victim (especially since attempts were considered equivalent to completed acts) were to be avenged by killing. Therefore the eye-for-an-eye principle, strictly speaking, breaks down here. In fact, the blood feud appears to have a spiraling effect, in which killing must be avenged by more killings and so on, until one family is wiped out.[11] The most important motivating factors in vengeance appear to be (a) a blind feeling of duty on the part of the victim or victim's closest relative to avenge the wrong by killing; (b) the belief of the victim's family that the victim, or if dead, the victim's closest relative is unclean until the offense is avenged.

There is, therefore, both an individual urge to kill in vengeance and a strong social pressure to fulfill a tradition. In ancient times these two forces, individual urge and social pressure, were often combined into one, thus unleashing one of the most frightening and powerful punitive forces in society: collective punishment. Stoning to death is the oldest form of collective punishment, and beheading is probably the oldest form of individual vengeance. Specific mutilations were also commonly carried out in vengeance killing. Let us now turn to the sacred forms of these two kinds of punishment and to other forms which are often variations of those basic types.

Beheading

Beheading is an ancient form of death penalty which can be traced well into pre-Christian times. One of the earliest instances of beheading was the execution of Brutus's son described by Livy.[12] He was first stripped naked, bound to a stake, hands tied behind his back, and scourged. Only then was he thrown to the ground, and his head cut off with a single blow of an axe.[13] We should note that during Greek and Roman times this form of punishment was not often used on criminals, but was the most commonly used form of execution of those conquered in war. There are several theories as to the origin and ritual function of beheading.

SACRIFICE THEORY: There are many documented cases of ancient beheadings in which the heads were preserved and stuck up on high poles.[14] This practice, it is thought, was a sacrifice to the god of lightning.[15] There are three arguments supporting this interpretation. First, the manner of beheading was similar to that of sacrificing animals, and the techniques used for such sacrifices were transferred to humans.[16] But this assumes that animal sacrifice preceded human sacrifice, for which evidence is inconclusive. However, it is very well documented that the ancient Teutonic people widely practiced the beheading of all manner of animals, placing the heads upon a pole or a tree. Second, in these cases, the offender was unclothed—a religious ritual with very old roots: "with the stripping of the body's clothing there falls too, the envelope of the soul, or the fate and secret of everyday life. . . ."[17] Indeed, some form of stripping remained an essential part of torture and execution throughout the whole of the Inquisition.[18] Finally, one is referred to the mythological headless horseman, descended perhaps from the Nordic God Wotan who drove on his chariot through the clouds swinging his axe and so cleaving the hills. The head was seen as the soul, the most precious part of man, and offered up to the gods. But if this practice were a sacrifice, from all the descriptions of these practices, it appears to have been a rather casual one at that—not surrounded by extensive rituals and procedures that usually accompany a sacrifice. Apparently only the stripping of clothing was part of the "ritual," and this may be interpreted from a simply functional point of view. To sever the head cleanly, the executioner needs a clean blow—unhampered by any loose clothing that may get in the way of the swing.

APOTROPAIC THEORY (warding off evil): A more plausible explanation takes note of another important observation: that many beheadings, perhaps even the first beheadings, were conducted *after* the victim was dead.[19] This observation has two important implications. First that the choice of beheading as a means of killing was not necessarily made for "functional" reasons—for reasons of efficiency, etc. Second, it means that the separation of the head from the body was the significant symbolic act in this form of execution, not the actual killing itself. We are once again able to refer to the dominant theme of death: the cult of the dead and the cult of ancestors. The physical killing of a man was seen as only the beginning of a process. The victim's soul still lived on. Yet, to the ancient mind, the division between soul and body was difficult to maintain; on the one hand the body appeared dead, but on the other, the spirit lived on. How to confront this problem? Separate the spirit from the body to cut down its mobility. If the soul had no body, so hoped the ancient mind, it could not move about. This is why, indeed, the separation of head from body was seen as creating a "magical dividing wall between head and trunk."[20] And it did not stop there: extensive mutilation of corpses was also a very common practice.[21] By destroying the physical image, hopefully the ghost was given a more difficult time.

REFLECTION THEORY: Many punishments of the Teutons throughout Europe during the middle ages were a kind of reflection of the offense.[22] Ploughing off the head was a very early form of beheading for a person who trespassed across a boundary line. The offender was buried at the place of trespass up to the neck, and then a circular plough was driven over him, thus striking off the head. Another example of the death penalty by reflection in medieval Weistumer was the chopping off of the heads of those who unlawfully struck off the tops of trees![23] In Teutonic languages, "ploughing" the head precedes other words used to describe decapitation.[24] There are many examples of reflecting punishment which we shall consider below. It does, perhaps, explain partially the practice of quartering the victims on the block and the gallows in medieval England somewhat later. Although it often is assumed that the placing of heads upon London Bridge or Temple Bar was done for deterrence purposes, there were a number of cases in which each of the four quarters were sent for display to particular areas of England where the offender was known to have committed his offenses. Although this is not exactly a "reflection" of the crime, it still represents an attempt to translate an offense concretely into its punishment.

HONOR THEORY: All of the above theories remain to some extent plausible. However, none appears to address itself to one fact of beheadings—that since the Greeks and Romans,[25] to die by the sword, especially to be decapitated, has always been considered the most honorable form of execution. In England the block was reserved for those of high status—hanging or sometimes the low block was used for the robber.

William the Conqueror introduced beheading to England, and the first to lose his head was the Earl of Northumberland in 1076. A succession of lofty figures followed him to their broken graves over the next six centuries, including: Archbishop Scrope (1405); Earl of Surrey (1547); Duke of Somerset (1552); Duke of Northumberland (1553); Lady Jane Grey (1554); Lord Guildford Dudley (1554); Mary, Queen of Scots (1587); Earl of Essex (1601); Sir Walter Raleigh (1618); Earl of Stratford (1641); Charles I (1649); Lord William Russell (1683); Earl of Kennun (1716); Earl of Kilmarnock and Lord Balmerino (1746). In 1644 Archbishop Laud petitioned to be beheaded rather than hanged, but his petition was denied. The last to be beheaded was Lord Lovat on April 9, 1747. After 1747, hanging became the sole form of public execution, but beheading and quartering of the body continued up until 1820.

Both the sword and the axe are significant sacred symbols. The axe and hammer especially were used by the Greek gods, and the sword was the symbol of valor in battle at a time when fighting was the most important social occupation that a young Greek or Roman could engage in. Thus to die in battle, usually by the sword or axe, was a most honorable death: in fact, the best way to go. The use of the tool of beheading is thus explained, as is the consistently high social status of those beheaded, since these people were the champions of battle and war throughout the ages.

But why must the head be severed? There are a couple of possible explanations. First, since the punisher never felt easy until the head of his enemy was completely severed, thus eliminating the possibility of the victim's ghost marauding the countryside, why should he not feel the same way about himself? It should not be assumed that because one feared the marauding soul of the dead, this condition was seen as a desirable state to be in after death. On the contrary, much religious literature from Greek through Roman to medieval times refers constantly to that terrible middle state of restlessness between death and Hades or Hell. Roman Catholics called it purgatory. Mystics refer to the restless, aimless wandering of the soul.[26] There can be no peace. Thus, to sever the head puts the soul to rest. It is a desirable state for all—both executioner and executed. The educated upper class understood this; the poverty-stricken, ignorant lower classes did not. Hanging and other lesser forms of execution were appropriate to a class that was held in disdain. Never was this displayed so keenly as by the French aristocracy in the face of the jeering crowds during the French Revolution. They rarely flinched or showed a flicker of emotion, which angered the crowds even more.[27]

A final conjecture. Nobles throughout the ages have always seen themselves as closer to the gods. Certainly during the heroic period in Greece, Homer's heroes were part god, part man. Is it not possible that to have oneself beheaded is to offer up one's soul to God, especially when one's executioner obligingly places it up high so that it may be lashed by wind and rain and other godly elements?

Stoning

Stoning is the oldest form of popular justice and the historical prototype of collective punishment so often talked about by sociologists, especially Durkheim.

The significant difference between this and other individual forms of death penalty is that here the people of the community take a direct hand. Collective action has also been noted in other forms of punishment: the use of the Halifax Gibbet (an ancient contraption resembling the guillotine), for example, during the sixteenth century in England, where those involved as victims of the crime were permitted to operate the machine.[28] We may note also the operation of the reflecting principle, since it was the practice that if an animal, such as an ox, sheep, or horse, were part of the offender's crime, these animals were used to draw out the pin that operated the machine.[29]

A more formal form of collective punishment is the firing squad commonly used in the military and also in the state of Utah. In this case, five citizens, who remain incognito, fire at the criminal. Supposedly, since one of the five has been issued a blank, no one knows for certain if he has fired a fatal shot.[30] This procedure is, of course, purely ritualistic, since the marksman can usually tell by the lesser recoil of the rifle if he has been "lucky" enough to fire the blank.

Collective punishment allows avoidance (real or imagined) of individual responsibility for the actual killing—a theme that we will come across again and again in the history of punishment.

There are various other explanations of the ritual origins and functions of stoning.

THE STONE AS SACRED: The stone was probably man's first weapon. There have been many stone cults in Egypt, Syria, Phoenicia, and Palestine,[31] and the worship of stone deities is extensively documented.[32] The stone had the power to kill; it appeared to be imperishable; and meteoric stones could only be sent from the gods. Many oaths and curses were made holding a stone. "Per Jovem lapidem" quoth the Romans, just before sacrificing an animal.

STONING AS A SACRIFICIAL FUNCTION: In Homer, the wrathful Hector berates Paris: "If the Trojan's weren't cowards, they would long ago have fitted you with a dress of stones."[33] Stoning the offender was a symbolic way of "feathering him" and thus turning him into a sacrificial animal. The practice of tarring and feathering is seen also to have its primitive origins here.

There is also evidence of a human parallel to the stoning of animals, at least as late as the seventeenth century. One, Judith Mandor, for being a Protestant:

> . . . was fastened to a stake, and sticks thrown at her from a distance, in the very same manner as in the barbarous custom formerly practiced on Shrove Tuesday, of throwing at cocks. By this inhuman proceeding her limbs were beat and mangled in a most terrible manner, and at last one of the bludgeons bashed her brains out.[34]

INCAPACITATION: By stoning, and thus virtually burying the offender, the soul of the dead was imprisoned beneath sacred stones and could not escape to do harm to others. This was an old Nordic belief.[35]

CLEANSING: The Greeks favored the stoning of criminals as a "radical defensive penal action," in an effort to remove pollution from their society.[36] At the time, the criminal was seen as an infected individual, as were lepers and other "unclean" people. But the cleansing ritual is more clearly illustrated in the method used by the Jews from very, very ancient times. It was prescribed in Mosaic law for all crimes which aroused the anger of God, such as blasphemy and idolatry.[37] The stones were missiles of individual sins, transferred to the criminal. Not only was Hebrew society cleansed of the polluting criminal or blasphemer, it was cleansed also of its own sins. Remember Jesus' words: "He that is without sin among us, let him first cast a stone at her" (John 8:7). His warning apparently went unheeded, since stoning was continued as a common practice well through to the Inquisition.

LYNCH JUSTICE: As I noted, the most significant aspects of stoning are its most ancient origin and the direct collective nature of the action. Although I noted previously that Moses specifically prescribed stoning for various offenses, it never appeared in the codified laws of the Romans. Rather, the Romans tended to turn a blind eye when it suited them, should the Jews decide to administer such collective punishment on one of their own transgressors.[38] Thus, stoning became the prototype for lynching.

Some have suggested that it is the collective, sudden revulsion of the community to a crime that is at the primary origin of this form of punishment. All else, the sacrifice, the cleansing, the incapacitation of the soul, all of these are secondary, ancillary forms of the punishment. By this interpretation, sacred rituals are said to be less important to the evolution of punishment forms.[39] One may argue, of course, that collective behavior itself may have sacred origins, as we saw in Chapter 2.

Hanging: The Common Man's Fate

In contrast to beheading, throughout history being hanged has been a disgrace, particularly if one were also stripped naked.[40] Hanging was used very little by both the Romans and the Greeks, although there is some disagreement about the latter.[41] It was not an official form of punishment by Roman law. Nor was it used among the Jews, though postmortal hanging is mentioned in the Bible.

SACRIFICIAL THEORY: Two main sources have been used to support the sacrifice interpretation of hanging. It is well documented that in a holy grove in Upsala, men were sacrificed by being hanged on sacred trees. These victims were dedicated to the Nordic god Odin, who became known as Lord of the Gallows. Odin was said to have been sacrificed to himself:

> *"I know that I hung on the windy tree*
> *For nine whole nights,*
> *Wounded with the spear, dedicated to Odin,*
> *Myself to Myself."*[42]

Might this god not be called the god of suicide? Again, it is well documented that the most strongly favored form of suicide during the middle ages[43] appears to have been hanging. Furthermore, hanging in effigy—especially of gods suspended from sacred trees—has also been widely practiced since Greek times, apparently a practice used to revive or resurrect a god.[44]

May we explain now why hanging is seen as such an ignominious death? Perhaps it was because one resembled a dead god or because it resembled the especially disgusting and sacrilegious form of death —suicide.

Dogs were commonly hanged alongside the criminal.[45] This is further support for the idea that hanging, at least in Germany in the middle ages, was very much a sacrificial ritual. The hanging of other animals has also been reported, especially of wolves,[46] and the hanging of dogs at the execution of a Jew was an old practice.[47]

When a tree was used, it had to be an old and dried up tree, for it was believed that if a person were hanged on a healthy, leafy tree, it would wither and die. Several chronicles have referred to this practice among the ancient Teutons.[48]

APOTROPAIC THEORY: Another important mythical notion had to do with "the evil eye." Death by hanging makes the eyes bulge, and thus the necessity to place a hood over the criminal. This practice is reported as early as Roman times by Cicero and has been a practice in hangings ever since. Perhaps it is the thought of these staring, bulbous faces that has encouraged the nightmarish idea of the devil's army, or the "raging army," as it was called in medieval times:[49] a mind-boggling army of executed criminals and traitors, restlessly seething under gallows hill like maggots in liver—grotesque apparitions. Little wonder that hanging was seen as such a terrible fate.

One final point concerning the mythical meaning of hanging deserves mention. For much of the middle ages, the criminal was dragged on a leather hide to the place of execution, and great care was taken that his feet should not touch the ground. This is stated in a number of officially worded death sentences used in Germany and Switzerland during the middle ages.[50]

I alluded briefly in Chapter 2 to the worship of and belief in the virtue and power of the earth in relation to the seasons and fertility, and it is well documented elsewhere.[51] The practice of requiring the criminal to be kept from the earth until hanged thrusts him into the gulf between heaven and earth. The earth is saved from the criminal's demonical powers. He is left to swing in the wind—to be cleaned by the elements of nature. Indeed, it was not until comparatively modern times that the body of the hanged criminal was cut down and buried. Rather, in the earliest period, it was left there to decay and eventually to be "returned to dust" by nature, and later it was subjected to a wide range of practices aimed at assisting nature in her task (e.g., burning, dismembering).

Breaking on the Wheel

It is likely that three other different forms of punishments have their origins in this ancient Greek punishment. These are crucifixion, gibbeting, and garroting. It is also closely related to hanging—especially in England.

Excavations in Greece have revealed the remains of several bodies dating to pre-Homeric times which had been pegged to wooden boards by metal bands. Although there is some disagreement about it, the practice of breaking on the wheel in classical Greece was called *apotympanismos.* However, a wheel was not necessarily employed. The culprit was laid out on a flat board, or sometimes crosspiece, and pegged to it with irons. The executioner then systematically broke all the major bones of the wretched criminal with sharp blows from an iron bar. When it was taken up in Roman times (called *in rota mittere*), expert executioners were employed who were able to break the bones without tearing the skin. Following that the practice varies considerably. Sometimes there was a hole bored through the board behind the offender's neck, through which was passed a leather cord, and this was repeatedly tightened until the victim was strangled: the forerunner of the terrible Spanish practice of garroting.[52] Others report that a death blow was usually administered to the stomach;[53] others that the prisoner was simply left out in the weather to die a slow and horrible death. In the practices of crucifixion and gibbeting alive, the unfortunate offender was simply pegged out and left to die of starvation and exposure without the previous beating. However, with gibbeting, especially in England, there was a good chance that the culprit would be hanged in chains as well. Indeed, it was most commonly used as a means of preserving the exhibition of an already hanged criminal, whose body had been parboiled in pitch or water to preserve it for the wonderment of passersby.

Other variations of the wheel were that of running a cart wheel over the arms and legs, thus crushing the bones, and then tying the body to the wheel, raising it up, and leaving the offender to die;[54] or pegging him out on the ground and running over him with a spiked wheel;[55] or tying him to the broad side of the wheel itself and rolling it down a mountain.[56]

Two theories are used to explain this ancient ritual:

SACRIFICE THEORY: The wheel is the symbol of the sun—which is well documented both in Greek and Roman mythology.[57] But more important, there are myths of punishment which clearly tie the two together. Ixion, after having murdered his father-in-law and become drunk with nectar, demanded Hera as a mistress. But Zeus played a trick on him so that instead of his mistress, he embraced a cloud. Ixion's punishment for his wild demand was to be bound to a glowing wheel and driven eternally around the earth. Thus was treated the first murderer in Greek mythology. The Nordic god Odin—god of thunder, lightning, and the storm, master of stars and sun (which is his eye)—has traditionally received sacrifices of animals and men. Lawbreakers have been traditionally offered up to him. Sacrifice theory seems at its strongest in explanation of this punishment—but the breaking?

APOTROPAIC THEORY: This theory can explain both the breaking and the wheel. In early Teutonic times, the wheel had to have nine spokes—a well-known magical number for defending against bad spirits.[58] In addition, not only is the wheel a symbol of the sun, but the circle is also an ancient apotropaic symbol. It has also been suggested that the breaking of the bones is an attempt to break the culprit's ghost.[59] The bones are seen as the most enduring, lasting part of the body, so by breaking the bones it is believed the culprit's spirit will be prevented from getting around too easily. There is also considerable evidence to show that bones, especially the marrow, were seen by the ancient primitive as sacred, wherein lies the permanent and sacred abode of life.[60]

A final and very important observation may be made about this form of punishment. The victim is characteristically left to die, on his own. There is evidence that the Greek practice of delivering the fatal blow was rare and in the majority of cases the culprit was left to die at his own pace.[61] The same practice also applied to crucifixion, where there is much evidence that persons crucified stayed alive for some time—even days—and then delivered speeches to the crowd below.[62] The practice of gibbeting alive also allowed the criminal to die at the hands of the elements of nature. That is, the criminal died, fantastically, by no one's hand.

This leads us to two apparently quite different forms of punishments, which are, however, closely tied by the practice of leaving the victim to nature. These are burial alive and drowning.

Burial Alive and Drowning

For a moment, let us return to the description I gave earlier of stoning to death. I noted that a major feature of that punishment was the collective involvement in the punishment. There is another less agreeable way of putting that: it permits the punishment of the miscreant without any individual having to shoulder the responsibility. But in stoning, the killing is done quite directly; with burial alive and drowning, although the punishment is not necessarily collective, an attempt is made to avoid any direct responsibility for the killing.

The most famous earliest example of burial alive is the punishment of vestal virgins who broke their vows. To the Romans, the fortunes of Vesta were inextricably tied to the fortunes of Rome. Plutarch describes the punishment:

> If one lost her maiden honor, she was buried alive near the Colline Gate. There is there, still inside the city a rise in the ground . . . here a subterranean room is built of small proportions and with an entrance from above. In it there is a complete couch, a burning light and a small quantity of the essentials of life, i.e., bread, water

in a jug, milk, oil, in order, as it were, that they should not be guilty of giving a person consecrated to the most important religious offices over to death by starvation.

The delinquent herself is placed in a sedan chair which is closely covered up and fastened with straps, so that not even her voice can be heard any longer. Thus she is carried over the Forum; everyone steps silently out of the way and in the silence of deepest mourning accompanies her. There is, indeed, no other spectacle so gruesome, nor a day of such grief as this day. When the chair reaches the place, the servants undo the straps, the Pontifex Maximus says some secret prayers, raises his hands to the Gods and lets the deeply veiled woman step out and put her foot on the ladder which leads down into chamber. When she has climbed down, the ladder is withdrawn and the chamber covered up, and earth shovelled over it until the place is levelled up with the rest of the ground.

This is the punishment of Vestals who have abandoned the sacred honour of maidenhood.[63]

Tacitus also mentions burial alive among the Germans. And here also, it was common to "put off" the time of death, by inserting an air tube into the mouth of the offender. By the middle ages, the punishment had pretty much died out or perhaps been overtaken by a similar form of punishment: impalement. With this punishment, a grave or pit was dug, and a stake was driven through the person to be buried. Impalement of corpses is a much older practice than impalement of the living.[64] In any event, the most significant aspect of this punishment was that the offender was nailed securely to the ground. This practice illustrates the fear of the "dangerous dead." The ghosts of the impaled, it is said, appear on dark nights as ravens, with a big hole in their chests through which shines the moon. This form of penalty was common in the middle ages in Germany as punishment for rape and the murder of children by their mothers. The practice was linked to many dark superstitions. Women who died in childbirth were often staked into their graves, along with the child.[65] It was also common, up until the sixteenth century in Germany, to place the culprit on a bed of thorns.[66]

Drowning and a similar punishment, sinking in a bog, also allow for interpretations similar to those just described. Drowning, traditionally used as the punishment for sorcery, effected the "magical removal" of the polluted person who was thrown into the water never to be seen again.[67] Bogs were also seen as the abode of spooks and ghosts, a bottomless morass. Sinking criminals in these terrible places sent them back to where they came from. In contrast to drowning, however, burial in a morass appears to have been predominantly postmortal, carried out with considerable ritual accoutrements, such as covering the body with wattle, or driving a stake through the coffin.

Other early practices of drowning the offender are of interest and point directly to the similarity of burial alive. There are reports of several instances of criminals being placed in a tub and set adrift at sea.[68] In England it was also common during the middle ages for sailors guilty of offenses to be tied to a stake at low tide and left to drown in the incoming tide. Both these variations of drowning were designed in accord with the principle (never stated or even recognized, of course) of indeterminate punishment:[69] that is, the desire to subject the criminal to punishment yet avoid personal involvement in or responsibility for the punishment. The tub punishment especially is an extreme example of this principle; occasionally the culprits were fortunate enough to be washed ashore and saved and justice was considered to be done. In other words, nature was left as the final arbiter. Or as Sophocles in strangely modern words explained in his drama in which Antigone is buried alive: "She should have food enough to exonerate the state from guilt. . . ."[70]

How can we interpret these forms of punishment? The usual competing theories have been advanced.

SACRIFICE THEORY: The instances of the punishment of deviant vestal virgins have been used to support this view. The many instances also of "walling in" a sacrificed victim (usually a child) into a new bridge, wall, or building is also used to support it.[71] However, the latter categories, at least, were never criminals, and it would seem that criminals as such were never walled in. We may consider the deviant vestal virgin as a criminal, since a wrongful act by a vestal virgin was tantamount to high treason. Yet it is difficult to conceive of her execution as a sacrifice. Rather, it was a straightout punishment.

APOTROPAIC THEORY: One theory suggests that these punishments were designed to rid the society of a plague.[72] Considerable evidence is available that persons were buried alive to avoid plague. But even here, these persons were innocent in the sense that they had not committed criminal offenses. Again, it was common to bury children for this reason. However, we do find more evidence for the apotropaic theory in sinking in a morass and drowning. We have noted the elaborate apotropaic rituals related to sinking in a morass. Drowning was also accompanied very early by complicated rituals. The Romans administered an especially nasty punishment for patricide. The criminal was tied in a sack—to exclude water, air, and earth—with the aim of sending him back to the beasts. He was tied up in the sack along with all manner of beasts: vipers, cocks, dogs, and even apes.[73] Or he was sewn into an ox-skin, his head covered with a wolf skin (preferably a she-wolf's uterus), and scourged with red-hot rods. We should be clear, however, that they were not sacrifices, but punishments clearly designed to make the "punishment fit the crime"— i.e., patricide was a crime against nature and so should be dealt with by sending the offender back to nature's beasts.[74]

Burning

"If a man abide not in me, he is cast forth as a branch, and is withered; and men gather them, and cast them into the fire, and they are burned."

Burning to death is an extremely old form of execution. It was practiced very early by the Hebrews against transgressors, by the ancient Germans, the Celts, the Babylonians, and many, many primitive tribes all over the world.

There are two curious features about the ritual use of fire and the burning of corpses. One is that some civilizations and tribes have so adored and worshiped fire that it has been the preferred way to dispose of the dead. The stories of ancient sacred funeral pyres of the Greeks and Romans provide obvious support for this observation. The pyre constructed for Caesar from the furniture and personal belongings of the people of Rome is perhaps the most famous example of this sacred practice. Yet others have considered the disposing of the dead by fire to be utterly terrifying—this applies especially to the Jews.

Why should this occur? The answer is probably that different peoples have different conceptions of and relationships with their gods, and for a great hero to be consumed in a funeral pyre along with his servant, horse, and various other trappings of life, was seen as sending him up to the gods; he was transformed into fire to become as near to a god as a human could become.

But this was burning *after* death. Burning alive was a different matter and was reserved by the Romans for the most hated of enemies. At first, under Roman law, burning to death was a "reflected" punishment for arson—a crime considered from ancient times to be equivalent to malicious murder,[75] akin to treason or rebellion. Nero had Christians denounced as the perpetrators of the great fire in Rome during which he is said to have fiddled, and which he perhaps started himself.[76] Thus the Christians were treated to the most horrendous execution: clothed in animal skins, torn by dogs, nailed to stakes or crosses, then burned to death.[77] Sometimes the stake was driven up through the body so that it came out the mouth. Nero wished to propitiate Vulcan, the god of fire.

There are several possible interpretations of this form of punishment.

REFLECTING PUNISHMENT: We can see that there is some limited validity to this interpretation in view of the Roman punishment for arson. However, there are many other crimes besides arson for which burning alive as a part of the execution has been most common: the ancient Hebrew God Yahweh recommended it for incest and prostitution;[78] the Inquisition of the middle ages used it extensively for witches and heretics; the English used it together with hanging for punishment of traitors and especially female murderers and coiners.[79]

SACRIFICES: There is an account of the sacrifice of criminals to fire gods, based on observations left for us by Caesar and Posidonius.[80] Burning to death is said to have begun with the ancient Celts of Scotland and Gaul. A great festival took place every five years, and the Celts saved their criminals or, if there were not enough, captives were taken at war.[81] When the festival came, huge wicker-work images of wood and grass were constructed, which were filled with live men, cattle and various animals. Sometimes the sacrificial victims were shot through with arrows, or impaled. But eventually, the wicker effigies were set alight and their victims burned alive. Frazer notes that the burning of giant wicker effigies has been a central attraction at midsummer festivals throughout Europe for many years and suggests that the similarity of these rituals to the ancient Celtic custom is too great to be ignored. It should be pointed out, however, that criminals were sacrified not because they were seen as demons or devils, but because they were available: i.e., since criminals occupied the lowest position in social life, they were expendable and could be used as sacrificial victims. They were not burned to death as criminals, but rather as human sacrifices to the fire gods.[82] In fact, there are more cases on record of the sacrifice of the innocent than of the guilty.

APOTROPAIC THEORY: An obvious interpretation is that burning provided the complete physical and metaphysical destruction of the criminal.[83] Criminals were burned and their ashes thrown to the four winds and sometimes sprinkled over the gallows. The dim beginnings of most religions of modern civilization appear to have given the worship of fire a central place.[84] And this, of course, is not at all surprising when one considers the important place fire must have taken among the primal horde. Fire is a Janus head: it opens the way for an enormous array of benefits to the man who can control it; but it can never be tamed, and when it breaks free, it turns its horrible, insatiable, unquenchable side toward us: it devours and destroys all in its path. We have little difficulty therefore in understanding how fire was so worshiped in the vague beginnings of civilization; how it remains a central symbol in virtually all modern religious rituals; and how it may be seen as the perfect treatment of those forces, tangible and intangible, which have frightened men throughout the ages: witches, heretics, sodomists, blasphemers, lunatics, criminals, wolves, were-wolves, and so on. "With his sharp, bright eyes he sees the hidden demons, seizes them with his tongue, with his brazen teeth. . . ."[85] This theory does not, however, explain why the culprits are burned alive. It only explains why burning is used to dispose of the corpse. Our next interpretation tries to take this into account.

DIVINE RETRIBUTION ON EARTH: Although it is perhaps difficult beyond a certain point to argue that any one of the forms of punishment so far described is more cruel than any other, since they are all so horrendous, I am inclined to think that burning alive has been the most awful. The method was at its height during the Italian and Spanish Inquisitions, which together lasted almost five centuries. From the descriptions available to us, one can only draw the conclusion that is was the intention of the executioners (or their bosses) to inflict as much pain, suffering and torture on the unfortunate culprit as was "humanly" possible. The celebrated description by Henry More of the burning of the Lord Bishop of Gloucester (Dr. John Hooper) in 1555 for heresy speaks for itself:

> The place of execution was near a great elm tree, over against the college of priests, where he was used to preach; the spot round about and the boughs of the tree were filled with spectators. Bishop Hooper then knelt down and prayed. Having closed his devotional exercises, the Bishop prepared himself for the stake. He took off his

gown, and delivered it to the sheriff; he then took off his doublet, hose, and waistcoat. Being now in his shirt, he trussed it between his legs, where he had a pound of gunpowder in a bladder, and under each arm the same quantity. He now went up to the stake, where three iron hoops were brought, one to fasten him round the waist, another round his neck, and another round his legs; but he refused to be bound with them, saying, "You have no need to trouble yourselves; I doubt not God will give me strength sufficient to abide the extremity of the fire without bands; notwithstanding, suspecting the frailty and weakness of the flesh, but having assured confidence in God's strength, I am content you do as you think good." The iron hoop was then put round his waist, which being made too short, he shrank and put in his belly with his hand; but when they offered to bind his neck and legs he refused them, saying, "I am well assured I shall not trouble you." Being affixed to the stake, he lifted up his eyes and hands to heaven, and prayed in silence. The man appointed to kindle the fire then came to him and requested his forgiveness, of whom he asked why he should forgive him, since he knew of no offence he had committed against him. "O sir (said the man), I am appointed to make the fire." "Therein," said Bishop Hooper, "thou dost nothing to offend me: God forgive thee thy sins, and do thy office I pray thee." Then the reeds were thrown up, and he received two bundles of them in his own hands, and put one under each arm. Command was now given that the fire should be kindled; but, owing to the number of green faggots, it was some time before the flames set fire to the reeds. The wind being adverse, and the morning very cold, the flames blew from him, so that he was scarcely touched by the fire. Another fire was soon kindled of a more vehement nature: it was now the bladders of gunpowder exploded, but they proved of no service to the suffering prelate. He now prayed with a loud voice, "Lord Jesus, have mercy upon me; Lord Jesus, have mercy upon me; Lord Jesus, receive my spirit"; and these were the last words he was heard to utter. But even when his face was completely black with the flames, and his tongue swelled so that he could not speak, yet his lips went till they were shrunk to the gums; and he knocked his breast with his hands until one of his arms fell off, and then continued knocking with the other while the fat, water, and blood dripped out of his finger ends. At length, by renewing the fire, his strength was gone, and his hand fastened in the iron which was put round him. Soon after, the whole lower part of his body being consumed, he fell over the iron that bound him, into the fire, amidst the horrible yells and acclamations of the bloody crew that surrounded him. This holy martyr was more than three quarters of an hour consuming; the inexpressible anguish of which he endured as a lamb, moving neither forwards, backwards, nor to any side: his nether parts were consumed and his bowels fell out some time before he expired. Thus perished, in a manner the most horrible that the rage of hell itself could devise, in a manner more barbarous than that exercised by wild

American Indians to their prisoners taken in war, the right reverend
father in God, Dr. John Hooper, for some time Bishop of Worces-
ter, and afterward of Gloucester.[86]

It later became the practice throughout Europe to strangle the
criminal first, and usually this was seen as a humanitarian step as
was noted by Strutt in 1775 in his description of the burning of Anne
Williams for the poisoning of her husband in 1753:

> The letter of the law to this very day, I believe condemns a
> woman, who doth murder her husband, to be burnt alive, but the
> sentence is always mitigated, for they are first strangled. In the case
> of Catherine Hayes (who, for the murder of her husband, some
> few years ago, was adjudged to suffer death at the stake) the in-
> tention was first to strangle her; but as they used at that time to
> draw a rope which was fastened round the culprit's neck, and came
> through a staple of the stake, but at the very moment that the fire
> was put to the wood which was set around, the flames sometimes
> reached the offenders before they were quite strangled—just so it
> happened to her; for the fire taking quick hold of the wood, and
> the wind being brisk, blew the smoke and blaze so full in the faces
> of the executioners, who were pulling at the rope, that they were
> obliged to let go their hold before they had quite strangled her;
> so that, as I have been informed by some there present, she suffered
> much torment before she died.[87]

It is to be noted, however, that by this time, such punishment was
used more for criminals, particularly female criminals, and less for
heretics and witches, since the Inquisition had mostly passed. But,
as we shall see in Chapter 5, the religious imagery of punishment
lived on. And what imagery! The hell of the middle ages was seen
as the most loathesome place of perpetual fires, where there lived all
manner of ugly demons and disgusting serpents, who took great
pleasure in tormenting and torturing victims sent to them. We need
only look at the many artistic works which depicted hell during that
time, such as Fra Angelico's *Universal Judgment* or the works of
Bosch. All of them depict the most terrible scenes of hell. It is, therefore, not too far fetched to conclude that the Inquisitors were trying
to bring the wrath of God to earth, to reflect as closely as possible
the most terrible punishments that they imagined were inflicted by
the devil. Hence, the emphasis on burning, torture, and suffering.
Burning becomes a sort of divine reflective punishment, which easily
explains why burning alive was such a central aspect of the punishment, since after the heretic was dead, he would be treated to the
roguish punishments of hell; the Inquisitor wanted to give the living a taste of hell before he passed on.

We should note in closing this section that some have suggested the Inquisitors were motivated to inflict horrible tortures for other reasons, both institutional and psychological, which have little to do with ritual. This is quite possibly true, and we will take this up in later chapters. In this regard, ordeal by fire is sometimes seen as a ritual punishment by some writers.[88] But it is not so much a ritual punishment as it is a ritual judgment. This applies especially to the use of torture by the Holy Inquisitors.

Quartering and Other Mutilations

Authorities appear to be agreed that the earliest origin of the punishment of quartering was disembowelling[89] or other practices which tore out internal organs. The sacred role of entrails during ancient Roman and Greek times is well known. "It is not so much the skinning and cutting up of the body that is the chief thing, but the fact that a way is forced into the last stronghold of all life, the heart."[90] A few interpretations of this practice present themselves.

PUNISHMENT OF BODILY ORGANS: From the many cases of disembowelling, it seems that certain organs of the body were thought of as the seat of the crime. Thus, it was for a long time the practice in England to have the hearts of traitors torn from their bodies and various other parts of the body treated as though they were the objects responsible for the crime:

> That the traitor is to be taken from the prison, and laid upon a sledge, or hurdle, and drawn to the gallows, or place of execution, and there hanged by the neck until he be half dead, and then cut down; his entrails to be cut out of his body, and burnt by the executioner; then his head is to be cut off, his body to be divided into quarters; and afterwards his head and quarters are to be set up in some open places directed; which usually are on the City Gates, on London Bridge, or upon Westminster Hall. And to render the crime more terrible to the spectators, the hangman, when he takes out the heart, shows it to the people, and says, here is the heart of a traitor.[91]

Several similar cases are reported in Germany and Switzerland, one in which kidneys were torn from the body with red-hot pincers, since they were seen as the seat of the criminal's wicked disposition.[92] Another case was the terrible execution of Balthazar Gerard, murderer of the Prince of Orange.[93] "On the first day he was flayed and rubbed over with salt, and needles stuck into his fingers. On the next day his flesh was torn with red hot pincers." Then his heart was cut out and impaled on his hand, to the words, "The treacherous murderer of his own master might rightly get such a terrible reward." He was then quartered, and his parts dispensed to various places. In yet another case, the heart was torn from the body and thrust in the face of the criminal with the words, "See . . . your heart!" There are also cases in which the quartered parts were put on display at the scenes where the criminal was said to have committed his crimes.

Other punishments, not intentionally leading to death, but clearly meant as punishments of particular "guilty" bodily organs, are of interest. It was customary to amputate the right hand for coining false money during the reign of Henry I and usual for one hand to be cut off previous to execution for arson and murder during the middle ages. It was also common to either cut out the tongue of blasphemers, or, as in the case of one of the Huguenots, the "tongue was pierced and attached to his cheek with an iron pin."[94] The ears were cut off, nose cut, and brandings applied often to those assigned to the pillory, but these were not so much punishments of specifically guilty organs as a means of ridicule. We shall consider these practices in a later chapter. Many other mutilations have also been practiced for the purpose of torture, which we shall consider in Chapter 4.

RETRIBUTION: Although we will have much to say about retribution later in this book, we would do well to note that one of the most primitive manifestations of this principle of punishment is the attempt to reflect the crime in the punishment. Punishment of particular bodily organs specifically involved in the commission of crimes, as we have just described, may be seen as a form of retribution by reflection.

When we consider the conglomeration of a wide variety of tortures involved in execution by quartering, we are moved to think that this method is the cruelest yet, since there seems to be no end to the barbarous cruelties laid on. The descriptions left to us by contemporaries all seem to refer to especially serious crimes, such as particularly gruesome murders, parricides, or the murder of a master by a trusted servant. So, although the horrifying descriptions make us feel that the punishment was inflicted because the punishers enjoyed the spectacle, there have been genuine attempts to make the death penalty equal the atrocity or severity of the crime. I would not want to overstate this point, since the most notorious description of drawing assunder is enough to make anyone turn green, and it is hard to avoid the conclusion that it was done for any other reason than to inflict torture of the most beastly variety. The last execution in France by drawing assunder was that of Robert François Damiens, in 1757, found guilty of *lèse majesté* and parricide. A special "extra" to his execution was the court's order that he be subjected to *question ordinaire et extraordinaire* to make him confess the names of his accomplices. The court ordered:

> . . . that he be taken to the Greve and, on a scaffold erected for the purpose, that his chest, arms, thighs, and calves be burnt with pincers; his right hand, holding the knife with which he committed the said parricide, burnt in sulphur; that boiling oil, melted lead, and resin, and wax mixed with sulphur, be poured in his wounds; and after that his body be pulled and dismembered by four horses, and the members and body consumed by fire, and the ashes scattered to the winds. The court orders that his property be confiscated to the King's profit; that before the said execution, Damiens be subjected to *question ordinaire et extraordinaire,* to make him confess the names of his accomplices.[95]

The awful tortures were administered one by one, until finally each of his lacerated limbs was attached to a horse and the executioners gave the order for the farm horses to drag the limbs from his body. But the sinews of his body were so tough that the limbs would not come apart. In the end, the executioners were forced to quarter the still living body with a knife. This method of execution was unknown in England, but was used extensively throughout France and Germany. Indeed, the hangman or executioner in many districts of Germany has been known in popular and thieves' slang as the "butcher" or "meat carver," at least since the fifteenth century. This leads us to a final interpretation of this terrible practice.

ANIMAL RITUALS: It has been noted that there is an amazing similarity between the quartering of humans and that of animals, as evidenced by the pictures of animal quartering in the Fehr collection in the Nürnberg German Museum.[96] The bowels of the human were burnt, as was the custom with animals.[97] It was also a punishment in early Teutonic times for the wanton destruction of trees—it will be remembered that we earlier observed the worship of trees as sacred and holy in those times. If a person killed a tree by stripping off its bark, as much of his bowels as was necessary to cover the damaged area was taken from the culprit's body.[98]

The practice of drawing is also related in some way to dragging at the horse's tail, which was a common punishment for religious heretics especially as a preliminary to crucifixion. It was later common for the criminal to have his feet tied to a horse's tail and his back bound onto an ox-hide or sled on which he was dragged to the gallows. This practice later gave way in England to the procession of the criminal taken to the gallows in a cart. And, of course, Achilles dragged the body of Hector round the walls of Troy. It has been suggested that the reason for dragging is to wipe out the footprints of the criminal, so that the dead person will be unable to find his way back from the execution site.

Conclusions

We may make a number of general conclusions concerning the sacred origins of the death penalty:

CRIMINALS AS SACRIFICIAL LAMBS: In general, criminals have not been sacrified to gods because of their criminal deeds, although this is not to say that it has not occurred—probably by hanging. They have most often been sacrificed along with others of less defensible social position. Indeed, more often than not innocents, namely children, have been sacrificed as offerings to various ancient gods.

CRIMINALS AS THE PURVEYORS OF EVIL: To some extent, this has been a predominant preoccupation in the punishment of criminals, though once again it is not clear whether such persons are penal or religious criminals, since the historical relationship between religion and crime is quite complicated and they have overlapped during many periods in history. There seems to be reasonable evidence suggesting that punishment has taken on the specific forms it has because of the punishers' fears of what the criminal would do after he was killed. We should be clear, though, that this fear was related to *any* dying or dead man and was simply heightened when a man was intentionally killed—whether justified or not. The killing of a criminal, therefore, invokes a double fear, since it is clearly an intentional killing and of one who is evil or unclean. Thus, provided the proper apotropaic methods were used, the community was rid of an evildoer, yet it also paid a price for the killing.

INDETERMINATE PUNISHMENT: Because of the difficulties involved in the intentional killing of a wrongdoer, various forms of punishment have evolved which, at least symbolically, allow the offender to be killed by nature, rather than directly by the accusers.

COLLECTIVE PUNISHMENT: This, the oldest form of punishment, gives vent to the immediate, bloodthirsty feelings of the community which attempts to rid itself of the uncleanliness of both the evildoer and a general feeling of evil in the community. It is a practice which "cleanses" the collective sentiment. However, we should note that it is the oldest form of punishment and has mostly been superseded by other forms, most of which avoid the direct participation of the public in inflicting the penalty. Its later form, the ribald public executions in the seventeenth and eighteenth centuries, served different purposes, which will be discussed later in the book.

APOTROPAIC RITUAL: It would seem that rituals in many forms accompany the death penalty, and these are most easily accounted for as a means to ward off evil of various kinds. The breaking of bones; sacred use of the nine-spoked wheel and the magic circle; burning and casting the ashes to the wind; drawing and quartering; drowning and sinking in a bog; staking to the ground; beheading; hanging— all of these may be interpreted as forms of defense against evils.

RETRIBUTION AND REFLECTION: Some forms of death penalty have been tied to specific crimes in an attempt either literally to deal out *lex talionis,* as in burning for the crime of arson, or to do it symbolically as in ploughing off a trespasser's head. A primitive form of retribution has also been identified: the direct assault upon a specific bodily organ, such as "the heart of a traitor" being torn from his body. Another modified form of retribution also identified was the attempt to recreate the punishment of hell on earth. This was seen as the most apt explanation of the hideous punishments of burning and drawing and quartering alive.

I must repeat that these are not presented as sole or exclusive explanations for the punishment of death presented in this chapter. Differing forms of punishments serve many purposes, often social and political, which may most usefully be surveyed from the point of view of their institutional forms. It is to the evolution of these institutional forms of punishment that we now turn.

4

Punishment and Obedience: Punishing Women, Children, Slaves, and Soldiers

We saw in our survey of the various speculations concerning the origins of civilization and punishment in society that a vague model was posed of a kind of loose group termed, for better or worse, a "horde" and injected with a structure resembling a family in the sense that there was a father, wives, and sons. Obedience to the father was an absolute and obedience to the clan a sacred obligation.

It is extremely important to note that the horde or "family" existed *before* the criminal law and its punishments. Therefore, while we may trace the particular forms that punishment has taken according to the evolution of the institution of criminal law, its procedures, and so on, it is most likely that many of the forms of criminal punishment should have been adopted from punishments that already existed, prior to the concept of criminality.[1] It is also likely that many of the justifications of punishment will be traceable to the use of punishment within social institutions that preceded modern criminal law. In this respect, we may make a distinction between two early institutional models of punishment, a distinction that is crucial to an understanding of the justifications and philosophical discussions of punishment that arose during the nineteenth and twentieth centuries. These two models are the *obedience model* and the *reciprocity model*. The prototype for the obedience model was punishment used within the primal family: punishment required to maintain obedience, first of the sons to the father, and later obedience of all to the primitive prohibitions of the incest taboo, totemic systems, and other sacred rites. The later more formalized institutional application of this obedience model was that of the military, epitomized by the city-states of Greece and Rome and enhanced by the recurring wars throughout history to modern times.

The reciprocity model has its origin with the feud, where wrongs were negotiated and treated in kind by each offending or offended party. The crucial difference between this and the obedience model is that in the obedience model there is an inherent difference in status between the punisher and punishee: the punisher is invariably socially and economically (and usually politically) more powerful. In the feud, in contrast, each party to the punishment is of equal status: thus the mutual and reciprocal nature of vengeance. I will argue later[2] that this reciprocal model of punishment is the sole social basis of the retributive philosophy of punishment.[3] We shall see that according to this principle much of what leading philosophical defenders and critics of retribution claim to be retributive in fact is not: it is punishment masking an obedience function. One reason for this is that purely reciprocal (or retributive) punishment disappeared with the feud. Although traces of feuding law may be found in modern criminal laws,[4] the fact is that the obedience model not only preceded the reciprocity model of punishment, but also subverted it both in ancient times and again in the late middle ages after feuding had reinstated itself in the period of social chaos following the burning of Rome.

There is little doubt that the obedience model of punishment both preceded and eventually completely dominated criminal punishments. We shall have more to say about this shortly. Our present task is to examine the institutional forms of the obedience model of punishment.

The Slave and Family Punishment

Women, children, and slaves have enjoyed throughout history an intimate relationship. In fact, I would go so far as to say that until the early middle ages there was virtually no distinction among them in terms of status and, subsequently, of the conditions under which they could be punished. It may seem that I am playing on popular rhetoric to equate women and children with slaves. Be assured that I am not suggesting that they are equivalent today. Much has happened in the space between now and Homer in the evolution of social life. But originally, they all occupied a similar social and legal status. As civilization developed, different institutions of control emerged, resulting in different kinds of punishments and systems of punishments which became applicable to each. The three institutions that eventually developed were the institutions of the family, of the school, and of slavery.

In addition, the reader is warned that there is considerable controversy right now concerning the sociohistorical evolution of the family. A great deal of criticism has been made of the myth that the family is our oldest social institution. Aries in his *Centuries of Childhood*,[5] probably the most influential book in this field, claims that the concept of the family was unknown until the fifteenth century. In my view, however, he is using the word in a very restricted sense, the modern sense, to mean a family group that is bound by strong emotional ties that transcend the simple genealogical system Aries sees as the only aspect of family existing before that time. It is also unclear if he means that the concept of "family" did not exist in the minds of people (which it certainly does today). Aries probably overstates his case, since he was dealing with a restricted period from the late middle ages on. He does not recognize that a lot happened before that time. Certainly, the bulk of Roman civil law revolved around the concept of the family, almost to a pathological degree.[6] Many religious rites were also centered on the home and its sacred hearth.

But one can agree with Aries that there is something very, very new about the popular image of the family today, especially the isolated, nuclear family. In fact, both the idea and the reality of this kind of family is probably less than a century old. During preceding centuries, families were never so isolated and always included fringe members who were, nevertheless, central or at least very important to the social and psychological make-up of family life. Apart from the constant physical presence of cousins, grandparents, and other strata of the extended family, the inclusion of servants, slaves, nannies, wet-nurses, and lodgers has been a most common practice. Psychohistorians have only just begun to document and analyze the importance of these additional elements of family life.[7]

As a constantly evolving, adapting, changing institution, there is no doubt that the family is the oldest social institution, and as such it is the source of the institution of punishment.

During the period of the early Roman Empire, the concept of *patria potestas* dominated Roman civil law and, in an indirect way, its criminal law also. The Romans did not have a very well developed criminal law, because it was mainly ancillary to civil law. This was because most problems of law were seen in terms of private litigations and responsibilities, even including crimes such as homicide.[8] *Patria potestas* was translated into practice as the *paterfamilias* doctrine, which gave the father of the household unlimited power. The household, by the way, legally included slaves, as well as members of the family. During the early Roman Empire, *paterfamilias* gave the father the power of life and death over all members of the household, the power of sale of any member, the power to veto marriage, and the right to recover a child whom he may have disposed of earlier —there were many complicated rules about this. At a later time, only the sale of newborns was permitted. Of course, slaves could be bought and sold at will.

The father was most definitely the agent of punishment both in terms of criminal law and socially. He could torture or punish any member of his family without any interference.[9] Nobody else could lay a hand on his "chattel." If a slave did something wrong, the matter would be referred to his *dominus* (master), and the father would decide on punishment. It should be noted, however, that slaves and sons especially had inherent economic value, and therefore the chances of their being overly physically abused were less. But women, and especially daughters, were not of economic value; in fact daughters were a distinct economic liability, since dowries had to be paid to the husband in order to marry them off. This is probably why girls were more often exposed on the hillside or plainly murdered. In fact, the practice of killing infant girls is well documented up until the middle ages throughout Europe[10] and is attested to by the higher proportion of males to females in the population throughout that period.

As monogamy gradually evolved, wives gained somewhat in status and economic value, but they were never emancipated to the slightest degree. Up to her marriage, the girl was subject to the home discipline of the father, and then after marriage to that of the husband, though the husband did eventually lose the right to punish the wife at home.[11] Prior to the early empire there were many reports of "home punishment." Livy reports one such case. There had been an epidemic of witchcraft, and a secret society of women was uncovered. The women were ordered to be executed, and Livy reports, "the condemned women were handed over to their relations or those in whose charge they were in order that they should themselves carry out the sentence in private. . . ."[12] A private execution was seen as a concession to family feelings because a public execution (i.e., one carried out by someone other than the *dominus*) would have been a disgrace.

After the Roman Empire, women were chosen as the special objects of religious persecution as part of the Holy Inquisition, and we shall look at the reasons for this in the following chapter. However, as far as criminal punishment is concerned, it must be said that women were probably by and large eventually treated much better than the men during the middle ages. In a fascinating study of female crime for the period 1300-48 for the counties of Norfolk, Yorkshire, and Northampton, Barbara Hanawalt[13] found that of a total of 10,607 felons brought to trial, the ratio of females to males was only 1:9. Furthermore, only 16 percent of women brought to trial were convicted compared to 30 percent of the men. The only aspect in which women were discriminated against was in the form of death penalty. If women killed their husbands (a common crime as it is today) this was considered tantamount to treason (since it was killing the "Lord") and the wife was burnt alive at the stake. The rest of the penalties and criminal procedures were identical for men and women.

The close affinity between children and servants is also well documented for Roman times. Not only did children wait on tables,[14] they were also mostly in the care of slaves who were either their nannies or tutors. Indeed, they were subject to be beaten by their slave tutors. To be in that position—to be beaten by a slave—has to be the lowest position on the social ladder!

But we must not carry this comparison too far. Although children and slaves were equally at the mercy of the *dominus,* the law discriminated much more against slaves, and in general the punishments were much more severe. During the early empire, if the master was murdered by a slave, all slaves in the household were put to death as a matter of course. Worse, if the master were murdered by someone outside the household, the slaves were still held responsible for the killing, since it was considered that devoted slaves should have prevented it![15]

By far the most terrible punishment was that of torture of the slaves as witnesses. This was probably an extension of the Greek practice of holding evidence from slaves inadmissible unless obtained under torture.[16] The forms of torture were those with which we will become familiar when we look at religious punishments: the whip, the rack, the thumbscrew, and the wheel.

Forms of punishment were basically the same for slaves as for free men, except slaves did not have the right to voluntary exile. Therefore, while many free men could avoid terrible punishments, the slaves could not. For gross violence they could be sentenced to death or sentenced *in metallum* to work in the mines, quarries, or making roads. The slave could be condemned *ad bestias* to fight in the arena, a punishment that lasted until A.D. 325 when it was abolished by Constantine. For theft, the slave would be scourged, then thrown off the Tarpeian Rock.

A word of caution is relevant here. Slaves were valuable pieces of property which, if lost, had to be replaced. When the *paterfamilias* doctrine held sway, my suspicions are that it would be unlikely for a *dominus* to deprive himself of his own property unless it was an especially bad investment—something like trying to decide whether to replace an old car that needs repairs. One doubts, therefore, that the actual carrying out of the death penalty for slaves would have been very common. It is very difficult to assess "vulgar Roman law," i.e., the law as it was practiced as opposed to the laws that were pronounced in various articles.[17]

There is no doubt, however, that slaves and servants were whipped unmercifully. In general, slaves and servants were whipped by another slave with the terrible Roman *flagellum:* a several-stranded leather thong, with knots tied in the leather strands, sometimes with weights and nails tied in. Not only were male slaves whipped as a matter of course, but also female slaves, and this most commonly at the whim of the aristocratic lady of the house.[18] At the beginning of the Roman Empire it was common for masters to beat or whip their slaves to death, in spite of their economic value. In later Roman law, the master lost the right to punish, which was taken over by the public flagellator. Excessive punishment of slaves was then discouraged and flogging of female slaves which resulted in death within thirty days was made unlawful.[19]

The conditions of slavery have remained pretty much the same up to modern times. The treatment of slaves in the American South is perhaps the most well known and documented, as well as the treatment of convicts in the colonies during the days of transportation, since these unfortunate convicts were virtually slaves and certainly treated as such. The law bears a striking resemblance to the Roman law of slavery, upon which it was probably based. It was, of course, designed to protect the owner, not the slave. According to the civil code of the state of Louisiana at the time, "the slave is entirely subject to the will of his master, who may correct and chastise him, though, not with unusual vigor, nor so as to maim or mutilate him, or to expose him to danger of loss of life, or to cause death."[20] Laws by the eighteenth century at least specifically forbade the mutilation of slaves (putting out eyes, tearing out tongues, etc.), but whipping was always permitted. The widespread use of severe flogging is amply documented and easily proven by the reports and records of doctors who examined Negroes wishing to enlist in the federal army at the time of the American Civil War.[21] Many terrible scenes of the treatment of slaves have been described in books. While I do not suggest that the most terrible scenes were the most typical, the reasonably common occurrence attests to the widespread milder use of the whip. The following is one of the celebrated descriptions:

> Solomon Bradley describes the following as the most cruel punishment he ever saw inflicted, by one Mr. Ferraby, owner of one of the largest South Carolina coast plantations, near Port Royal. Attracted by the noise of fearful screams in Mr. Ferraby's own yard, he went up, and saw a slave girl stretched on the ground on her face, her hands and feet tied fast to stakes, her master standing over her, beating her with a leather trace from a harness, every blow of which raised the flesh if it did not gash it, and now and then kicking her in the face with his heavy boots when she screamed too loud. When he had become exhausted by this benevolent exertion, our "patriarch" sent for sealing-wax and a lighted lamp, and dropped the blazing wax into the gashes; after which, finally, his arm being rested apparently, he switched the whip out again with his riding whip. Two grown-up Miss Ferrabys were all this while watching the humane series of operations from the upper windows. And the offense of the girl was burning the waffles for her master's breakfast.[22]

We may heave a sigh of relief that open slavery has been virtually abolished from the globe, at least in the Western world. However, some have argued that although the status of slavery has been abolished, the forms of punishments used on slaves have remained. This hypothesis has been given support in Professor Thorsten Sellin's book, *Slavery and the Penal System,* in which he showed that many of the horrendous forms of punishment such as I described in the previous chapter, were used first against slaves and only later against free men. Many of the Burgundian and Frankish laws that developed during the middle ages were meant specifically to discriminate against those of lower status. Thus, free men could buy off their punishment, whereas slaves (and serfs) could not. Just as in Roman times, free men sentenced to death could choose voluntary exile, but slaves had no such choice.

But, one may ask, why make this really obvious point? Virtually by definition, slaves are supposed to be discriminated against, and so it is surely no surprise that they should fare badly when it comes to punishment. It is perfectly understandable that they should have experienced most forms of punishments before free men. The significant fact here is that the punishment of slaves had virtually no limits. The institution of slavery demanded total obedience. Punishment became pure and primitive tyranny—the repetition of the Freudian myth of the primal horde. It was a tyranny using limitless violence to punish a hugh mass so totally subjected that to rise up against their "leader" was, except in the most unusual circumstances, an utter impossibility. We find in slavery the political basis of punishment in its rawest form. We will see in the following chapter how punishment took on a more "civilized" tyranny under the nurturance of the Italian Inquisition.

The status and conditions of life for the slave were so low that it was a punishment in itself, so that very early slavery (i.e., various forms of forced, chained labor, such as the Roman, Spanish, and French convict galleys; road and quarry gangs; and later forced industrial and public labor in France and England)[23] was used as a punishment for criminal offenses.

Not only have many slave-related punishments remained in the penal system, but they also remained within other institutions, such as the family and school, of which slaves were an integral part: whether in ancient Roman times or in the more recent antebellum South.[24] Flagellation has been the most common punishment within families and in schools. The story of the flagellation of children is perhaps one of the most interesting aspects of punishment, since it is here that legal corporal punishment still persists. Indeed, it is comparatively widespread, and the U.S. Supreme Court decision of April 19, 1977, has upheld the right of teachers to chastise their pupils.[25]

To gain a clear understanding of the role of obedience in the use of punishment against children, we must first understand the social and political conditions of the child through history. Such factors are well known in regard to slavery. They are less known and more difficult to interpret in regard to childhood.

Home Discipline and Schooling Punishment

Although I have written at some length concerning the totalitarian structure of the Roman family, this is not to say that this structure was confined to Rome. The model has been applied among all Christian peoples; a similar structure has existed from time immemorial in Moslemic civilizations. Early Jewish religion certainly permitted the wholesale power of life and death over the child by the parents, as Philo stated:

> It is right that parents should rebuke their children, and reprove them with considerable severity, and even, if they do not submit to hearing threats, to beat them, disgrace them, and imprison them. But after these expedients have been tried and the children still rebel . . . the law permits that they even be punished with death.[26]

In Alexandria, during the Roman occupation, parents could take their uncontrollable child to the village gate where the elders would stone him to death.

I have already referred to the extensive use of infanticide throughout classical Greek and Roman times, up until the fourteenth century.[27] By 1890 dead babies were still a common sight in the streets and dung heaps of London. There was a widespread practice of abandoning children, selling them, and often more surreptitiously letting them out to wet nurses who were expected to kill them either by design or neglect.[28] And, of course, the use of children in mines and other forms of labor during the nineteenth century is so well known we need not go into it at all.

I present these facts so that one may keep in perspective the evolution of the child in the school and his punishment by the teacher, since it has become common law that the teacher acts *in loco parentis*. What happens in the home, as far as punishment is concerned, is therefore not only of crucial social importance, but also of legal importance.

"In medieval society, the idea of childhood did not exist," says Aries.[29] He enumerates many situations and occasions in which children "did not count." He shows that up until the seventeenth century there was no clear distinction between children and adults in work, play, or dress. The evidence he uses to support this is an examination of iconographic material at the time (there was an inability to represent the form of a child except in adult proportions) and through the diary of Louis XII's doctor Heroard, who recorded the minute details of little Louis's life. While one can accept much of his evidence, Aries nevertheless overdraws his case. Louis was after all, whipped most often for a variety of common domestic offenses (such as refusing to eat). He was even whipped on the day of his coronation at age eight. He was also subject to the sexual abuse of adults.[30] Children were still objects—either of pleasure or property. "Little ones" certainly did "not count," as Molière observed,[31] since they could be sold, abandoned, or killed, and so many babies simply died from neglect or illness. The acceptance of a very high infant mortality rate as a natural state of affairs would no doubt lead a parent to consider a very young child as a quite temporary member of the family until he grew stronger. In addition, children were easily replaceable. John Marshall gave up his son to King Stephen, saying he "cared little if William were hanged, for he had the anvils and hammers with which to forge still better sons."[32]

While children may have joined in a much wider variety of society's activities prior to the seventeenth century, this does not necessarily mean that there was no distinction between child and adult. Children were the objects of punishment. Although there is no doubt that their parents were also objects of punishment whether for religious or legal reasons, they at least had some leeway to avoid it. Children could not: they were always available to be punished. If they were not being whipped by slaves as in Roman times, they were being whipped by parents who were the "slaves" of other punishing systems of religion or law. Nor is this mere speculation. The sickest, and most telling practice of all, which clearly demonstrates the intricate interrelationship between various punishment systems, was the widespread practice in the seventeenth century of taking children to see hangings or gibbeted corpses and whipping them soundly on the site.[33]

If the middle ages were a period of sexual license and abuse of children, the sixteenth century ushered in a new emphasis upon modesty. The rise of this new preoccupation came hand-in-hand with a new, more intentional hardness of attitude toward the child. In part, this was a reaction against the perception of children as objects of amusement as they had been used in the immediately preceding decade or two. Said Montaigne at the turn of the sixteenth century: "I cannot abide that passion of caressing new born children."[34]

By the seventeenth century, children were no longer to be treated as objects of pleasure. Religious doctrines of both Catholicism and Protestantism played an important part in the advance of two apparently conflicting images of the child: the child as innocent and the child as the product of sin. The description of a nurse in an East European village in the eighteenth century, to whom babies were given on the understanding that she would kill them, demonstrates clearly the religious imagery:

> In her own strange, helpless way, she loved them all . . . but when the luckless infants' parents or the latter's relatives could not or did not pay the customary small sum for their keep . . . she disposed of them. . . . One day she returned from the city with an elongated little bundle . . . a horrible suspicion seized me. The baby in the cradle was going to die! . . . when the baby cried, I heard her get up, and she nursed it in the dark, mumbling, "Poor, poor little one!" I have tried many times since to imagine how she must have felt holding to her breast a child she knew was fated to die by her hand. . . . "You poor, poor little one!" She purposely spoke clearly so I would be sure to hear. ". . . fruit of sin through no fault of your own, but sinless in yourself . . . soon you will go, soon, soon, my poor one . . . and, going now, you will not go to hell as you would if you lived and grew up and became a sinner." . . . The next morning the child was dead. . . .[85]

Innocent children, simply because they lived, became sinful. They were the product of sex, conceived in sin. Thus, complete and tireless supervision and discipline became necessary. "I would rather have a dead son than a disobedient one," said Luther.[36]

The principle of total supervision was introduced in Jesuit schools and soon spread to other schools. Also, until this time, serious offenders in the Jesuit school were "stripped in front of the whole community and beaten until they bled."[37] It is to be noted that this punishment was carried out by a special assistant (often an older student) called the "corrector." A priest could not punish with his own hands. How familiar this pattern of punishing was to become! The student was "abandoned to the secular arm"—to use the words of the Holy Inquisition.[38] Later in the seventeenth century, as the idea of modesty developed, complete stripping of adolescents was not permitted for whipping. Only sufficient lowering of the breeches for the whipping was allowed. This was a sign of the growing dread of puberty that teachers have harbored to this day.

It was not until the sixteenth century that classes in schools were divided according to age. Prior to this, all ages and abilities were completely mixed up. It should also be realized that the medieval schools initially did not teach "reading" and "writing." These were skills that were either taught at home or more likely in an apprenticeship. The medieval schools started with the teaching of Latin. They were basically there to satisfy ecclesiastical recruiting. We find, however, that with the early beginning of classification in the school, there was also a growing tendency on the part of the masters to exaggerate the puerility of their pupils. This was a process that was to reach a crescendo during the eighteenth and nineteenth centuries, and in many school systems it continues today.

Whipping became the main and central means of "discipline." The school was organized around it. And this included college or university.

The Jesuits were quick to develop a highly formalized system of discipline, obsessed with supervising the details of each student's everyday life. They laid out a system of punishments which, in 1598, were more or less copied into the code of conduct for the University of Paris.[39] An older school student was selected to administer the beatings with either birch or cane. A system of informing was developed in the seventeenth century which extended the doctrine of eternal vigilance. If the informers failed to report offenses, they were punished as though they had committed the acts. The spy system was extended to the streets as well as within the schools. The monitor system was also introduced, and, shrewdly, it was the elected monitor (called this time the "excitor") who administered the whippings.

We should note that whipping was not a "scholastic punishment" (i.e., a punishment for learning failure) until the sixteenth and seventeenth centuries. Up until that time, it was administered only for acts of violence.[40] But by the seventeenth century, it was a basic teaching aid. Thomas Platter complained, "My master used to beat me horribly; he used to seize me by the ears and lift me off the ground,"[41] and it was well established that the child should be beaten harder if he screamed. Later, with the rise of Napoleon, the schools easily adapted to a militaristic model, and discipline, uniforms, toughness, drill routines, "captains," and "corporals" were infused into the school systems of France and also in England, where they stuck fast. Corporal punishment of school children was abolished in France in 1882. It had just reached its zenith in England at that time and is still widespread.

But it was not all one way. The history of schooling from the pupils' view is one of periodic turbulence, chaos, violence, rebellion, and poverty. If the masters kept the upper hand, they periodically paid for it. With reasonable cause, they insisted (as they do today) on the heavy use of corporal punishment to maintain order and protect themselves.

In the seventeenth century, a large number of students in France were armed, and it was common for them to have to check in their weapons when they entered school.[42] Armed revolts were common, and masters literally feared for their lives. Students were by and large a fringe group. They subsisted by professionally begging and thieving. People were frightened to walk past schools for fear of being attacked. The fighting of duels was most common, which was subsequently institutionalized within the British system in the form of boxing and wrestling "grudge" matches.

Mutinies continued in England well into the nineteenth century, and it is said that they were as common at Eton as was whipping. The last one at Eton, in 1832, ended in the flogging of eighty boys.[43] In 1818 two companies of troops with fixed bayonets had to be called into Winchester College to suppress a student riot.[44] Similar mutinies occurred at England's other prestigious public school, Rugby.

We should draw a distinction between violence as a part of the prevailing social milieu, such as dueling in the seventeenth and early eighteenth centuries and the general roughness of life during that period, and violence that occurred as a direct result of a political (for the children) nature.

In England these uprisings can be traced back to 1669, to the children's petition, which "was presented by a lively boy . . . to the speaker, and to several members of the House,"[45] with a view to requesting a bill to control the use of corporal punishment. The story of the gradual move to abolish corporal punishment in England since that date is a remarkable testimony to the resilience of this form of punishment. A series of reports on the use and effects of corporal punishment in England's schools was conducted in 1952, 1961, and the influential Plowden Report of 1968. And there were many other local reports as well.[46] On all occasions, the recommendation of the reports was to abolish the punishment. And on all occasions, teachers' organizations adamantly opposed the ban.

At least, however, limits were applied. Most school districts established rules as to where the child could be hit and the maximum number of strokes permitted. A punishment book was required to be kept in all schools and details of all punishments had to be recorded therein.

By 1968 the pressure for abolition was growing. The main defense that teachers' organizations used was that it was needed as an ultimate threat: the identical argument used for the retention of the death penalty. Members of Parliament who wanted to avoid direct confrontations argued that there was no need to act on something that was dying out anyway, and the myth developed that corporal punishment was rarely used in the schools.

Of course, it was not true. Various surveys and examinations of the punishments recorded in the punishment book revealed that nothing could have been further from the truth.[47] A study in 1967-68 showed that of selected secondary modern schools, 25 percent of the pupils were caned, evidence that the cane was certainly not used as a "last resort" as suggested by the Plowden Report.[48] In the analysis of one school, fourteen of the sixteen teachers used the cane, and four of these teachers accounted for over half the canings. The stories behind the canings reported on the pages from the punishment book are pitiful in the utterly pedestrian nature of the offenses. We find such common entries as gross insolence, leaving the football field, disobedience, climbing through a window, talking after a warning, absent without permission, leaving seat, leaving school without permission, loud-mouthed insulting behavior, and the list could go on. The common punishments for these misbehaviors were "two on hand"! As one distressed parent asked, "How can men do this to little boys?"[49] Of course, we already know part of the answer to this: history was having its day!

In another survey, it was also found that half the schools did indeed administer corporal punishment to girls—another myth shattered. The "offenses" for which the cane was used in one secondary modern school in England included, in order of frequency, cutting lessons or leaving class or school without permission; interruptions by talking, silliness; insolence, abusive behavior, defiance; throwing objects; disobedience; damage to property, fighting, persistent lateness; trespassing while truanting; smoking; and not showering without excuse.[50] Many other surveys have demonstrated the widespread use in Britain of "scholastic punishment."

Here was a nation that was finally able to bring itself to abolish capital punishment for all but a tiny number of crimes, but never managed to abolish corporal punishment of children. The London Education Authority, against much teacher opposition, finally managed to abolish it in 1973. But it continues in most other school systems in England, and the suppliers do a brisk trade. In the rest of Europe, corporal punishment in schools is long gone. It was abolished in Poland in 1783, Holland in 1958, Sweden and Denmark in 1968, and now it is abolished in Soviet Russia and most of West Germany.

It is significant that most of the English-speaking world retains corporal punishment of school children. In the United States, only the New York City, city of Chicago, and District of Columbia education districts have abolished it, and many state codes expressly condone it. The only states to expressly forbid corporal punishment are New Jersey (1968), Hawaii (1973), and Massachusetts (1974). Recent cases such as *Bramlet* v. *Wilson* (49 F.2d 714, 8th Cir. 1974) and *Ingraham* v. *Wright* (493 F.2d 248, 8th Cir. 1974), although refusing to assert that corporal punishment is a violation of the Eighth-Amendment guarantees against cruel and unusual punishment, nevertheless have affirmed this principle as a means to restrict its use.[51] And, as was noted earlier, the U.S. Supreme Court affirmed the decision in *Ingraham* v. *Wright* that teachers had the right to chastise their pupils.

The use of corporal punishment in the United States would appear to be widespread, and it has been since colonial days.[52] In a survey reported by the National School Public Relations Association in 1973, of those reporting, 237 school districts said that they used it, 164 that they did not. Those who reported its use emphasized that it was used only "as a last resort"—an assertion with which we are familiar. In another survey in the same year, it was found that 55.5 percent of secondary school teachers and 65.3 percent of elementary school teachers favored the "judicious use" of corporal punishment. The United States has been on the brink of abolishing capital punishment. But it is nowhere near the abolition of the beating of school children.

Aries concludes at the end of his book that by the end of the nineteenth century:

> The solicitude of family, church, moralists and administrators deprived the child of the freedom he had hitherto enjoyed among adults. It inflicted on him the birch, the prison cell, in a word, the punishments usually reserved for convicts from the lowest strata of society.[53]

This is a grand conclusion, but it is too simple and has led to a number of misunderstandings and some well-deserved criticisms. The reason for this criticism is that in one paragraph Aries mixes up the concept of freedom with the practice of punishment. It is made even more difficult by the ambiguous meaning of the word "freedom."

Aries sees the move from immodesty to innocence as one of loss of freedom in the sense that the child was kept a child longer and for the first time was separated from adults. The implication is that for a child "to be free" he must be treated not as a child, but as an adult, as he was in the middle ages. Aries hints, but never states, that "something was lost" in this transition. If it was, I can see nothing worth caring about. The child, as an adult, in that rough world, was clearly taken advantage of and abused in every way. Surely the transition from that period was a desirable developmental stage. Today, we do not sell children, dump them in the garbage or the gutters, or beat them in schools till their blood runs. They are no longer treated as convicts. Although corporal punishment has not been abolished, it has been severely limited and controlled. Where there are no official rules stated in school districts, many common law cases have clearly established limits beyond which a teacher (and to a lesser extent, a parent) cannot go.

One might also bear in mind that children for a long time, from the beginning of civilization, suffered a status *beneath* that of the criminal and more akin to the slave. Thus the observation that legally he can be corporally punished whereas a convict cannot comes as no surprise to us. One may also observe that, considering the child's original position at the bottom rung in civilizations all over the world, he has come a long way over the centuries.

Today the child's situation is very complicated. We have extended the period of childhood to a ripe age. The child is subject to fewer beatings. Yet the necessary lesser status of the child remains. It must therefore be difficult for the child to know his place. Before, the brutal punishment that he received clearly conveyed the truth of his position at the bottom of society's ladder. George Orwell has explained that feeling better than anyone:

> I had fallen into a chair, weakly snivelling. I remember that this was the only time throughout my boyhood when a beating actually reduced me to tears, and curiously enough I was not even now crying because of the pain. The second beating had not hurt very much either. Fright and shame seemed to have anaesthetized me. I was crying partly because I felt that this was expected of me, partly from genuine repentance, but partly also because of a deeper grief which is peculiar to childhood and not easy to convey: a sense of desolate loneliness and helplessness, of being locked up not only in a hostile world but in a world of good and evil where the rules were such that it was actually not possible for me to keep them.[54]

Orwell did not make the same error as Aries. He saw that punishment is not the cause of the unfortunate low status in which the children find themselves. It is an endemic part of the social life and order, and as such is not the cause of that order but the expression of it. Corporal punishment in the past has merely communicated this fact to the child in no uncertain terms.

Punishing Soldiers

One doubts if there is any army in which the right to discipline is not also an intrinsic right of command. The two are inseparable. It is not a statutory right (though it may be circumscribed by statute), but rather is embedded in the fundamental structure of military life and organization.[55]

The study of punishment in the militia is of special interest to us for a number of reasons. First, it may have been the first form of state control of citizens. Second, it may show us how a system of punishment operates within a closed organizational setting. Third, it allows us to fill in the rest of the picture of society's systems of punishment. The military is, after all, the backbone of every state.

If we return to the early classical period of Rome, we find that only slowly was the city government separated from military command. This observation is highly significant as far as the Roman citizen was concerned, especially in light of the punishment provided by the criminal law of Rome. It points up the fact that, although on the books the criminal law of the state did not intervene in private lives of citizens a great deal, the disciplinary procedure did. Magistrates of various types were empowered to issue edicts which had to be obeyed. If they were not, then the machinery of law would take over. The concept of utter obedience to the leader was a clear carryover from the time when the general or leader of the army also was the leader of the city. This is why colonial occupations always appear more despotic, because the governor is often an army official of high rank. However, at least for Roman citizens, appeal against the rulings of magistrates was possible.

In the army it was not.[56] Discipline of the Roman soldiers was raised to the level of an ideal, almost worshiped. Livy[57] tells the story of Manlius Torquatus and his son, Titus Manlius. Titus Manlius, while leading a squadron of cavalry in his father's army, came upon a group of enemy cavalry, and after much provocation from them, Manlius engaged the enemy chief in single combat and killed him. But when Torquatus was told of the deed by his proud son, he turned away in disgust at such an "idle show of honor." To set an example of his son who had disobeyed orders not to get into this battle, Torquatus solemnly declared his love and admiration for his son, but nevertheless, for the purpose of maintaining complete discipline, ordered the young Manlius to be tied to a stake and executed by beheading.

Beheading was also the summary punishment for soldiers caught without arms, standard-bearers without standards, or soldiers quitting their posts.

The most common military offenses then, as now, were desertion and misconduct in battle. Other offenses revolved around the breaking of oaths. The soldier was required to take religious oaths and observe various rites meticulously. The soldier was also required to take an oath swearing he would not indulge in theft. The reaping of loot and booty were a major part of war and its distribution always a difficulty. With such large numbers of soldiers living close together, theft became a most difficult problem to control.[58] Five levels of punishments were applied to offenders: (1) deprivation of pay; (2) reduction in rank; (3) disgrace, which included dishonorable discharge, being made to camp outside the fortifications, forbidden to eat or drink in public, standing with a sod in one's hands in front of the commander's tent, standing barefoot in public places; (4) corporal punishment, flogging with the Roman *flagellum* was the common punishment, most often for inattention to duty; (5) death: two methods were commonly employed—beheading by the axe of the lictor or beating to death (*fustuarium*). Polybius describes this punishment as follows: "The tribune takes a cudgel and just touches the condemned man with it, after which all in the camp beat or stone him, in most cases dispatching him in the camp itself."[59] This punishment was used for those who did not attend properly to their night patrol. Polybius adds that as a result of this penalty, the Roman night watches were scrupulously kept.

Other punishments such as reduction to slavery, mutilations and onerous duties were also used but apparently not to any great extent. In the case of mass misconduct, such as may occur in battle, decimation was used: i.e., every tenth man was executed. There was one occasion, however, when 370 deserters from Hannibal were recaptured. They were all flogged and thrown from the Tarpeian Rock, the usual punishment for traitors.

There is a dearth of information concerning the development of military punishments after Roman times until we are able to pick up the story again in 1189. In England at this time Richard I announced three punishments for offenses at sea: for murder, the offender would be tied to the corpse of the victim and thrown overboard; for assault, ducked three times in the sea; and for theft, his head would be tarred and feathered.[60] Decimation continued well into the seventeenth century in cases of mass misconduct. Offenders were either selected by ballot under the gallows or they threw dice to decide. The direct link with the Roman practice is clear.

The Earl of Northumberland, in 1640, also continued the Roman custom of *fustuarium* in his pronouncements for discipline in the Royal Navy. At this time a wide range of painful corporal punishments was commonly applied to criminals, including mutilation and torture. Much the same punishments were applied in the navy, except that running the *gantelope* was added. Although this punishment took on varying forms, it was commonly conducted by parading the offender stripped to the waist, between two columns of troops who were invited to rain blows with whips or thick pieces of cord. A drum-major would walk slowly in front and one behind, with the point of a bayonet against the offender's body, so that he could not hurry through. The offenders were very often beaten to death. The practice was continued up to 1710.[61] Other colorful punishments used commonly for soldiers which were not used quite so much for criminals were the *strappado*, a punishment originating with the Inquisition, in which the offender is hoisted with his arms tied behind him, then let fall with a jerk, thus dislocating his shoulders (in the Inquisition, weights were also tied to the offender's feet); hanging by the thumbs; tying neck and heels together; riding the wooden horse, in which a wooden apparatus like a horse was set up, and the offender was sat upon it, weights tied to each leg, and sometimes beaten; the picket, in which the offender was suspended by one wrist so that he was just above the ground, then one spike was set for him to place his foot on to take the weight of the body; cobbing, beating the offender with a stick or cross-belt on the posterior; blistering, in which boiling water or oil was poured on the backs of drunkards; booting, flogging the soles of the feet with a belt. And a common punishment for infantry men was to be removed to the navy![62]

Until 1761, all of these punishments were administered summarily without a trial. After that date, courts-martial were necessary for serious offenses. They were, however, very summary in nature. A soldier would commit an offense, a court-martial would be held among a group of officers, and the punishment would be meted out promptly. Toward the end of the eighteenth century, appeals were possible, and there were a number of cases in which damages were obtained by some who claimed to have been unjustly punished.[63]

At the time when these improvements came about, the most terrible form of punishment reached its height: whipping with the cat-o-nine tails.[64] By 1812 it was estimated that the average number of lashes per month dealt out in India was 17,000. Significantly, it was in this year that the American Congress officially abolished flogging in the U.S. Army. Substituted were extra drill, extra duties; drinking salt water and restricted rations, gagging, the stocks, the "dry room" (confinement without grog); and the black hole.[65] During its height, the use of flogging was, to say the least, incredible. One thousand lashes and more was a common punishment for quite minor offenses. Often, this meant a virtual death penalty. The offender would be taken down because he had passed out before the 1,000 strokes were completed. He would be taken to the hospital where his pulped back would be "dressed" (other patients complained of the stench from the festering sores), then after five or six weeks when it was healed, he would be taken back for the remainder of his punishment. The flogging occurred as follows:

> The first stroke of the cat occasions an instantaneous discoloura-tion of the skin from effused blood, the back appearing as if it was thickly sprinkled with strong coffee even before the second stroke is inflicted. Sometimes the blood flows copiously by the time the first fifty or one hundred lashes are inflicted; at other times little or no blood appears when two hundred lashes have been inflicted. During the infliction of the first hundred and fifty or two hundred lashes, a man commonly appears to suffer much, considerably more, indeed, than during the subsequent part of a punishment, however large it may be. The effused blood in the skin, or, perhaps, some disorganization of the nerves of sensation, seems to occasion a blunt-ing of its sensibility, and thereby lessening the acuteness of the pain arising from the application of the cat. Left-handed Drummers, whose cats are applied to a portion of sound skin and Drummers who have not been sufficiently drilled to flogging, spread the lashes unnecessarily, and excite an unusual degree of pain. Delinquents frequently call out to the Drummer to strike higher, then lower, and sometimes alternately.[66]

Surgeons, always on hand, reported, "some persons suffer much more than others from the same amount of punishment," and com-monly in the more severe cases, "when the wounds were clear, the backbone and part of the shoulder were laid bare."

Typical offenses and their punishments occurring throughout this period are presented in Table 1, pages 74-75.

Opposition was, however, growing toward this punishment. A Royal Commission was conducted in 1835, which examined all aspects of the controversy and produced a report strikingly modern in its observations. It was concluded, for example, that there were many men who had been whipped and had gone on to make excellent officers. But it was also observed that "when indeed inflicted on one of confirmed bad habits . . . it has failed in effecting their reform."

It was strongly urged at the time that imprisonment be substituted for whipping, but the Commission was quite clear that this would be most unsatisfactory. Not only had it discovered from talking to servicemen that they preferred the quick, sharp punishment of the whip to imprisonment, but also that imprisonment would contribute to the serious problem of drunkenness, since as soon as they were released they would spend their accumulated pay on drink. The Commission also observed that the standardization of prison would be too difficult to achieve. It did, however, favor transportation as a substitute.

A common observation at the time was that England's army was a volunteer army, and a detailed comparison was made to the French Army which was conscripted and had abolished whipping. The reason this was possible, so the argument went, was that a conscripted army insured a generally higher class of recruit, whereas a volunteer army, because of the poor pay and conditions, necessarily attracted the rougher elements of the labor force, so that severe discipline was absolutely necessary. It should be borne in mind, by the way, that, although many of these floggings were carried out in a tyrannical, despotic fashion and no doubt many "innocent" or "good" men were unduly flogged for trifling infractions, nevertheless ". . . the majority of the thousands who had corporal punishment . . . were a type of human closely related to our modern gangster, rapist, gun-man. . . ."[67]

Pressure to cease flogging continued. In 1825, one man in fifty-nine was flogged, but the same number also received other forms of punishment. In 1834 (before the Commission) only one in 111 was flogged, but the number of offenses had increased considerably. In 1850, the infliction of flogging a second time was declared illegal. In 1868, its use in peace time was forbidden and the maximum in war time set at fifty lashes. It was completely abolished in 1881. The caning of boy seamen, however, continues to be legal. This is, of course, consistent with the use of corporal punishment in schools.

The situation today is different, but how different it is very difficult to ascertain. The military prison has taken over as the solution for major punishments, but we actually know very little about it. The military complex is so separated from the other institutions of society that very few professionals from outside have bothered to research

TABLE 1

Sample of Crimes and Punishments from Admiralty Courts-Martial Records

When Tried	Names of Persons Tried	Qualities	Ships	Nature of Charges or Offenses	Purport of Sentences
April 27, 1778	——Brown	Boatswain	"Launceston"	Indecent behaviour and disobedience of orders.	Dismissed the ship.
Dec. 30, 1778	Benj. Brots	Serj. Marines	"Shrewsbury"	Theft, and other infamous behaviour.	Reduced to a private, and to receive two hundred lashes.
Dec. 30, 1780	Twenty-three	Seamen and Marines	Different Ships	Desertion.	From fifty to five hundred lashes.
Jan. 18, 1781	Wm. Brannon	Seaman	"Ajax"	For mutinous behaviour.	Five hundred lashes.
July 25, 1781	Sam Wickham	2nd Lieut.	"Lizard"	Contempt and disrespect to the Captain on the quarter-deck.	Dismissed His Majesty's Service.
Dec. 24, 1782	Thirty men	Seamen	Different Ships	Desertion, drunkenness, etc.	Fifty to five hundred lashes.
Aug. 18, 1783	John Mitchell	Seaman	"Chaser"	Writing a mutinous and seditious letter.	To be hanged.
Nov. 8, 1783	John Burn and Arthur Rice	Seamen	"Adamant"	Mutiny.	Six hundred lashes.
April 29, 1784	John Cumming	Seaman	"Trusty"	Striking Daniel Ford, Boatswain of the said ship.	To be hanged at the forward-arm.
July 30, 1792	James Allen	Clerk	"Medusa"	Insolent and mutinous behaviour.	Broke and rendered incapable of ever serving again, and to receive 100 lashes.
April 6, 1793	Rob. Brown, John Gordon	Pilots	"Fox"	Running the said ship on the Gunfleet Sand.	Both rendered disqualified from hereafter taking charge of any of His Majesty's ships, and to be imprisoned six calendar months in the Marshalsea.

Year	Name	Rank	Ship	Offence	Sentence
1829	T. Lapham	Marine	"Magnificent"	Disobedience of orders and contempt to his superior officer.	100 lashes, to be mulcted of all pay due to him, and to forfeit and lose all claims of every description which he may be entitled to by reason of his previous servitude.
1829	J. Bathie, J. Lada, W. Scott	Seamen	"Cruizer"	Desertion.	150 lashes each.
1830	H. M'Vea	Marine	"Winchester"	Theft, and an attempt to desert.	100 lashes.
1830	W. Mitchell	Seaman	"Champion"	Attempting to desert.	50 lashes.
1831	J. Horsley	Marine	"Nimble"	For a breach of the 2nd, 19th, 22nd, 23rd, and 27th Articles of War.	100 lashes and lose three years time.
1831	F. Thomas	Seaman	"Firefly"	Mutinous and insulting language towards Lieut. J. H. M'Donnell, commanding the "Firefly."	50 lashes, to be mulcted of all pay due to him, and discharged from the Service.
1835	J. Pascoe, T. Barnett, W. Hawkes, J. Hilborn, C. Webber	Seaman, Marine, Marine, Marine, Marine	"Caledonia"	For a breach of the 19th Article of War.	T. Barnett acquitted. J. Pascoe, 60 lashes. W. Hawkes and J. Hilborn, 100 lashes each, and to be discharged with disgrace from the Service; and C. Webber, 80 lashes.
1839	G. Tarm, J. Lodge	Seamen	"Castor"	Mutinous and contemptuous behaviour.	100 lashes each round the Fleet or alongside H. H. S. "Castor"; G. Tarm to be imprisoned one year and J. Lodge six months in the Marshalsea.
1841	W. Ansfield	Marine	"Cambridge"	Disobedience of orders, making use of threatening and mutinous language.	48 lashes.
1842	J. Bingham	Marine	"Pickle"	Leaving his post while in charge of prisoners.	60 lashes.

this problem. The military would appear today to be undergoing considerable pressure, from both outside and within, to loosen up its disciplinary system. This pressure would seem to have arisen in response to various incidents, such as that of Private Bunche in 1968 being shot and killed trying to escape from the Army Presidio Stockade in San Francisco. Twenty-seven prisoners sang freedom songs in response to this incident, and they were subsequently charged with mutiny and sentenced to up to sixteen years hard labor. From the little available research on the topic, it would seem that the main thrust of the judicial military punishments is toward reclaiming errant soldiers through "restoration training," which is the military's term for "rehabilitation."[68] There is also, of course, the usual tension between the rehabilitative ideal and the requirements of retribution.

Perhaps of more interest is the status of "nonjudicial punishment," which is, and has always been, the mainstay of day-to-day military discipline. Once again, the military has been under attack because of particular incidents, such as the cases of a mentally retarded private who died as a result of "extra details" and of the West Point cheating scandals.

The U. S. Uniform Code of Military Justice, Article 15, spells out the authority of the commanding officer to administer nonjudicial punishment or, put more bluntly, punishment without trial. To quote a common handbook interpretation: "It is *not* a trial . . . the commanding officer does not convict or acquit; he either punishes or dismisses the charges. . . ."[69] The supposed advantage of this system is that it allows the officer to punish the offender without the record being placed against the offender's file, as a "previous conviction." It does, of course, cut both ways, since the offender is told that he may appeal the punishment by demanding a trial, but should he lose the case, then it *would* be a conviction. It has also been held that the offender must undergo the punishment even while he is appealing it. Appeal beyond the nonjudicial level, therefore, is clearly not something that one would undertake lightly.

Types of nonjudicial punishments are: admonition and reprimand; restriction to limits (maximum of sixty days); extra duties (maximum forty-five days); correctional custody (maximum thirty days); confinement on bread and water or diminished rations (maximum three days); forfeiture of pay (maximum two months); detention of pay (maximum three months); and reduction of one grade. The punishment may run concurrently or consecutively, but must not exceed the maximum limits for which there is a special table of equivalents.

We can see that there has been continuity in the forms of punishments administered in the military sphere since Roman times. Its severity has been closely associated with the idea that punishment is inherent in command. Without it command could not exist. Although many of the forms of punishment throughout the ages were similar to those applied to civilians for like offenses, the added offenses of desertion and disobedience make for a much harsher system of punishment in the military. It is of particular interest, however, that some scholars have argued that early Roman cities were indeed governed by the military. Therefore, we should expect certain aspects of military justice to continue in the civilian sphere.

The impression is that it did. The behavior of criminal justice practitioners throughout the ages parallels in large part the attitude of the military model. Until basic "rights" were spelled out for the defendant, his arrest and trial were often a forgone conclusion. His failure to cooperate resulted in such trials as *peine dure et forte* or he was simply left in a cell until he complied. Obedience, once the offender was inducted into the criminal justice system, has always been important and, indeed, became essential with the rise of prisons.

It is now time to add one more piece to the network of institutional forms of punishment. We have seen that the institutions of family, school, and military in their early stages demanded absolute obedience from their subordinates. There was another social institution that demanded not only absolute obedience, but constant and visible affirmation as well. This was the church. When it became an empire, it brought together both the sacred and the institutional forms of punishment to create the most terrible system of punishments ever devised by man.

5

The Terror of Punishment

Although I have presented a number of explanations for punishments which might reasonably be termed religious in origin and form, in this Chapter I want to emphasize religion as an institution. By this I mean that we must see religion not only as some kind of vessel into which we dip our hands and pull out various beliefs, myths, superstitions, and sacred rites, but also as an organized formal social system with a hierarchy, laws, an economic structure, and, of course, sanctions. The amount and type of punishments used should always be seen against this institutional backdrop. Social institutions generate their own needs, so one would assume that they would generate their own special system of sanctions. But social institutions also respond to pressures or demands from the people. We need, therefore, to study the institutional forms of punishment in religion as a constantly evolving phenomenon, fluxing in response to both institutional and people needs.

The obvious beginning is with the Holy Inquisition, a system of punishment that has been grossly distorted by many religious historians and other sensationalists. For example, during the nineteenth century, many religious historians tried to whitewash the church by insisting that the Inquisition never put anyone to the torch. Strictly speaking, this is true, since the law required that those sentenced (by the Inquisitors) to be burnt, were handed over to the secular arm for the actual punishment to be carried out. But there is absolutely no question at all that the Inquisition *was* responsible for their deaths. This is another example of the familiar practice that we have noted throughout this book of those actually responsible for the punishment shifting the burden to someone else.

The Holy Inquisition: An Empire of Punishment

Professor H. C. Lea,[1] whose balanced and thorough account of the Inquisition may be relied upon, points out that the Holy Inquisition got off to a very sluggish start. The first law to be passed condemning heretics to death was in A. D. 382[2] when Inquisitors were appointed to carry out the task, though these Inquisitors were lay people.

Upon Charlemagne's visit to Rome in A. D. 800, an immediate welding of canon law to civil law occurred. Previous to this time, canon law had developed its own system of sanctions and was considered superior to the Roman civil law, which as we have seen emphasized private regulation. The religious view of the world saw the individual as an abstraction, a mere part of the totum (society). It was a thoroughly collectivist doctrine. Roman civil law had therefore fallen into disuse also, of course, because the structure of the Catholic church required a strong central hand for the administration of justice. There was no litigation as far as justice was concerned; the church was the *sedes justitiae.* Charlemagne adopted all the instrumentalities of Roman civil law that could be used to maintain order in his empire. He ordered all his bishops and secular officials to "prohibit all superstitious observances and remnants of paganism." Subsequently, the study of Roman law underwent a great revival and became thoroughly enmeshed in canon law.

It would appear, however, that after the fall of Charlemagne's empire, the bishops displayed no great enthusiasm to stamp out heresy. The church had recognized the danger of the inquisitorial process, where the judge was also the accuser, and therefore it was established that proceedings were only begun if the offender were popularly believed guilty. This virtually left it up to the masses, who did not disappoint. The case of the Cathari, who confessed at Liege in 1144, is a prime example. They had to be rescued from the mobs who sought to burn them. In 1167, William Abbott asked an assembled crowd what he should do with some confessed heretics he had on his hands. The unanimous shout came back: "Burn them! Burn them!," and the order was duly executed. In 1114, the crowd broke into a prison while the bishop was away and burned a number of heretics who had been found guilty by the water ordeal. (That is, the accused was thrown into the river. If she floated, she was guilty, if she sank, she was innocent. See Chapter 6, concerning the ducking stool.)

The number of heretics appears to have become greater and greater, yet until 1220 the bishops remained indifferent to the problem. The ruling classes especially were demanding suppression of heresy, but because there was no really centralized system or organization, the efforts were piecemeal.

The next important step, indeed a great irony, was that Frederick II, feeling the pressure of the people and the ruling classes on him, enacted laws during the period 1220-39 requiring the persecution of all heretics. They were to be processed by the church, delivered to the secular arm and burnt, all their property to be confiscated. Frederick, an adamant enemy of the church, constantly complaining of its excess of riches, excommunicated twice, became the first to underwrite the legal basis of the Inquisition. From that time on, the Inquisition enjoyed a close and cooperative relationship with the state, although tensions were to arise when the Inquisitors gained far more power than the secular arm had bargained for. The strange and powerful mix of church and state in the administration of a basically theocratic law is attested to by the common phrase by which laymen addressed the Inquisitors: "Your religious majesty." For a long time, though, no states other than Italy would accept the financial responsibility for the Inquisitor, except for the cost of the burning itself. Confiscation of property, therefore, became an extremely important part of the Inquisition.

The cost of the Inquisition must have become enormous. By the middle of the fourteenth century, the Inquisition had assumed immense powers and a colossal system had developed. Highly detailed records were kept of every step of the proceedings. Records of everything said during interrogation had to be made, as well as detailed descriptions of suspected heretics. The cost of maintaining such records must have been considerable. It guaranteed, however, that there could be no escape through flight. The organization was so well developed that there was every chance that one would be caught. Not only were there the records, but there was also an extensive system of spies and informers (termed "familiars"). Furthermore, friends and family were encouraged to report on each other, and they often did for fear of being accused of harboring a heretic.

How did the system get out of hand? One may ascribe all sorts of sinister sexual and psychological motives to the Inquisitors, as some do,[3] but it seems to me that it is not enough to say that the Inquisitors were "sadists." They were part of an enormous legal system which had grown up partly in response to the clamor of the people to protect them from heretics. As the system grew, it seemed the people had brought upon themselves a mighty terror. Initially, the church had been cautious in persecuting heretics. The dangers of the inquisitorial system had been recognized and safeguards even introduced. But as safeguards were introduced, they were quickly circumvented. For example, Inquisitors were not permitted by the church to administer torture, for if they did they would become "irregular" and require absolution by the bishop. Torture after all, was clearly foreign to Christian doctrine. Indeed, Gratian had asserted that no confession by torture was acceptable in canon law. It was only after the intensive examination of the Roman civil law by the Lateran Council of 1215 that the need for torture was seen. But it was most inefficient for the torturer to have to go to the bishop for absolution, so Pope Innocent IV, in 1245, gave the Inquisitors and their families the power to absolve each other.[4] The church now began to champion its system of punishment.

We now come to the Inquisitors' brilliant use of torture that has set an example for many regimes and police systems right up to today. One should realize that their central and overwhelming aim was to extract a confession, as is usually the aim of most organizations that use torture. The confession was so important to them that a priest or familiar always accompanied a heretic right to the stake in the hope that he would finally recant. There were instances when some did and were saved from the flames, only to spend the rest of their days in prison. If the offense were very serious, the heretic might be burned whether he confessed or not. But no effort was spared to extract a confession.

The Inquisitors refined the use of two basic elements of the inquisitorial process: time and terror. As the Inquisition developed, it became clear that it was the intention of the church to paralyze the people with terror.[5] A number of factors contributed to this: the complete secrecy in which the interrogations were conducted; the elaborate secret police system; the horror of the torture chamber; the absolute separation of the prison which held the condemned from the rest of the community. Indeed, by the time of the Spanish Inquisition, the prison was always located in the same building as the Inquisitors —in which they both slept and conducted interrogations. This meant that, once an offender was taken in, he may never be seen until he appeared at his hearing. He could be called on at any hour of day or night. The Inquisition had complete and absolute control. Furthermore, the offender, under torture, was encouraged to name others who might be suspected as heretics. One never knew, therefore, if one's name was embedded in the mass of records that the all-knowing Inquisitors kept.[6]

It would be a mistake to assume, as popular writers of the Inquisition suggest, that the Inquisition existed for the sole purpose of killing and administering torture. This is far from the truth. It was the dread of torture that was most often successful along with brilliant verbal interrogations, in which Inquisitors were well trained. In a moving passage, Professor Lea describes their sophistication and dedication:

> Trained through long experience in an accurate knowledge of all that can move the human breast; skilled not only to detect the subtle evasions of the intellect, but to seek and find the tenderest point through which to assail the conscience and the heart; relentless in inflicting agony on body and brain, whether through the mouldering wretchedness of the hopeless dungeon protracted through uncounted years, the sharper pain of the torture chamber, or by coldly playing on the affections; using without scruple the most violent alternatives of hope and fear; employing with cynical openness every resource of guile and fraud on wretches purposely starved to render them incapable of self-defence, the counsels which these men utter might well seem the promptings of fiends exulting in the unlimited power to wreak their evil passions on helpless mortals. Yet through all this there shines the evident conviction that they are doing the work of God. No labour is too great if they can win a soul from perdition. . . .[7]

Prisons assumed a very important part of the process. Offenders could be left to await their interrogations, after the initial accusation, months and sometimes years. All the more time for them to anticipate the horrors that lay before them. All manner of ruse and trickery were used. The offender may be fed well, allowed to see his family in an attempt to gain his confidence, then, tricked into admissions. False promises would be made, he may be shown the torture chamber. He may be starved for a period and then fed wine, so that he would be drunk and caught off his guard. The probability, therefore, is that the majority produced confessions without getting anywhere near the torture chamber.

This is not to say that torture was not widely used. Of course it was; there is no doubt about that. In similar fashion, it is popularly believed that a confession of heresy automatically meant burning at the stake. Again this is not true. The stake was used as a last resort—the most important aim of the Inquisition was to extract a confession. If it were extracted, there was a good chance that the stake would be avoided. In fact, according to Professor Lea the stake was mainly used for relapsed heretics, that is, those who had confessed and been punished in some other way but later relapsed into heresy. Burning was a mandatory punishment in these cases. The variety of punishments used is clear from the register of Bernard Gui the Inquisitor, compiled from 1308-22:[8]

Delivered to the secular court and burned	40
Bones exhumed and burned	67
Imprisoned	300
Bones exhumed of those who would have been imprisoned	21
Condemned to wear crosses	138
Condemned to perform pilgrimages	16
Banished to Holy Land	1
Fugitives	36
Condemnation of the Talmud	1
Houses to be destroyed	16

One can see quite clearly from this, and many other records that the *real* curses, the most terrible punishments in terms of frequency, were the dungeons, confiscations, humiliating penances, the saffron crosses, and the invisible police force. The prisons especially were crammed full of confessors. Their use was so widespread and so central to the whole system of the Inquisition, especially later during the Spanish Inquisition, that one is forced to consider them as a major form of punishment from the middle ages on. It is common in modern writings on prison to assume that it is a relatively recent (since 1800) method of punishing criminals.[9] Prison has been with us for centuries, not just as a holding place for persons awaiting trial, but as a punishment as well. Why is it that historians of prison have overlooked this fact? Most probably because it has been overshadowed by the whole idea of burning at the stake:

> The deliberate burning alive of a human being, simply for differences of belief, is an atrocity so dramatic and appeals so strongly to the imagination that it has come to be regarded as the leading feature in the activity of the Inquisition. Yet, frequent as recourse to the stake undoubtedly was, it formed but a comparatively small part of the instrumentalities of repression.[10]

This observation is in contrast to the report of a contemporary historian Llorente, based upon an examination of Inquisitors' records for the period 1481-1517. Llorente claims that some 13,000 persons were burnt at the stake in Spain, and the number burnt for the period 1481-1808 was 341,021.[11] However, statistics on crime and punishment in modern times are very difficult to interpret, so those reported from the middle ages should be treated with considerable skepticism.[12]

It would seem, though, that the Spanish Inquisition was much more severe, under the guiding hand of the infamous Torquemada. Here the secrecy and complete separation of the process of the accused from the rest of the world was accomplished. The offenders were kept in heavy chains, usually with metal gags, since it was feared that their utterings may contaminate other prisoners awaiting trial. Yet Professor Lea also points out that the conditions of inquisitorial prisons were no worse than those run by the secular arm; in fact, they were probably better. There is evidence that, at least in 1561, inquisitorial prisoners received every "necessary" care.

Also very common in the Spanish Inquisition was the whipping of offenders. Although this was used during the earlier Italian Inquisition, public whipping of the penitent was a most common punishment in the Spanish Inquisition.[13] Here we have linked up again with a very old punishment.

Faith and Flagellation

Whipping has been a central element in the Christian religion, almost from its inception. As early as A. D. 508, Saint Cesaire d' Arles prescribed whipping as the punishment for nuns who failed to observe the regulation of their order. The punishment became extended to all manner of disobedience,[14] and the amount and severity of the flagellation was left to the discretion of the abbot. Two forms of discipline were used: superior and inferior. Superior was applied to the upper part of the back, and inferior to the buttocks and belly. The universality of the practice is clearly attested to by the fact that it was the custom in many monasteries to wear a special shirt that opened at the back, although in cases of severe penalties (usually related to sexual promiscuity or liberties) the monk or nun was required (appropriately!) to completely disrobe and be whipped in public.[15] It would seem, although ample documentation is not available, that the whipping of nuns became an especially widespread practice, especially if administered by monks.

One should be aware, though, of the fine line between whipping as punishment and whipping as pleasure. Monks and nuns, after all, were supposed to live a cloistered existence of self-denial. They were constantly tempted by pleasures of the flesh—whether of sex or food. In most cases, they *wanted* to be whipped, and there are many cases in which they whipped themselves—many saints especially indulged in this practice. For example, St. Pacifus regularly scourged himself to such an extent "as to fill all those with horror who heard the whistlings of the lash, or saw the abundance of blood which he had shed during the flagellation." And there are many other examples from Christ and St. Paul down. There is a point at which it is not possible to say whether self-flagellation or even flagellation by another is really punishment.

Flagellation became such a central part of monastic life that it became popularly known as "the discipline" and was automatically a part of life whether or not one had committed specific misdeeds or had specific evil thoughts.

> . . . the Carmes are to discipline themselves twice a week; the Monks of Monte Cassino, once a week; the Unsuline Nuns, every Friday; the Carmelite Nuns on Wednesdays and Fridays; the Nuns of the Visitation, when they please; the English Benedictines, a greater or lesser number of times in the week according to the season of the year; the Celestrines, on the eve of every great festival; the Capuchin Friars, everyday of the week, etc.[16]

We may not call this pleasure, but it was certainly not a punishment in the sense of being applied to a specific wrong. Instead, it was taken as a necessary part of life.

Pleasure was also sometimes involved. There is the famous case related by Doctor Krafft-Ebing of the Carmelite Nun, Maria Magdalena of Pazzi, who lived toward the end of the sixteenth century. She was being publicly whipped on her bare buttocks, when she cried, "Enough! Fan no longer the flame that consumes me: this is not the death I long for; it comes with all too much pleasure and delight!"[17]

There are many, many stories (and rude jokes) of monks and nuns indulging in all sorts of sadistic, masochistic, and licentious behavior. The majority of these stories refer to indecencies and liberties taken by monks on nuns and young female penitents. The problem must have been quite serious, since all sorts of regulations and advice were provided by the church to prevent these temptations. Priests, when hearing confessions of a woman, were advised to have quotations from the Psalms posted up before their eyes.[18] Or, during the Inquisition, the Inquisitor should never be alone with a female inmate. Indeed, there were punishments for this, and during the Spanish Inquisition, there was a mandatory death penalty for anyone having intercourse with a female inmate.[19]

Professor Lea, our only reliable source in this regard, does report a number of cases of priests taking sexual advantage of their female penitents, but they are few (occurring in the seventeenth and eighteenth centuries). The popular works and imagination (fanned especially by the works of the Marquis de Sade, whose writings are full of such stories) maintain that it was widespread. The secrecy in which confessions were conducted, especially in relation to the Inquisition, stimulates the suspicious mind of the ordinary person and at the same time serves to prevent any record or investigation of "what really went on." On the other hand, the punishments for abusing the office were extremely severe, so that one doubts if many Inquisitors would have succumbed to temptation. The only way around the regulations would have been for a whole order to act together. Even then, because of the rigors of the inquisitorial system, the chances of being caught would have been very high.

We have seen, then, that the Holy Inquisition, for the first time in the history of Western civilization developed a comprehensive, centralized, well-organized system of punishment. The forms and justifications of punishment had been already established in Roman civil law. At the same time, the church attempted to avoid direct responsibility for the killing of heretics by handing them over to the secular arm, which was in most cases only too happy to cooperate. In theory, the church did not put heretics to death, it only "withdrew the protection of the church." It did, however, develop an elaborate system of interrogation based on threats and torture, which has been used by various other institutions, especially political, to this day. We saw also that the development of this system of terror depended upon a delicate and complicated relationship between church and state. Without the backing of the state, the Inquisition certainly would not have begun. There is clear evidence of this in the fact that it never gained a substantial hold in England, except for a brief period when the monarch (Mary Tudor) cooperated.

The Special Objects of Religious Punishment:
Jews, Women, and Animals

Professor Lea is strangely quiet concerning the extent to which Jews and women were the objects of persecution, yet it is widely believed that women were the main objects of punishment for heresy, especially for witchcraft. It is furthermore argued that Jews were practically exterminated in the peninsula of Europe during the height of the Inquisition. There were many superstitions about Jews, which were very similar to those about witches.[20] It was believed, for example, that Jews fattened up little boys, then crucified them. In 1144, 100 Jews were tried for such an offense and hanged. Similar cases have occurred as recently as the case of Leo Frank in 1915 in Atlanta, Georgia. It is not surprising that Jews should have comprised a large portion of the heretics. They were given the traditional choice: conversion or martyrdom. Many assumed superficial orthodoxies while carrying on their own true religion in secret. Such persons were termed Marranos, and they became the object of much activity of the Inquisition since they represented the epitomy of the Inquisitor's fears: that the heretic may confess but not really mean it. This contributed to another important justification for torture. In 1481 six Marranos were burnt at the stake and this continued on and off for three more centuries.[21]

The role of women as the objects of persecution is, of course, obvious. The personnel of the Inquisition, after all, were men, or at least one assumes that this is so since women are never mentioned as Inquisitors in any of the histories. The Inquisitors were quite convinced of the innate defects of women which led female heretics naturally to lies, deceit, and concealment. The *Malleus Maleficarum,* the official handbook for the conscientious Inquisitor, published in 1487, noted:

> ... there was a defect in the formation of the first woman since she was formed from a bent rib, that is, a rib from the breast, which is bent as it were in contrary direction to man. And since through this defect she is an imperfect animal, she always deceives.[22]

Erick Midelfort's thorough study, *Witchhunting in South Western Germany, 1562-1684,* makes quite clear that witch trials were used to deal with what he calls a "socially indigestible" group, unmarried women. Midelfort suggests that this group had grown quite large because of changing marriage patterns at the turn of the sixteenth century.

Women were seen as temptresses, seducers, and most important as having a firey tongue. A great many proceedings against heretics and witches were based on what heretics were supposed to have said. The centrality of verbal interrogation (Professor Lea calls it "verbal digladiation") must not be overlooked. It was probably here that women were given the stereotype that continues today of being "talkers." This gave rise in later years to the specific crime of "scolding" and the curious punishments that arose to deal with it. Certainly, the witch trials at Salem, Massachusetts, all involved women who would not keep quiet. We shall have more to say about scolding shortly.

The criminal and religious punishment of animals during and after the inquisitorial period makes one of the more bizarre yet significant chapters in the history of punishment. The punishment of animals fills in the larger picture of the extent and form of punishment throughout the whole of society. Animals of various kinds, after all, have been pretty much a part of our families for many centuries. We are also aware that many of the legal arguments concerning insanity and mental defectiveness as excuses from criminal punishment were preceded by similar arguments in defense of "irrational animals."

The cases of animal punishment fall into two groups. The first of these comprises animals and insects that are beyond direct human control, more or less "nondomestic." The other group of animals that were dealt with through the ecclesiastical courts of the middle ages were the domestic animals that committed acts of violence, usually homicide. These included pigs, cows, mares, asses, and dogs. The picture of a pig being placed in a dock in court and undergoing a criminal trial strikes us today as being completely absurd. However, the practice was perfectly reasonable for the society of the middle ages.

In the sixteenth century at the court of Anton, in France, a bright young lawyer called Chassenee was commissioned to defend a large group of rats that had been charged with "having feloniously eaten up and wantonly destroyed the barley crop of that province."[23] Chassenee conducted a spirited defense, using a number of standard legal arguments: his clients were unable to attend the hearing because they were frightened that cats might kill them on the way; to make matters worse they had been summonsed in Latin; and the question was raised as to whether they were rightly summonsed to ecclesiastical court as against the secular court. The final verdict of the court is unknown, but judging from the verdicts of many other such cases conducted throughout the middle ages in ecclesiastical courts, the chances are that they were found guilty and an anathema (a curse) was placed upon them. This took the form of a pronouncement, in appropriate ecclesiastical language, that the offenders cease what they were doing, and quite often a specifically selected plot of land was chosen for them to go to. This happened in 1545 in the case of a plague of weevils that ate the vine crop of the wine growers in St. Julia, France. After "due process" in the ecclesiastical court, an anathema was announced and they were banished to a carefully selected piece of land on the outskirts of the village.

Similar trials were conducted throughout the middle ages. The Council of Worms, in 864, decreed that a hive of bees, having caused the death of a human, should be smothered to death in the hive; anathemas were pronounced, after due process, against a plague of locusts in Rome in 886; serpents were prosecuted at Aux-les-Bains in the ninth century; field mice and caterpillars at Laon in 1120; flies at Foigny near Laon and horseflies at Mayence in 1121; eels at Lausanne (because they were biting swimmers) in 1225; Spanish flies at Mayence in the fourteenth century; rats and bloodsuckers at Berne in 1451; and an assortment of weevils, moles, caterpillars, worms, beetles, snails, grasshoppers, gadflies, and locusts up to the last recorded case in 1866, when a plague of locusts was anathematized at Pozega in Slavonia. An anathema was even pronounced against an orchard, because its fruits were tempting the children!

There was absolutely no doubt at all that the church could effectively get rid of these pests; at the same time the insects were seen as having a right to an adequate means of subsistence, since they were not exterminated but given a special place to live. However, with the rise of Protestantism, the later practice was to appoint a "spoiler" to assist the anathema and actually exterminate the nuisances. This occurred in Dresden in 1559, when the church "put under ban the sparrows, on account of their increasing and extremely vexatious chatterings and scandalous unchastity during the sermon. . . ." The use of the curse, a central and perhaps the oldest punishment in Western civilization, was the central feature of this system of punishment, and though it is mostly known to us through the Bible, it should not be assumed that it is purely Judeo-Christian in origin.[24] Curses were a mainstay of Greek and Roman moral life. The classical Greeks especially pronounced curses on weapons and other lifeless things.

Another reason for the ecclesiastical punishment of animals was the belief in demons. The middle ages was a period rife with symbols and images, especially of hell. The doctrine was that demons were waiting to be sent to the fires of hell, but this would not happen until the day of the last judgment. The soul of each person and animal who died and were marked for hell had a long time to wait for judgment day. Therefore, these demons had to look for a place to bide their time, and animals and insects were their chosen places of residence. This is why early baptism of an infant was seen as so important, to prevent the demon from entering it. It is a simple matter then to understand why people should try to deal with plagues of insects and pests by calling upon the divine powers of the church to issue a curse or anathema: the church was, after all, the only recognized authority to deal with demons. Exorcism was a well used and important method, closely related to the criminal punishment of insects. There was indeed the case in 1559 near Joachimsthel of a girl who swallowed a fly and immediately began to speak in strange voices. She had, of course, swallowed a demon that had taken up residence in the fly. Mephistopheles introduces himself to Faust as:

> *The Lord of rats and of mice*
> *Of flies and frogs, bed-bugs and lice.*

It is also not surprising that people should believe that plagues were visited upon them because they had sinned in some way. I uncovered the primitive origins of this belief in the second chapter. Once again, the church was the logical vehicle to deal with such a problem.

The second group of animal defendants, the domestic animals, were prosecuted in the secular courts. Plato long ago observed that domestic animals must be punished for homicide: "If a draught animal, or any other beast kill a person . . . the kinsmen of the slain shall prosecute the said homicide for murder—and the overseers . . . shall send the offender beyond the boundaries of the country." The same applied, according to Plato, to a lifeless thing if it so took a life.[25] One sees the familiar theme of vengeance: a death *must* be appeased, regardless of the reason for the death.

There were generally two groups of criminal animals that were prosecuted: those charged with homicide, and those charged with sodomy in union with a human. Both crimes were subject to the death penalty. Ninety-three such cases were recorded in France from the twelfth to the eighteenth century, but it is thought that many more were probably never recorded.[26] The most celebrated case is probably that of the sow which was charged, in 1386 by the tribunal of Falaise, with having torn the face and arms of a child, thus causing its death. The tribunal appropriately ordered that the sow should also suffer to be mangled in the head and forelegs and then hanged. At the execution, conducted in the public square, the sow was dressed in a man's clothes and the executioner given a new pair of gloves.[27] Pigs appear to have been the most common class of offender, and in every case reported they had killed and partially eaten young infants. In fact these comprised the overwhelming majority of the homicide cases, which makes one a little suspicious, in light of the evidence presented in the previous chapter concerning the strong tendency toward infanticide among the people of the middle ages.[28] The offending sows were hanged, quartered, burned alive, and even gibbeted. The earliest cases were in the beginning of the thirteenth century and continued until the last case in 1906 in Switzerland. The cases had, however, undergone a certain amount of change. By the middle of the tenth century, most owners of the offending animals were also fined for the animal's offense, but the owner could appeal to the court not to destroy his animals. An example of this occurred in 1379 when three sows who were with a large herd suddenly charged at the farmer's son and killed him. The rest of the herd were found guilty as accomplices, but the owner appealed on the grounds that it would ruin him if they were executed, and the court granted a pardon.

The final case in 1906 is of interest, and quite different. Here, a man called Scherer and his son, along with their fierce dog, attacked a man, killing and robbing him. The two human offenders were sentenced to life imprisonment and the dog received the death penalty.

The other group of cases comprises a series of sodomies, for which both man and beast were usually burnt alive. There were fewer cases in this category, most of them occurring after the fifteenth century.[29] The most notorious case was reported by Cotton Mather in New Haven. One Potter, a staunch pillar of the church for twenty years, was executed for buggery. "This monster lived in most infandous Buggeries for no less than 50 years together, and now at the gallows there were killed before his eyes a cow, two heifers, three sheep and two sows, with all of which he had committed his brutalities."[30]

Why were animals subjected to criminal punishment? Some have suggested that it was a result of the personification of animals—that is animals were seen to have human attributes. This is probably not accurate. It is certainly true that during the middle ages stories were often told about animals that had many human attributes. *Reynard the Fox,* for example, was clearly used to display all the despicable human traits: he lied, cheated, stole, murdered in cold blood, and so on. But this was not a personification of the fox. Rather it was more likely the animalization (if one will excuse the word!) of the human. No one really believed that the fox was that adept at lying. It was simply a convenient way to lay bare human folly. Furthermore, it is clear that the animals were simply not seen as humans, since the arguments used in their defense were most often those testifying that they were not sentient or rational beings and therefore could not be held responsible for the crime.[31]

One should realize, however, that our attitude toward these practices today is rather snobbish. When one considers that there were really very few cases over several centuries, that the plagues especially must have been very severe, and the people at their wits' end, the need to appeal for help beyond the realm of reason runs very deep. After all, only as recently as 1976 special church services were held throughout Europe and England to pray for rain to alleviate one of the worst droughts in history.

Vengeance is another explanation. One of the very basic elements of punishment, underlying the whole structure of the criminal law is the need for, indeed duty of, vengeance. A death, no matter how caused, has to be accounted for. It is a practice that goes back to the early Greeks. What is surprising is that there are no cases reported where the owners of an animal that committed a homicide were not also subject to the vengeance of feud. This only occurred in mild form late in the sixteenth century, when fines against the owner were introduced, and a portion of this money did go to the victim's family. One could also argue that the practice was a very primitive forerunner of insurance, from which perhaps derived *deodands* referred to by Blackstone and others.[32] *Deodand* was the term given to property forfeited to God as a result of some accident or injury. "If a man falls from a boat or ship in fresh water, and is drowned, it has been said that the vessel or cargo are in the strictness of law, a deodand." This law was abolished in England only during Queen Victoria's reign. It was clearly a way to make somebody liable for accidents and perhaps constitutes the underlying rationale of property and many other kinds of insurance.

Finally, there is the theory of animal persecution. Modern writers on animal liberation have referred to the criminal prosecution of animals in the middle ages as a prime example of persecution, another demonstration of man's cruelty to animals.[33] Nothing could be farther from the truth. The animals were indeed fortunate, since they received due process of law every bit as good as that provided for humans. They were certainly not executed summarily, as would be the case today of an animal that ate a baby. In fact, the prosecutors were so careful to apply the law equally to animals, that they even placed them on the rack and tortured them for a confession.[34] There was even the case of a hangman who summarily executed a sow for infanticide, without a trial. He was hounded out of town. Animals were clearly not persecuted during the middle ages. They were only treated cruelly by the criminal law to the same extent that humans were.

It is of interest that today's "animal liberationists"[35] (the champion of whom is Professor Singer) argue that our attitude toward animals is a form of racism, which Singer calls "speciesism."[36] Singer argues that animals should receive consideration equal to humans. One wonders where this advocacy will lead—perhaps back to the middle ages.[37]

Punishment and Puritans

The story of punishment at the hands of institutionalized religion does not stop with the Inquisition, nor has it been solely a function of the Catholic church. Protestantism has also played its part. The word "puritanical" immediately conjures up images of harsh, rigid, unrelenting punishment. Indeed, Protestantism and Anglicanism were no doubt responsible for many terrible punishments. Yet one hesitates to label the punishment dished out by these churches as part of a system of terror like the Inquisition. There are two important reasons for making this distinction. The first is that much of Protestant punishment was highly localized. The second is that in England, at least, where the Inquisition did not gain a foothold, there was no clear separation of church and state: the duties of prosecution were mixed between the two, and indeed, as we shall see in later chapters, the clerics became mere puppets of the state.

Elizabeth I displayed a distinct tendency to behead those Catholics who showed any tolerance for Mary Tudor. In 1559 Queen Elizabeth handed down the act requiring uniformity of common prayer, service, and administration, and the bishops were charged to insure uniformity. Indeed, this was the start of the enormous local powers that bishops attained and which they subsequently abused, especially after Elizabeth's reign. Each could boast of his own gallows, drowning pool, and gibbet. Under Whitgift, Archbishop of Canterbury, "the commissioners were empowered to inquire into all misdemeanors, by all such ways and means as they could devise, and thought necessary; to examine persons upon oath, and to punish those who refused oath by fine or imprisonment."[38]

Although the commands issued by the Archbishop of Canterbury have an uncanny similarity to the commands given by Charlemagne to his bishops, a system like the Inquisition never developed. The reason, I suspect, was that the administration of the Church of England was highly localized and lacked a centralized force such as the Inquisition received from the Pope. Elizabeth had too much to do to allow her concern for the uniformity of worship to dominate the whole of her polities. In fact, she was careful not to do so, for fear it would divide her people.[39] As later events were to prove, her judgment was, as usual, impeccable.

A great deal of blood was shed, however, during the Interegnum, under the Lord Protector Oliver Cromwell. The lives that his "reign" cost both Protestants and Catholics were many, even though prisoners and wounded were spared during the skirmishes of the civil war. But Cromwell was responsible for the murder of thousands of Irish, whom he believed, after a loose interpretation of the Old Testament, God had told him to exterminate. His shameful Irish escapade reached its peak with the massacre of 3,000 men, women, and children in Drogheda in 1641. Because he saw the Irish as close to animals and beasts, "no quarter" was given.[40] These battles with their heartless slaughter of innocents were repeated many times over, and the number killed would surely equal those killed as the result of the Holy Inquisition. We tend, however, to regard the Inquisition as more evil, since it lasted for six centuries and was so systematic in its tyranny. In contrast, Cromwell was impetuous, unpredictable, and lasted a short time, but he managed to dispose of a great many Irish Catholics.

One may, of course, in defense of the Protestant church, argue that these atrocities were the product of politics and not religion (as an institution, that is), since the early Protestants had insisted that there be no church hierarchy or organization. In England, it is difficult to separate the two, since the church and the state were more or less welded into one under Queen Elizabeth with the 1559 act requiring the uniformity of worship. In addition, during his early escapades, Cromwell claimed only political justifications for his acts and not those of religion.[41]

However, if the organization were not there, the willingness was. Luther, although he opposed the burning of heretics, approved doing everything else to them, including whipping, imprisonment, and banishment.[42] He advocated banishment of the Jews and the burning of their synagogues. In 1554, Calvin went further and defended the lawfulness of putting heretics to death.[43] He imprisoned his enemies when possible, and even went as far as sending evidence to the Inquisitors to have one of his enemies, Servetus, convicted of heresy. In Berne, Basle, and Zurich at this time heresy was punishable by death. In Holland some were beheaded and others given life imprisonment.[44]

Nor were the puritans in America very tolerant of religious deviants. Apart from the well-known witch hunt in Salem, they were most openly hostile to the Quakers. There was, in fact, a law against Quakers coming to New England. For the first offense, they had to forfeit £100 and were committed to prison. For a second offense, the men lost one ear and were sent to a house of correction, and the women were whipped. For a third offense, their tongues were bored through with a red hot iron, they were sent to a house of correction, and then transported.

We can see that the institution of religion has played a very large part in the evolution of forms of punishment, especially concerning to whom they were applied. In Europe, there was a clearly separate church organization for the administration of punishment. In England the situation has been more complicated, since both the laws and their administration were closely intertwined beginning in the Tudor period and continuing through the seventeenth century. A highly systematized method of punishing heretics and other religious deviants did not arise in England because of the highly localized nature of the administration of punishments by the church. The localized punishment allowed a number of "curious" punishments to surface which were widely used according to the many records that are available. I would not want to suggest that they were found only in England—they were used also throughout Europe. But it is from English history that the largest volume of records of these punishments exists.

Curious Religious Punishments

The classification of the following punishments as religious rather than criminal is admittedly a little strained. They were very often used also for "crimes" according to the criminal law. However, my argument is that they issued from various religious attitudes and practices. The punishments with which we may deal here are: the scold's bridle, doing penance, the ducking stool, and variations on all of these.

THE DUCKING STOOL: The many illustrations and reports of the ducking stool on record[45] suggest that this form of punishment was very widespread throughout England during the sixteenth and seventeenth centuries, and throughout the colonies in America till the eighteenth century.[46] There is some disagreement as to its origin and also its distinction from the "cucking stool." One researcher conducted a detailed etymological search and concluded that the two words were of the same origin.[47] There are reports of a few early uses of the cucking stool which did not involve the ducking of the person in water. Rather the punishment was simply that the offender was conducted on a chair through the village and subjected to ridicule. The offenses for which this punishment was used were mostly those of giving short weights in a sales transaction or selling bad beer. There is some evidence to suggest that the ducking stool was used for these "consumer crimes," and it has been argued that this was essentially a reflecting punishment in that the balanced ducking stool contraption represented the scales of a shop.[48]

All authorities agree, however, that its most common use was for the punishment of "scolds." "The tongue is a fire, a world of iniquity." There exists a mass of religious writings on the government of the tongue, the most significant being Edward Ryner's *Rules for the Government of the Tongue* (1656-58). The sins of the tongue were frequently regarded as branches of the sins of wrath. It was necessary that wrath be submerged—as Dante so colorfully showed. Thus the wrath of the scold was submerged, and the firey tongue was put out in water: "They place the woman in this chair, and so plunge her into the water, as often as the sentence directs, in order to cool her immoderate heat."[49]

It is also possible that the practice originated from trial by water, a common method during the Inquisition for trying witches. These offenders (most always women) were bound and thrown into the water. If they floated, they were innocent. If they didn't—well, too bad. It is quite possible that since this was a punishment reserved for women, it was continued with the variation of the ducking stool.

That the offense was both religious and public is amply supported by the many cases described by the antiquarian writer, Andrews. For example, it was seen as a form of penance: "Jane Johnson adjudged to the ducking stool for scolding, and commenced her penance," was the judgment of a court in Elizabeth's reign;[50] "scolds, brawlers, disturbers, and disquieters of their neighbors, to the great offense of Almightie God and the breach of Her Majesty's Peace . . ." (1597). In contrast, in colonial America the stool appears to have been administered by nonchurch persons, or the secular local government. In fact, there is no evidence for its use in early American puritan communities. Rather, it was widespread in "the cavalier" colonies of Virginia, the Carolinas, and, somewhat surprisingly, Quaker Pennsylvania. Although the court at Massachusetts Bay ordered the ducking of scolds, there is no evidence that it was carried out. However, a dozen towns in Maine were fined for not having a cucking stool.[51]

The Statute Books of Virginia from those times read:

> Whereas often times many babbling women often slander and scandalize their neighbors, for which their poor husbands are often brought into chargeable and vextious suits and cast in great damages, be it enacted that all women found guilty be sentenced to ducking.[52]

The last case of a person sentenced to ducking as a common scold was the famous case of Mrs. Anne Royal, during the time of John Quincey Adams. A very colorful woman, she became editor of a Washington, D. C., newspaper called the *Washington Paul Pry* and spared no public official her abuse. In her own life, she had been stolen by Indians as a child, and was raised by them for fifteen years; she was eventually married to a Captain Royal who taught her to read and write. She lobbied so relentlessly and plagued congressmen so much that she was finally arraigned before Judge William Crauch, who sentenced her to be ducked as a common scold in the Potomac River. This was, perhaps, one of the earliest examples of a woman in the nation's capital unable or unwilling to keep her mouth shut![53]

In conclusion, our most interesting observation is that ducking was a mixture of religious and public punishments of scolds, who were mostly all women. The religious element of the punishment was clearly evident, but it would appear to be absent from the American colonies.

THE SCOLD'S BRIDLE: Scolds were also punished by being made to wear various metal branks or bridles, which, depending upon the particular locality and severity of the offense, could be quite painful. A bridle consisted of an iron cage that fitted over the head, with a sharp front plate, often spiked, that fitted into the mouth of the scold. She was then led through the streets by a chain, and subjected to the jeers of the villagers. Again, Andrews describes a great variety of bridles, and it is clear that they were widely used. However, from the descriptions of the cases he presents, it is not so clear that the bridle was used on women for religious reasons. It is more likely that it was used by men to keep women in their place, especially any that might question their position or take to task a drunken husband. Andrews gives an account of a practice at Congleton, in which the collusion among men is quite clear:

> In the houses . . . there was generally fixed on one side of the large open fire-places a hook, so that, when a man's wife indulged her scolding propensities, the husband sent for the town jailor to bring the bridle, and had her bridled and chained to the hook until she promised to behave herself better for the future. I have seen one of these hooks, and have often heard husbands say to their wives: "If you don't rest with your tongue I'll send for the bridle and hook you up." The Mayor and Justices frequently brought the instrument into use. . . .[54]

In another case, when a woman told a clergyman and other men that it would "look better of them if they would look after their own houses, rather than going looking after other folk's," she was immediately marched off to the mayor and magistrates where it was unanimously decided that she should be made to wear the town's bridle for scolding women.[55]

In early America, the situation seems to have been a little different. The bridle and its variations were used just as much for men as women. Petty surveillance seems to have been rife. One citizen in Salem complained sarcastically that if he were to lie abed in the morning, he supposed the magistrates would haul him up. They did, and he was fined for sarcasm and a cleft stick put on his tongue.[56] The same was applied to a number of drunks in 1639 and to others for swearing. In 1671, Sarah Morgan struck her husband who "ran whining to the constables." She was ordered to stand in the public meeting place with the gag in her mouth, her offense written and placed on her head.

This punishment as a punishment for "scolds" died out much earlier in America than in England, although the cleft stick was used in the eighteenth century in Providence schools to punish children for talking or swearing. The wooden contraption became known as the "whispering stick."[57]

PENANCE: There is an entry in the Roxby Parish Register which states: "Memorandum—Michael Kirby and Dixon, Wid. had 2 bastard children, one in 1725, ye other in 1727, for which they did publick penance in our P'sh Church." Penance, of course, is almost solely religious in origin; the extreme forms, one supposes, are those of public self-flagellation to which we referred earlier. The central feature of penance was that the individual must humble himself publicly and was usually put through a mild physical ordeal—parading barefoot, lightly clad in a white sheet, required to proclaim one's offense and request forgiveness. Apart from the more famous instances of penance, such as Henry II's penance at Canterbury to pay for the murder of Beckett or that of Jane Shore, one of Edward IV's mistresses,[58] the majority of penances were ordered of ordinary people for such crimes as adultery, gambling or drinking on the Sabbath, and "unchastity." That it was widely used in the seventeenth and first half of the eighteenth century is well supported by the many records in Parish Registers, especially those accounting for the costs of the punishment. Special repentance stools were also used in some churches, upon which the sinner was urged to stand or sit and renounce his sins before the congregation.[59]

Public penance was widely used in Colonial America. Sir Thomas Dale in Virginia passed a statute that said:

> No man shall unworthilie demeane himselfe unto any Preacher, or Minister of God's Holy Word, but generally hold them in all reverent regard and dutiful intreatie, otherwise he the offender shall openly be whipt three times, and ask publick forgiveness in the assembly of the congregation three several Sabath daies.[60]

Offenders had to stand in church wrapped in white sheets with white wands in their hands. Many cases for similar misdeeds were reported in New England.[61] Judge Sewall was perhaps the most famous early American to do penance at his own behest. The judge passed judgment upon the offenders of the Salem witchcraft trials and many years later became convinced he had been mistaken. His confession was read aloud at the Sabbath service in the Boston Church, "while the white-haired judge stood in the face of the whole congregation with bowed head and aching heart."[62]

One can see that institutional religious punishments have been responsible for very severe, often horrendous forms and systems of punishments. In Europe, during the middle ages, they dominated the scene of punishment of both religious and criminal deviants, since acts that today we would consider "crimes" were often dealt with by the ecclesiastical courts. In continental Europe, religious punishment was dominated by the Holy Inquisition. In contrast, in England, although religion was closely related to extensive persecutions and punishments, religion was much more an ancillary to politics and did not achieve a highly systematized tyranny of its own. The tyranny in English history from the middle ages on was not of religion, but of politics, formerly of the monarchy and later of Parliament. Naturally, the economic base also played an important part in shaping the evolution of punishment. It is to the evolution of criminal punishments in England, in all their political, economic, and religious aspects, that we now turn.

TITUS OATES

6

Punishing Criminals

I have so far concentrated on death and other bloody punishments from the point of view of their sacred origins or their rather narrowly defined use in the service of obedience within family, school, or religion. It is now time to place the use of punishment into a broader political perspective, by analyzing the relationship of punishment to the economic and social structure of society. I will do this very briefly for the period prior to the middle ages, and then concentrate specifically on the development of criminal punishment in English history.[1]

Punishment up to the Middle Ages

If I have given the impression so far that the major forms of punishment in ancient times were those of bloodthirsty physical injury, I must apologize for a little sleight of hand. In proportion to other punishments that we would consider mild today, such as fines or compensations, severe physical punishment was not the most common form used in ancient times. The death penalty, for example, was used rarely in classical Greece, although often pronounced for serious crimes. In Athens the more common punishment was to banish the criminal by the vote of 6,000, and if the criminal refused banishment, then the death penalty followed. Socrates could have elected exile had he wished. This practice was continued on a much greater scale by the Romans, who encouraged those under death sentence to go into voluntary exile. In general, in classical Greece only those criminals caught in *flagrante delicto* were executed, and this was done on the spot by special commissioners appointed for the purpose.[2]

In classical Rome the death penalty was almost never inflicted,[3] although there is some disagreement in the literature as to whether this applied also to slaves. The only crime for which capital punishment was administered arbitrarily was for *furtum manifestum,* a thief caught in the act, who was executed on the spot, preferably by the accuser. This apparently overzealous punishment is directly related to the central part that the Roman house and family played in Roman law. Free men were certainly rarely executed from second to first centuries B.C.—the height of the Republic. And it was not until A.D. 250 and 257 that the great persecutions of the Christians occurred under the Emperor Valerian, and this again only for a very brief period.[4]

It is also clear that only under very special circumstances was homicide dealt with by the public authorities in classical Greece. The execution of the offender was essentially looked upon as a private affair, and no officially coded law was ever written which required the state to punish a murderer without there being an accuser.[5] Roman law was also based on this premise, although it gradually gave way toward the end of the empire when the dictators took over.[6]

If free men were able in most cases to avoid the death penalty, and the truly harsh physical punishment was applied mainly to slaves, what punishments did free men of ancient times actually receive? Of course they received economic sanctions.

Early Origins of Economic Punishments

By the fourth and fifth centuries B.C. in Greece, the Gortyn[7] code had developed an extensive system of fines for a wide variety of offenses. Greater fines were leveled against richer people, but they were intended as vindictive punishments rather than as restitutions or compensations[8] and could be administered for such offenses as assaults on slave girls, arson, housebreaking, or for failure to fulfill jury duty. It is to be noted that these codes do not mention homicide at all —further evidence to suggest that it was dealt with privately, probably through the blood feud.

The fines against failure to perform jury duty were summary fines with a legal limit of fifty drachmas and could be levied administratively by the magistrates, though they could be appealed. For fines below ten drachmas, the magistrates possessed sole jurisdiction.[9] We should note also that fines not only were levied against the offender, but if the plaintiff failed to get a fifth of the jurors' votes, he was ordered to pay a fine of 100 drachmas. Thus, we see the essentially private aspect of criminal proceedings. This practice continued right through the classical period. Crimes such as slander, robbery, and assault depended on the actions of private citizens who often hired professional speakers or, as we would call them today, "prosecutors" to deal with the case. The cases were brought by individuals as a "matter of public duty," but the prosecutors were paid substantial portions of the fines levied against the offender.[10] Other crimes dealt with in this way were all laws relating to commerce, customs, and mining; cutting down more olive trees than allowed by law; and recovery of state property unlawfully in the possession of individuals. Originally, these prosecutors proceeded avowedly out of a public duty; but gradually as the financial gains became a major factor, they became known as "sycophants" and were held in derision by the Athenian citizens.

The Romans continued this essentially private way of dealing with crimes. There was no well-developed system of criminal law, but simply a multiplicity of penalties for a multiplicity of crimes. Most of these were dealt with through private redress. The public authority only intervened if the defendant refused to pay the restitution ordered by the civil court to the plaintiff. Although a fixed fine (*taxatio*) was levied in such cases,[11] the most common procedure was the confiscation of the offender's goods and property and their transfer, in proportion to the offense, to the plaintiff. This process was available virtually for all crimes: treason, homicide, theft (*furtum*), robbery with violence (*rapina*), adultery with slaves, incest, and many others. Although harsh death penalties were prescribed for such serious crimes as treason and incest, these were rarely carried out, since the magistrate was free to give the offender the choice of "voluntary exile." Since this meant the confiscation of the offender's property, with the resulting financial benefits to both the plaintiff and the magistrate, choice of exile was often granted as a matter of course.[12]

The Middle Ages

The period from the decline of Rome up to the middle ages is a gray area in the history of Western civilization. It was a strange period, "where blood feud raged along the banks of the placid Cher, where saints were banished, where kings were foresworn, where generations of nameless ruffians lurked in the forests and prayed upon the Frankish beeves."[13] The way in which the criminal law developed, its rules and its administration during this period has been the subject of painstaking research of many German scholars, such as Brunner, Amira, Wilda, and many others. There is a great deal of controversy over the interpretation of the period, so in my brief discussion of it, I must necessarily oversimplify to some extent. When in doubt, I have relied upon Professor Goebel's brilliant and exhaustive work, *Felony and Misdemeanor.*[14]

The early middle ages is an extremely important period in the development of Western criminal law, for in this period the very slow delineation between felony and misdemeanor was forged. Professor Goebel remarks upon the mischievous and stultifying effects that this classification was to have on later, and indeed current, Anglo-Saxon criminal justice.[15] The death penalty came to be prescribed for all felonies by the seventeenth century in England, and the list of felonies had, as a result of the tyranny of a succession of kings and barons, become all-embracing.

Between the period of the Romans and the beginning of the middle ages (roughly the fifth to eleventh centuries A.D.), society consisted of feuding families and tribes. There was a slow but clear force among the people to seek a solution to the violence of blood feud, and much of the old Roman law continued through this period making it possible to introduce certain procedures into the feuding process. One of these procedures was bargaining, in which each side bargained for various punishments due to each other. This naturally led to the attempt to conclude feuds by exchanging property and goods. Some have argued that a feature of early feuding called outlawry—where an offender was expelled from the group and declared *persona non grata,* his property and every part of his existence completely destroyed—was the forerunner of confiscation. However, this is not confiscation, strictly speaking, since the property was not transferred to others but destroyed.[16] It is more in keeping with a ritualistic interpretation of the kind suggested in Chapter 3.

At the same time another force for order also developed, that of the "King's Peace,"[17] or, to use a more modern term, the growth of the public sector in the administration of justice. Crimes became a strange mixture of private and public wrongs. The threat of confiscation was used by the public office to insure that a party fulfilled his obligations to another in the matter of a dispute. Here, the borrowing from Roman law is clear: the defendant's property was sequestered for one year. If he did not fulfill his obligation, it was confiscated.[18] Originally, both at Roman law and early Frankish law, the fisc, or public office, retained only a small portion of confiscated property.

During the early Frankish period, the king's ban was sixty shillings and the court's ban was fifteen shillings. These were fixed sums, wielded mainly as a threat against certain forms of misconduct and intended to promote specific royal interests. At the same time, private parties were also accustomed to paying the public authority a fixed sum for its services in dealing with a complaint. It can be seen that these "laws" clearly safeguarded the ordinary person and placed limits on the extent to which the crown could use its position to accumulate property. But as various militaristic states gradually developed, they usurped these laws and amassed large estates at the expense of the masses of "coloni"—serfs oppressed into a virtual slave status.[19]

There was also a very gradual increase in the part played by the public office. While it hesitated for a long time to administer penal punishments for many crimes (indeed, as we have seen earlier in this book, the criminal law of ancient Rome was more than overshadowed by a voluminous civil law which dealt with most crimes as we know them today), the public office was not backward in encompassing the economic aspect of crimes. By 809, it was enacted in Frankish law that when a man was sentenced to death, all his property went to the public authority.[20] During the reign of Charlemagne, the fiscal power of the public authority in the realm of criminal law extended considerably, and this formed the basis of the blatant tyranny, after the Norman Conquest of Britain, that the barons, lords, dukes, and abbots were to use to build their personal fortunes.

In this regard, the gradual evolution of the concept of felony is worth considering. The contract between the lord and the vassal was the central point of feudal law, the oath around which many duties were regulated. If the vassal broke his promise, "established by his act, desertion in battle or the like," he was subject to punishment by the lord, the ultimate one being loss of the land.[21] During the twelfth century, this breach of faith came to be known as *felonia*. The important feature of this feudal law (as opposed to criminal law) was the oath, upon which most of Norman law was built and around which the notion of infamy—failure at battle or ordeal—developed. Under feudal law, the punishments were originally forfeiture of chattel and land. But as the public authority gained more and more prerogative, eventually the theory of *bannus,* the right of the court to have complete control over the wrongdoer including his body and goods, allowed also for the death penalty. By the time William was to cross the channel, the basic forms of punishment were already established for the later development of English law: forfeiture of goods and land, the death penalty, and the powerful concept of felony. It remained for subsequent English kings to centralize the power to punish crime and to develop the trial procedure.

Criminal Punishments under the Tudors

From the time of William the Conqueror until the turn of the eighteenth century, the amount, severity, and type of criminal punishments were moulded by three great forces, or perhaps more accurately, institutions. These were the monarchy, the religions of Catholicism and Protestantism, and the economic structure.

The English monarchs, especially during the powerful reigns of Henry VII, Henry VIII, and Elizabeth I, used their unique styles to further their command of the land and put the law to work for their own ends. Although it is true that little by little Parliament managed to acquire more independent power, even under the reign of Elizabeth I (often considered the strongest of monarchs), never has criminal law been used more as an instrument to further the ends of individuals than during this period. We often read of the reverence with which the body of the common law was (and is) held in England from the eighteenth century on. Yet, although the common law did build upon previous law, the directions it took depended heavily on the instrumental gains that could be obtained through it by each successive monarch. The idea of the law in itself being "just" could not arise. It was just only in relation to the monarch's end. Not until the beheading of Charles I—the great signal of the end of monarchy as law—and the gradual forging of parliamentary democracy (after shaky beginnings) did the law itself assume a position of immense importance, and even reverence. (It was during this very period, though, that the law seemed at its most unjust, as we shall see in the following chapter.)

Up until the end of the fifteenth century, the amount of crime fluctuated considerably, probably according to many factors such as the effectiveness of the monarchy, poverty, the return of soldiers from foreign wars.[22] The popular picture of the "ordinary man" during these centuries is one of utter poverty, subject to the whim of the lord, with a multitude of criminal bands roaming the forests and lawless highwaymen robbing the rich. Like most popular ideas of history, this one is highly romanticized and only half true, although the grains of truth are there.

The economic situation certainly presented a problem to both the common man and the monarchs. The enormous growth in demand for cloth placed great pressure on England's old feudal farming system to raise sheep and sell wool. Henry VII was able to capitalize on this demand from Antwerp, and through the system of enclosure (the annexation of common land to run sheep) and general pressure on his subjects to raise more and more sheep, a great and profitable trade was developed, and Henry ended his reign a most solvent king indeed. He was, though, the last one to do so. Subsequent monarchs found the furthering of their pleasures, the defense of England, and the fighting of foreign wars a colossal drain on the royal coffers, and most were continually in debt. Taxes were a sure means of raising money, as was melting down the coin. But these solutions simply complicated matters further, resulting in various uprisings among the people, including the nobles who were placed in the middle position of having to extract money from their serfs in order to feed the realm's endless need for money.

But these observations can be overdrawn. At the beginning of the Tudor period (1485) "the peasantry who made up the majority of Henry VII's subjects were still warmed by the golden rays of the medieval sunset."[23] Most had risen above the ambiguous, quasi-slave status to that of yeomen or freeholders. They were, therefore, largely independent persons who had to be bargained with by landowners who, for the next several centuries, bore considerable political pressure from above and economic pressure from below.

Furthermore, the Tudor period was to see the growth of a very English trait: the feeling of closeness by the common people to the monarch. In many ways the history of Tudor England can be written as a history of London, since the London people felt a personal intimacy with their king—and it was, after a fashion, reciprocated. The people never shrank from judging their monarch's behavior both morally and socially. The monarch, if popular, set an important and exotic standard of behavior against which the people judged themselves. This is why only monarchs who were strong either politically or in personality (usually both) were able to go against tradition and bring about change. Even the strongest would not go too far. Henry

VIII, for example, although breaking with Rome on the matter of divorce, nevertheless retained the formal trappings of the Roman church. To have broken completely would have divided his people and thus spelled his own demise.

The idea of an unruly, highly disorganized society during the Tudor reign is also false. On the contrary, beginning with Henry VII, the machinery was set in motion to control the countryside and the city to an extent that was never achieved before in England. Although Henry VII had to rely on volunteer magistrates and clergy to administer local governments, Henry VIII's removal of many of the clerics' privileges and the gradual introduction of paid servants of the crown (especially Sheriffs) brought about a degree of control hitherto unknown.

Increased control at the local level, would, of course, serve to accentuate disorders which had previously been ignored. Indeed, up until the fifteenth century, chroniclers of crime (usually monks) recorded only those that directly affected their own "house." There is therefore no reliable way of knowing the amount and extent of criminal violence in general during this period, except through occasional reports of persons directly affected.[24]

The general impression is that during feudal times the high fluctuations in criminal violence, which are the crimes most commonly referred to, were due to the continuance of the blood feud process carried over from the early Frankish and Norman periods. The only difference here was that the feuds were given a more "formal" appearance, since they were mostly fought on a grander scale between warring magnates, such as that between Thomas Courtenay and William, Lord Bonville, in 1440, over an administrative error appointing the former to the same position as Lord Bonville,[25] and there are many others. These hostilities are, however, compared with the ancient feuds, better defined as civil wars, the most serious of which during this period were those fought in quest of the crown. The greatest battle and most important of the middle ages was the battle of Bosworth, in which Henry VII defeated Richard III, and so ended thirty years of sporadic wars: the Wars of the Roses.

Fluctuations in violence, then, were more a product of wars between nobles than the "plight" of the peasants, who went about their business of feeding, clothing, and warming themselves.

Outlaws indeed existed, and were often levied to serve in various battles. Outlaws were customarily dealt with "by the purse," which meant that the outlaw could purchase a pardon. There is the report, for example, of one outlaw, John Fitzwalter, an "habitual offender," who bought his pardon for £847, 2 shillings and 4 pence-half-penny.[26]

Indeed, right up until the fifteenth century an elaborate system of pardons had developed. Although various excuses were used by the king to provide a pardon (e.g., that the defendant was accused out of malice[27]), probably the most significant reason was that pardons were useful as a source of revenue for the king. As one would expect, of course, pardons were not granted to notorious or persistent offenders. Although pardons were early allowed for homicides and even treasons, by a petition in the commons of Parliament in 1390 it was laid down that pardons were not henceforth permitted for treason, rape, and murder with malice. It must be remembered that pardons were the special prerogative of the king. For example, in Staffordshire between 1409 and 1414 only nineteen pardons were given out of 158 felons who presented before the local justices. In contrast, the general pardons issued directly by Henry VI from 1437-60 numbered roughly 12,000.[28] It has been argued that the difference is more than made up by the fact that local juries acquitted at a high rate, and there was also a very high rate of nonappearances.

Criminal bandits also continued to exist throughout the Tudor period. But we should again be careful not to assume that all of England was violent, just as we popularly believe today that all of New York City is violent. Indeed, one nineteenth-century criminal-law historian insists that there was less crime in England at the end of the sixteenth century than at any previous time in English history.[29] This, by the way, includes the period in which Henry VIII is said to have executed 72,000 of his subjects for theft and robbery alone. This figure, originally appearing in *Holinshed's Chronicle,* has been seriously questioned by a number of authors.[30] Again, one is inclined to believe that although the peasant classes may have suffered materially in terms of fines, taxes, and forfeitures, their heads were quite safe during the Tudor period and even well into the seventeenth century. The most severe punishments were administered to those who stood in the way of the monarch: these were treated loosely as traitors or according to other trumped up crimes (as Henry VIII managed to do with at least two of his wives) and summarily relegated to the chopping block. Indeed, Henry VIII created more treasons than all his predecessors put together. It was not until after Henry's death in 1547 that Somerset repealed the Six Articles which comprised these repressive laws.

I have said little, so far, concerning the effects of the institution of religion on criminal punishments. The reason is that, compared to the rest of Europe, the horrendous religious punishment that accompanied the Holy Inquisition barely obtained a foothold in England. There are two related reasons for this. The first was the all-important break with Rome over Henry VIII's divorce and the subsequent tension between church and state within England, and between Pope and monarch throughout the Tudor period. Although Henry VIII did not actually break with the traditions of the Catholic church (though he did establish his own church), by the end of Elizabeth's reign, the Church of England—a totally independent church, recognizing only the English monarch as its head—was well established. Few people were burnt throughout the Tudor period for such inquisitorial crimes as heresy and witchcraft.

Only during the reign of Mary Tudor was the Inquisition imported to England. Mary Tudor revived the heresy laws and abolished the limitations on ecclesiastical jurisdiction, so carefully developed by Cromwell under Henry VIII. The persecution was a small one by contemporary European standards, but it still stands as the most terrible period of religious persecution in English history: "even if we regard the two hundred Catholic victims of Elizabeth's reign as martyrs to their faith rather than as traitors to their realm, their death rate of eight a year does not compare with the Marian figure of nearly ninety."[31]

The second reason is that, as far as can be ascertained, there was no well-developed use of torture in England. Indeed, it was clearly forbidden by common law.[32] Inquisitors who were imported from Europe to deal with the Templars complained that they could not locate persons sufficiently versed in the use and techniques of torture, nor were there sufficient implements of torture available.[33] Related to this was the constant tension between church and state in England. The system of the European Inquisition depended to a considerable extent on the cooperation of the public authorities for its operations, especially in the matter of carrying out the executions.

The Rise of "Curious" Punishments

We saw in Chapter 5 that the institution of religion brought its own special tortures and curious punishments, and now we have noted that England was largely insulated from this movement until well into the Tudor period. Yet England also developed its own conglomeration of "curious" punishments that appear to have been largely Anglo-Saxon in origin, and which probably originated some time in the middle ages. Their rise was related, as one would expect, to the social and political conditions of the time.

I have suggested that the middle ages was a period in which the English economy blossomed. The feudal system had worked well. Toward the close of the middle ages, with the accession of Henry VII and the policy of enclosure, a highly localized criminal justice system had evolved into a situation where social unrest could, and did periodically, break out. Although there was periodic violence in the form of civil wars, this was not sufficient to disturb the rhythm and security of feudal life. The subsequent Tudor period is a story of constant battles between monarchs and nobles, of whom the latter, as we now know, eventually won. It took a strong, resolved, and brilliant politician to keep the crown, and as it happens history produced at least three such monarchs during the Tudor period: Henry VII, Henry VIII, and Elizabeth I. Successively, these great monarchs unified England and centralized the administration of justice, while at the same time emphasizing its local control. This was necessary for each of them in turn, mainly because they needed to control both the economy upon which they placed great demands for resources and the behavior of that always hungry strata of lords and nobles, many of whom would not hesitate to seize the crown if given half a chance. Indeed, there were many instances in which this occurred, culminating in the abortive and pathetic attempt of Lord Essex to seize the court and the tower in February 1601.

The picture that we have of the Tudor period in terms of criminal punishments is of a series of illustrious lords and nobles and pretenders to the crown being confined to the tower or being beheaded on the high block. Some of them were executed in public. Many of the more illustrious were sent to their death behind the high walls of the tower.

What of the ordinary people? We have seen that up until the Tudor period, by far the most common punishments were those of fines, forfeitures, and purchasable pardons. Physical punishments of any sort appear to have been very rare during the middle ages.[34] Hanging is the punishment most commonly mentioned, and this was reserved for felonies and therefore fairly rare, since felonies at this stage were reasonably circumscribed, including only homicides, robbery, and rape. However, because of the highly localized nature of criminal justice, each town had its different tradition of execution, and most forms of the death penalty described in Chapter 3 were used at one time or another. It is true that the public hanging and disembowelling of traitors was practiced throughout this period and that the onlookers appear to have enjoyed the spectacle. But it would be wrong to consider such spectacles a central part of the everyday lives of the people. This was not to be the case until the end of the Tudor period, when the gallows and the gibbet became common landmarks.

The forms of punishments, then, were highly local and intended to serve immediate and specific purposes within the small community. Perhaps this is why physical punishments persisted and were used more extensively in the small towns.[35] The punishments that I am about to describe are punishments of small communities where the assumption was that everyone knew each other, if not by name, at least by sight. One may note that these forms of punishment persisted somewhat longer and for a wider range of crimes in the early colonial period in the United States,[36] perhaps also because this early period was one of small, tightly knit communities.

THE STOCKS: The stocks were originally intended as outside restrainers or "jails," not as punishments to turn the offenders into an object of ridicule—the purpose to which they were eventually put, as is commonly known. Stocks were the equipment of every jail by the fourteenth century and were used mainly as a restraining device while the prisoner awaited trial.[37] The Statute of Laborers in 1351, which was intended to "curb the malice of servants who . . . were idle and unwilling to serve without securing excessive wages. . . ,"[38] ordered that such offenders be punished by "imprisonment of their bodies" in the stocks. While the statute clearly stipulates this as a punishment in itself, another authority claims that the main purpose these early stocks served was to display the prisoners, most of whom were runaway servants, so they could be identified and claimed by their masters.[39]

That the stocks were seen mainly as an outside prison is demonstrated by the lines of a local poet of Ellesmere:

> *A tailor here! confined in stocks,*
> *A prison made of wood-a-,*
> *Weeping and wailing to get out,*
> *But couldna' for his blood-a-*[40]

The sight, in a small community, of someone restrained and helpless in this way was surely enough to encourge an increasing amount of joking and ridicule. Stocks became a popular attraction in all English villages, and indeed they became a "status symbol" of the village. The act of 1405 required each village to build stocks. There are reports of a number of instances of contemporary historians noting that a town was a mere hamlet and not a village if it had no stocks.[41] It is to be noted, however, that by far the largest number of descriptions and instances of the use of the stocks as punishments came not from the middle ages, but from the seventeenth and eighteenth centuries. We are indeed seriously lacking information on the use of punishments during the Tudor period. It would seem, if we may depend on the somewhat antiquarian works that deal with these punishments, that the stocks during the Tudor period were used mainly for those who displayed "ribald" behavior and for petty or nuisance offenses in the village, such as "tearing the hedges," abusing one's wife on the Sabbath, "stealing two puddings," and drunkenness. In 1623 the stocks were officially designated as the punishment for drunkenness in England and their use persisted up to the early 1800s. The last recorded instances in England appear to have been in 1860 for gambling on Sunday and in 1872 at the Butter and Poultry market at Newburg for drunkenness.[42]

The use of stocks in colonial United States deserves special mention. Here, however, it would seem that they were preceded by the wide use of bilboes, or "laying by the heels." This apparatus was used extensively in the colonies and British ships to restrain deviant sailors and, more often than not, slaves. The term is derived from Bilboa in 1588, where the Spaniards manufactured them to shackle their English prisoners for voyage.[43] They were simple and effective restraints: a metal shackle was attached to the base of the leg, thence to a chain, the end of which might be attached high up the wall or to the floor. They were also used extensively in Virginia and other slave states, for the shackling of slaves for the night.

Stocks soon superseded the bilboes, and the Boston magistrates of early America commissioned a carpenter to build a set of stocks. The carpenter was promptly placed in them himself for charging too much to build them! Again, virtually all reported case of the stocks being used were for the period of the seventeenth century, for petty offenses such as slandering, signing a rebellious petition, bigamy, stealing yarn, stealing an Indian child, lying idle, drunkenness, vagrancy, and resisting a constable.[44]

All in all, during the seventeenth and eighteenth centuries drunkenness was by far the most common offense for which a person was stocked. That it was not seen as a serious offense is apparent, but that it should have been considered an offense at all is of particular social significance. Since it was such a public crime, and often a spectacle, the stocks were an obvious and apt punishment. The drunk having made the community suffer his ribaldry, was now made the object of a similar community action. It was, therefore, both a collective and reflected punishment.

We have seen how the stocks evolved from a primitive outside prison to the object of spectacle and ridicule. We turn now to the punishment that clearly established solely with the intention of creating a spectacle.

THE PILLORY: There are reports of the use of a pillory-like apparatus by the ancient Greeks and the Gauls[45] for the punishment of drunkenness. The pillory was used frequently in country towns during the Tudor period, but it did not reach its zenith until the seventeenth century. Unlike the stocks, the pillory was used solely to punish and ridicule, and its use led in a number of instances to the death of the criminal. Again one notes how the antiquarian sources refer to the fifteenth and sixteenth centuries as being the period of widespread use of the pillory, but it is apparent that most of the cases they report are from the seventeenth century and later.[46] One is particularly struck by the descriptions of brutal treatment during the seventeenth century. The most famous case of such brutality, the more famous because the offenders (Bastwick, Burton, and Prynn), having been convicted of libel by the Star Chamber, excited the compassion of the people who came to see them not as criminals but heroes. They were sentenced to the pillory to be branded and to have their ears cut off. The punishment occurred in 1647, and the treatment of Burton was described thus:

> . . . when the executioner had cut off one ear which he had cut deep and close to the head in an extraordinarily cruel manner, [Burton] never once moved and stirred for it. The other ear being cut no less deep, he then was freed from the pillory, and came down, where the surgeon waiting for him presently applied a remedy for stopping the blood after the large effusion thereof.[47]

And when Bastwick's ears were cut off, "His weeping wife stood on a stool and kissed his poor pilloried face, and when his ears were cut off, she placed them in a clean handkerchief and took them away, with emotions of unspeakable and undying love."[48] During this period, the penalty was common for such crimes as libel, giving short weight, thefts not exceeding twelve pence, all manner of frauds, and a wide variety of petty crimes. It was also often used as an additional or preliminary punishment to a term of imprisonment for more serious crimes. Often, it was ordered that the ears should be nailed to the wood on either side of the headhole. To emphasize the ridicule, sometimes additional punishments were ordered. In the case of Robert Ockam, for example, in 1543, it was required that he be mounted on horseback, facing the tail, with papers on his head stating his misdeed, and thus to ride about Windsor, Newbury, and Reading and stand in the pillory at each town.[49] One can easily imagine the fun and joking that such a procession would invoke from the onlookers.

It was also not uncommon for those sentenced to the pillory to be killed at the hands of the angry spectators. This was so in the case of criminals who were especially disliked for having committed serious crimes or offenders who were professional witnesses who would, for a reward, swear falsely against accused criminals. Such was the case of Egan and Salmon, who were assigned to the pillory in 1751 as part of their sentence for robbery and murder.[50] The mob pelted them with turnips, potatoes, and stones. Egan was struck dead by a stone, Salmon died soon after. In 1732 John Waller died at the pillory of the Seven Dials, London, of injuries inflicted by the angry mob. One is struck here by the similarity between this and the ancient form of punishment referred to in Chapter 3: stoning to death.

That the pillory allowed the continuance of a rough mob justice is also demonstrated by the famous case in 1635 of Oates, guilty of perjury, "inventor of the Popish Plot." He was to be exposed for three consecutive days. The first day almost cost him his life at the hands of the angry mob, but the next day his own supporters and partisans rallied together to protect him.[51] It was a common practice for any supporter of a criminal to place carts in the way of the streets leading to the pillory to forestall any attack from onlookers.

The equally famous case of Daniel Defoe, who had been placed in the pillory for writing a satire against the church entitled, "The Shortest Way with the Dissenters," demonstrates the compassion of the mob, especially when it comes to resisting the powers of the state. He was not pelted with rotten eggs, but rather flowers. His *Hymn to the Pillory,* partially reproduced in the introductory chapter of this book, is to this day a poignant commentary on the injustices of criminal justice.

The pillory was also used widely in the colonial United States, especially for various economic crimes such as counterfeiting, forestalling, and frauds of any kind. There was even a case of electoral fraud in 1671, of one Mr. Thomas Withers for "surriptisiously endeavoring to prevent the Providence of God by putting in several votes for himself as an officer at a town meeting,"[52]—two hours in the pillory. Up to at least 1803 the pillory enjoyed a central place in most of the major towns of the colonial United States. The forms of the punishment were mostly similar to those in England: ears were cut off or nailed to the board, and the angry and ridiculing mob reaction was the same. A case is described in Boston in 1771:

> A little further up State Street was to be seen the pillory with three or four fellows fastened by the head and hands, and standing for an hour in that helpless posture, exposed to gross and cruel jeers from the multitude, who pelted them constantly with rotten eggs and every repulsive kind of garbage that could be collected.[53]

One further punishment often used in relation to the pillory and the stocks was branding. This practice can be traced as far back as the reign of Edward VI, and was discontinued under George III in 1829.[54] It was also widely used in colonial America. Once again, however, one is impressed by the fact that virtually all the instances of branding reported by the antiquarians refer to the seventeenth century. Although used for some petty offenses such as vagabondage or drunkenness, it was also often used in conjunction with other punishments of the pillory or imprisonment. For example, the "Mad Quaker," James Nayler, as punishment for blasphemy, had his tongue bored through, and the letter B stamped on his forehead with a hot iron.[55] The forehead, cheek, shoulder, or hand were common places upon which to apply the brand. Those claiming benefit of clergy were often allowed to receive the brand on the hand, and in the eighteenth century this became the most common place. One need hardly mention the obviously stigmatizing nature of this punishment, the indelible nature of the criminal record. Indeed, it became customary during the eighteenth century to command offenders in the courts to raise their hands to show whether they had any previous convictions.[56] It is quite likely that this practice was the forerunner of the modern swearing of witnesses requiring one hand on the Bible but the other raised with an open palm.

Branding was used in colonial America in most states. Its major use would appear to have been as a commuted sentence for those claiming benefit of clergy but convicted of serious crimes. The General Quarter Sessions of New York bear many records of those branded on the left thumb with a T in open court and then discharged, instead of receiving the gallows. In Maryland, branding was widely used well into the eighteenth century. The letters S. L. stood for seditious libel, M for manslaughter, T for thief, R for rogue.

One is reminded here of Franz Kafka's story "In the Penal Colony," where a major principle was that the sentence should be written upon the body by Kafka's weird punishment machine, the Harrow. The use of branding appears to have reached its height toward the end of the eighteenth century.

In the seventeenth century, also widely used was the "scarlet letter," or sewing onto the garments of the criminal a letter or inscription stating the crime. This was especially common for blasphemers and drunkards, and it was used extensively in New York and Massachusetts.

> 1634. Robert Coles, for drunkenness by him committed at Rocksbury, Shalbe disfranchized, weare about his necke, and soe to hange upon his outwd garment a D made of redd cloth and sett upon white; to continyu this for a yeare, and not to have itt off for any time hee comes among company, Vnder the penalty of Xls for the first offence and V£ for the second . . . also he is to wear the D outwards.[57]

Further failures to comply were often followed up with a whipping.

In conclusion, we may make a couple of important observations about the pillory and its related stigmatizing punishments. It was an ideal punishment for small communities in which everyone sought to know the other's business. However, as towns grew larger and social relationships became less intimate, and the state at the same time took a larger and larger role in the social control of behavior, the pilloried criminal became not so much an object of community concern as an anonymous figure that could be treated cruelly by a mob with comparative impunity. In contrast to the punishment of stoning, which was a quick response of a community's revulsion to the misdeed, here it is more a response of derision and pleasure that it is "better him than me." Unlike the pillory, branding allowed for a continued stigmatization of the criminal, which, once again starting in small communities, was equally effective in larger populations since it readily identified the person for life. Perhaps this explains why it was so popular in colonial America, where there was a constant influx of strangers—it served as a prophylactic device to keep the community "pure" of criminals. Indeed, branding was often used in conjunction with an order that the criminal be sent to "Barbados or some far away place."

WHIPPING AGAIN: A NOT-SO-CURIOUS PUNISHMENT: Whipping must be one of the oldest and most widely used forms of corporal punishment. By "widely used," I mean used and experienced by the bulk of ordinary people throughout the history of Western civilization. I have already reviewed its use on slaves, children, soldiers, and within religious orders. Its wide use has much significance for criminal punishment because, although it was used to create a public spectacle, it is also apparent that most people could probably identify with it, especially during the period of its greatest use, the three centuries from 1600. The chances are that most spectators of public whippings had personally experienced a whipping either as a child or a servant. It was, therefore, essentially a universal punishment and not community centered as were the pillory and the stocks.

Although whipping was used prior to the Tudor period, particularly for vagrants, it was not until the reign of Henry VIII in 1530 that the Whipping Act was passed. Apart from his marital and religious difficulties with the Pope, two major preoccupations also dogged Henry VIII: how to pay for his expensive foreign wars and how to keep the ever-present pretenders to his throne at bay. The latter problem he solved by expanding the list of treasonable offenses in his Six Articles. The former problem of revenue was of equal importance. And in the end, there was only one source as there is in today's modern state: the work of the ordinary man. Vagrants therefore were considered by Henry as a direct threat to his crown. The Whipping Act required that vagrants were "to be tied to the end of a cart naked, and beaten with whips throughout such market town, or other place, till the body shall be bloody by reason of whipping."

We should beware of imputing to Henry's reign the widespread use of corporal punishment. Although the act was passed in the sixteenth century, once again the majority of cases reported by antiquarians are from the seventeenth century and later.[58] The payments for using the lash formed an important item in municipal records, and here also there appear to be more extensive entries for the seventeenth century than before. Further evidence that it reached its zenith after the Tudor period comes from the poet John Taylor's observation in 1630:

> *In London, and within a mile, I ween,*
> *There are jails or prisons full eighteen*
> *And sixty whipping-posts and stocks and cages.*[59]

In 1597, toward the end of Queen Elizabeth's reign, the Whipping Act was revised. The body was no longer to be naked, but stripped only to the waist. A whipping post was substituted for the cart. Subsequently, combination pillory, stocks, and whipping posts became a common sight throughout most English market towns. These changes do perhaps suggest the early effects of puritanism—the concern for public nakedness, for restraint (the procession at the cart's tail was considered unseemly), and for dispassionate administration of punishment. Whipping gained in popularity during the following two centuries, reaching its zenith in the early American colonies, where it persisted well into the twentieth century.

We are fortunate enough to have a well-documented report on whipping in the American colonies, especially Delaware, provided by Robert Caldwell.[60] From the records that are available, the use of corporal punishment throughout the colonial United States and later was much more prevalent than in England. This has led some to conclude that punishments were more severe because of early American puritanism.[61] This is true only to a limited degree, because it must be considered in the light of the fact that of the early criminal codes[62] in the colonies, only eleven crimes were classified as capital offenses, compared to many, many more in England. In other respects, however, the range of criminal punishments was similar to that in England: pillory and double damages for forgery; fine or corporal punishment for fornication; larceny of more than ten shillings, a whipping and fine to cover damages or costs. In Delaware in 1677, one Francis Jackson received twenty-one lashes and was confined to the stocks, for calling Captain Billop "son of a whore and son of a bitch." And so it went on.

As we know, there was a brief period when the criminal laws were made more lenient, with a greater use of imprisonment and less corporal punishment, when William Penn introduced his "Great Law" on December 4, 1682. But corporal punishment, especially whipping, was still retained for the more serious offenses, and gradually severer penalties were again introduced as the influence of the Quakers waned.[63] By 1719, there was little left of the liberal elements of Quaker penology: only the prisons. The act of 1719, which reintroduced more serious punishments, brought Delaware into line with the then current explosion of death penalties, brandings, mutilations, and whippings. By 1742, the punishment for stealing less than five shillings in value was fifteen lashes. Delaware was the last state to rid itself of whipping as a criminal punishment.

Eventually, these laws did disappear, but whipping remained for a long time an important and cruel nonjudicial punishment—on estates to discipline slaves—and well into the twentieth century it found a comfortable home in the privacy of a new punishment, the prison yard.

PEINE FORTE ET DURE (PRESSING): A survey of curious punishments would not be complete without consideration of *peine forte
et dure,* a punishment unique to England's criminal law. We might
call this an "adjudicatory punishment" in the sense that it was applied to offenders who refused to plead "guilty" or "not guilty." The
punishment consisted of the following:

> That the prisoner shall be remanded to the place from whence he
> came, and put in some low, dark room; that he shall lie without any
> litter or anything under him, and that one arm shall be drawn to
> one quarter of the room with a cord, and the other to another, and
> that his feet shall be used in the same manner, and that as many
> weights shall be laid on him as he can bear, and more. That he
> shall have three morsels of barley bread a day, and that he shall have
> the water next the prison, so that it be not current, and that he
> shall not eat. . . .[64]

The origins of this punishment are unknown. It is tempting to
draw an analogy between this type of punishment as a torture and
the inquisitorial process, with its absolute necessity of extracting a
confession from the accused. In one sense they are the same: they
are punishments (or tortures) used as a means to an immediate end.
But we can trace the inquisitorial methods well back into Roman
law. We are unable to do so for *peine forte et dure,* nor is there any
similar method of punishment used by the Inquisitors. It is most
likely, therefore, that pressing is unique to English criminal law, and
we must look to English history for an explanation.

A similarity to the religious punishment of trial by ordeal suggests itself. This principle may be applied to English soil, since there
are extensive records of "trial by battle" during the very early years
of the middle ages. It will be remembered that I referred to the early
formation of the concept of felony, its link to the crime of infamy,
which was defined in one way as failure to prove oneself to one's
master in battle: a trial by ordeal. There are many instances of trial
by ordeal in the order of religious punishments, but these often relied on nonrational, supernatural signs to decide guilt or innocence.
The difference with trial by battle, trial by duel, and trial by *forte et
dure* is that they depend upon the personal strength and fortitude of
the accused. This is admittedly speculative, and more so if one wants
to use it to explain why pressing itself became the form of the ordeal.
There were, after all, many other slow tortures well refined by the
Holy Inquisition that would have served just as well.

Yet *peine forte et dure* was also meant to speed things up a little, since its forerunner was simply to leave the accused in a stinking prison cell to starve until he would plead.

There was, as one would expect, a very practical reason why defendants chose not to plead in the face of this horrible torture. Throughout the period of its use, a person found guilty of a felony not only went to the gallows, but had all his property confiscated by the crown as well. Thus, if the accused refused to plead, he could not be found guilty, and his heirs would not suffer. A number of cases are also reported of persons of incredible durability who withstood the punishment for so long they were eventually set free.

Conclusions

Contrary to the popular opinion of historical penologists,[65] the bulk of punishments up until the beginning of the seventeenth century have been economic sanctions either in the form of fines, confiscations, or restitution.

Although repressive laws were passed during Tudor times, especially by Henry VIII, there is no clear evidence that this was a period of extreme severity in criminal punishments, the only exception being the period of Mary Tudor. Death penalties were not often used during the middle ages, but during Tudor times when they were carried out, especially for treason, they were usually accompanied by quartering and disembowelling alive.

Corporal punishments were probably more widespread in the American colonies than in England. The reasons for this were (a) there were generally fewer capital crimes in the colonies than in England, during the seventeenth century, although this changed somewhat during the eighteenth century, (b) curious punishments were seen to be more a function of small, community actions, and (c) the effects of puritanism were to treat even minor offenses as serious.

The effects of the Italian Inquisition on Anglo-Saxon criminal punishments appear to have been minimal.

The gradual escalation of capital and corporal punishments began more markedly in the early seventeenth century, coinciding with the rise of parliamentary power and the weakening of the monarchy. This occurred after the Tudor period, and it is to this fascinating period of criminal punishment that we next turn.

7

Death and Delirium: Punishment Rears Its Ugly Head

We come now to what, in my view, is the most turbulent period in the history of punishment in the Western world, a period in which the fears of death and killing that lay in the darkest recesses of Western culture burst into the open. Public executions were, of course, not new to the seventeenth and eighteenth centuries, but the public reaction to them was. Death sentences were pronounced by judges of the assizes with great severity and sternness; the pomp and splendor of these occasions was enough to strike awe into even the most feckless of highwaymen. The judge sat up on high, bedecked in great wigs, scarlet robes, pronouncing the sentences along with a booming, resonant speech calculated to impress the audience.

These terrible sentences were not often carried out, for reasons that we shall see. But they were carried out often enough for a whole culture of hanging to have evolved. Many jocular and amusing colloquialisms arose in reference to the gallows. The criminal was "turned off," he "danced in the air," or "danced the Paddington frisk." A hanged man will "piss when he cannot whistle." A young pickpocket was a "Tyburn Blossom." The hanging day was known popularly as a "hanging match," a sheriff's ball, or a "hanging fair." The contemporary phrases "gala day" and "gala occasion" derive from the word gallows.[1] The three-hour procession to Tyburn from Newgate Prison became a great ritual. So much so that the authorities came to see it as detracting from the hanging itself, and so the procession

125

was eventually abolished in favor of public hanging in front of and later inside Newgate Prison.

The Procession to Tyburn

The "mob" at the procession and around the triple gallows tree at Tyburn has always been characterized by antiquarian historians as a sodden, drunken, angry lot: "what was a morbid curiosity among a certain section of the upper classes became a fierce hungry passion with the lower . . . a ribald, reckless, brutal mob. . . ."[2]

The ritual began in court when the great judge boomed out the sentence that the criminal be hanged until he were "dead, dead, dead." If he were a famous criminal, he would be placed on public display at Newgate Prison, and people would pay a handsome price to see him. If he were rich enough, the condemned man could entertain his friends and guests at Newgate with feasting and merry making the night before. Then, when the time came, he would be mounted on an open cart, seated beside his coffin, the halter that was to hang him wound around his chest, his arms pinioned. The gates of Newgate Prison would open, and he would begin the slow procession to the traditional sound of the church bells of St. Sepulchre.[3]

The procession was led by the city marshal on horseback, other officials, and a company of pike-men for protection against the unruly mob or against any attempts (especially if it was a well-known highwayman to be hanged) of a gang to rescue him. The most quoted description of this procession is this:

> . . . no solemn procession, it was just the contrary; it was a low-lived blackguard merry making . . . the whole vagabond population of London, all the thieves, and all the prostitutes, all those who were evil minded, and some, a comparatively few curious people made up the mob of those brutalizing occasions.[4]

Various descriptions of the demeanor of the condemned have been handed down to us. Most suggest that they displayed anything but remorse—rather an attitude of belligerent defiance which was approved and applauded by the mob. This applied especially to the "pop" stars at the time, the highwaymen.

Always traveling in the cart was the Ordinary (the clergyman) whose duty, theoretically, it was to prepare the condemned for his fate. It seems that in practice the Ordinaries turned a neat profit by prevailing upon the criminals to tell their story along with their confessions, which the Ordinary then had printed as broadsides and sold either during or after the hanging. Many hundreds of these broadsides were sold at the time, and they were avidly read by those who could read.

The crowds did, however, show some discrimination. The people hated Jonathan Wilde, perhaps the father of organized crime, and were pleased to see him at last punished for his tyrannies. On the other hand, in the case of Dr. Dodd, a clergyman of good reputation who was executed for forgery, the crowd was most angry. To make a blanket statement, therefore, that all processions were carnival-like and all hangings invited the enmity of the crowd against the "tyranny" of the law is quite misleading. The fact is, the people believed in the law and did not see it as tyrannical, the reasons for which I shall explain in a moment. Their behavior at the gallows and during the procession is, therefore, best explained by other factors—at this point, I suggest, by the details of the particular case. A browse through the *Newgate Calendar*—the fascinating volumes that contained the more interesting cases of the "bloody assizes"—is sufficient to show that each case was indeed a story in itself. There were cases of callous, brutal murders, such as the case of Elizabeth Browning who tortured her female apprentices to death. There were cases fascinating to the public, as they would be today, such as that of Hollings who killed his lover; the frequent cases of women charged with killing their babies (a common practice and a common charge); those of the notorious highwaymen such as Dick Turpin, himself a violent thug; and that of the unfortunate forger Dr. Dodd. All of these cases, as far as I can ascertain, were treated on their merits. Some invited a solemn procession, others anger from the crowd at a sentence that seemed too severe. And others excited ribald behavior in conjunction with a ribald person, such as Turpin. There were other causes of the mob behavior at the gallows which we shall look at soon. But first, let us continue with the procession.

The procession crossed a narrow stone bridge over the Fleet River, climbed the gradual slope of Holborn Hill to the top of Shoe Lane. Here crowds of people peered out of the windows of the famous inns and taverns. The condemned man stopped for a last drink at the Crown Inn at St. Giles-in-the-Fields, an ancient custom dating back to when there was a lazar house on this spot that offered a charitable bowl of ale. He could even stop in on a friend and have a good-bye drink. Captain Stafford promised an innkeeper that he would pay for his bottle of wine on the way back. No doubt some of those condemned played up (or down!) to the crowd.

Time soon ran out. The crazy cavalcade reached its end between what is now the wall of Hyde Park and the bottom of Edgeware Road. There stood the grimly simple instrument of execution: the triangular gallows or "triple tree," with the astounding capacity to hang twenty-four persons at a time—eight on each bar of the triangle—a feat which was performed by William Lowen on June 29, 1649, when he hanged twenty-three men and one woman for robbery and burglary.

The cart was backed under the gallows, the rope attached to the bar and knotted around the criminal's neck. The Ordinary made a speech, and the condemned criminal was also invited to speak—preferably to confess his terrible deeds and exhort the people to learn from his example. After admiring the condemned person's clothes, which were often new and the best available (the executioner by law claimed them as his own after the criminal's demise), the executioner pulled a white cap over the criminal's head to hide the facial contortions and death agonies from the crowd, then whipped the horses away. A letter written by a country gentleman who was visiting London at the beginning of the eighteenth century provides such a penetrating description of the scene that it is worth reproducing in full:

> I have this day been satisfying a Curiosity I believe natural to most People, by seeing an Execution at Tyburn. The Sight has had an extraordinary Effect upon me, which is more owing to the unexpected Oddness of the scene, than the affecting Concern which is unavoidable in a thinking Person, at a Spectacle so awful, and so interesting, to all who consider themselves of the same Species with the unhappy Sufferer.
>
> That I might the better view the Prisoners, and escape the Pressure of the Mob, which is prodigious, nay, almost incredible, if we consider the Frequency of these Executions in London, which is once a Month; I mounted my Horse, and accompanied the melancholy Cavalcade from Newgate to the fatal Tree. The Criminals were Five in Number. I was much disappointed at the Unconcern and Carelessness that appeared in the Faces of Three of the unhappy Wretches: The countenances of the other Two were spread with that Horror and Despair which is not to be wonder'd at in Men whose Period of Life is so near, with the terrible Aggravation of its being hasten'd by their own voluntary Indiscretion and Misdeeds. The Exhortation spoken by the Bellman, from the Wall of St. Sepulchre's Church-yard, is well intended; but the Noise of the Officers, and the

Mob, was so great, and the silly Curiosity of People climbing into the Cart to take leave of the Criminals, made such a confused Noise, that I could not hear the Words of the Exhortation when spoken.

All the way up to Holborn the Croud was so great, as at every twenty or thirty Yards to obstruct the Passage; and Wine, notwithstanding a late good Order against that Practice, was brought to the Malefactors, who drank greedily of it, which I thought did not suit well with their deplorable Circumstances: After this, the Three thoughtless young Men, who at first seemed not enough concerned, grew most shamefully daring and wanton; behaving themselves in a manner that would have been ridiculous in Men in any Circumstances whatever: They swore, laugh'd, and talk'd obscenely, and wish'd their wicked Companions good Luck, with as much Assurance as if their employment had been the most lawful.

At the Place of Execution, the Scene grew still more shocking; and the Clergyman who attended was more the subject of Ridicule, than of their Serious Attention. The Psalm was sung amidst the Curses and Quarrelling of Hundreds of the most abandon'd and profligate of Mankind: Upon whom (so stupid are they to any Sense of Decency) all the Preparation of the unhappy Wretches seems to serve only for Subject of a barbarous Kind of Mirth, altogether inconsistent with Humanity. And so soon as the poor Creatures were half dead, I was much surprised, before such a number of Peace-Officers, to see the Populace fall to halling and pulling the Carcasses with so much Earnestness as to occasion several warm Rencounters, and broken Heads. These, I was told, were the Friends of the Persons executed, or such as, for the sake of Tumult, chose to appear so, and some Persons sent by private Surgeons to obtain bodies for Dissection. The Contests between these were fierce and bloody, and frightful to look at: So that I made the best of my way out of the Crowd, and, with some Difficulty, rode back among a large Number of People, who had been upon the same Errand as myself. The Face of every one spoke a kind of Mirth, as if the Spectacle they had beheld had afforded Pleasure instead of Pain, which I am wholly unable to account for.

In other Nations, common Criminal Executions are said to be little attended by any beside the necessary Officers, and the mournful Friends: but here, all was Hurry and Confusion, Racket and Noise, Praying and Oaths, Swaring and singing Psalms: I am unwilling to impute this Difference in our own to the Practice of other Nations, to the Cruelty of our Natures; to which Foreigners, however to our Dishonour, ascribe it. In Most Instances, let them say what they will, we are humane beyond what other Nations can boast; but in this, the Behaviour of my Countrymen is past my accounting for; every Street and Lane I passed through, bearing rather the Face of a Holiday, then of that Sorrow which I expected to see, for the untimely Deaths of five Members of the Community.

One of the Bodies was carried to the Lodging of his Wife, who not being in the way to receive it, they immediately hawked it about

> to every Surgeon they could think of; and when none would buy it,
> they rubb'd Tar all over it, and left it in a Field hardly cover'd
> with Earth.
>
> This is the best Description I can give you of a Scene that was
> no way entertaining to me, and which I shall not again take so much
> Pains to see.[5]

So, to the constant tunes of hell-fire and eternal damnation, the unhappy victims of the criminal law leaped to their fate before a swooning, delirious crowd. It was observed from time to time that there were many women and adolescents in the crowd who fell commonly into a trance. In the case of Hollings, considered quite mad, a great deal of public interest was aroused and an enormous crowd gathered. A young woman who was helped up onto the platform swooned when she placed the dead man's hand to her bosom.[6] There were many examples of trance-like states and strange behavior motivated by all manner of superstitions, such as that the touch of a hanged man's hand cured warts, and that a piece of the rope brought good luck—the hangman sold the rope by the inch.

What was it about English society that made its treatment of public executions such a spectacle? Was the criminal law and its administration as bloodthirsty as most historians purport? To answer these and other questions, we must retrace our steps to some important events of the seventeenth century, for it was then that the foundations were laid for the mass psychology that was to follow.

Sociohistorical Foundations of Gallows Behavior

First, some important observations about the seventeenth century as a whole. Although some statistics have been produced purporting to show that the average number of executions per year under the Commonwealth was lower than any since before Henry VII or the century following, this number—as in most statistics used historically—is grossly misleading as an indication of the spirit of the times,[7] especially in regard to crime and punishment. In fact, the seventeenth century was probably the most sanguine in all English history. Certainly it was the most turbulent politically and for the people as a whole, as Sir Charles Firth has noted in his biography of Oliver Cromwell.[8] It was the century in which the English gentry came into its own, and, spurred on by the spirit of puritanism, upset the delicate balance between Catholicism and Protestantism that

Elizabeth had so skillfully maintained. She had been careful to make herself governor of the Church of England, but not the head of the church.

The English gentry (the class immediately below the peers) were becoming professional men, merchants, and industrialists. Under Elizabeth, important trading contacts had been extended, and the traditional English industry of the manufacture of woolen cloth continued to boom in the seventeenth century. A minor "revolution" in agriculture, including the raising of sheep, had occurred along with a rapid rise in the coal industry. By 1618, Londoners were burning coal instead of wood. Already the beginnings of those smog-ridden pictures of eighteenth-century London were being prepared. Many other industries, such as glass, ship building, and salt, continued to thrive. Those who helped these industries to succeed were the often aggressive gentry who had been brought up on the puritan teachings of hard work and diligence. More important, Parliament had become a powerful political and social body. Previously, under Elizabeth, it had been a way into the royal court. But she had known how to control Parliament and, furthermore, the puritans during her reign were a small though noisy minority. The succession of two weak monarchs, James I and Charles I, much less skilled than Elizabeth, helped England toward that ever-increasing slide to becoming a republic. By the time of Charles I's reign, the House of Commons was heavily loaded with puritan gentry, and it was here that the trouble brewed.

We cannot hope to analyze all the factors that brought about the demise of Charles I, the Civil War, and the behavior of Cromwell, that much-derided, much-praised figure of English history. It is usually argued that Cromwell did not wish to bring civil war to England, but he was forced to do so, originally on the grounds of the political liberty of the people. It was only later, so it is believed, that the explicitly religious connotations or justifications for his actions were introduced.

Be that as it may, the two—the political and the religious—are probably not clearly separable. A central teaching of the Calvinist doctrine was that each individual must independently interpret the scriptures for himself and the church (or anyone else for that matter) had no business interfering. It was a simple and inevitable step that the ideology of independence—an extreme individualism—should overflow into the political sphere, when much of the politics and social institutions of the country was controlled by clerics of one kind or another and the church had been pronounced the Church of England. The two were inextricably related.

Thus the Civil War of 1640–49 was fought against Charles I, and Cromwell, with his highly trained cavalry and absolutely devoted army, eventually brought the war to a close on Tuesday, January 30, when at four minutes past two the head of Charles I tumbled from the low block before a silent audience of London citizens. At the time, Cromwell and his followers no doubt saw the end of political and religious tyranny achieved in one blow. This was not to be. Instead, this terrible act brought about a period of psychological and political turbulence such that England had never seen before. A people that had once loved its monarchy had risen up and killed its king. The psychological repression of hundreds, perhaps thousands, of years had been stripped away by this incredible reenactment of the primal crime.

The Interregnum of 1649–60 was to be one of the most fascinating for subsequent political theorists, since all manner of political theories was tossed about, especially by the Levellers. Some suggested that there should be no such thing as private property, and Hobbes announced that the "universe is material . . . all that is real is material, and all that is not material is not real."

The tragedy was that, in the midst of this "ferment of ideas,"[9] Oliver Cromwell could never find a constitutional basis for his government. He was forced, time and again, to fall back on the army which underwrote his power. The loyalists distrusted him because they wanted a Stuart as monarch. The Levellers and other independents distrusted him because his place as "Lord Protector" was too much like a monarchy. Moderates feared that he planned to destroy private property. In 1658 he died at fifty-nine, prematurely old, his death no doubt brought on by the increasing impossibility of his task. On May 29, 1660, Charles II was invited to return from Holland to reclaim his throne. The monarchy was never to be the same again, although theoretically nothing had changed constitutionally.

Cromwell's body was later dug up and publicly hanged. It had been a period in which the violence of killing, both in the name of order and against order, had become commonplace. It is small wonder that Hobbes saw the "war of all against all" to be so imminent. It was also the period in which Milton wrote his *Paradise Lost*.

The church also was never the same again. The burst of religious enthusiasm and the untrammeled examination of religious ideas had brought up the urgent need in Parliament for reforms. It set about to transform the Episcopal church into the model for the Church of Scotland, with one difference: the head of the Presbyterian Church of England would be Parliament. Bishoprics were abolished, and land and hierarchies dependent on them were reapportioned. It was an almost total transformation.

So it went on, through wars with the Dutch, a shaky reign of Charles II whose timely death probably averted another civil war, and then another crisis that would transfer more power to Parliament. This was the glorious revolution of 1688. Although the House of Lords was mainly Tory, and the Commons two-thirds Whigs, in the name of religious liberty, these men arranged for the "invasion" of England by William of Orange, and James II was forced into exile. Some have argued that this "glorious revolution" was a revolution not in the name of freedom but of men of property, and that Locke's view of property ("Government has no other end but the preservation of property"[10]) was the later apology for it.[11] That the revolution benefited the propertied classes there is little doubt, since all of Parliament was composed of those persons of influence. Parliament, after all, had always been composed of men of influence, even when it was heavily controlled by the monarch. The difference now was that the member of Parliament was in a position more than any other to use his post to advance his own interests, and those of his class, at the expense of the masses.

Was this situation all that different from the time when the great Tudor monarchs extracted and squeezed money and services out of their subjects? The answer is clearly "yes." During the Tudor period the monarch valued and prized his personal relationship with the people. The monarch represented to the people stability, security, and the rhythm of English life. Now there was a growing sovereignty of Parliament. Depending on one's point of view, one might call it a tyranny. And by the eighteenth century it had produced the kind of tyranny that we today find familiar: Parliament enacted a huge arsenal of laws, both criminal and civil, to shore up its interests. The rule of law had become institutionalized at last. It became indeed a government of laws, not of men. And again, depending on one's point of view, it might be called a tyranny of laws.

The founding of the Bank of England in 1694 transferred even more power to Parliament[12] and heralded the beginning of the advanced, fluid, flexible modern economic system that was to make England the most advanced trading nation of the world. It would make possible the extravagance and luxury of trade that Henry

Fielding, novelist and criminal court magistrate, sixty years later complained was the downfall of the poorer classes.

At the beginning of the seventeenth century, the population of England and Wales was over 4 million and the population of London was 200,000. By 1700, it was close to 400,000 compared to the total population of 5¼ million. One-fifth of the total population lived in the Thames valley. The incessant progress toward what today we call "urbanization" had begun to produce a city at once beautiful and dreadful. As far as the level of crime is concerned, we have no reliable information. There is little doubt that the number of executions was as high as and possibly higher than in the eighteenth century. It was during the seventeenth century that England—London especially—attained dubious renown for its common practice of hanging. Gibbets and gallows were an extremely common sight and widely known landmarks. The dark, feared image of "Jack Ketch," the mythological name of the executioner, arose during the reign of Charles II.[13] The greatest number of persons ever hanged at one time was, as we noted, during Cromwell's protectorship. The processions to Tyburn were well established before the eighteenth century, and indeed many of the more horrendous stories published in the *Newgate Calendar* refer to the seventeenth century. Furthermore, from the end of Charles II's reign to 1819, 187 new capital offenses were added to the criminal law, compared to only thirty from Henry VIII to Charles II.[14]

In sum, the colossal changes of the seventeenth century virtually turned the ordinary people inside out. They had lost their traditional life supports. Their personal feeling for their sovereign had been battered by the successive humiliating failures of monarchs in the face of the powerful Parliament. Their old religion was completely undermined, whether Catholic or Protestant. Catholicism suffered at the hands of the Cromwellian puritans and the later Presbyterians. Protestantism had been buffeted in all directions by the independents and nonconformists. Parliament, in the end, controlled that too, to the extent that the clergy came to serve their own and Parliament's interests. The clergy were cut off from the old traditions of Christianity and thrust into battle for property, a transition made easy for them by the Christian rationalist and defender of private property, John Locke. The feudal, medieval rhythm of life—the unhurried, detailed work of the master craftsman, the leisurely raising of sheep and spinning of cloth, the quiet tilling of the earth—was deeply disturbed. The merchants, traders, and industrialists were beginning to take over. The people were being thrust headlong into the business of production.

To make matters worse, the ordinary people were constantly embattled by wars, civil and international. The civil war, though fought with dignity, nevertheless was a war. And wars cannot circumvent the horrors of death. As if this were not enough, the people of England were visited frequently by terrible plagues—the worst one being the black death of 1666, followed soon by the Great Fire of London. Death was all around them at the time when the social and economic life of the country began to throb. All of the basic fibers of English life had been subverted: economy, religion, politics, the lot. By the end of the seventeenth century, we can say safely that medieval England had indeed died and the foundations of modern society as we know it today—laws, pollution, industry, commerce, religious toleration, urbanization, political parties—were established. And in the crowded city of London the specter of death and killing loomed larger than ever.

It is little wonder that by the time the eighteenth century was under way, the ordinary Londoner, soon to become known as one of the "working class," found himself gazing dumbfounded or yelling hysterically with the crowd at the foot of the gallows. And the small group of aristocrats that watched the executions with quiet, morbid curiosity—what could it be thinking? That this was in some way the demonstration of freedom saved from the clutches of the tyrant monarchs of old?

Let us take a closer look at what happened to criminal punishment in this frightening eighteenth century. Tyburn was a strange vision indeed. Especially when it appeared that for the first half of the eighteenth century, the common people thoroughly approved of it all.[15] Yet, with the exception of an occasional criminal of respectable background, those who journeyed to Tyburn were those of the feckless, confused lower class. In short, they were much like their audience: in a simple sense, popular heroes of the day, much like modern pop record artists.

Religious Foundations of Gallows Hysteria

From 1715 on, bishops were at the mercy of the politicians. They were "employed" by Westminster. Their influence over the people was well recognized, yet by politicizing them, their religious influence was deeply undermined. On the payroll of Westminster, the priests and curates tended to do everything but attend to their own decaying institution. Agricultural prosperity brought leisure to the parish priests, and the growth of industrial suburbs and towns had no relation to the traditional pattern of parishes. The clergy had also been sucked into the materialism of the previous century, and sermons revolved around the theme of the inherent goodness of the business life. The church was out of touch with the masses—indeed, they had now truly become "masses" and no longer parishioners. The church ignored the poor, both religiously and ideologically.

Not so John Wesley. The religion that this amazing man preached explains a great deal of what went on at the gallows hill. One would have thought that the masses, the growing poor decrepit mass of wage-earners, would have found a religious leader who would ease their squalid lives. But the opposite was the case. Wesley was absolutely conservative politically: "The greater the share the people have in government, the less liberty, civil or religious, does a nation enjoy." The French Revolution he saw as the direct work of Satan.

Instead, what he offered his greatly devoted followers were hell-fire and brimstone sermons; a call to a relentless, selfless Christian life; a life of abstinence, hard work. In short, it was puritanism again, but this time purged of its radicalism. What an incredible model to live up to! A great challenge to those who would try to uplift themselves.

Wesley also preached a wide range of crazy, superstitious practices and beliefs: he believed in witches, the corporeal existence of the Devil, and many of the more exotic superstitions that have from time to time been attached to Christianity. They reflected mostly the beliefs and superstitions of his audiences. His hell-fire sermons frequently instigated hysterical sobbing, weeping, and laughing. He reproduced in his church gatherings mob behavior identical to that of the gallows. When he preached of death and hell to his rougher audiences, people fell with convulsions and hysteria.[16] With the help of Wesley, the mob beneath the gallows seemed to understand. There were many occasions when the hanging was treated like a wedding,[17] something like a nuptial mass where the hero was the bridegroom and death the bride. Charles Wesley, the brother of John Wesley, preached at a Wapping hanging: "Well is the spirit compared to a mighty rushing wind: we heard the sound of it now, and the flame was kindled. Many felt the pangs of a new birth. Behold, a cry: 'The Bridegroom Cometh.' "[18] This was the most profound religious conversion possible: death into life.

Wesley could dredge up the unconscious fantasies of the masses. Death, or more exactly, violent death became a kind of justification for religion. How far civilization had come! In the darkest beginnings of civilization that I outlined in the second chapter, we saw that the killing came first, followed by various religious rituals. Rituals arose as atonement, in a sense as a justification, for the killing that occurred in the primitive tribe. The weight of this early killing—and much subsequent violence—has hung like a millstone around the neck of Western man. We have developed elaborate rituals and institutional devices to cope with this necessary but frightening activity. Religion had been one such important facet of civilized growth. It had suffered many setbacks, culminating, in eighteenth-century England, with being turned on its head. Religion was no longer the justification for violent death; hanging was instead the justification of religion. The orthodox clergy had become nothing more than gallows birds, empty and corrupt, feeding off the carcasses of criminals and abhorred by the masses.

The clergy, having gone over so fecklessly to material existence and given up the moral intonations that are the basis of any religion, had only one material fact to offer their parishioners: the material fact of death. Even here, they dealt with it not morally, but with a view to material profit. In short, they knew not what to do with death. One might add, though, that the doctrine of predestination could not have helped the Ordinaries take their jobs seriously.

With death closing in all around, the mob was happy to see that some control was possible. At Tyburn a life could be turned off at will, and not just any life but the life of a hero and an idol. But there was renewed hope, if Wesley were right, that life would be turned on again, if one worked hard, because Wesley had thrust aside the Calvinist doctrine of predestination. For the ordinary onlooker, with no personal involvement in the case, the public hanging of a criminal was a deeply spiritual experience. He liked it, but he knew not why.[19]

There were still other factors that contributed to the brawling scene at the gallows, and these were related more to the character of criminal law and its administration, the character of the judiciary, and the rapid rise of another important profession of the well-to-do classes—medicine.

Criminal Justice and the Gallows

The eighteenth century brought with it a continued increase in the number of capital offenses. George II added thirty-three more capital offenses, and George III added sixty-three. But in actual fact, the possible number of capital offenses could be multiplied by five, since the enactment of various emergency laws allowed for their wide application and extension by judicial decision. Indeed, criminal law was in a sorry state. The same punishment was provided for different kinds of crimes of varying degrees of severity. The Waltham Black Act, enacted in 1822 in response to robbers who blackened their faces and preyed upon the people of Waltham, provided the death sentence for anyone found with his face blackened in specific places at specific times. Sir Leon Radzinowicz estimates that there were probably fifty crimes punishable by death at this time, but seven groups of offender types, which makes about 350 possible capital crimes![20] This "emergency" law remained in force until Sir Robert Peel abrogated it in 1823.

If there were so many capital offenses in the judiciary's arsenal, they were certainly used with constraint, when one considers the extremely high rate of street crime during the period and the temptation for harsh punitive reactions. We must also remember that England throughout this time probably had one of the lowest murder rates in Europe. In London and Middlesex, for the period 1749 to 1771, only 10.6 percent of death sentences were for murder.[21] Burglary and robbery together accounted for by far the highest proportion—close to 70 percent. Understandably, an age preoccupied with property and the "luxuries" of trade and commerce, applied its most severe laws to those who threatened these cherished ideals. Historians have often remarked that this century was remarkable in its level and acceptance of violence—usually noting the practice of violent sports such as bear-baiting and cock-fighting to support their claims. It is true that some highwaymen employed violence to further their ends (Dick Turpin is the most quoted example), yet it is also clear that the highway robberies did not commonly lead to murder of the victims; at least, the *Newgate Calendar's* catalogue of crimes rarely refers to such cases. Most murders appear to have been of the kind that are familiar today: love triangles and the occasional sadistic or mass killer. Murder during the course of a robbery was probably less common then than it is today.

TABLE 2[22]

Proportions of Those Sentenced to Death Actually Executed
(London and Middlesex)

Date	Percent Executed
1710-1714	35.0
1749-1758	69.0
1790-1799	29.5
1800-1810	13.0

From the criminal statistics available for the period, one must presume that the judiciary knew what it was doing, that it purposely did not enforce the enormous range of capital offenses, and, more important, that it was responsive to current opinion. The data of Table 2 clearly demonstrate this. We can see that the proportion of those actually executed of those sentenced to death rose astronomically for the period 1749-58—the period during which Henry Fielding, the influential and upright magistrate, pleaded for stricter enforcement of the law and elimination of pardons and commutations. His *Inquiry into the Late Increase in Robbers* was published in 1751. Various writers, especially the Reverend Madan, were also arguing for the "doctrine of maximum severity." They observed the high rates of crime and the mild application of a truly severe criminal law, severe only if enforced. The obvious conclusion was that "hanging was not punishment enough," nor was it applied often enough.

It is also of interest to observe the fluctuations in those sentenced

TABLE 3[23]

Percentages of Those Committed to Trial on All Charges
Sentenced to Death and Executed
(Home Circuit)

Date	Percent Sentenced to Death	Percent Actually Executed	Percentage of Those Sentenced to Death Actually Executed
1688-1718	12.7	6.7	50.0
1754-1784	16.3	4.6	25.0
1785-1794	12.4	4.1	30.0

and those actually executed for the Home Circuit, which might be taken as "nonurban" areas. Table 3 demonstrates a slight, but significant difference in comparison to London and Middlesex. We can see that on the Home Circuit the number of death sentences peaked about the same time as London and Middlesex, but the proportion of those executed actually dropped during the period of Henry Fielding's pleas for increased severity. Although the periods are not exactly comparable, these data do suggest that there may have been marked differences between city and country regarding the administration of justice. From what we know about the administration of justice today, this is what we would expect.

Why were so few executed? There were many reasons. The judiciary, completely consumed by their laws, preoccupied with the "rule of law" rather than men, indulged in ridiculously narrow interpretations of the law. As a result many obvious cases where offenders were probably guilty were dismissed for insignificant reasons. There is little doubt that the judge tended to give the benefit of the doubt to the offenders. The reasons for this tendency were summarized by Henry Fielding in 1751: their lives were threatened by gangs; they were just plain indolent; they were avaricious and very poorly paid, so easily susceptible to bribes; and, worst of all, they were tenderhearted.[24] These remarks applied both to judges and prosecutors. It is amazing indeed that judges boomed out their sentences of death with such grandeur and sincerity, yet immediately recommended pardons and commutations for the majority of cases. Circumstances that were taken into account were: first offense or not, previous good character, offense unattended by violence, driven to it by necessity, no weapons involved, the object stolen had been returned, and conviction based solely on confession. In addition, perhaps the most important reason was the youthfulness of the offender, because then, as now, crime was an activity of the young. Of every twenty executed, eighteen were under twenty-one![25]

Finally, another very important reason for there being so few capital convictions was that the juries began to refuse to convict by understating the value of the property stolen to make the offense a misdemeanor rather than a felony. They were often aided in this by the prosecutor, who, as we have seen, also tended toward leniency. Table 4 shows the interesting flow of the criminal justice process in England and Wales for 1805. It has often been argued that there were insufficient alternatives to the death penalty available during the eighteenth century. This must surely be false. There were the

TABLE 4

Criminal Justice Process, England and Wales, 1805

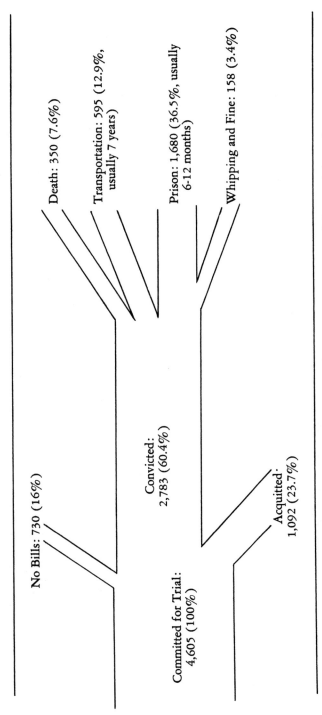

No Bills: 730 (16%)

Committed for Trial: 4,605 (100%)

Convicted: 2,783 (60.4%)

Acquitted: 1,092 (23.7%)

Death: 350 (7.6%)

Transportation: 595 (12.9%, usually 7 years)

Prison: 1,680 (36.5%, usually 6-12 months)

Whipping and Fine: 158 (3.4%)

Adapted from Sir Leon Radzinowicz, *A History of English Criminal Law* (London: Stevens and Sons, 1948), passim.

wide range of criminal punishments that I recounted in previous chapters, plus the possibility of transportation, and toward the end of the century, the rapidly growing new solution to punishment: prison.

The Gallows and the Good Doctor

We come now to one final aspect of the hanging practice: dissection. For the first half of the eighteenth century it had been the practice of anatomists to purchase the bodies of executed criminals, and the beadles and servants of medical men were sent to fight for or buy the bodies. With the work of the Hunter brothers, anatomy had become a central part of the training of English physicians and surgeons, especially with the requirement that the student doctor learn from the experience of actually dissecting a cadaver. Therefore, the demand for bodies was very high. The only problem was that the public found the practice an outrage, although many appeared to enjoy the public spectacle of dissection performed in the great Surgeons Hall (next to Newgate Prison). To those who were close friends or family of the executed criminal, the thought of dissection was terrifying. In 1752, dissection of the body was made a mandatory part of the death sentence. Thus, friends and family of the convicted appeared at the gallows not only to pull on the legs of the unfortunate criminal to help him die more quickly, but to save his body from the anatomists. Recent historians have suggested that a large proportion of rough brawls fought around the gallows involved sailors trying to snatch their hanged comrade away from the anatomists.[26] There is no doubt that the free-for-all was largely a function of the various interest groups fighting for the corpse which had, in keeping with the age, been reduced to a piece of property worth about three pounds, seven shillings. The beadles for the barber surgeons fought for the corpse; the representatives of the public hospitals fought for it; the servants of the private surgeons fought for it; tough free-lancers fought for it with a view to making a profit; and the family and friends of the corpse fought for it, to allow "a decent burial." Indeed, the body of Dick Turpin, having been buried, was stolen by servants for anatomizing, and then grabbed back by his friends who reburied it.

It is to be noted that until this time, the medical profession had not enjoyed a particularly high status in the social hierarchy. It was their treatment of death, their callous practice of cutting up bodies —and in public too—that thrust the profession into the incredibly high status that it now enjoys. Medicine at that time revolved completely around death and attained most of its knowledge from dead people.[27] The profession has thus developed an honored, ritualistic position in modern society.

For the ordinary person, the doctor exudes mysterious, life saving powers. In the eighteenth century most doctors cut up cadavers. But some also got in on the act of hanging and attempted to circumvent the law by reviving those already hanged. If the medical man was to have absolute power over death, the mere display of his mastery of it by cutting up cadavers was not enough. Could he not overcome death and bring people back to life? With so many more bodies available after 1752, some medical men fell to conducting a number of eccentric experiments.

In 1803, the body of George Forster was assigned to Dr. Aldine for "galvanic research." Application of galvanism was found to bring about strange movements of various parts of the body. One onlooker died of fright when an application caused one eye of the corpse to open. There were a number of amazing cases. In 1650, Anne Greene, after having hung by the neck for a half hour or more, was about to be dissected by Sir William Petty, the anatomy professor at Oxford, when he heard a noise in her throat. He bled her, and she completely revived.[28] And there were a number of other famous cases of persons recovering from a hanging—the cases of "half-hanged Smith" and "half-hanged Meg."

Then in 1729 there was the incredible case of William Gordon, who was approached by an eccentric surgeon, Chovet, with the proposition of making an incision in his windpipe so he would still be able to breathe when the rope tightened around his neck. Chovet had experimented successfully by cutting the windpipes of dogs and hanging them. Unfortunately, although Gordon was alive when taken down from the gallows, after hanging three-quarters of an hour (others hanged were quite dead), attempts to revive him later failed. The method was immediately given a specific name—bronchotomy. This method was used in a number of other cases, apparently sometimes with success. It is little wonder that the superstitions surrounding hanging and dissection were so rife.

In general, though, it should be remembered that the possibility of revival after hanging was to some extent realistic. The hangman could be bribed to cut down the offender early, to tie the knot in a different place, or, as in the famous case of Dr. Dodd, to pretend to pull on his legs while actually supporting the waist.

Gradually, and very likely at the instigation of both the medical profession and advocates such as Fielding and Madan, a hard line was taken toward executions. The notorious Jack Sheppard, who had escaped from Newgate twice in 1724,[29] was buried at St. Martin-in-the-Fields after a riot over who had right to the body. His friends were not permitted to try to revive him; nor was dissection permitted. In 1750, the traditional parting drink at St. Giles was forbidden. In 1752, the act required dissection and/or mounting of the body on a gibbet. In 1783, the procession was eliminated, and the place of execution was an open space in front of Newgate Prison. At this time the drop was adopted as the standard method of hanging.

These changes, though eliminating the ribald behavior of the procession—indeed the aspect that Dr. Johnson felt was needed by the criminal for his moral support in the face of death—continued the execution as a public spectacle. For the execution of Holloway and Haggerty in 1807 there were 40,000 spectators. And for the execution of Fauntelroy, 100,000. People suffocated in the crowds and were trampled to death. Windows sold at two pounds each. The governor of Newgate didn't help. He traditionally held a private party on each hanging day, and his invitations read: "We hang at eight, breakfast at nine." Public executions, as such, were abolished in 1868. The extent to which they were "private" is questionable, though, since many persons were still invited to witness the hanging inside the prison walls. But the specter of public hanging was removed from public sensation amid considerable debate and argument. Whether it was a "humane" step is another question. Some have argued that it was not. I will have more to say about the abolition of public executions in Chapter 9.

The "Culture" of Hanging in the United States

Public hanging was popular in the early American colonies up to the nineteenth century. The Americans in the early colonial days were probably less severe in their penal punishments than were those of Mother England. The influence of the Quakers in Pennsylvania even caused capital punishment to be abolished for a short period under William Penn's governship.[30]

Nor did religious fanatacism run rampant. According to one estimate,[31] the total number of witches hanged in colonial times was thirty-five, half of them at Salem. In comparison, 30,000 were put to death in England, 75,000 in France, and 100,000 in Germany. In America, hanging was the most common form of execution for witches and heretics; it was also reserved for the usual serious crimes of violence, especially for infanticide which was very common. The massive capital statutes promulgated under both Kings George during the eighteenth century also theoretically applied to all colonies under common law, although most of them developed their own codes. The preoccupation with the defense of property was also great, but once again, the strict application of these sanguinary laws was rare. The tradition of reprieves, pardons, and commutations was very common, and, according to one authority,[32] they were often timed to be announced at the very last moment at the gallows.

From the descriptions we have of these public hangings, they were of a very different tenor from those in London. Although they were still "enjoyed" as a spectacle, the behavior around the gallows was more sedate and orderly. Nor was it the scene of delirium as the London hangings. The sermon was taken more seriously, and hymns were solemnly sung as the offender was sent on his way. In contrast to the English practice which published the criminal's confession, the American practice was to publish the sermon, which was full of hell fire, and undoubtedly by the end of the eighteenth century hangings were well suited to the spreading of Methodism throughout America.

In fact, the first "book" to be published in Boston was a sermon preached by the Reverend Increase Mather at a public hanging in 1675, titled *The Wicked Man's Portion*.[33] There was no hypocrisy or cynicism here, as there was at Tyburn. The reverends were not humbugs: they preached what they believed, and the people took it all very seriously. Perhaps they took it all too seriously, since it took the United States a long time to move from public to private executions, even though moves toward abolition preceded the English. In 1787 Benjamin Rush published a paper denouncing public executions, and by the 1830s and 1840s, many states began to conduct their executions inside the prison walls—though large crowds were usually allowed to attend inside. The last public execution in the United States occurred in Kentucky on August 14, 1936, when a twenty-year-old Negro was hanged before an audience of 20,000, for criminally assaulting a seventy-year-old woman.

Yet, although there was no delirium or hysteria attached to hanging, there is little doubt that hanging in America has become the subject of a "perverted" romanticism. In the United States, more than anywhere else, a huge number of folk songs and ballads have evolved over the years, especially the eighteenth and nineteenth centuries, referring to the sorry lives of criminals and their seemingly inevitable end on the gallows. The best known ballads are those of the hero outlaws of the old West, such as Jesse James, Billy the Kid, and many others. The lives (or deaths) of Bonnie and Clyde were also immortalized by Bonnie's Ballad, "It's death to Bonnie and Clyde," and there are ballads of many other "modern" criminals. Most of these ballads, though indulging in a certain amount of hero-worship, nevertheless note that "they got what was coming to them." The following verse is from the ballad "The Death of Charlie Burger." The Burger boys fought the Shelton gang for the bootleg traffic in southern Illinois. Charlie was hanged on April 19, 1928.

I'll tell you of a bandit
Out in a Western state,
Who never learned his lesson
Until it was too late.
This man was bold and careless,
The leader of his gang,
But boldness did not save him
When the law said, "You must hang."

  * * * * *

The Ten Commandments show us
The straight and narrow way,
And if we do not heed them
Sometime we'll have to pay.
We all must face the Master,
Our final trial to stand,
And there we'll learn the meaning
Of houses built on sand.[34]

The United States also holds the record for mass hangings during the eighteenth and nineteenth centuries. In 1741, eighteen Negroes were hanged and eleven burnt at the stake, along with four whites hanged, on the charge of having conspired to burn New York City. A special holiday was announced: but in contrast to England, the holiday was not for the day of the hanging, but for the day after to thank God for deliverance. On December 26, 1862, thirty-eight Sioux Indians were hanged as penance for a whole tribe that slaughtered 500

men, women, and children. By the turn of the century, young
Negroes had become the main objects of public execution. The old
idea of vengeance figured very strongly in the execution of blacks,
as the following stanza, published anonymously in a Memphis newspaper in March of 1868 suggests:

> *Thrice has the lone owl hooted,*
> *And thrice the panther cried;*
> *And swifter through the darkness,*
> *The Pale Brigade shall ride.*
> *No trumpet sounds its coming,*
> *And no drum beat stirs the air;*
> *But noiseless is their vengeance,*
> *They wreak it everywhere.*
> *   —Ku Klux*[35]

Conclusions

We have seen how criminals were hanged in their own glory; how
their bodies were callously bought and sold and dissected; how the
gallows of the criminal justice system were far greater than its bite;
how laws came to tyrannize men; how a Parliament completely consumed with its own affairs of trade, property, and industry enacted
these laws with serenity and indifference; how the orthodox clergy
forsook their church and the poor; and how Wesley saved the masses
by giving them hope and providing meaning to death. In the eighteenth century all of the ritual, sacred, and primitive features of punishment that had been so carefully played out and buried in the
unconscious erupted in the courtroom, gallows hill, the procession,
and the Great Hall of the Barber-Surgeons. Punishment in Western
civilization had reached its blazing adolescence.

I have told the seamy side of the eighteenth-century story of punishment. There is a "brighter" side. Just as great scientific discoveries
often occurred as a result of several scientists working independently
on a similar problem, so did great developments occur in criminal
punishment.

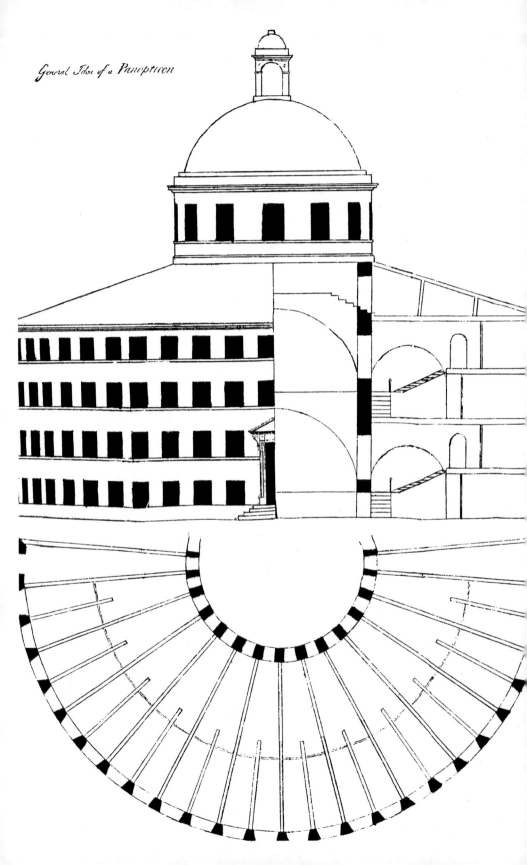

General Idea of a Panopticon

8

That Wonderful Utilitarian Punishment Scheme

It has been said that "reform consists in taking a bone away from a dog."[1] The first clear call for reform came from Beccaria's *On Crimes and Punishment,* published in 1764, yet no decisive legislative reform occurred in England until the decade of 1820-30, when suddenly everything gave way. There were two great forces that pulled at the bone: the force of ideas and the force of the masses. They may not have often acted in concert, and perhaps that is why Parliament was able to hang onto the bone for so long. But both were concerned to eliminate the same thing: the oppression of the criminal law and, in the wider sense, the oppression of Parliament.

In this chapter we will look at the veritable torrent of ideas that flowed from the pens of the utilitarians and other reformers of the eighteenth century. As far as punishment was concerned, the major theoreticians of the period were Beccaria and Bentham. The major pragmatist was Henry Fielding, a criminal court magistrate.

Although the pragmatists and the theoreticians took opposite positions on many issues concerning the reform of criminal punishment, all of these great thinkers expressed an unmistakable humanitarian aim and a new sensitivity to the conditions of the poorer classes. This was part of a great "philanthropic urge" that had spread throughout Europe, partly as a result of the incredibly industrious work of the Encyclopaedists in France, centered on the genteel salons of such intellectuals as Montesquieu.

The passing of medieval society had left its mark on the consciousness of the "better off." No longer was the division between master and servant, lord and serf, external and unchanging. In the eighteenth and nineteenth centuries there were new rich; there were those who had been rich and were now poor; and the numbers and visibility of the poorer classes were increasing dramatically. The position of the upper class was no longer a natural social law, but rather something that could be fought for with diligence, thrift, and intelligence. As the eighteenth century drew to an end, the violence and unrest of the masses, the American Revolution, and the French Revolution had made clear to the intellectuals of the "better off" classes that the masses did indeed possess the power to overthrow the government by force. The new sensitivity toward the suffering of the poor therefore grew out of the removal of the absolute psychological barrier between lord and vassal existing in the feudal mind.

It is one thing to recognize the plight of the masses and another to advocate what should be done. We shall see that the increased sensitivity toward the poorer classes resulted in a reaction from many of the "better off" to advocate more oppression and more severe treatment of the poor—a reasonable response if one sees oneself in danger of being overrun by a belligerent mob.

Many of the new ideas on punishment also arose from the increasing rationalism of the period. Progress in the natural sciences had been tremendous. The world as material, as Hobbes had laid down in the previous century was studied as material. What had previously been taken to be a world of confusion, basically a supernatural world that only God could understand, was found under the close scrutiny of scientists to be ordered and intelligible. Yet, unlike the natural sciences, the closer one looked at the social world, the more chaotic it appeared. There was no readily observable rationality to social relations, social institutions, or politics. It would be necessary therefore to impose a rationality on them.

It was a special kind of rationality, one which required the strict application of Aristotelian logic to the solution of social problems, and one that blindly accepted two apparently inherent truths upon which to build: the principle of utility and the pleasure-pain principle. Jeremy Bentham devoted his life to the construction of such a system.

In the list that follows, I have pulled together the ameliorative suggestions for reform proposed during the eighteenth century. It will be seen that, although many of the reforms were recommended on the basis of the "greatest happiness" principle, many were not and in fact were advocated by individuals who had quite different perspectives on crime and punishment. A forceful opponent of many utilitarian proposals was Henry Fielding, the only one of the early reformers who had any firsthand practical knowledge of the criminal justice process. Other reformers, such as Paley and the Reverend Madan, were deridingly called apologists by the utilitarians.

It is common to ascribe to Beccaria the lofty place as the first criminal law reformer, with his famous essay *On Crimes and Punishment*. He achieves this position, not because he was first with the ideas, for it can be shown that most of his suggestions had been put forward by many of his contemporaries and predecessors, but because he produced a brilliantly concise, clear document that brought all these arguments together into one forceful indictment of the tyrannical criminal law. His essay was also expressed in a modest and restrained manner, undercutting response from critics that it was the writing of a raving radical. There was one point that did set him clearly apart from all other writers at the time: he advocated the abolition of capital punishment. In general, however, the arguments for reform of criminal law were reactive arguments—that is, they were stimulated by the obvious contradictions, injustices, and tyrannies of the existing criminal law and its administration. We must also remember that the movement toward reform took its ideological basis from Europe, where the system of criminal law was still dominated by the methods of the Italian Inquisition. Although English social life was verging on chaos during many periods of the eighteenth century, there was still an unshakable belief in the eternal nature of English criminal law and a well-founded satisfaction that it provided much more liberty and freedom to individuals than did the inquisitorial system in Europe. It is no surprise, then, that the most moving early criticisms came from Europe.

In piecemeal fashion, most of these ideas preceded Jeremy Bentham, England's great utilitarian, so I have excluded any reference to him for the moment. It was Bentham who later incorporated these principles within his fantastic utilitarian system. Since his contribution can be shown to have been far more extensive and effective in subsequent legislation, we shall deal with him separately.

Reforms and Apologies

ELIMINATE UNNECESSARY CRUELTY: Most forms of the death penalty described in Chapter 3 were still in force either in England or in various parts of Europe. As late as 1762, for example, Voltaire defended Jean Calas of Toulouse, who was broken on the wheel,[2] and gibbeting continued well into the nineteenth century.[3] Certainly all the corporal punishments and mutilations that I have previously described were prevalent throughout the whole of the eighteenth century. In general, the abolition or even weakening of corporal punishments was not advocated by leading thinkers. Beccaria still favored corporal penalties for violent crimes.[4] Thus it was not so much an horrific reaction to the violence of corporal punishment itself that motivated the Europeans to advocate moderation of punishment, but rather the tyrannies that they saw went with them. After all, Beccaria argued that life imprisonment was more severe than execution and, therefore, life imprisonment should substitute for the death penalty. Montesquieu, Beccaria's predecessor in many ways, argued that excessive cruelty would deter prosecutors from prosecuting to the full, whereas moderate punishments were more likely to encourage responsiveness of the people as witnesses and cooperators with justice.

In Europe, torture was commonly used to extract confessions from both the accused and witnesses—a hangover from the days of the Inquisition. The closest corollary to it in England was *peine forte et dure,* when an accused refused to plead. In any event, the Encyclopaedists and the English reformers all argued for the elimination of cruelty used in the process of investigation or trial. A corollary of the use of torture to extract confessions was the use of secrecy in the conduct of trials, a practice that was a central and necessary feature of the inquisitorial process. Once again, this was not the case in England. Justice was done in the open—almost with a vengeance.[5]

In sum, the argument was for moderation—certainly the opposite of the proposed doctrine of maximum severity, or "deterrence by terror," put forward by some English thinkers, such as the Reverend Madan, in 1785, in response to what he saw as an alarmingly high rate of violent crime. But if the punishments were to be moderate, there had to be a way of determining just how moderate. The utility principle provided the answer (or perhaps the need for) this question.

THE PUNISHMENT MUST BE PROPORTIONATE TO THE CRIME: There are many ways of interpreting this dictum, but it first requires one to specify the crimes in such a way that they may be proportioned. Traditionally, the criminal law of England had developed a large conglomeration of laws which arbitrarily (though for definite historical reasons, as we saw in Chapter 6) divided crimes into two levels of "seriousness"—misdemeanors and felonies. The utilitarians solved this problem by arguing that the measure of gravity of an offense depended on the extent to which it was injurious to society. In this way, they were able to extend their materialistic view of the world and avoid the question of whether any crimes were inherently grave to some predetermined degree—which, of course, only God could reveal. Since the utilitarians, especially Montesquieu, saw the principal object of punishment to be the establishment of order in society, it was easy enough to argue for a scale of punishments to fit each crime, whether a crime of violence or of property. The tendency also was to try to derive the form of punishment from the form of the crime[6]—a practice which we have seen has a long history. Thus, Beccaria naturally enough advocated corporal punishments for violent crimes and fines for many property crimes.

As far as one can tell, the argument for assessing the gravity of the offense by its injury to society has never gained acceptance in criminal law, mainly because it cuts across a most cherished, and one of the oldest, concepts in the criminal law of both England and Europe: the concept of intent, the idea of the guilty mind. Beccaria argued against this as a criterion for assessing severity on the grounds that it was too changeable and, therefore, allowed too much discretion to the judge. He virtually dismissed as criteria for deciding seriousness the amount of sinfulness and the rank of the injured person.

In short, the Encyclopaedists and Beccaria advocated that (1) a punishment should closely conform to the nature of the crime, so that the link between the crime and the penalty is clear, (2) there should be a moderate upper limit to the most serious punishment, (3) a punishment should also be proportionate to other penalties, (4) the overriding key to assessing the gravity of an offense, thus the proportionate punishment due, was to be the amount of injury done to society. To achieve these goals, it is clear that a whole *system* of criminal laws would have to be developed. None of these utilitarians did this—least of all Beccaria, who had little first-hand knowledge of the law and was not educated in law. This task Bentham would later tackle.

CELERITY OF PUNISHMENT IS DESIRABLE: None of the reformers or "defenders" of the system disagreed over this. Henry Fielding was most critical of the English criminal justice administration which allowed months to elapse before the hanging of criminals. He argued that the atrociousness of their crimes was often forgotten by the time they reached the gallows, so they appeared as heroes rather than the villains they really were.[7] Fielding advised that the death sentence be carried out immediately after the sentence. Both Montesquieu and Beccaria advocated celerity of punishment for the same reason: that the public would clearly see the connection between the penalty and the offense.[8]

A DISAGREEMENT OVER THE CERTAINTY OF PUNISHMENT: There was considerable controversy over this question, as there continues to be today. The Reverend Madan and Henry Fielding called for the strict enforcement of the law—every law—so the people would learn that justice will be done. Severity according to Fielding was a more wholesome virtue than mercy, and besides it saved more lives—i.e., more were deterred when they saw that criminal law meant business.[9] Fielding and Madan, Beccaria and Montesquieu all argued for the certainty of punishment to the point of strongly criticizing the practice of pardoning. This was in keeping with the latter's view that the law should be, beyond anything else, clear in its letter and certain in its application, without room for discretion which to him meant partiality. Besides, the optimistic Beccaria saw that as punishment became milder, clemency would be less necessary.

There were, however, those who disagreed with this view, and one of them was Paley, the English criminal law theorist who wrote extensively in 1785. Paley has been deridingly called the apologist for the existing system, since he accepted many of the utilitarian arguments concerning the estimation of the severity of offenses and the preventive aim, but he insisted that complete enforcement was not necessary to achieve the deterrent effect.[10] This view had been the contention of Sir Edward Coke, Paley's predecessor by many years, who argued that the more frequently one punished crimes, the more common one made them. Both these theorists claimed that the system of a mammoth range of capital offenses was never intended to be enforced to the letter.

It is of considerable interest that the European utilitarian reformers were strong on the moderation of punishments, yet they were also very strong on enforcement. They advocated, in fact, a strict, highly controlled model of criminal justice. This is probably why most of their reforms were never adopted. It is also why twentieth-century utilitarians later came under considerable criticism, when similar arguments were used to support the "treatment" model of punishment.[11]

It is also of great interest to note that the defenders of the already existing eighteenth-century system never based their defense on the principle of retribution, as has become the case in the twentieth century. On the contrary, they adopted the same defensive base as the reformers: that their system would prevent more crime than the utilitarians.'

DISCRETION AND THE SPECIFICATION OF LAW: Beccaria saw the judiciary as exercising enormous discretion to the extent that judges were able to behave as petty monarchs and tyrants. He rejected their discretionary right on the grounds that they were not legislators and therefore were not fit to interpret the laws. This is, of course, a somewhat forced argument, since the judges were supposedly trained to do just that. Furthermore, his observations may have applied more to the European scene, where the judiciary, because of the inquisitorial system, held a great deal more power. In England, this was not the case, and in fact one may argue, as does Sir Leon Radzinowicz,[12] that the judges had precious little discretion at all and they suffered from a necessity to stick too closely to the letter of the law—so much so that many cases were dismissed for trifling inadequacies (an incorrectly filled out form, for example). The jury system also added considerable restraint on the judge in finding the accused guilty and even in the crimes for which he would be charged, since the jury could underestimate the value of the property stolen.

This perceived discretion as a necessary corollary of tyranny, Beccaria felt disposed to criticize severely, along with two further recommendations: that interpretations of the "spirit of the law" should be avoided at all costs, since it allowed for too much discretion and therefore partiality; and, finally, that the laws should be written in such a way that they be clear and simple. Obscure laws only encouraged discretionary interpretation and, therefore, abuse on the part of the judge. It is to be noted, however, that these are generalities and that neither Beccaria nor any of his contemporaries provided any specifics on how laws might be simplified and made clear and discretion might be avoided. Perhaps this is why his small book attained instant fame and was immediately applauded in many countries throughout Europe: it expresses admirable sentiments in a refined logic at a sufficiently general level to find applicability to a great many of the diverse criminal law systems throughout Europe. But to actually apply it to the specifics of criminal laws and procedure was another matter. The document was a statement of intent rather than a detailed plan of attack. Nor was there any recognition of the individual case where the individualization of punishment might be reasonable and, therefore, discretion appropriate. Once again, it was Bentham who later addressed this question.

THE PURPOSE OF PUNISHMENT IS TO PREVENT CRIME: Not one of the reformers or even apologists of the existing system of punishments questioned this premise. It was axiomatic—so ingrained in fact, that one wonders what happened to the basic concept of retribution whose main aim, as I have suggested earlier, was the correction of wrongs rather than the prevention of crime. Of course, prevention of one kind or another has always been a central element of criminal punishment, whether preventing others from committing the crime, a principle that can be traced as far back as Plato,[13] or preventing disasters it was thought would occur if punishment were not carried out. The difference between the apologists and the reformers was the way in which punishment was seen to work. It had to be admitted that at the time of the controversies it was an article of faith on the utilitarian's part that reduction in the severity of punishments would reduce crime, especially in the face of the social violence and chaos that the legislators and officers perceived all around them. Fielding summed up the judge's position by noting that "pardons have brought many more men to the gallows than they have saved from it."[14]

It is clear that it was general prevention that was uppermost in all minds, since criminal punishments in England at least were all highly visible and in many cases presupposed an intimate public participation. The pillory, stocks, branding, bridles, and so on all involved the public, as did the public executions. All these criminals were examples, first to others and secondly to themselves. It has only been in more recent times, especially since rehabilitative and treatment ideologies have been introduced, that punishment as an individual deterrent became the central object of concern.

We must also not forget the trying political times in which these punishments were conducted during the eighteenth century. The government was frightened by what the masses might do when they got out of hand. It was natural for the government therefore to view criminal punishment as having the educative function of teaching the masses a lesson and setting an example. Never was this so obvious as in the punishment of the traitor Brandreth and later the Cato Street conspirators, about some of whom we will speak in the next chapter.

Punishment as the general preventive measure was therefore the supremely unquestioned assumption of reformers and conservatives alike. The idea that it might be "just in itself" (i.e., retribution) never arose. In fact, the utilitarians went a step further. They had to justify the right to punish.

THE RIGHT TO PUNISH: It had never occurred to such practitioners of the law as Fielding or criminal law theorists such as Blackstone that one had to justify the right to punish. The criminal law of England was revered by judges and legislators alike. Fielding was convinced that the legislation was fine, but the execution of the laws was at fault.[15] And, with the centuries of precedents of laws to fall back on, how could a respectable criminal law theorist such as Blackstone even question the right to punish? Surely the right was a natural one which issued directly out of the eternal brick of England: its accumulated common law.

Why, then, should the utilitarian reformers find it necessary to justify the use of punishment? This is a crucial question, since we shall see later that it became the central feature of philosophical discussions of punishment in the twentieth century. The eighteenth century, it will be remembered, especially the latter half, was a period when a great deal was said about individual liberties and freedom, words that became the catch-cries of both the French and the American revolutions. On the other hand, the utilitarians still believed the Hobbesian model of the war of all against all, since they understood individual behavior according to the pleasure-pain principle. With all individuals pursuing their own pleasure, a picture of society perpetually on the brink of chaos was easy enough to imagine; and in fact with the new "pleasure-filled" life imputed to the poorer classes, it seemed that English society provided daily evidence for Hobbes's argument. It was clear, however, since Hobbes and now with Rousseau, that individuals must give up a little of that pleasure (a liberty to pursue pleasure) so that society may be established and order maintained. For how could one gain a measure of pleasure out of chaos? The possibility was hardly imaginable to these philosophers, with perhaps the exception of the more extreme thinkers such as the Marquis de Sade, who advocated the unbridled pursuit of pleasure.

In any event, because these utilitarians had placed individual liberties before the rights of the sovereign (or the government), they saw that it was necessary to justify the use of punishment (infliction of pain, the perceived opposite to their guiding principle of life: the pursuit of pleasure). And the justification was readily available in the form of that grand generalization, the social contract. Thus individuals gave up a small portion of their liberty (i.e., they agreed to be punished) so that order could be maintained and society established. It is not clear whether or not they did this freely, although it seems to be suggested that in primitive times it was done of necessity after men grew "weary of living in a continual state of war. . . ."[16] On the other hand, Beccaria observes that "no man ever freely sacrificed a portion of his personal liberty merely in behalf of the common good." In any event, Beccaria concludes: "the sum of all these portions of liberty sacrificed by each for his own good constitutes the sovereignty of a nation. . . ."[17] And it is by this right that the state punishes. We can see that this was a highly general and artificial precept. Yet it also had fantastic implications. It meant that Beccaria and other utilitarians saw the criminal laws as direct reflections of the public will, or at least that they *ought* to be direct reflections of the public will. They introduced, therefore, a new tension into the state of the criminal law—a negation of its history in favor of its adaptation to the present. Indeed, the writings of the utilitarians, especially Bentham, largely disregarded history which was, of course, the backbone of the criminal law. It was indeed a brazen attack by the utilitarians, especially when many of them had little knowledge of the criminal law itself. Once again, we are not surprised that so few of their recommendations were accepted and that, of those that were, it took almost 100 years.

THE BOUNDARIES OF THE CRIMINAL LAW: All of the utilitarians developed some kind of classification of "wrongs." Depending on their particular positions, the classifications varied, but they were all in the same direction: toward the secularization of the criminal law. Helvetius, for example, argued that there was no absolute right and justice changed according to custom. Holbach was convinced that crime was caused by bad government and religion, and morality was a function of biology. Montesquieu divided crimes into four groups— religious, moral, public order, and individual security—and suggested particular punishments for each class of offenses. Beccaria used a similar classification, but dismissed religion as having no proper place in the criminal law, and argued that the words "virtue" and "vice" had become "extremely vague notions of honor" since their meaning had changed through history according to the fashions of the time. Thus crimes should only be called crimes if they fall between two points: on one end, the extent to which they directly destroy society, and on the other, the extent to which they injure private security (i.e., his life, property, etc.). Any act that fell outside this domain should not be punished, because it could not possibly affect individual liberties and there was therefore no right to punish. Offenses that concerned God and that did not endanger public security should be left to God. By the same reasoning, the criminal law should keep out of the sphere of individual morals; it has business only for the prevention of crimes that are injurious to society, individual security, or public order. One may note that similar discussions concerning criminal law's functions in the area of morality and "victimless crimes" continue today.

PENOLOGICAL THEORY: "A man's notoriety, his flight, his non-judicial confession, the confession of an accomplice, threats and the constant enmity of the injured person, are proofs sufficient to justify imprisonment of a citizen."[18] Beccaria insisted though, that this be written as law and that a judge should never have the discretion to imprison awaiting trial. Also those accused should be separated from those already convicted so that they will not be corrupted by hardened criminals. Punishments should be chosen that will make "a lasting impression on the minds of men, and inflict the least torment on the body of the criminal. For a punishment to attain its end, the evil which it inflicts has only to exceed the advantage derivable from the crime," and "a spectacle too atrocious for humanity can only be a passing rage, never a permanent system. . . ."[19]

Banishment appears to have been favored by Beccaria as a form of "civil death" for anyone who had committed, or against whom there was considerable evidence that he had committed, an atrocious crime against the public peace. However, Beccaria opposed the practice of confiscation of the offender's property (a practice that was common throughout Europe and England at least until the eighteenth century) on the grounds that it encouraged tyranny of the administrators: "confiscations put a price on the heads of the weak, caused the innocent to suffer the punishment of the guilty. . . ."[20]

As I noted earlier, Beccaria advocated corporal punishments for violent crimes. He does, however, advocate that for crimes of "pride" these should not be applied, since the offenders often gained glory from the pain itself. He advocates instead public ridicule—but not too often or public opinion will become too used to it. As for prison, the utilitarians had not a great deal to say except that the convicted should be separated from the accused and that conditions in the prisons should be habitable and humane. Once again, it was left to Bentham to take up this question.

We can see that the range of punishments suggested by the utilitarians was not especially broad and certainly not innovative. Indeed, many punishments were retained which today would be considered *not* humanitarian. But seen against the backdrop of the punishments used during the eighteenth century, they were indeed milder. Again the principle was moderation. The idea of punishment as a reformatory device was rarely considered.

THEORY OF CRIME CAUSATION: All thinkers, both reformers and defenders of the system, were agreed on one point: that idleness was a leading cause of crime. Both Montesquieu and Beccaria held that crime depended largely on the "manners" of society, which were in turn related to fiscal and economic policy and educational standards.[21] They did not, however, go into the details of an economic plan that would help reduce crime, except to advocate the repression of idleness. In England, idleness had been considered a serious problem at least since Henry VII, and a series of "poor laws" since that time were intermittently enacted, culminating in those of Elizabeth I. They were generally designed not only to punish idleness, but also to restrict and control the movements of the poor. Workhouses were established in which the poor could "earn" a little to eat. As Henry Fielding so poignantly summed up the attitudes of the times: "Labor is the true and proper punishment of idleness, for the same reason . . . death is the proper punishment for cowardice."[22] However, Fielding complained that the poor laws, just like the criminal laws, were hardly ever enforced. And, confronted with the daily parade of "excesses of luxury," he could not help but conclude that crime was caused by these excesses of the rabble:

> It must be Matter of Astonishment to any man to reflect that in a country where the poor are, beyond all comparison, more liberally provided for than in any other part of the habitable globe, there should be found more beggars, more distressed and miserable objects than are to be seen throughout all the states of Europe.[23]

Fielding advocated strict enforcement of the poor laws, especially the restriction of travel so that the idle could more easily be identified and put to work. He divided the poor into three classes: those unable to work, those able and willing to work, and those able and not willing to work, of whom the latter was by far the most prevalent. The failure to punish receivers of stolen goods he saw as also encouraging a criminal underworld. Finally, he complained that the environmental design of London—its narrow streets and dark alleys—created a vast forest for robbers.

It is clear, then, that there was a very early acceptance of the economic theory of crime causation, though the theory was at this time very superficial. The Encyclopaedists failed to go into the question in any detail, except to make the observation that there was a relationship. Fielding appeared unclear about the exact dynamics that the economic system had on the production of crime. He saw idleness as a direct cause of crime and commented at length on the "luxury" of the poor classes, complaining that pleasure appeared to be their dominant want. This he related to the fantastic amount of trade and mercantilism that typified England in the eighteenth century. It was also related to drunkenness—another "pleasure" that was pursued by the poorer classes. There is little doubt that this was indeed a serious problem. One historian has estimated that in 1750, 7,000 out of the 12,000 quarters of wheat in London were turned into alcohol! Fielding notes that there was no crime of drunkenness in England until the reign of James I, when a fine of five shillings was introduced. Fielding recommended prohibition.

There would appear, therefore, to be two kinds of relationships between poverty and crime. On the one hand, the idle committed crime because they were idle, and they were also poor because they were idle. On the other, crime resulted from the near chaotic pursuit of pleasure produced by the abundance of "luxury" resulting from trade. Indeed, the behavior of the lower classes must have appeared very close to the Hobbesian paradigm come true. The idea was to remove these causes, and then crime would be averted and punishment would become less necessary. Perhaps Fielding was not quite so optimistic, but Beccaria was. He appeared to believe that there was a force that impelled men toward well-being—a force as fundamental as gravity.[24] As time went on and the sensitivity of the people increased, punishments would become less and less necessary.

CONCLUSION: A better summary of the utilitarian position cannot be found than that given by Beccaria himself at the end of his treatise:

> In order for punishment not to be, in every instance, an act of violence of one or of many against a private citizen, it must be essentially public, prompt, necessary, the least possible in the given circumstances, proportionate to the crimes, dictated by the laws.[25]

Jeremy Bentham's Grand Design

Before we look at Bentham's theory of punishments, it is well to look at the grand design of his work, since it was enormous in scope, ranging over pretty much every area of social problems. Furthermore, his work, in my opinion, has been unfairly maligned either on the basis of being a "bourgeois" theory, because it failed to address the question of social change, or adopting a "superficial psychology." The former charge is, of course, a purely ideological criticism and is to be accepted or rejected according to one's political preferences. The latter has arisen mainly because his views on punishment have often been cut away from the rest of his work for inclusion in various criminology textbooks. The superficiality has, in fact, been thrust upon the work by its users.

Unlike all the other utilitarian criminal law reformers referred to in this chapter, Bentham did not merely write in reaction to a series of perceived inequities in criminal law but rather perceived that the whole basis of that system was wrong and that it was also related to many other aspects of the "social system," as we would call it today. He therefore embarked on a massive life's work, to develop a comprehensive system, that would tie together all the complex arms of government: criminal law, penological practice, system of government, universal suffrage, social welfare, and a host of others.

His most important insight into punishment and the criminal law, which the other utilitarians did not have, was that if the utilitarian principles were to have any impact, their utter contradiction of the basic premises of criminal law would have to be resolved. The other utilitarians had seen fit to announce their criticisms and leave it at that. Bentham, having attended Blackstone's lectures on criminal law when he was sixteen and done his own devastating commentaries on Blackstone's *Commentaries* (probably the most venerated criminal law textbook of the time), knew that he would have to do more than that. He accurately saw that the law involved a set of morals, which to him were chaotic and senseless but, nevertheless, moral premises. He also saw that the criminal law assumed a set of psychological principles, which also appeared to him as chaotic and senseless. Bentham therefore set about constructing his own system of moral psychology which would span the gap between those two great languages, the law and psychology, or as Bentham put it from "gulph" to mountainside, with philosophy above and law below—"between these two lies a dreary waste: trackless. . . . I propose to take [it] in hand for cultivation and in so doing to open a communication between them. . . ."[26]

Bentham's theory is, I suggest, the only truly systematic theory of legal psychology in existence. Today, many theorists complain of the apparent incompatibility between law and psychology—especially that they speak different languages.[27] To achieve his aim, Bentham virtually invented a new language, his *Novum Organum.*

He was clearly aware of the highly tendentious, even fictitious nature of his work. It was his "art-and-science"—art because he was creating a language of morals and psychology; science because he was using a strictly Aristotelian logic coupled with acute observation. The result was a work of vast proportions, but also a work often ponderous with its relentless exhaustion of alternatives and its neologisms. To understand him, one has to take the time to learn his language.

One final significant observation is in order. Bentham was the first social theorist to argue that punishment was an absolute evil. This had possibly been implicit in much of the utilitarians' writings, but they had never fully recognized it. Bentham criticized Montesquieu, for example, for saying that criminals deserved to be punished. This was simply never possible in Bentham's system. No one could "deserve" to be punished, it was always administered as a matter of necessity, not as desert. Bentham would have preferred alternatives to punishment if they could be found—thus, he suggested indirect legislation and various educational principles in an effort to prevent crime before it began. The importance of this insight of Bentham cannot be overstated. It was the first time in the history of the Western world that anyone had felt that the use of punishment against criminals had to be justified. The age-old problem, the unconscious guilt of punishing an offender felt for centuries and displayed by attempts to shift responsibility for the final punishment from man to nature, had now been brought into the open. Bentham had dredged up a profound piece of cultural guilt and subjected it to a rational analysis. In doing this, the way was made for later twentieth-century philosophical discussions about punishment and retribution, for the Italian positivists to develop their theory of social defense, and for modern psychologists to conduct a scientific analysis of punishment.

It would be nice if we could divide Bentham up into his theory of behavior, theory of morals, and theory of law. Unfortunately, it is not so easy, since the very nature of his theoretical system is to join all three together. "A choir of proofs must have its commencement somewhere,"[28] said Bentham in reference to the principle of utility, so it is with this principle that we will start.

THE PRINCIPLE OF UTILITY: It will be remembered that the utilitarians argued that (1) mankind is governed by the pursuit of pleasure and avoidance of pain, to which are attached the moral labels of good and evil, respectively; (2) it follows that society should be organized according to the principle of the greatest happiness for the greatest number; and (3) as far as the criminal law is concerned, the gravity of an offense should be measured by the injury done to the society.

Bentham recognized that these were generalizations, almost fictitious, that had to be analyzed and applied to concrete observations of individual and social life and to a system of legislation, including criminal law. His recognition of the very general nature of these assertions is clearly demonstrated by his definition of community, which modern sociologists would do well to consider:

> The interest of the community is one of the most general expressions that can occur in the phraseology of morals: no wonder that the meaning of it is often lost. The community is a fictitious *body*, composed of the individual persons who are considered as constituting as it were its *members*. The interest of the community then is what? —the sum of the interests of the several members who compose it.[29]

The principle of utility he understood to mean the "property of an object, whether it tends to produce benefit, advantage, pleasure, good or happiness . . . or to prevent mischief, pain . . . [etc.]."[30] He admits that this principle is not susceptible to any direct proof because it is used to prove everything else, leaving nothing to base its own proof on. In short, it is an absolute, from which, using the Aristotelian method of exhaustive bifurcation *per genus et differentiam,* his whole system flowed.

THE SOURCES OF PLEASURE AND PAIN: A modern psychologist would immediately begin by referring to man's basic biological needs of hunger, thirst, sex, but not Bentham, since he was concerned equally with developing a set of moral principles. Therefore, though such "needs," as we might call them today, might serve as "motives" (we will discuss this term shortly) to action, they were not themselves the sources of pleasure and pain. Instead, Bentham proposed four categories or "sanctions" (defined as "anything which serves to bind a man" to a particular mode of conduct),[31] which he seems to have adapted from Blackstone's *Commentaries.* These were (1) the physical sanction, (2) the political sanction, (3) the moral or popular sanction, and (4) the religious sanction, each with its own particular forms of pleasures and pains. He locates the sources of pleasures and pains as *exterior* to the individual. As his first basic step, he avoids an individualistic psychology.

THE STRUCTURE OF HUMAN ACTION: Bentham's theory of action must surely stand as a first as far as modern psychology is concerned. Although basically teleological in structure, his theory nevertheless was sufficiently flexible to allow for motives which not only "propelled" the person to action (today we would call a theory of human behavior that adopted this meaning of motive a theory of psychological determinism, e.g., instinct or drive theory), but also "tempted" or induced persons to action. These motives made up an important aspect of intentionality, the central ingredient of action. The other three ingredients of action were: the act itself, the circumstances surrounding the act, and the individual's consciousness.

One can immediately see that Bentham has incorporated into his theory of action a basically legal structure, but the way he analyzes its contents is completely different. For example, there are no "good" or "bad" intentions. Intentions, as a category of action, are neither good nor bad since these terms can only be attached to pleasure and pain respectively. Thus, Bentham develops a complex but systematic analysis of all the possible combinations of intentions with consciousness and circumstances, to establish the amount of pain or pleasure produced by various acts. In fact, from this basis, he is able to develop a classification of types of action which are also moral types. His analysis of motives is also based on the pleasure principle, but this is no simplistic or superficial analysis. Once again, there are no motives that are good or bad in themselves, but it is possible to arrange the major motives according to their production of pleasure and pain, and in this sense it may be possible to assess the goodness or badness of particular motives. Even so, many motives may conflict with each other (either internally as propellants to behavior or externally as tempters to behavior). There may be struggles between motives and there may be restraining motives. All of these Bentham catalogues, giving concrete examples. We can now easily see that this is no superficial psychology, certainly not the much derided "lightning calculus" of pleasure-pain that is the usual charge made against his utilitarian model of human action.

There is much more. Bentham, as if aware of this "lightning calculus" criticism, also posits the idea of human dispositions, by which he means ". . . a kind of fictitious entity, feigned for the purpose of discourse, in order to express what there is supposed to be *permanent* in a man's frame of mind. . . ."[32] In other words, men not only act in relation to circumstances and motives at the time, but also develop habits of acting in particular ways; i.e., they have a history. It is this idea that allows Bentham to answer "Yes, certainly," to the question, "Is there nothing about a man that can properly be termed good or bad?" Without this notion of disposition (perhaps today we would call it "personality"), he cannot address the question of whether there are such types as good men and bad men, since till then he had analyzed action in the abstract. He notes, however, and it is clear from the quotation above, that the disposition can only be *presumed:* it must be based on the observation of many past actions of the individual, and it depends heavily on *how the actor perceives his own action*.[33] Once again, Bentham plays out all the possible combinations of good and bad dispositions in conjunction with the range of intentions, motives, consciousness, and circumstances. Of course, the goodness or badness of a person's disposition is evaluated according to the effects it has (1) on the individual's own happiness and (2) on the happiness of others.

It is now necessary to assess what is meant by "effects" or consequences, which Bentham does for what he terms consequences of a mischievous act.

THE NATURE OF MISCHIEF: The consequences of a mischievous act may be primary or secondary. A primary consequence is the effects on an individual, such as the victim of a robbery. The secondary consequence applies to those persons who are closely related to the primary victim and who suffer pain or "danger" (Bentham means mental or even financial anguish) as a result of his victimization. The victim's family, for example, may go hungry because all his money was stolen. We need not go into it here, but once again by playing out all the possible combinations, Bentham develops a systematic theory of victimization.

In sum, this is Bentham's moral theory of human action: the terms "good" and "bad" can only, strictly speaking, be applied to pleasure and pain. The sources of pleasure and pain—the physical, moral, political, and religious—are *external* to the individual. They are responded to by motives, of which there are a wide variety and which struggle against each other and may impel or restrain. These motives are in some way (unspecified) transformed into intentions, which in turn may or may not be carried out in action, depending on the actual circumstances, the consciousness or awareness of the individual of these circumstances and, in some instances, of the intentions and motives themselves (e.g., the young or insane). This chain of causes and effects produces the final consequences of the act, the mischievousness of which may be assessed through the effects on the happiness of the individual and the community and, in the case of the latter, especially the strength, constancy, and extent of its effect.

These are the natural consequences and facets of behavior. Now Bentham turns to what he calls the artificial consequence, that of punishment. It is artificial because it is imposed by a political authority and does not follow naturally from the acts.

BENTHAM'S THEORY OF PUNISHMENT: Bentham begins with Beccaria's dictum that since punishment is an evil it should only be used to exclude some greater evil. Now, applying his utility principle, he is able to make a host of recommendations concerning the use and types of punishment. Clearly, he suggests, there are four cases in which punishment should *not* be used:

1. Where there is no mischief for it to prevent;
2. Where it cannot act to prevent mischief;
3. Where it would be too expensive, i.e., it would produce more mischief than it would prevent;
4. Where, if left alone, the mischief may cease of itself.

We are able now to list very briefly the circumstances which Bentham thought necessary to consider in deciding the proportion of punishment in relation to the offense. Throughout, it should be remembered that to each word Bentham has given a precise meaning, most of which rest on the extensive theory of action just discussed. The factors that must be taken into account are as follows:

I. *On the part of the offense:*
   1. The profit of the offense,
   2. The mischief of the offense,
   3. The profit and mischief of other greater or lesser offenses, of different sorts, which the offender may have to choose out of,
   4. The profit and mischief of other offenses, of the same sort, which the same offender may probably have been guilty of already.

II. *On the part of the punishment:*
   5. The magnitude of the punishment: composed of its intensity and duration;
   6. The deficiency of the punishment in point of certainty;
   7. The deficiency of the punishment in point of proximity;
   8. The quality of the punishment;
   9. The accidental advantage in point of quality of a punishment, not strictly needed in point of quantity;
   10. The use of a punishment of a particular quality, in the character of a moral lesson.

III. *On the part of the offender:*
   11. The responsibility of the class of persons in a way to offend;
   12. The sensibility of each particular offender;
   13. The particular merits or useful qualities of any particular offender, in case of punishment which might deprive the community of the benefit of them;
   14. The multitude of offenders on any particular occasion.

IV. *On the part of the public,* at any particular conjuncture:
   15. The inclinations of the people, for or against any quantity or mode of punishment;
   16. The inclinations of foreign powers.

V. *On the part of the law:* that is, of the public for a continuance:

17. The necessity of making small sacrifices, in point of proportionality, for the sake of simplicity.[34]

And now, there are 11 desirable properties of punishment which are:

1. Variability: ease of adjustment to the gravity of different offenses.

2. Equability: what we would call "equity" today. Bentham's wish was to make the effect the same on all; thus age, sex, condition, fortune, habits, etc. would have to be taken into account.[35]

3. Commensurability: where two offenses are in competition, the punishment for the greater offense must be sufficient to induce a man to prefer the lesser one. Thus, the punishment for the lesser offense could be made an ingredient of the punishment for the greater offense.

4. Analogy: the punishment should as far as possible be characteristic or analogous to the offense. We see here preserved the old precept of punishment by analogy or reflection, to which I have referred several times throughout this book. The most obvious analogous punishment, according to Bentham, is retaliation. But as an alternative, Bentham suggests searching out the motives of the offense and basing the punishment on that.

5. Exemplarity: "It is the idea only of the punishment that really acts on the mind . . . it is the apparent punishment therefore that does all the service." Therefore it must be clear to the people that the punishment is indeed a punishment, and the easiest way to do this is to punish by analogy.

6. Frugality: no superfluous pain should be inflicted. Thus, the death penalty especially should be applied only in very extraordinary cases.

7. Reforming Tendency: punishment most apt to produce individual reform should be used.

8. Incapacitation: but this may violate the property of frugality since, if you prevent a man from doing bad, you probably also make him unable to do good.

9. Compensatory Properties: whether it is possible for compensation or restitution to be made to the victim.

10. Popularity: a punishment should not shock the sensibilities of the public.

11. Remissibility: in case of errors, it is desirable to remit punishments. Thus branding, maiming, whipping, and capital punishments are irremissible.

Finally, it is of course obvious that no one type of punishment is likely to have all eleven qualities, so it is a good idea to mix different kinds of punishment to suit the offense. Some, however, are more applicable than others. Bentham therefore provided a classification of kinds of punishments; but this time, he broke with his Aristotelian logic and gave a more "practical" classification. These punishments were:

1. Capital.
2. Afflictive—corporal punishments such as whipping, starving, etc.
3. Indelible—of permanent bodily effect, e.g. branding, amputation.
4. Ignominious—exposing to contempt of the spectators.
5. Penitence—awakening shame but not to the extent of ignominy.
6. Chronic—banishment, transportation, imprisonment.
7. Restrictive—prohibiting the exercise of a certain profession.
8. Compulsive—obliging a man to do something from which he would normally be exempted; present himself at regular times to an officer of justice.
9. Pecuniary.
10. Quasi-pecuniary, such as depriving an offender of certain services of individuals.
11. Punishment by analogy.[36]

Afflictive penalties he thought were not often suitable, since it was difficult to apply them to only a slight degree. The indelible punishments were similarly handicapped, with the addition that they were irremissible. However, Bentham thought ignominy had great possibilities and could be applied creatively to concentrate public indignation on the offender. New methods would have to be developed, however, since existing ones, such as the pillory, were inequitable because they could lead either to death or fame for the offender, depending on the crowd.

Banishment and transportation were not desirable punishments since they also allowed for unequal effect (because of differences in the offenders' age and sex, the family suffered differentially). Transportation was especially undesirable to Bentham because it involved the buying and selling of bondage and hard labor with no proper supervision, resulting in vicious habits.

Finally, Bentham criticized the present state of prisons in England. They encouraged idleness and included "every imaginable means of infecting both body and mind." Indeed, a great mess required a great design which only Bentham could offer, to solve the problems of prisons in England, and eventually elsewhere. This led to an important period in his life—his middle years—when he designed the Panopticon. They were also the most bitter years of penal reform in the nineteenth century. Bentham's role in this reform is part of a larger story to which we must now turn.

The Reformation

From about the middle of the eighteenth century there were vocal demands for reform in most areas of social life. There were moves for an inquiry into child labor which had reached its peak with the most abominable conditions in factories around this time; there were calls for the planning of cities and improvement in housing conditions; and there were calls for reforms in the penal system. These are but a few. There can be no doubt that reform in the use of criminal punishment was but a small part of a wider movement for reform in every sphere.

Apart from the tireless efforts of the utilitarians, three great streams of events helped shape the reforms of this period. These were the industrial and agrarian revolutions, the strange role of religion, and the development of what E. P. Thompson in his classic, *The Making of the English Working Class,* calls "the illegal tradition."

A Sordid Revolution

The period from 1760 was characterized by a rapid rise in the urban populations and a commensurate decrease in agrarian workers. Small family economics and factories persisted for some time, producing a large strata of "little businessmen" who played a special part in promoting the economic conditions of the time. These businessmen were mostly Methodists, utterly convinced of the goodness of hard, uninteresting, backbreaking labor, especially for the "idle" (i.e., the workers or poorer classes) and even more justifiably for children, who were better kept busy than have their heads confused with education.[1] As widespread as family factories were, a large number of poorer-class families who had previously relied on small crafts or family weaving economies could no longer compete with industrial production. Family economics were broken up as each member converted his work into wage labor and left the family to work in factories. Children had, of course, worked quite hard within the families prior to the industrial revolution, and much of this work had been what we would call today "cruel" (e.g., treading cotton eight hours a day). We know from Chapter 4 that children have always (until the twentieth century) been relegated a quasi-slave status; but until 1800, this had been slavery within the family. The use of children in factories, especially the coal pits, introduced a high degree of specialization, in which children were used for the most menial, backbreaking, and uninteresting tasks:

> . . . the bald place upon my head is made by thrusting the corves, my legs have never swelled, but my sisters' did when they went to the mill; I hurry to corves a mile and more underground and back; they weigh 3 cwt . . . sometimes they beat me if I am not quick enough. . . . I would rather work in a mill than a coal pit.[2]

The condition of the cities grew worse and worse. Small-time speculators built poor housing; the amenities were not well planned and, though at the beginning of industrialization (*ca.* 1760) they were probably better than what their inhabitants, recently from the country, were used to, by the time the eighteenth century was under way they were in a terrible state. Crowding and unsanitary conditions, bringing disease, became commonplace. Many more examples can be given of the conditions of the working class in the eighteenth century, and they have been well documented,[3] especially in Friedrich Engels's classic, *The Conditions of the English Working Class.*

One would have thought conditions were ripe for revolution, especially since two had already occurred in America and France, and even more so since Pitt's Parliament, which ruled England for some fifty years after it took office in 1784, staunchly resisted reforms: a great irony, since William Pitt was a disciple of Adam Smith who was the friend of William Wilberforce, the most ardent spokesman for reforms. Elected just four years after the Gordon Riots—the most savage riots in London during the eighteenth century—Pitt steadfastly managed to check reforms either of Parliament or any other area during the whole of his "reign."

Yet it was not just Pitt and his Parliament. The masses were also involved, in a strange and twisted way. Their involvement is largely a story of the psychology of the lower middle class, and in some ways it bears a striking resemblance to observations about this same class in Germany during the rise of Nazism, where a Communist revolution was expected but the opposite happened.[4]

E. P. Thompson has characterized the period 1790-1820 as the period during which the people were reacting to the failure of a revolution in England—in sharp contrast, of course, to those in America and France. This fact, he says, had a profound psychological effect on the masses, bringing them to the brink of despair, forcing them into a frenzied search for hope. Methodism would provide an answer.

A Painful Repression

Methodism had become a religion not only of the masses, as it began with Wesley, but also of the rising middle class. It was incorporated easily into the middle-class utilitarian ethic, since it emphasized work, frugality, efficiency. As we have seen, all the utilitarian reformers condemned idleness. Methodism did also. But, more important, after Wesley's death the Methodist church developed a heavy authoritarian structure and efficient organization and began the business of preaching salvation through work (*hard* work), acceptance of one's lot, no matter how terrible, and concomitantly the ultimate importance of submission to authority. Submission, in fact, was the message. And how else could one manage to live a life like this, unless one submitted to the world, a life in which Methodism had turned everything upside down? It taught love of death, suffering, sorrow, in short, love of pain. What a fantastic irony, when we find the middle-class utilitarians basing their philosophy directly on the pleasure-pain principle! It is no wonder that the two classes got on so well together and the "class" in between—the lower middle class, those who administered directly the factories—had to develop the brutal insensitivity of what they were doing to those they employed:

> I saw two mills blazing like fury in the valley. Their inmates, poor little sufferers, had to remain there until 11:30 o'clock, and the owner of one of them I found to be a noted, sighing, praying canting religionist.[5]

And:

He related the story of a boy whom he had recently interred who had been found standing asleep with his arms full of wool and had been beaten awake. This day he had worked 17 hours; he was carried home by his father, was unable to eat his supper, awoke at 4 a.m. the next morning and asked his brothers if they could see the lights of the mill as he was afraid of being late, and then died. (His younger brother, aged 9, had died previously, the father was "sober and industrious," a Sunday school teacher).[6]

A final aspect of the religious sentiment that neutralized the masses was sexual repression. Under the Methodists, sexuality was repressed in a volatile, hysterical manner. Sexual asceticism and the work ethic had long been linked under puritanism.[7] But here the repression of sexuality took a new turn. The extreme sinfulness of the male sexual organs was more and more believed, especially as women came to be seen as not feeling the "lust of the flesh." Now Christ, logically enough, became the object of love, a *female* object, and in Charles Wesley's hymns, the imagery of this is clear:

> *O precious side-hole's cavity*
> *I want to spend my life in thee . . .*
> *There in one side-hole's job divine,*
> *I'll spend all future days of mine.*
> *Yes, yes, I will for ever sit*
> *There, where thy side was split.*[8]

Eternal life is a return to the womb. Death is rebirth. And violence (repressed) takes the place of sexuality:

> *We thirst to drink thy precious blood,*
> *We languish in thy wounds to rest,*
> *And hunger for immortal food,*
> *And long on all thy love to feast.*[9]

What more can one add? The vital force, energy, call it what you will, upon which social movements must depend for their success and sustenance was sapped away—spiritually by the Methodist demands of sexual repression, obedience to authority, and worship of death; physically by the utter submission to physical toil. One wonders where the "mob" found its energy to live the ribald, "dangerous" lives that the middle-class observers imputed to them. How could a population that was always tired rise up in revolt? As far as punishment is concerned, we can see very clearly why the move to alleviate it did not come from the poorer classes, even though the larger portion of those punished came from their ranks. Punishment had come as close as it could to "divine punishment."

Some did try to rise up and it is to a few of these instances that we must now turn. Together they make up what Thompson has called the "illegal tradition."

The "Illegal Tradition"

We may usefully begin with the case of John Wilkes. This man, the epitomy of the new eighteenth-century Englishman, was one of the *nouveaux riches*, his father having been a wealthy distiller. He published a journal, the *North Briton*, and, having become aligned with Chatham against George III's foreign policy, printed an insolent attack on the king's speech in 1763. Though a member of Parliament, Wilkes was arrested on a general warrant and lodged in the Tower. But he fought back through the courts, widely publicizing the case, so that eventually Judge Lord Camden found in his favor even though at common law he need not have. Wilkes was released and "became the idol of savage London."[10] But George and his ministers pursued the matter further and, after a series of incidents involving Wilkes being wounded in a duel and writing an obscene poem, he was deprived of his parliamentary privilege. Wilkes was charged with outlawry and fled to France.

The government, especially its system of justice, had been publicly ridiculed, its arbitrariness and partiality exposed. And, since most of Parliament relied on the public's belief in the justice of its rule, this was potentially a serious blow to order.[11]

Four years later there was a general election, and in 1768 Wilkes brazenly returned and offered himself as a candidate first for London and then for Middlesex. He was enthusiastically elected, and the outlawry charge was quashed. George III then proceeded to make some serious mistakes in judgment. He insisted that Wilkes remain expelled from Parliament and that he serve twenty-two months in prison on the earlier charge. The public, almost hysterical, deluged the prison with gifts and campaigned relentlessly for his release. During these protests, Wilkes's supporters were killed and their murderers pardoned. Time and again the Middlesex freeholders elected Wilkes, yet finally the House declared a little-known man with a minority of votes the duly elected candidate. Although Parliament was probably legally within its rights, the public was not interested in such niceties. To them, Wilkes personified liberty.

After his release from prison, Wilkes began to publish reports of parliamentary debates or proceedings which Parliament was quite within its rights to stop. But Wilkes led Parliament on until it made the serious error of finally reversing the decision of a court of law.[12] This was the ultimate tyranny, "the acts of a mob not a parliament," Chatham called it. London was on the verge of open rebellion; the government retreated.

Why had Wilkes succeeded against a powerful government, even when it had the law on its side? The answer is that public opinion, especially organized public opinion, had come into its own. The period from 1750 on had seen a rapid rise in literacy and a fantastic increase in printing, with publications of books, brochures, and journals. No longer would the public take the actions of the government as "just" simply because they were the acts of government. The English people, through Wilkes, had learned to dissent.

But Parliament had also learned, and when the Gordon Riots occurred in 1780 it reacted with restraint by only punishing a small number of the rioters though many more were involved. This riot had begun as a small, "gentlemanly" demonstration in London against Popery. It ended up a free-for-all of mob violence, involving mostly the poor, some criminals, journeymen, and apprentices. Armed support to quell the disturbance was late in coming, and local authorities were noticeably reticent—mainly because it served London well to display a resistance against the king. At the last minute after much violence, armed support appeared, and ironically Wilkes, now city alderman, appeared on the steps of the bank. The riot subsided very quickly.

One hundred and thirty-four persons were tried for their participation in the riots, of whom fifty-eight were found guilty, and twenty-five executed. Four of these were women.

Much has been written about the Gordon Riots, especially on who made up the mob. It was traditionally believed that it consisted of criminals and other useless individuals. It is now clear that although such types were involved toward the end of the riot, many persons of substantial working- and middle-class backgrounds were involved earlier. The trouble was that they had not yet learned how to organize themselves, how to conduct a demonstration to achieve results.[13] From this time on, the government became more and more embattled in the eyes of the "mob": an increasingly literate and increasingly disobedient mob.

It has been noted by one English historian[14] that "1797 marked the lowest ebb in Britain's fortunes." There were many instances in the army and navy when, as we have seen in Chapter 4, flogging and the death penalty were meted out with brutality even for trivial offenses. Britain was on the verge of defeat in the war against France. This had grave effects at home. The price of food soared, and the poor were on the brink of starvation. Food riots broke out throughout England; food was scarce because of Napoleon's blockade. Some riots were well organized, especially during 1801-02. Even when the fortunes of the war with France eventually turned, the riots kept coming and going. Secret societies had long existed in England, and "oath-taking" was a capital offense. All of this came to a head with the discovery of a plot to overthrow the government, led by Colonel Despard, an Irishman deeply committed to the Irish cause.[15] In 1803 before an aghast London crowd, Despard's bloody head was held aloft by the executioner Calcraft, who called out the traditional cry: "Behold the head of a traitor." Despard had been hanged, disembowelled alive, beheaded, and quartered, according to the ancient statute on treason. Although it seems that Despard did in fact engineer a plot and was in fact guilty, the public, now wary and suspicious of the government, was angry, believing that Despard may have been innocent. It should be noted that the crowd was not the delirious crowd we have heard so much about at the scaffold. It was aghast at the horrors of the execution procedure as much as it was angry at the execution itself. This was to continue for another two decades: decades of violence on the scaffold and throughout England.

Among the crowd that witnessed Despard's execution was Jeremiah Brandreth who, some fourteen years later, would suffer the same fate. The circumstances that led to the execution of Brandreth cannot be told in full here, because they are too complex, full of intrigue, myth, and tortuous machinations of government, capitalists, and the secret organization of the "mob." But there are a few points that are important if we are to understand the backdrop against which penal reform was set—or, perhaps more accurately, set behind!

There are two important aspects. First, many of the manufacturing districts must have appeared as what we would call today "police states." In the areas of rioting, in 1812, there were upward of 12,000 troops—more than Wellington had in the penninsula! Second, there is no doubt that a very elaborate spy system was established by the government, supposedly as a "preventive" police method to stop riots before they began. Why were such extreme measures necessary?

The presence of troops in such large numbers was the final recognition by the government, still dominated by the landed aristocracy, that the battle of the industrialists against the Luddites was also *their* battle. At first, the Luddites, an organization of artisans and others, systematically broke up the new machines of the growing number of factories. But the breaking of machines lasted only for a brief period of their activities, for they soon developed into a well-organized insurrectionary body that became a threat not only to the machines of the industrialists but to the social order itself.

There is, as well, the great story of intrigue and treachery of Oliver the Spy, who helped "set up" a series of uprisings, of which one was to be led by Brandreth. Instead of the government stepping in to prevent the violence, it allowed it to go on and then stepped in to punish. Many of those who partook in the riots were captured, along with Brandreth. The widely read *Leeds Mercury* disclosed the treacherous role of Oliver (today it would be called "entrapment"), so the juries refused to convict many of those tried. The public once again had its say: it was outraged by the use of secret police tactics.

Brandreth was to be the government's bloody deterrent. He had killed a man during the course of the Pentridge uprising and so was prosecuted on that basis, the government taking care to keep Oliver out of the trial and to carefully pick a compliant jury. Brandreth was found guilty and died at the hands of Calcraft on November 1, 1817. The Reverend Charles Cox provides us with a graphic description of the execution, and the now characteristic animosity and outrage of the crowd:

> On November 1st, the Prince Regent signed the warrant for the execution of these three misguided peasants, remitting that part of the sentence that related to quartering, but ordering the hanging, drawing and beheading. . . . Two axes were ordered of Bamford, a smith of Derby. . . . On the morning of Friday, November 7th, the three prisoners received the Sacrament. . . . The hurdle or sledge was then brought within the gaol; . . . A horse was attached to it, and each of the three condemned men was dragged round the gaol-yard, their hands being held to prevent their being jolted off. . . . They hung from the gallows for half-an-hour. On the platform, in front of the gallows, was placed the block and two sacks of sawdust, and on a bench two axes, two sharp knives, and a basket. . . . The body of Brandreth was first taken down from the gallows, and placed face downwards on the block. The executioner, a muscular Derbyshire coal miner , . . was masked, and his name kept a profound secret. Brandreth's neck received only one stroke, but it was not clean done, and the assistant (also masked) finished it off with a knife. Then the executioner laid hold of the head by the hair, and holding it at arm's length, to the left, to the right, and in front of the scaffold, called out three times—"Behold the head of the traitor, Jeremiah Brandreth." The other two were served in like manner. . . . The scaffold was surrounded by a great force of cavalry with drawn swords, and several companies of infantry were also present. The space in front of the gaol was densely packed with spectators.

"When the first stroke of the axe was heard, there was a burst of horror from the crowd," says an eye witness, writing to the *Examiner*, "and the instant the head was exhibited there was a terrifying shriek set up, and the multitude ran violently in all directions, as if under the influence of a sudden frenzy."[16]

The Reverend Mozley further described the reactions of the crowd:

At that hideous spectacle the whole crowd, with a confused cry of horror, reeled and staggered back several yards, surging against the opposite houses. My father came home sick and faint. For many days after the small shop windows contained coarse and vivid representations of the scene.[17]

At least the offenders were not disembowelled while still alive, thanks to the efforts of the reformer Sir Samuel Romilly, to which we may now turn.

Steps to Reform

Against this no less than tragic picture of the social and political conditions of England for most of the eighteenth century and the beginning of the nineteenth century, the move to penal reform must be seen. It is easy to see why the ideas for reform preceded their enactment by almost seventy years—yet one can also see why change was, in the long run, inevitable.

Pitt died in 1806, and virtually no reforms had been achieved. Many proposals had been made, only to be headed off by Pitt requiring that they be approved first by the judiciary. Of course, since the reforms deeply affected the old ways of the judges themselves, the reformers would have none of it. And so a stalemate had resulted. But there were some moves toward reform—and at this stage we should retrace our steps to 1751 and Henry Fielding, and be careful to ask ourselves what we mean by "reform." There is no doubt that Fielding wanted "reform," but it was a reform of a different order from those whom we traditionally consider to be the great criminal law reformers, such as Bentham and Romilly.

A committee was set up by the government, probably stimulated by Fielding's treatise on the *Late Increase in Robbers*. In his treatise Fielding had recommended, among other things, a tightening in the enforcement and administration of the law; increased control over the poorer classes in an effort to eradicate the social causes of crime; and the execution of the death penalty away from the public eye to increase the shame and terror of the punishment. The committee did adopt his suggestions for tightening the administration of the criminal law and for controlling the "dangerous classes," but it said nothing on public executions and, in fact, recommended that "it would be reasonable to exchange the Punishment of Death, which is now inflicted for some sorts of offenses, into some other adequate punishments."[18] We should note that this was the first sign, ever so slight, of a move to moderation of punishment, and it occurred fourteen years before the publication of Beccaria's treatise. The alternative punishment that the committee recommended was that of "confinement and hard labor in his Majesty's dock yards."

None of these recommendations was implemented. The violence of robbers continued, made worse by the increasing number of riots for the reasons that we have seen. In 1770 another commission was formed at the instigation of Sir William Meredith, who was concerned that it was essential "to leave no one in doubt that equal justice was administered to every delinquent." Recommendations for the repeal of eight very different capital statutes were made, two of which were successful in the House of Commons, only to be defeated in the House of Lords. None of the offenses mentioned was for larceny.

In 1787 another motion for an inquiry into the criminal law was made, requesting a complete revision and adoption of a new classification of offenses according to their gravity. Pitt cut off the proposal, labeling it "dangerous," and it was here that he announced that any motions for reform should be "fully weighed and settled" by the judges.

Sir Samuel Romilly, every year from 1810 to 1818, introduced bills to repeal the capital penalty for stealing forty shillings in a dwelling house and five shillings in a shop, and every year it was defeated. Romilly, unlike Bentham upon whom he undoubtedly relied for much of the impetus for reform, saw the futility of trying to hasten reform. Instead of attacking the whole of the system at once and asking for a completely new criminal code (Bentham's approach), he attacked the criminal law little by little, concentrating on small areas or groups of offenses at a time. In 1810, 1811, 1813, 1816, 1818, and 1820, Romilly even managed to convince the House of Commons that laws which allowed five-sixths of the persons sentenced to death to escape execution were in need of review. Such was the law for stealing in a shop over the value of five shillings. But the House of Lords overturned the bills each time, and, it will be noted, seven bishops including the Archbishop of Canterbury voted against it. The material and spiritual stake that the church had in supporting the aristocracy to retain the death penalty we have already discussed.[19]

Romilly's most eloquent opponents were Lord Chief Justice Ellenborough and Lord Chancellor Eldon, who steadfastly opposed all of Romilly's bills, usually on the simple grounds that they were dangerous innovations to a system of criminal law well tried and proved for a century and more. His attempt to have the ancient and horrible punishment for treason changed ever so slightly (to allow the offender to be dead before disembowelling and quartering) was steadfastly resisted by Lord Chancellor Eldon.

As we have seen, these were frightening times for the lords and the gentry. They pushed through more and more capital offenses. But there is a sense in which the behavior of the House of Lords, and also the Commons to some extent, should not be looked upon as "reactionary," although they were quite definitely conservative. Sir Leon Radzinowicz notes that there were a number of bills introduced into the House which requested aggravated death penalties for other crimes besides murder and treason, and these were thrown out. One such bill sought to extend mandatory dissection to other executed criminals besides murderers, and this passed the House of Commons, but was thrown out by the Lords.[20] Even in the bill introduced in response to Luddite activities, which requested the death penalty for breaking into a house and destroying a stocking frame, was reduced to a penalty of transportation from seven to fourteen years. And there were several other bills in which opposition to increased severity was clearly displayed in Parliament.

At least, in 1812 and 1814, Romilly did manage to get the capital sentence reduced for very obsolete crimes and to have disembowelling as part of the punishment for treason abolished.

We should therefore not impute bloodthirsty intentions to the members of Parliament. Furthermore, one very real reason for resistance to reduction in the number of capital crimes was the absence (in their views) of any feasible alternative punishments. After 1776 convicts could no longer be transported to the American colonies, and although Australia was available, the arrangements were laborious and complicated, necessitating the virtual "selling" of convicts or deck hands to the captains of trading vessels, who then sold them at the other end. What prisons and workhouses were available everyone agreed were abominable. And the idea of forced labor was rejected as an insult to British ideas of liberty (even in contrast to death!) because it was too much like the galleys of France and Spain.

It was Jeremy Bentham who offered Parliament a creative solution to the problem, and Parliament received it favorably. It was the

Panopticon, and although never adopted in England, it created a model for the building of many prisons throughout the world. The plan was for a polygonal building, with cells on every storey of the circumference, joined to a center building (the warden's office) from which vantage point the warden could survey all prisoners without their seeing him.

The architectural design was only a small part of the idea. Bentham proposed a contractual scheme of management, whereby the superintendent would be paid a fixed sum per inmate and have the right to use their labor as he wished and accrue any profits that may result. The prisoners should be well fed and cared for, and frequent inspection would be required. In fact, the superintendent would also be liable to pay a certain sum for each prisoner lost by death or escape. Such was the utility principle (we would call it an incentive plan today) put into practice! It seems that even Pitt was impressed, and in 1794 an act was passed to adopt the scheme and to obtain sites for penitentiaries. Bentham offered to build and run the first one himself, and received a grant of £2,000 to retain some labor. Unfortunately, he had already spent £6,000, and began spending at the rate of £2,000 a year. No money was forthcoming from Parliament, and in fact George III never got around to signing the final papers. Bentham devoted a large part of his middle years to the Panopticon and was brought to economic ruin over it. His great supporter in Parliament, Sir Samuel Romilly, explained to him why the scheme never got off the ground: the public didn't care tuppence for prisons or prisoners at any time, let alone during critical years of riots, French wars, and near starvation. "And Parliament, the Home Office or the Treasury took their cues accordingly."[21] By 1811 a committee finally rejected the whole proposal, condemning especially the use of inmates for profit by private individuals. Instead, the Millbank Penitentiary was established in 1816. In 1813 Bentham received £23,000 compensation for his losses—an irony of all ironies, as Bentham saw: "Oh, how grating, how odious to one is this wretched business of compensation! Forced . . . to join myself to the blood-suckers and contribute to the impoverishment of the public. . . ."[22]

Some have suggested that as a result of the Panopticon tragedy, Bentham developed more and more radical ideas, but others have argued that the radicalism was there from the start.[23] Whatever the reason, it is certain that he became more radical as he got older—and certainly more favorable to republicanism (having been a severe critic in his early years, of the American Bill of Rights). Yet here he was not an astute political observer: he indulged in bitter vitriol against

George III who had failed to sign the paper, but it was Parliament that always held the reign and Parliament that denied him.

On November 2, 1818, Romilly committed suicide, four days after his wife had died following a long illness and three months after yet another of his bills had been thrown out by the House of Lords. Bentham had lost a great friend and supporter in the House, but he continued through his friend Brougham to inundate Parliament with his ideas. He grew increasingly impatient, even with Brougham, and began to write scathing criticisms of many of the activities of Parliament. A favorite object of his scorn was Lord Eldon.

Yet the seeds of change were sewn. The Battle of Waterloo was fought on June 18, 1815, and Britain emerged from that decade the richest and most powerful nation in the world. At the same time, as we have seen, she was on the brink of social chaos—or was she? I think not. Parliament was in command of a large number of troops. It was firmly in command as repressive as the command was, and although we have seen that there was an extensive organization of rebellion going on, there was no binding ideology that would have forced a total revolution. Parliament therefore had sat tight all these years.

Romilly had many successors, the most notable of whom was probably Sir James Mackintosh. In 1819 Mackintosh was successful in having a new committee established to review the criminal law. The recommendations were sweeping, but due to various parliamentary maneuverings, it was not Mackintosh but Sir Robert Peel, new home secretary, who moved for the reforms and, in fact, for the next decade introduced an enormous number of revisions to the criminal law and its punishments. In 1823 Peel pushed through with remarkable speed the abolition of the death penalty for stealing forty shillings in shops and from ships in navigable rivers. So also was the Waltham Black Act at last repealed. Eventually, Peel was responsible for the repeal of 278 acts asking for the death penalty, consolidating them into eight acts.

Reform had begun. Acts were drawn up to improve every aspect of the criminal justice system, of which Peel is most famous for the establishment of a modern police force. As far as punishment is concerned, although the number of crimes punishable by death was drastically reduced, other secondary punishments remained in favor. Little attention was given to establishing a prison system or looking at what went on in prisons, and the reformative value of the treadmill and solitary confinement were given much emphasis. The use of whipping was considerably extended.[24]

Why did the reforms, so long in coming, happen almost all at once? Peel sensed the climate of public opinion and behaved accordingly. But the crucial fact was that now public opinion counted, thanks to the activities of the likes of Wilkes, Brandreth, and many others. Although the activities of radicals and "revolutionaries" had hastened the government's stand in opposition, they had also sensitized the people to the tyrannies of the government. The people, then, were also ready for it. Indeed, the momentum of reform went beyond Peel and beyond crime.

The Parliamentary Reform Act of 1832 has been described as the "most momentous event since the revolution of 1688."[25] It extended the franchise from 500,000 to 800,000 and wiped out one quarter of the existing English and Welsh seats—something that one could not imagine any modern legislature doing to itself! It increased the voting capacity of the middle class, and, as we have seen, the reform movement was mainly led by the middle class. Thus, when Peel wanted to retain the death penalty for forgery, Parliament forced its abolition, and by 1861 capital punishment was reserved only for a handful of offenses involving murder and treason. On March 10, 1840, William Ewart rose in the House and moved, for the first time, for the complete abolition of capital punishment.

That century of repression, the Victorian era, was about to have its way with punishment. Freud was later to observe that civilization pays a price for progress. The reformers were to pay their price for forcing the issue of total abolition, because, quite understandably, punishment went underground.

Although Ewart's resolution was defeated, it received such an unexpectedly large number of votes in its favor (ninety), that the press began to predict total abolition. It was wrong. A tortuous and often acrimonious debate followed for the next twenty years, both in Parliament and in the public forum through many newspapers and journals. The campaign was kept before the public by many reform societies and such public figures as Charles Dickens.[26]

In 1849 Ewart again tried for abolition and again the motion was defeated, but during the debate, Sir George Grey, home secretary in Lord John Russell's cabinet, made the seemingly remarkable concession that "a public execution is not absolutely necessary." Subsequently, the question of abolition was to be inextricably tied to the question of public versus private executions. The reformers' ranks were split. If they opposed abolition of public executions, they would be accused of callousness; but if they supported private executions, they knew that abolition was simply not a possibility, since it was the conservatives who supported private executions. In addition, the *Times* and other newspapers were ardently against private executions because of the insidious idea of the state doing its nasty work in secret and the doubts they were sure the public would have whether the penalty would be administered impartially. How could the people be convinced that an offender of the upper class really had been executed? Finally, even Charles Dickens went over to private executions amidst great bitterness among the abolitionist ranks. Apparently, he must have thought that private executions were at least an improvement over public executions. Eventually public executions were abolished in 1868. It would be another 100 years and many Royal Commissions before near-total abolition.

The Vanguard in America

Reform of the death penalty did not take quite the same tortuous path in the United States until much later. In 1787, Benjamin Rush presented a lecture in Ben Franklin's house recommending the construction of a "House of Reform," and this was followed by other lectures a year later, urging abolition of the death penalty. His arguments were based almost entirely on Beccaria's *On Crimes and Punishments,* published, it will be remembered, in 1764. In 1794 the death penalty was repealed in Pennsylvania for all crimes except "first-degree murder." We should note, however, that although before the Revolution the criminal law of the colonies was theoretically the same for the colonies as for England, the extent of capital punishment, as I have shown in Chapter 6, was considerably less in the colonies. In addition, we have seen that public executions did not take on the same hysterical terror in colonial America as in England.

However, the deeply ambivalent attitude toward capital punishment that we have seen maintained throughout the history of punishment in the Western world also applied very clearly in the United States. States such as Iowa, Colorado, Maine, Wisconsin, and many others abolished the death penalty very early, certainly far in advance of England and much of Europe. A number also restored it, and even reabolished it (Iowa, Oregon, and Maine). The deep ambivalence—the deep need for it—is demonstrated by what happened in Colorado, where abolition was instituted in 1830. A few years later, the public lynched offenders, apparently because prison was "not punishment enough." Ambivalence remains even today, when capital punishment's virtual abolition (in practice), having been with us for ten years or so, was broken in 1977 with the execution by firing squad of Gary Gilmore. We have even been treated by the media to the incredible sight of convicted murderers pleading on television for the death penalty.

The need for and the guilt over its use are also clearly demonstrated by the American search—through technology—for a more humane method of execution. Although there are many stories told about why the electric chair (the machinations of Westinghouse) and lethal gas were introduced, it is probably fair to say that these and other methods were investigated in a rather distorted attempt to make killing humanitarian. There is no doubt that it could be done more "humanely" by using lethal injections, but this would also no doubt be seen as an insidious 1984 type of solution. Besides, the British Royal Commission approached the British Medical Association to see if it would consider this—and the association would have nothing to do with it, nor would the American medical profession.

If we are to get on with the story, we must leave the death penalty here, because after the middle of the nineteenth century it was no longer the spectacular hub of criminal punishment. It therefore warrants less of our attention. The most important feature of punishment for the last 100 years or so has been the punishment that replaced the death penalty, which was, of course, imprisonment.

Mountains of books have been written on the subject of prisons, so I do not intend to look at it in any detail, but only make a few important observations of relevance to the theme of this book. Our survey of the history and slow delineation of principles of punishment—both theoretical and applied—has concentrated almost entirely on Europe and England. I have done this because these are where the main events affecting the rest of the Western world occurred. Although certain forms of prison (galleys and the like) have been in existence in Europe for centuries, whether by design or accident, they became the necessary alternative to the death penalty in England and Europe. Yet it was in the United States that a "rational" or concerted effort was made to develop a system of prisons. Experts from all over Europe were sent to the United States to observe and report upon the famous American systems.

Two competing systems were established in the 1820s. New York devised the congregate system at Auburn and later at Sing Sing, in which the prisoner worked with other inmates during the day, but could not converse and was kept in individual confinement at night. The Pennsylvania system, first applied at Pittsburgh in 1826, and then at Philadelphia in 1829, advocated complete isolation of the prisoner for the entire period of his confinement.

Regardless of the pros and cons of this debate, the important observation to be made is that these systems of prison developed out of the needs of the community and took on the forms they did as a direct reflection in society of its beliefs about the causes of crime:

> Convinced that deviancy was primarily the result of the corruptions pervading the community, and that organizations like the family and the church were not counterbalancing them, they believed that a setting which removed the offender from all temptations and substituted a steady and regular regimen would reform him.[27]

But this explanation only goes part of the way. We must remember that the nineteenth century was also a Victorian era and the repression of sex with highly moralistic overtones was the dominant theme in all middle-class circles—whether English or American. Like sex, punishment was also repressed—repressed into the secrecy of institutions and the unconscious of society. Prisons performed a major function by removing the filthy aspects of society from public view; public executions became private, prisons became places of maximum isolation and security. In addition, the systematic, rigid, and compulsive nature of both the systems, along with the widespread use of the whip to maintain obedience (and one suspects purity), connote unmistakably their repressed sexuality. In the past 100 years, this isolation has been increased many times by the massive bureaucracies that grew up to administer these prisons, thus burying them further beneath paperwork and personnel.

Punishment had gone underground. But it was reappearing in a variety of forms. Corporal punishment in prisons during the nineteenth and first half of the twentieth century was widespread—probably including the punishment of death. We are left with occasional eruptions of violence to attract our attention to the penal punishment that goes on in our society, but these quickly subside; and we are left with accusations by reformers that insidious torture or punishment of prisoners goes on behind the prison walls, about which the public knows nothing. But as Romilly noted to Bentham a century and a half ago, the public doesn't give tuppence for criminals. And why should it?

The next step in reform has begun: the move to abolish prisons altogether. This movement, too, ebbs and flows like the spring tide. One wonders if this is not asking for just a little too much too early, since it took 2,500 years or more to relegate the death penalty to the low level that it now has, and prison was the price that was paid for that reform. What will be the price for the abolition of prison?

"Let desert mount."

10

The Principles of Punishment

Philosophers and legal theorists have developed three basic moral theories to justify the use and distribution of criminal punishment. These are the theories of retribution, utilitarianism, and social defense. In keeping with my broad delineation of punishment, I will go a little beyond the usual philosophical arguments developed to support each camp. I will endeavor to analyze each of the justifications according to its historical origin and definition of punishment; its moral imperatives; the role of the state in punishment; the role of the individual; whether it emphasizes reactive or proactive punishment; the status of the offender in the punishment scheme; and the discretion in punishment that it permits. It should be clear that the three schools overlap considerably, although much of the writing on them has been directed one against the other, resulting often in a statement of what, for example, retribution is *not,* rather than what it *is.*

Of the three theories, retribution and utilitarianism are the oldest—indeed as old as antiquity. Social defense is comparatively recent, growing out of the very confusing nineteenth century, so full of the volatile ideas of reform, and propelled by the boom of scientific endeavor known as "positivism."

The Principles of Retribution

DEFINITION AND ORIGIN: Retributive punishment is punishment which adheres to the basic assumption that a wrongful act *must* be "repaid" by a punishment that is as severe as the wrongful act. Its most primitive form is that of vengeance, which probably has two early origins. One is the ancient feud, in which a "life for a life" was deemed the only solution to a wrong perpetrated upon another. However, we saw in Chapter 6 how this form of retribution gradually gave way to other kinds of punishments. The other early origin is religious. In its primitive form, retribution was a reflection, where the punishment was fashioned to resemble closely the criminal offense. We considered a number of examples of very ancient reflected punishments in Chapter 3. The "civilized" religious form of retribution is *lex talionis,* the "eye-for-an-eye," which is deeply embedded in Judeo-Christian religion.

There are many other variations of retributive punishment that we shall consider shortly. But before we do, it is well to consider an important historical fact about retribution. We have seen that it is an extremely ancient principle of punishment. We have also seen that it began to be transformed and taken over by various other approaches to punishment very early in civilization, certainly by the close of feudal times. The punishments of the Inquisition were largely done with other purposes in mind (i.e., the eradication of heresy) than that wrongful acts should be repaid by punishment. Further, the arguments of the eighteenth and nineteenth centuries over punishment, we have seen, were not motivated by desire for retribution, but by the expected utilitarian effects of punishment. The utilitarian principles of punishment have just as ancient roots as retribution, but unlike retribution, utilitarian punishment never receded into the background. Rather, it became more and more the central feature of punishment. It was not until the twentieth century that English philosophers began to attempt a systematic explication of a retributive philosophy. Even during the debates over the death penalty in the early nineteenth century, we saw that the reforms asked for were always argued on utilitarian grounds. One might argue that, had a retributive philosophy been advanced, that is, the punishment be proportionate (both in kind and amount) to the crime, the use of capital statutes could have been considerably reduced, since they would simply not have been applicable to the wide range of offenses then punished by death. The fact that the utilitarians were the most vociferous in their arguments for reforms left us with the popular idea that utilitarianism was humanitarian and in comparison retribution was a kind of primitive, vengeful punishment in which only tyrants indulged.

PUNISHMENT: THE CATEGORICAL IMPERATIVE: The trap question that retributivists are often asked is: "But why must a wrongful act be punished?" How does one respond to this question without providing a utilitarian solution? For example, it is tempting to reply, "to reinforce the legal or moral order," but we can see that this is a utilitarian answer. The most common response (and it appears to be the only nonutilitarian answer possible) is "because the act was wrong." One can see that this is merely a restatement of the assertion; it does not explain why a wrongful act must be punished. Retributivists are always embarrassed when confronted with this question, and usually as a last resort they refer to Kant, claiming that the statement "A wrongful act must be punished" is a categorical imperative. As Kant says: "The penal law is a categorical imperative, and woe to him who creeps through the serpent-windings of utilitarianism. . . ."[1] Then the argument usually turns to a discussion of the faults of utilitarianism, leaving one with a view that retribution is something negative: it is what utilitarianism is not. Again, in Kant's words: "for one man ought never to be dealt with merely as a means subservient to the purpose of another . . . punishment . . . must in all cases be imposed only because the individual on whom it is inflicted has committed a crime. . . ."[2]

Is it any more than a blunt assertion? Is it possible for a statement to be inherently right? Today the answer would be that, of course, no assertion unless tautologous could be inherently right. Fortunately, from our historical survey of punishment, we are able to shed some light on this problem and offer the retributivists a way out.

First, the statement "A wrongful act must be punished" is not just an assertion, it is a statement of fact. There has never been a time in history when wrongful acts (that were perceived as wrongful acts) were rewarded. In fact, such a possibility is plainly ridiculous. I have also argued earlier that punishment is not a moral value that has to be justified, but is a part of the natural order. Therefore, the insistent question asked by the utilitarians, "But why must a wrongful act be punished," may be dismissed as mischievous and symptomatic of the utilitarian's preoccupation with justifying punishment and his blunt assumption that punishment is evil because it is painful.

Second, I would go so far as to say that "A wrongful act must be punished" is not only a statement of fact, but verges on being a social law, which is the norm of reciprocity.[3] Sociologists and anthropologists have written a great deal about reciprocity, which they have seen as a central feature of economic and social life. Indeed, without the notion of reciprocal arrangements between individuals and groups or organizations, much of economic and social life would simply not be possible.[4] Yet few of these sociologists have applied the notion to the area of morals and law. Surely it is logical that such an all-pervasive social law as reciprocity should also be applied to the area of sanctions. It is perfectly understandable, therefore, that in the primitive feud, a wrongful act (e.g., homicide) was reciprocated in kind. The simplicity of these "reciprocal punishments" was, of course, destroyed when the state, or third party, intervened as the arbiter, when the civil or tort aspects of criminal punishments were more and more taken over by the state. Historically, the state turned out to have very definite utilitarian purposes in mind as far as punishment was concerned, so the pure reciprocity of criminal punishment has never really been given a chance. The result is that some have argued the state, in the name of retribution, dishes out a reciprocal punishment, but asks "a little more." Be that as it may, we may conclude that, as a principle, retribution has a great deal of social and historical support. That a wrongful act should be reciprocated by a punishment in kind is not a moral imperative (although it sounds like one), but rather the explication of a social law: that just as fair exchanges are conducted (and bargained for) in the social and economic sphere so are they in the field of morals and law.[5] Thus, for the retributivist, punishment restores an equilibrium that was upset by the crime.

Third, there is a sense in which "A wrongful act must be punished" may be tautologous, and therefore inherently true. For after all, how can one know what is a wrongful act unless there are sanctions that clearly delineate it as such? All moral or religious doctrines espouse a right way to live, and prescribe various sanctions against deviations from this "right." One may argue, therefore, that punishment is part of the definition of a wrongful act and certainly of a criminal act. The idea that a legislature could enact a crime with no corresponding punishment also seems nonsensical.[6]

ROLE OF THE STATE: Once again, in my view, the principle of retribution is incorrectly believed to be something awful that the state demands of the individuals in society. I have suggested that, on the contrary, the role of the state in punishment has, by and large, required utilitarian rather than retributive justifications of punishment. The reason for this confusion is that the two best known proponents of the retributive view—Kant and Hegel—viewed the state with a good deal more reverence than did the utilitarians of the eighteenth century, and so tended to mix in arguments for the right of the state to punish with the arguments for retribution. For example, Hegel insists that the state is a higher entity and therefore may justly lay claim to the life and property of members of the public; indeed, it demands a sacrifice.[7] Hegel has substituted the state completely for the injured party, so the reciprocation of retributive punishment is no longer between two opposing parties, as it was with the feud or with much of Roman criminal law, but is a matter entirely between the offender and the state.

Kant puts forward a more "sociocultural" argument. He suggests that a criminal must be punished so that "bloodguiltiness may not remain upon the people."[8] Again, this is a throwback to the old sacred origins of punishment that we discussed in Chapters 3 and 6. It demonstrates the deep, reciprocal arrangement between the people (society), the criminal, and punishment. But Kant goes still further and argues that the right to punish is invested in the sovereign; the head of state may punish his subjects, but also the head cannot be punished, since he is the supreme judge.

In my view, neither of these arguments is intrinsic or necessary to the retributive view; in fact, if anything, they tend to violate it. The retributive principle simply requires that punishment be done, and that it be proportioned both in quality and kind to the offense. Since retribution has its origins in early history where there was no state as we have known it in the last 2,000 years, the state's role in retributive punishment is certainly problematic. The state *should* demand punishment of offenders, on behalf of the individual members of the society, but not, as Hegel insists, on behalf of the state itself. The state has an obligation to the members of society to punish criminals.[9] The criminals are punished not on behalf of the state, but on behalf of the people. The criminals, therefore, are not "sacrificed" as Hegel says. Rather, they are punished as is their due, and it should be the role of the state as an agent of the people to see that this punishment is exacted. The criminal pays his debt to society; and the state, by punishing, also pays its debt to society.

This is the model of retributive punishment that *ought* to hold. It is virtually never upheld, however, because the state and its various sovereigns have not utilized punishment in this way since the criminal law developed into a law of the state and later the law of legislatures. We have seen in our historical survey that punishment was mostly used by kings, popes, and parliaments as a means to an end, for an ulterior motive, generally of repression. Ironically, the retributive principles of punishment were usually invoked as justifications for using criminal punishment for other purposes.[10]

ROLE OF THE INDIVIDUAL: A very important principle of retribution is recognition of the rationality of the individual by punishing him. Although this appears at first blush to be a contradictory statement, it is not. Not only do all individuals have a right to see that a criminal is punished, but they also have a right, if they break a law, to be punished themselves. This is seen as a "right" in the sense that punishment sets them apart from the state. Since punishment *exists* as a part of the natural order of society, an individual when he breaks a law is assumed to have chosen to be punished. Put in its most basic form, it is as Kant says: "if you kill another, you kill yourself," or "if you steal from another, you steal from yourself." The important point to be considered here is that he is punished only for his wrongful act, and no other factor is seen as relevant. The individual is not punished as a means to some further end (such as reforming him or setting an example to others), but rather within a very narrow framework for the wrongful act itself. The idea, then, is that the punishment leaves the individual intact; it avoids treating the individual as a means to an end (i.e., he cannot be "sacrificed" for some supposedly greater good); and it also allows for the separation of the individual from the state. Perhaps this last point needs a little more explanation.

Imagine a society in which there were no criminal laws and therefore no criminal punishments. Instead, there were a few general guiding principles which all people were effectively taught to abide by since childhood. What kind of a society would it be? It would be a dull society, a totally conforming society, for without laws and their concomitant punishments, there would be no way of separating oneself from the society. A totally socialized individual would not be an individual, but rather an abstraction of society. Thus laws, especially criminal laws, create the possibility for nonconformity. Punishment when used on children is used with the intention of inculcating obedience. That is, it is punishment befitting children. But with adults, criminal punishment should not be used to inculcate obedience, but rather to accentuate the individual's right to deviate. By punishing him, this right is upheld. By refusing to change him, his right to deviate is further upheld. Thus, all criminal punishments create the possibility both for deviation and conformity. In contrast to popular views of the retributive principle of punishment, retribution is therefore the highly radical principle and the utilitarian principle is not only deeply conservative, but deeply reactionary as well, since it concentrates only on one aim—conformity.

A final view of the role of the individual entertained by the retributivist is that the individual, and only the individual, is solely responsible for the act. By this is meant usually that the person is able to understand the relevant moral and legal obligations; that the person was the author of the act, that is, he *caused* the criminal act at issue; and, thus, that he is considered accountable for the act.[11] At issue, then, is the notion of free will or volition. The retributivist insists that criminals are "normal adults," who are rational and choose to act the way they do. It is the individual who is held accountable for the criminal act. We shall have more to say about this when we come to consider the social defense doctrine. It also follows from this view that an assessment of the severity of the crime depends upon not only the external or objective consequences of the act (e.g., an assault victim dies), but also the "mental state" (*mens rea*) of the offender. An assessment is made of the motivation of the offender, his "evil intent" and so on. Such factors play an important part in the assessment of the severity of a crime. For the utilitarians, these play a secondary part, and for some extreme adherents of social defense, the state of mind may have no place at all in assessing the severity of the offense. For a retributivist, then, an assessment of the "amount of harm done" by a crime can never be enough on its own; it must always accompany an assessment of the moral turpitude involved.

Although there is some argument about it, this aspect of retribution is somewhat more recent than the simple "eye-for-an-eye" model. We saw in Chapter 3 a number of examples where, especially in the feud situation, reciprocal punishment was exacted, even in the case of accidental death. However, the guilty mind was very much a part of Roman law and, of course, was (and is) central to Judeo-Christian religion. This is one aspect of retribution that has remained central in the criminal law and was never overtaken by utilitarian doctrine. In fact, one suspects that it was this concept that was the major stumbling block for Bentham's utilitarian model. It required him to invent a complete system of morals and human action to take into account the mental aspect of human behavior.

PUNISHMENT AS REACTIVE: A major principle asserted time and again by retributivists is no punishment without guilt. Punishment, they say, is never justified unless an offender is found guilty of a particular offense. It is "backward-looking," applicable only to past offense.[12] In this regard, the retributivist asserts that punishment is unjust (a) if it is applied to a person with the expectation that he might commit some future offense or (b) if a new law is applied to a person retrospectively. Once again, it can be seen that these are principles that assert the rights of the individual, the insistence on punishing only an actual offense and only the person who has committed that offense. The retributivist gets into a certain amount of difficulty here, because occasionally retributivists advocate that a second offense (of the same crime) should be seen as more severe than a first offense. Strictly speaking, however, a retributivist should not hold this position. Each offense should be treated separately and punished accordingly, and all priors ignored.[13] This, of course, rarely occurs in the criminal law administration.[14]

The retributive model is, perhaps, a little too general to allow its clear application to the law enforcement model that should follow from it. We may say that the establishment of the guilt of the offender is of prime importance, as is also the necessity that a crime must not go unpunished. Therefore, although the retributive philosophy is reactive in the sense that it is not invoked until a crime has occurred, once that crime has occurred it would appear to be of central concern to the retributivist to see that it was atoned for. However, unlike the utilitarian, for the retributivist it is essential that the person punished be the actual one who committed the crime. Thus, the English criminal law's traditional presumption of innocence applies. However, we should be careful to distinguish this presumption of innocence in the trial stage from the situation of discovering and arresting the criminal. It is surely perfectly obvious that if a policeman worked on the assumption of innocence he would never arrest anyone. The retributivist principle, therefore, does not appear to tell us how the law should be enforced, except to make the general requirement that a crime must never go unpunished. The model that the police adopt to effect this end may depend on other factors not related to retribution.

Does this mean that the retributive view expects "total enforcement" (an impossibility)? Probably not. The difficulty is that we have no modern retributive system from which to make observations. The idea of the early historical model of retribution was that a crime be avenged privately (the feud), and this was subsequently mediated by a formal criminal law. Perhaps this suggests that as far as law enforcement is concerned, only those crimes that create a public spectacle, or for which the people clamor for punishment, should be enforced and enforced at any cost. In this situation, law enforcement should seek out such crimes so that their perpetrators may be punished effectively. This extrapolation is, however, a little strained, and it must be said that the retributive model remains basically reactive and inert. It is the social defense and utilitarian theorists who have more to say about law enforcement.

A note on the use of torture may also be applicable here. I have argued that the retributivist does not arbitrarily assume that pain is evil, therefore he is more likely to consider the use of corporal punishment. Does it follow that he could also favor the use of torture? It is possible that in a few circumstances he might. He would favor torture as a punishment if it resembled the crime that was committed. If it was a particularly horrendous crime in which the criminal tortured his victim, one cannot see why the retributivist would object to a similar punishment being applied to the criminal. We should be clear, however, that this use of torture is done simply for the purpose of inflicting a punishment and not to achieve other ends, such as a confession or the names of accomplices. The retributivist, consistent with his principle of never allowing an individual to be punished as a means to an end, would adamantly oppose the use of torture for such ends. The utilitarians, before they categorically rejected pain as evil (i.e., before the eighteenth century), found no difficulty in justifying its use—as we have seen in the Inquisition where it was used to obtain confessions and names of further suspects.

STATUS OF THE OFFENDER: It is clear that, throughout history, the effects of punishment have been felt more by those of lesser social status. Sometimes persons were punished simply for being what they were (e.g., Jews). At other times, though subject to the same laws as "free men," the actual punishments were much more severe. Indeed, guilt was often presumed as a part of the status so that persons could be punished at will. A clear example of this arrangement was with the *pater familias* of Roman times, where the father could virtually punish members of his household at his whim and evidence from slaves was inadmissible unless obtained under torture—that is, they were presumed in advance to be guilty. A more recent example was the eighteenth-century law prescribing death for women found guilty of killing their newborn offspring and, a little earlier, of bearing stillborn babies. The women were presumed guilty, and the onus was on them to prove innocence—the only such law to make such a presumption in the history of English criminal law.

The retributive principle insists that all offenses be treated with punishments that resemble the offenses both in quality and quantity. The extent of guiltiness and severity of crimes has varied throughout different periods of history and also has been closely related to particular classes of people. Therefore, although in abstract theory one would have presumed that the same offenses would be punished by the same punishments, thus insuring equitable treatment for all, it has never happened in this way. Since particular classes of persons have from time to time been presumed to be inherently more guilty than others and since, according to the retributive principle, the degree of guilt is taken into account in deciding the severity of the offense, retributive punishments may occur that are, by today's standards, inequitably distributed among different classes of people.

In general, however, the retributive principle does not permit punishment of a person for what he is; punishment is justifiable only for what he has done. This position of the retributivist has occasionally been attacked as leading to inequity and injustice, since it is well known that the criminal laws, because of their economic, political, and social history, are designed to discriminate against particular kinds of crimes (e.g., street crimes, crimes of violence) which are those most often committed by disadvantaged groups. Punishing only the offense, and refusing to allow for other factors, insures that the disadvantaged groups will be punished more than the well-off groups who are freer to choose not to commit these crimes. In addition, the rigid punishment of a particular offense often entails the suffering of other persons (e.g., the criminal's family), indirectly, if the offender is sent to prison. Thus, it is argued, retributive punishment is both unfair and unjust.

The answer to this criticism is that it is not a criticism against retribution but against society's established system of distributive justice. The criminal law and its punishments cannot be held to be the cause of the inequitable distribution of wealth and power. On the contrary, one may agree with Marxist theorists that it is the product of society's system of distributive justice. Therefore, to attach the criticism of "unjust" to retributive punishment that attempts to distribute punishment equitably (i.e., the same punishment for the same offense) seems to me to be unfounded. The inequities that may occur, occur not because of the retributive principle, but because of the inequitable distribution of justice in the first place.[15]

As far as secondary suffering is concerned, the retributivist may reply that, indeed, this may occur and he is most concerned that this should not happen. This is why the retributivist, unlike either the utilitarian or the social defense theorists, would favor corporal punishment that can be quantified easily and administered quickly, so the criminal's family does not suffer economically for months or years while their breadwinner is in prison. The utilitarians, of course, would never consider this type of punishment, because they categorically reject pain as evil. The arguments against corporal punishment usually refer to punishing of soldiers and criminals in the period of the eighteenth century that we reviewed earlier. The punishments were no doubt horrendous, especially the whipping of sailors. But once again we should be mindful that such punishment was conducted with ulterior aims by the commanders: to instill obedience in the traditional military fashion by setting the example of terror. The use of punishment for such ends is anathema to the retributivist, as I have already argued. Responsibility for the excessive use of corporal punishment may be laid at the feet of the utilitarians, not the retributivists. We shall have more to say about this shortly. I should also add that the problem of secondary suffering is a difficult one for all models of punishment, including the utilitarians and the social defense theorists. The retributivist also offers another way out of the problem: that of judicial discretion.

DISCRETION: The above problem may be offset to some degree by another precept of retribution, that of charity or, in the judicial situation, mercy. We should be careful not to mix this notion up with the idea that retributive punishments may in some way equalize the inequitable distribution of justice in society. This is not the intention at all, and mercy must be seen as a secondary factor. However, because the retributive philosophy of punishment sees the individual (and only the individual) as responsible for his act, the retributivist can also display mercy or forgiveness toward the offender. In contrast, if the offender were seen as not responsible for his act (as may be the case especially with the social defense theorists), then one can hardly forgive him—rather, one excuses him. As far as the retributivist is concerned, there can be no excuse for crime.[16]

The retributive judge may make exceptions in the punishment he gives to the offender under circumstances where either charity or mercy are seen to be served. It is a gift given to the offender—it is not his right. Thus, mitigating or special circumstances may be taken into account by the judge when either pronouncing sentence or, as in the eighteenth and nineteenth centuries, recommending pardons or commutation of the death penalty.

We should note that some modern retributivists argue that there should be no discretion, since judges differ widely in what cases they view as warranting charity, so abuse and inequitable sentencing may follow. There is a move today to advocate mandatory and fixed sentences and take away the large portion of discretion allowed judges.[17] One must view this move not as a strictly retributivist principle, since by these new schemes the fixed and mandatory sentences are invariably increased for second and subsequent offenses. This does, of course, discriminate against those with prior sentences, thus breaking the retributive principle of same punishment for same crime. The only way in which the strict retributivist may deal with the question of individuals with prior offenses is to treat them as cases that do not warrant charity or forgiveness, which seems eminently reasonable. One might argue that by introducing mandatory or graded fixed sentences one is building the idea of "no forgiveness" into the system of punishment. But this has generally not been the principle espoused by its advocates. Rather, the principle used is generally a utilitarian or social defense one of incapacitating or deterring the "hard-core offender." Furthermore, we may note that in practice, if judges were behaving retributively, they would use their discretion in recommending charity only very sparingly (since if all or many are forgiven, the punishment becomes in effect a joke), and mandatory sentencing or some such system would become unnecessary.[18]

The Utilitarian Principles of Punishment

DEFINITION AND ORIGIN: It is popularly believed that the utilitarian theory of punishment began with Hobbes's dictum:

> In revenges or punishments men ought not to look at the greatness of evil past, but the greatness of the good to follow, whereby we are forbidden to inflict punishment with any other design than for the correction of the offender and the admonition of others.[19]

But if we take the most basic principle of the utilitarian theory of punishment, that we punish as a means to an end, then it is clear that this principle has probably held sway in Western civilization since its very beginning. In our picture of the primal horde, we saw that the horde was held in subjection at first by brute force, and then later by a combination of guilt and the threat of force. Although there is some disagreement as to whether the retributive model preceded the imposition of punishment by the state, it is clear that the retributive system was certainly overtaken by the state's punishment. In fact, I have suggested in Chapter 4 that the militaristic model of punishment has existed since man was able to organize himself sufficiently to wage war, and certainly it held in the Greek city-states. We can find a statement in Plato's *Laws*, virtually identical to Hobbes's, which Plato repeated several times in his other writings:

> . . . not that he is punished because he did wrong, for that which is done can never be undone, but in order that in future times, he, and those who see him corrected, may utterly hate injustice, or at any rate abate much of their evil-doing.[20]

However, with the somewhat extreme individualism of Roman law and its central focus on the *patria potestas,* the obedience model of punishment that we saw in the Greek city-states was somewhat abated and applied more to those specific groups where obedience was essential: i.e., the military, the slaves, and members of the household. A retributive model was more available to free men who were permitted (in fact, required) to exact atonement for crimes through a kind of formalized private prosecution. We have seen that this Roman practice was mostly lost with the rise of the Christian religion and the Inquisition, which incorporated into its own law only those aspects of the Roman law that were most typical of the obedience model (e.g., torture). This was because, in spite of its constant pronouncement (even to this day) that it believed in a retributive philosophy of punishment, the church in fact used this as an excuse for punishment as a means to an end: that is, the eradication of heresy, the enforcement of obedience, the reinforcement of the central (state) power of the church.

We saw also that in England criminal punishment was used largely as a means to an end—either to remove troublesome political enemies of the monarch or to set an example of terror for the general populace. Once again, it was the clergy who assisted the state in putting forward the smokescreen that it was punishing retributively. The clergy's preoccupation with repentance and confessions at the time of the public execution was meant to demonstrate to the people that the crime *had* to be punished and this was the only reason the state played a part. Of course, this was not the reason at all: rather, the reasons for punishment were quite clearly dictated by the desire of the monarch to control the people with the threat of terror and, later, for a tyrannical Parliament to keep the "mob" in check. While the thunderous pronouncements of the judges of the eighteenth and nineteenth centuries sounded retributive in expounding that the criminal deserved to be punished, there is little doubt that the whole system was a utilitarian system based on the doctrine of maximum severity: that maximum punishment would deter crime. The nineteenth-century utilitarians introduced reforms that modified this utilitarian principle, but they certainly did not question the basic utilitarian principle of deterrence through punishment that has existed since the beginning of civilization.

To repeat: the utilitarian principle of punishment is probably the oldest, or is at least as old as the retributive principle, and there is little doubt that it has always been the most dominant guiding principle of punishment in Western civilization. Much confusion over this point has arisen because very often the politicians, administrators, and students of criminal law have used the principle of retribution for utilitarian ends,[21] so people (including academics) have come to think of retribution as "evil" or "oppressive," and utilitarianism as "progressive" and "humanitarian."

In sum, the basic utilitarian principle of punishment believes that a past wrong cannot be corrected or undone by a present punishment. It rejects, or at least ignores, the law of reciprocity. Instead, the utilitarian principle adopts a model of obedience: the aim of punishing now in order to prevent future offenses by example both to the offender and to the people at large who may be (in fact, it is assumed that they are) contemplating an offense.

PUNISHMENT AS A UTILITARIAN IMPERATIVE: For the "modern" utilitarian, punishment as an end in itself can never be justified, since it is assumed that punishment is in itself evil (it inflicts pain, and pain is evil), therefore other motives or reasons sufficient to outweigh the evil of the punishment must be invoked to justify its use. I have noted, though, that this applies to the "modern" utilitarian. Prior to Beccaria and Bentham, the utilitarian punisher saw nothing wrong with pain and would use any measure to effect his ends: the effectuation of obedience. Furthermore, he did not feel the necessity to justify the use of excessive punishment, as does the modern utilitarian. Therefore, the justification for punishment was obvious to him: the ends were to eradicate political opposition and insure obedience of the populace. There were no limits on the amount of punishment allowed to achieve these ends, as long as the ends were achieved.

Yet, although the utilitarians have never used punishment as a "categorical imperative" in Kant's sense, there is little doubt that it has been seen as an imperative of some kind—a utilitarian imperative —in the sense that without punishment from a superior authority obedience (and thus social order) could never be maintained. We have seen that the most primitive form of retribution was the feud. The most primitive form of utilitarian punishment was most likely tyranny. The primitive utilitarian principle overtook the primitive retributive principle under the rationale of maintaining order, preventing the total destruction of whole groups and clans that feuding necessarily brought about. Thus, the utilitarian theory of punishment assumes that a certain amount of primitive oppression is necessary to maintain order and without it there would be, in Hobbes's words, "the war of all against all."

This particular utilitarian justification for punishment should not be confused with one occasionally used by retributivists that retributive punishment maintains order. For the retributivist, the maintenance of order issues only indirectly from the reciprocal use of punishment by reinforcing the social law of reciprocity and, thus, also society. However, retribution is an expression of the social law, it is not its cause. In contrast, for the utilitarian, punishment is the very cause of the social order. Without it, there would be chaos. Here is highlighted the moralistic view of punishment held by the utilitarians who see it as a kind of foreign, evil infliction on society; yet paradoxically that society is dependent on it for its existence. For the retributivist, punishment is a natural part of the social and cultural fabric, so it is neither good nor evil except to the extent that we may decide (on other criteria) that our culture or society is good or evil. For the utilitarian, punishment is an absolute evil that is absolutely necessary! It is upon these fundamental distinctions that the ultimate morality of punishment depends. We shall look very closely at them in the final chapter.

ROLE OF THE STATE: It is fair to say, I think, that the utilitarians have never satisfactorily resolved this issue. Historically, the cause of deterrence was accepted without question as a legitimate aim of punishment until the nineteenth century. Hobbes most certainly, amidst the political and social chaos of the seventeenth century, saw the state as the only solution to bringing about order, and one of its major tools was to be punishment. However, Bentham and other utilitarians failed to resolve the split that their philosophy brought about between the individual and society. Bentham's utilitarian theory of behavior sought to protect the rights of individuals from being abrogated by other individuals, and this was achieved through the social contract, in which individuals gave up part of their rights. The sum of such rights some have described as an artificial "state." In any event, there is little doubt that the modern utilitarian justified the imposition of a third and "higher" party into the business of punishment. To put it in concrete terms, the ideal utilitarian society of the social contract, was a fancy term for a system that we call today a protection racket, with the state holding the gun and issuing the threats.

I have taken, here, the more basic utilitarian principle of punishment, that of deterrence, in which two "simple" processes are said to operate:[22]

1. All individuals are deterred from committing a crime by the threat of punishment issued by the state. Thus, all persons are seen as crime-prone. This process is known as general deterrence.

2. Those who have committed a crime are punished with a view to deterring them from committing a second crime. A whole subtheory of punishment has developed in relation to this postulate, variously called the reformative or rehabilitative ideal. We shall defer discussion of this subtheory until our discussion of social defense, where it properly belongs.

Modern writings on general deterrence have sought to shake it loose from Bentham's supposed superficial psychology (though we saw in Chapter 8 that it is anything but that) and to suggest that it involves a much broader meaning, which for clarity's sake we will call general prevention, though the two are often used synonymously. General prevention[23] means that not only is the general public deterred from committing a particular offense by the threat of punishment (in fact it is now suggested that this may be in the minority of cases), but also only because the criminal law punishes at all do individuals learn "right" and "wrong." It is a generalized process that builds up over time so that people become accustomed to obeying the law and considering it right to do so. These processes are usually called the "educative," "moralizing," and "habituative" effects of criminal law. It is even suggested that these effects may be felt unconsciously, supposedly a further demonstration of this theory's ability to go beyond Bentham's psychology.

In view of the ancient roots of utilitarian punishment in the obedience model of the early militaristic states, these extensions of deterrence theory come as no surprise to us. Unfortunately, this elaborate principle leads the utilitarians into a very sticky problem, putting them in the position of having to argue that, if this general preventive process is successful, the people will obey the laws of their society whether they are just or not, and everybody knows there are both just and unjust laws. Professor Gordon Hawkins, a strong proponent of general prevention, uses, significantly enough, an example from Nazi Germany where Bruno Bettelheim observed that the middle classes "could not question the wisdom of the law and of the police, so they accepted the behavior of the Gestapo as just. What was wrong was that *they* were made objects of persecution which in itself *must* be right, since it was carried out by the authorities."[24] Hawkins then concluded that it was important for general prevention theory not to confuse "acceptance of and submission to authority with morality."[25] Yet Hawkins's view surely contradicts the other basic utilitarian principle that punishment must also be used to deter the individual law breaker from future offenses, since this presumably cannot be achieved short of reforming him. Thus, there is no way out. Even if one behaves "morally" by breaking an unjust law, the utilitarian state will punish with a view to deterring other future offenses—i.e., of eradicating moral behavior. Here is, perhaps, the starkest contrast with the retributive scheme which recognizes the independence of the individual from the state and has no interest in deterring his future offenses. This was exactly the dilemma that Bentham faced, which was why he attempted to construct a completely new system of legislation *and* morals. For he saw that it is only in a just society that utilitarian theory can be just. In an unjust society there is no way for the utilitarian but to insist that morality must be separated from authority; yet it is hard to see, if this is the case, how authority has the right to punish. In the last analysis, therefore, the social contract as a protection racket holds. One grudgingly gives up a little freedom in return for greater freedoms. But one never views this process as morally "right."

The modern utilitarian theorists' simple answer to this criticism is that there are many other institutions in society that teach moral or ethical behavior besides the criminal law, such as the church, family, school, and work. Depending on the particular political structure of a society, these institutions may punish and reward behaviors differently from the state so that alternate views of morality and resistance to blind obedience to the state may be developed. It is when the state controls *all* of these alternate institutions that situations such as Nazi Germany arise.

One final aspect of the utilitarian system is its advocacy of "system." Bentham invented the word "codify," and since his time, attempts to systematize, streamline, and increase the efficiency of criminal law and its administration have been many. Efficiency and economy were almost synonymous with utility for Bentham. We may conclude that the utilitarian theory of punishment lends itself best to a large state process, since the utilitarians would see efficiency and economy coming from one organization and one code of laws. For the utilitarians, the state is absolutely necessary for the administration of punishment. It always precariously depends on the approbation of the people; yet paradoxically this also means that the more it punishes, the less precarious is its existence, since, according to twentieth-century theorists, the people will believe that the state is "right" and will learn to "obey."

ROLE OF THE INDIVIDUAL: To the utilitarian punisher, the individual is basically a malleable object that is manipulated by the process of punishing provided by the criminal law. This does not mean that there is no concept of the individual in the utilitarian theory of punishment. It must be said, however, that since Bentham utilitarian theorists have been quite vague as to the psychological makeup of the offender or, in the case of general prevention, the would-be offender. Bentham's psychology was a highly sophisticated one. Its only major shortcoming, in my view, in comparison to modern twentieth-century psychology, was that there was no idea of the unconscious.[26] One should be mindful that there are many modern models of social psychology that refuse to recognize the importance (or even existence) of the unconscious and that use essentially a rationalistic, means–end schema, an inner–outer dichotomy that is strikingly similar to the Bentham model. The main difference between these modern theories and Bentham's is that they claim to be value free or objective–scientific analyses.[27] Bentham was concerned to make his analysis of human action a moral as well as scientific one. For Bentham, man was indeed an individual, a thinking, reasoning individual who weighed alternatives and tried to translate his basic needs into motives, to carry them out as well as possible (intentions) in the face of a world that offered strong temptations in several directions at once. The important point is that Bentham's man was not pushed by desires in the way that Freud was later to argue, but was rather pulled by temptations. Man, therefore, exercised rational choice by dealing mainly with the outside world. For Freud, man spent most of his time dealing with the inside world, a view that led very easily to the psychological determinism that was later to take over criminology for a period when the social defense model almost took hold.

The nineteenth-century utilitarian model of man, therefore, lent itself more easily to a utilitarian (as gross as it was) model of criminal law, which nevertheless had preserved within it the one retributive principle: the rational man of free will and intent. It is not surprising to us, then, that Bentham probably more than any other criminal law reformer had a direct influence on an incredible array of legislation.[28] He tore apart Blackstone's *Commentaries* but retained the part that he knew was essential to develop any moral system, the concept of volition.

There is an important sense in which this nineteenth-century utilitarian model of man when used within a deterrence model is not necessarily incompatible with the retribution principle. Provided one insists on the narrow meaning of the word "deterrence"—that persons are deterred, either from first offenses (general deterrence) or subsequent offenses (individual deterrence) by the threat of punishment, and that this is the only way they are deterred—one might argue simply that the fact that they desist from offenses does not mean that the punishment (or its threat) in any way changes them as individuals or that they come to obey because they see the law to be "right" or even "lawful." We are again faced with that common sociological problem: do people obey grudgingly or unquestioningly? If people obey grudgingly, then we may safely assume that punishments will not change or reform them as persons, and therefore their individuality remains intact—an important value for the retributivist. On the other hand, if we take the broader general preventive model (i.e., the "moralizing effect") one must assume that the individual is changed by legal punishment, and therefore the retributive principle of individuality is violated.

Deterrence, used under its more inclusive definition of general prevention, has become a major topic in criminal law and administration in the last decade,[29] which perhaps suggests the highly utilitarian direction that our criminal law is currently taking.

PUNISHMENT AS PROACTIVE . . . OR REACTIVE? One of the most common, and superficial, criticisms of the utilitarian principle of punishment is that, since it treats the individual as a means to an end (i.e., the individual is punished to prevent further offenses either of his own or of others), it therefore logically leads to the permissibility of punishing a person who has not committed an offense—surely an unjust punishment, certainly from the retributive point of view. As far as Bentham's theory is concerned, this could never have happened. This is clearly stated by Bentham in his listing of "cases unmeet for punishment," the first of which was: "where there has never been any mischief,"[30] and he goes on to point out that he includes as cases unmeet for punishments acts that are made illegal by an ex-post-facto law.

In theory, however, the point can be argued, since another utilitarian dictum is that a punishment should be used only in sufficient quantity to outweigh the mischief caused by the act. It is possible to imagine an extreme situation when, say, the hanging of an innocent man for a particularly heinous crime might save the lives of many from a belligerent vigilante mob. But this is an extreme example where the obvious weakness of the utilitarian philosophy of the preparedness to sacrifice the one for the many or the treatment of man as a means is magnified.

In sum, the basic utilitarian system of punishment should be seen, in practice anyway, as essentially *reactive*. It must wait for a crime to occur, a failing of deterrence, before it can punish for proactive purposes. Of course, there is an easy way around this problem if one wants to retain the resemblance of the retributive principle of no punishment without guilt: one can enact many laws, as occurred during the utilitarian period of the doctrine of maximum severity, so that there is a much greater chance that a sufficient number of persons will break the law. They can then be "justly" punished as an example. Thus, utilitarianism is most likely to be proactive legislatively.

It will also be proactive administratively, since it is driven by the overwhelming aim to prevent future offenses. It should do all it can to seek out current offenses and punish them. Indeed, utilitarian theorists since Bentham have worked out a basic, ideal system for the punishment of crimes. There are four central concepts to this system: certainty, severity, celerity, and publicity of punishment. Punishment of all crimes must be swift and certain, so we should expect a strong enforcement model of the administration of criminal justice. Much publicity must be given to the punishment, and the severity must outweigh the profit of the offense. The criminal or potential criminal must be made well aware that, if he commits a crime, he will certainly be punished, and swiftly. Our crime clearance statistics and complicated court system, along with an almost uncontrolled sentencing practice, makes all of these, with the possible exception of publicity, completely impossible today. We shall have more to say about these concepts of deterrence in the following chapter.

Our conclusion is that while in theory utilitarians would logically have to approve the punishment of an innocent man for the greater good, no traditional utilitarians have ever espoused this view, especially Bentham. In any case, this problem never arises in practice since there are always plenty of laws that persons can be found to have broken. Thus, utilitarians are able to adhere to a reactive response to crimes. But, since prevention is the single purpose of the utilitarian model, an efficient, full enforcement model of the criminal law should be their preference.

STATUS OF THE OFFENDER: Utilitarians have long recognized the fact of individual differences among offenders. Certainly Bentham recognized that all persons differ according to the way in which they feel pleasure or pain. There were two aspects to this: the quantum, or intensity of feeling, and the "bias," or quality of sensibility. These two differentiating aspects of individual sensibility reacted to many factors, of which Bentham listed thirty-two. These may include health, strength, intellectual powers, insanity, various attributes that we would today call "personality traits" (e.g., "antipathetic sensibility"), religious biases, habitual occupations, sex, age, rank, and education. Many of these, to a varying extent, Bentham was prepared to admit as an excuse from punishment. And subsequent utilitarian reformers developed a whole theory of the individualization of punishment,[31] which laid the groundwork for the later theories of social defense.

We must remember that the nineteenth-century utilitarian, especially Bentham, was not just concerned with the reform of the criminal law, but also with reform of the whole of society, especially the eradication of what were often seen as the causes of crime: the sordid conditions of the working class.[32] The abolition of confiscation in the eighteenth century and of imprisonment for debt in the nineteenth century was no doubt motivated by their ideals, in an attempt to alleviate the secondary punishment of the offender's family.

There is another aspect in which the utilitarian model is most applicable, and that is toward particular classes of offenders. As soon as one accepts the possibility of certain general conditions (e.g., age, sex, social conditions), it is clear that not only are there individual differences in proneness to commit crime, but also differences between particular groups.[33] Thus, according to today's crime statistics, for example, the youthful male, the black, and the poor are by far the most crime-prone groups in society. It follows that if my inference of the full enforcement model of a preventive system is taken seriously by the utilitarians, they should advocate an intensive application of the criminal law to these groups. They should, in fact, advocate a discriminatory application of criminal punishments; or if they do not have the heart to go this far, at least they should see that the punishment of criminals from among these groups is widely publicized. Yet today, the practice has evolved of keeping secret the age and identity of the youthful offenders and not reporting even the race of an offender in the newspapers.

I have shown repeatedly that throughout history the utilitarian use of punishment necessarily has involved its discriminatory application to particular "minorities" whether they have been women, children, slaves, soldiers, or animals. It is logically impossible for it to do otherwise. Its basic tenet is, after all, "the greatest good for the greatest number." It has never suggested the greatest good for *all*. More about this in the final chapter.

DISCRETION: It is not altogether clear whether the utilitarians favor judicial discretion or not. Certainly, Beccaria was a vocal opponent of pardons and other forms of judicial discretion on the basis that it allowed the judges to behave like tyrants, virtually punishing at will or whim. On the other hand, the "defender" of the English criminal law, Blackstone, favored pardons and the prerogative of mercy as an essential aspect of the retributive system of punishment. The problem, of course, was that, as Sir Leon Radzinowicz points out, Blackstone failed to recognize that pardons were used not as a comparatively rare exception (the principle of retribution it will be remembered) but almost routinely. Thus, pardons were not used retributively during the eighteenth and nineteenth centuries—they were used to soften the effect of the principle of maximum severity. Pardons were therefore used for utilitarian purposes.[34]

One must also infer from Bentham's work that he would permit no discretion unless it were highly structured. Since he allowed for main factors, such as age, religion, and personality, mitigating the application of punishments, it is difficult to see how a certain amount of judicial discretion could be avoided in individualizing punishment to the extent Bentham apparently envisioned. Yet, since Bentham so clearly loathed the judiciary, it is hard to see him leaving much freedom to them—he would no doubt have codified definite principles to guide their sentencing decisions. Bentham did, however, approve of the royal prerogative to pardon, provided it was used only rarely.

The Principles of Social Defense

DEFINITION AND ORIGIN: Social defense theory argues that society, if it is to survive, must protect itself by the repression of crime and treatment of offenders.[35]

I suggested earlier in this chapter that social defense constitutes an off-shoot of utilitarianism. While I consider this observation to be generally true, I must also point out that the principles of social defense go well beyond utilitarianism, creating a set of postulates that are uniquely its own. Certainly, Enrico Ferri, the original and most trenchant expositor of social defense, would be most upset at being labeled utilitarian, since much of his work was developed as a criticism against what he called the "classical school"—a school that included Beccaria and Bentham.

The origins of the school are comparatively recent. It arose at the end of the nineteenth century when it was once again recognized that, in spite of all the utilitarian reforms that had been effected in the criminal law, crime continued to increase and continued to be a major social problem. At the same time, two great schools of thought arose: the positivist movement both in criminology and in sociology and the Marxist method of analyzing social problems. Enrico Ferri found himself amidst the two. In his early years as a student and a professor, he developed a solidly Marxist analysis of society and suffered political discrimination in academia because of his Marxist adherence. However, what this training in Marx enabled him to do better than any other criminal law reformers before him was to perceive realistically the social facts of crime. He saw accurately that penal punishment was of extremely limited influence in eradicating crime—it was seen, he complained, as a panacea, especially by the classical school. Thus, he recommended "penal substitutes," state measures to eradicate the social, economic, and political conditions of crime, because "social reforms are much more serviceable than the penal code in preventing an inundation of crime."[36] In fairness to Bentham, though, it must be pointed out that the use of penal substitutes (Bentham called it indirect legislation) was a central element of his system also. However, where Bentham was certain that the severity of punishments would gradually decrease as society improved under his system, Ferri took a much more realistic, even pessimistic view.

The reason, of course, was Cesare Lombroso's influence. Lombroso had, using "the scientific method" (i.e., measurement and classification), isolated a class of criminals that were biologically atavistic. Ferri called them "born criminals" and was quite convinced that it was useless to punish them since they were not capable of changing or learning from the punishment. In fact, Ferri suggested that, in relation to punishment, there were three main groups. First, there was the majority of people who would never commit crime, because of their moral and religious upbringing, and no penal code was necessary for them. This is at once a radical departure from the utilitarians who have usually assumed that *all* people need to be deterred (general deterrence). Second, there were the morally destitute, primitive types, the criminals against whom punishment was useless. Third, there were those in between, the occasional and perhaps habitual criminals, who were a little of both. It was against them that punishment might be effective.

Thus, Ferri was a realist: he recognized that to make punishment effective on the level envisaged by utilitarians one would have to take it to absurd lengths that would be totally unacceptable to humanity. For instance, he argues that the only sensible use of the death penalty would be the complete elimination of the born criminals, but since this would have required about 1,000 executions per year in Italy (instead of the then 7 or 8 in 1900), it would be a completely unrealistic practice.

We find, then, that the essential distinguishing features of the social defense theorist from the utilitarian are his social realism and his aim to defend society against an inevitable amount of crime, which, though reducible through social reforms, is almost never reducible by penal punishment. It is essentially a holding pattern.

This was the definition and meaning of social defense in the 1920s. It was later extended considerably to include, in addition, the two basic features now well known in penology: the protection of society not only by the repression of crime, but also by the treatment of offenders.[87] Treatment and rehabilitation have since become the central features of the social defense school, although their relationship to the early positivists is not often recognized. It was a logical extension of Ferri's work. Although Ferri recognized reform of the offender as a worthwhile goal of punishment, he relegated it to secondary importance. The first in importance was the defense of society against crime. Yet his acceptance of the reformative ideology was always implicit in his work, especially as evidenced by his advocacy of the indeterminate sentence. But we are getting ahead of ourselves.

PUNISHMENT, THE NEGATIVE IMPERATIVE: For the social defense theorists, punishment is a bottom-line, protective device. They have given up the utilitarian idea of eradicating or preventing all crime. However, even after social reforms have been applied to eliminate the causes of crime, there will still be the born criminal with which to deal. Society has the right to protect itself. The Marxist premise of societal right superseding individual right is evident, although the Marxist would probably argue that individual right flows automatically from societal right. Therefore, society is entirely justified in punishing individuals, since by protecting itself it protects individuals.

Although Ferri argued that "force is always a bad remedy for force,"[88] he nevertheless constantly berated the classical school for diminishing the effectiveness of punishments by (a) decreasing the severity to absurdly low levels and (b) upholding the traditional structure of the criminal law that never allowed for implementing the celerity of punishment, which all utilitarians (including Ferri) saw as essential if punishment were to be made to work. Ferri, therefore, strongly doubted the deterrent effects of punishment.

He saw punishment as a negative, stopgap measure whose main function was to incapacitate dangerous criminals, largely by separating them from society. Treatment could follow later, but the imperative to Ferri was to protect society, to defend it against the criminal element. And the most efficient and realistic way to do this was to direct the punishment against the *offenders,* the criminal types, and not against the *offenses* as both the utilitarians of the classical school and the retributivists had always done. It can be seen that this is simply an extension of the utilitarian notion that the criminal must be treated as a means to the end of preventing crime—thus he may be subjected to indeterminate sentence and reformative measures. There is also an element of the retributive notion that the offender be treated as an end in himself, in the sense that he is seen as the sole object of punishment. But this is as far as the similarity goes. For the retributivist it is punishment that is the object, not the offender.

With the onset of the "medical school" of the 1950s-60s, Ferri's idea of punishment as a negative imperative was dislodged, and it came to be believed that the offender could indeed be treated, even while he was incapacitated.[39] Thus it was that punishment came to be seen as a positive imperative, and now the two words "punishment" and "treatment" became hopelessly confused. Punishment came to be seen as curative, as Plato had argued long ago.[40] The idea of "treatment of the offender" was used to alleviate the obvious moral technical problems involved in incarcerating persons indefinitely, their release left purely to the discretion of prison or parole personnel. Under this system, an offender could easily (and did) spend much longer in prison for an offense that might be seen as mild by retributive standards, because he was diagnosed as "dangerous" or given some other such "disease" label.[41] Ferri, in my view, suffered no such illusions. He justified the lengthy incarceration of an offender, not on the basis of treatment needs, but of the need to protect society by incapacitating him.

ROLE OF THE STATE: Ferri has insisted that the state has a very important role in the administration of criminal punishment. Not only should it busy itself with the identification and separation of the dangerous criminal, but it should also make its primary role the compensation of victims of crime. Once again, we should note that Bentham also recommended this and thought it preferable to other forms of punishment. However, Bentham was pessimistic as to the practicability of effecting compensations from offenders who were usually destitute. Ferri also saw this difficulty, but he stuck to his insistence on the state's responsibility to see that the victims of crime were adequately compensated. He observed sarcastically that the state extracted a fine from the offender and pocketed the money, when in fact it was the state that had failed to prevent the crime in the first place. Therefore, the least it could do was to compensate the victim. The way in which such a system might be enforced, Ferri suggested, was to develop prison labor, in which prisoners would be paid a competitive salary, out of which they would then pay for their keep and pay off reparations to the victims.

The potential tyranny of the state under the social defense system is, of course, obvious. The system would logically allow for the adjudication of offenders before they have committed an offense (i.e., if they were diagnosed as potentially dangerous, so that the division between crime and mental illness would become extremely blurred). People could be put away for their lives, not upon the basis of a criminal law process that has evolved an explicit system of moral concepts throughout history, but upon the psychiatric or diagnostic process which is still in the process of coming to grips with its own morality (if it has any!).

One might observe that Ferri's idea of crime victim compensation and his insistence on the state's responsibility to see that it is carried out have appeal from both a retributive and a political point of view. One recalls that an essential element of retributive punishment is the reciprocal arrangement of punishments and how this scheme developed into a workable one for a period in the middle ages when severe punishments were uncommon. However, with the rise of the complex state of today, this retributive scheme is obviously too simple to work. But with the state backing it, perhaps retribution could be revived. The important point is that the state does not become the sole boss of a protection racket as with the social contact, but rather the arbiter of the dealings between the offender and victim.

ROLE OF THE INDIVIDUAL: Ferri has characterized the social defense school as seeking to establish an equilibrium between individual and society. We have seen in our discussion of utilitarianism how central this problem was and that it was never fully resolved. The "solution" offered by Ferri and another contemporary social defense advocate, Lady Barbara Wootton,[42] is to substitute a concept of social responsibility for legal responsibility. By social responsibility, Ferri means that the idea of legal culpability should be discarded and replaced by the assumption that the offender is "responsible" for a criminal act simply because (a) he has performed it and (b) he is a member of society. The major criterion for determining severity of acts, therefore, becomes the measure of the harm done to society and, especially in Ferri's terms, the offender's dangerousness. In fact, it becomes pointless for the social defense theorist to assess the gravity of a particular offense. Rather, he focuses on the "gravity" of the particular offender. This has fantastic implications since it denies what is the very essence of the criminal law—the idea of wickedness or, to use more legal terminology, the "guilty mind." This ancient idea, going back at least to Roman times and probably before, insists that the gravity of forbidden actions is made much more serious if the actor acts on purpose. The distinction in terms of morality is so basic, and provides such a continuous thread to the cultural heritage of the criminal law, that one is amazed that brilliant students of the criminal law such as Ferri and Wootton could suggest such a thing. Certainly Wootton is much more extreme than Ferri in this regard. The change would have the effect of emasculating the criminal law of its moral fiber. It would also require the complete rewriting of the criminal law to frame the offenses in such a way as to exclude the idea of "guilty mind," which is built into the very description of many offenses. Bentham understood this problem, and so invented a new language of morals which would allow him to develop a measure of the harm done to society and also incorporate the mental element.

For Ferri and Wootton, the mental element is also of crucial importance, not, according to them, as a moral or judicial evaluation, but as a "determinant of cause" of the offender's behavior. Because of the predominance of positivism, the social defense theorists thought that this assessment of the psychological plus physiological and social causes of the offender's behavior was objective because it was scientific. Thus, it followed that the offender would be dealt with objectively, rather than primitively, and science would effect a cure. Although as we have seen Ferri was not optimistic about the effectiveness of treatment, this rationale of the social defense school provided the justification for the proliferation of the indeterminate sentence, extensive psychiatric processing and other diagnoses of offenders, and even the attempt in Sweden to substantially alter the criminal law to allow for the eradication of guilty mind. Lady Wootton also reminds us that many crimes on the English statutes are already of this kind (often termed crimes of "strict liability"), such as driving above the speed limit or with blood alcohol above a fixed level. In fact, Wootton argues that "indeed almost certainly, the majority of the cases dealt with by the criminal courts are cases of strict liability in which proof of guilty mind is no longer necessary for consideration."[43] Although it is true that there have been many changes in the criminal law that have increased the extent of strict liability, it is still hard to accept Wootton's claims as true. The changes have been with specific laws (e.g., drunk driving determined by blood alcohol level; "illegal use" for joyriding where intent to steal the automobile could not be proved) or where specific additions have been made to existing laws (e.g., assault is automatically assumed to be a more serious crime if performed with a deadly weapon). The criminal law has indeed made some accommodations to the social defense doctrine. But it has not made the next crucial step: replacing the judicial examination of the mind with the psychiatric examination.

PUNISHMENT AS PROACTIVE: Any strategist knows that the best defense is offense! And this is the strategy recommended by the social defense theorists. Once the focus has been shifted away from offenses on to offenders, it is a simple matter, equipped with the paraphernalia of modern social and psychological science, to develop techniques to identify in advance those persons who are likely to commit crimes. The social defense school, therefore, takes an extremely proactive approach to the administration of criminal sanctions. The many attempts to predict delinquency and crime in the 1950s-60s fall within this school. Once again, Ferri, the realist, saw that the process of criminal justice was severely hampered in its attempt to protect society from dangerous criminals. It seemed perfectly clear to him that a person who had committed prior crimes was a particular kind of person and the law should treat him as such. Thus, the presumption of innocence, the supposed backbone of the retributive penal system, should be abandoned where such persons are involved. Instead, it is reasonable, in fact it is the duty of the state in order to protect the rights of law-abiding citizens, to assume in the enforcement and investigatory process that an accused who has a prior offense is guilty so that the bureaucratic and inefficient machinery of "due process" can be dispensed with and the criminal quickly incapacitated. Logically, he suggested that severity of punishment should be increased considerably with each relapse.

The jury system was also more a hindrance than a help in attaining the levels of social defense. Ferri saw it mostly as an ameliorative mechanism to a bad law and quotes approvingly Bentham's dictum that he would rather have "a remedy in law than subversion in law."[44] Furthermore, since the evaluation of the offender was to be no longer moral or judicial, but scientific, there was no place for lay people to make these kinds of sophisticated judgments.

Taken to its extreme, then, the social defense theorist would pursue his protection of society beyond the law as we know it. He would approve the incapacitation of persons on the grounds of their probable dangerousness;[45] he would approve a strong enforcement model which assumes guilt of offenders with prior offense records; he would rewrite the criminal law to define crime in terms of harm to society rather than individual moral culpability. This is, however, the extreme. Ferri, in fact, did construct a model penal code based on his social defense theory which does indeed recognize the basic distinction between offenses committed by "malice" and by "impudence." He does, however, justify this distinction not so much on the ethico-juridical ground that "malicious intent" makes an act more wicked or evil, but rather that it reflects on the increased dangerousness of the offender.[46] To pursue this fascinating problem further would take us beyond the bounds of the book, but it is clearly an important area in need of study. Unlike Bentham, Ferri did not construct a completely new system of morals. Instead, he stuck with the existing Italian criminal code and tried to redefine it from his social defense perspective. The result is a delicate blend of the juridical and scientific analyses of behavior. His model code was rejected by the Italian government as far too radical, which of course it was in its implications. One cannot abolish wickedness by calling it by another name. Or if one thinks one has, sooner or later it will be rediscovered.

STATUS OF THE OFFENDER: It is abundantly clear that in order to achieve society's protection against crime, straight out discrimination against particular types of persons in society is warranted. Those most discriminated against are the habitual and dangerous offenders, who should be separated from society as efficiently and swiftly as possible. However, once separated, all the social defense theorists agree that the offender should be treated humanely,[47] although the meaning of this word varies from one theorist to another. For some, it has automatically been assumed that to "treat" (medically, psychologically, etc.) is *prima facie* more humane than to punish. Thus, treatment was seen as ameliorating considerably the long, indeterminate prison terms recommended by the social defense theorists. There are, of course, problems with the assumption that treatment, even in nonpenal conditions, is "humane," and this mainly has to do with infliction of pain or violation of the body.[48] For Ferri, collective work and the criminal's repayment of damages was the humane treatment. He was especially critical of the cellular systems of American prison practice.

One may logically take the dangerous offender focus to even further extremes, as does Ferri. If the causes of criminal behavior are biological (inherited), psychological (family relationships), and social (economic conditions), then it follows that a truly preventive social defense will countenance the punishment of not only the offender, but also his family. Ferri takes us, approvingly, back to Plato who argued: "admitting the principle that children ought not to suffer for the crimes of their parents, yet, putting the case of a father, a grandfather, and a great grandfather who had been condemned to death, their descendants should be banished, as belonging to an incorrigible family."[49] It follows that the modern social defense theorist who is concerned with prevention, should approve, if not of the banishment, of the treatment of the children of the offender's family. This argument for the secondary punishment of the offender's family is not so wild as it seems. Wootton and others have argued for the punishment of the parents of delinquents. It is now well established that many cases of child beating are generational, passed on from parent to child. Family therapy sees the responsibility for the treatment of the patient as going beyond the patient himself.

Now we see the true meaning of social responsibility. The social defense theorists do not eradicate moral responsibility at all. They keep it and add to it a series of other responsibilities—social, psychological, and biological. You are responsible for what you are. Therefore it follows that you are responsible for what you do, since you are what you do.

There is, finally, no way of avoiding the idea that to the social defense theorist the criminal is a kind of enemy. It is therefore difficult to see how he can be treated "humanely" from this perspective or even how a doctrine of social individualism can work in practice. Admittedly, the level of protection may be high, but the costs in terms of power to the state and the risks of one's victimization by the system (as opposed to the offender) may also be prohibitive. But to those living in the high crime areas of the inner city, the social defense approach must surely seem appealing. The costs and dangers may not be as serious as they appear, however, as we shall see in the final chapter.

DISCRETION: If the juridical elements of the criminal law were retained (e.g., the concepts of intent), then judges could be expected to be encouraged to use considerable discretion in evaluating each individual case. However, under an extreme social defense system, the judge's role would be reduced simply to ascertaining whether a crime had occurred or not and whether the accused was its author. The evaluation of the mental element would be carried out by experts in the medical, psychological, and social sciences in order that the offender could be diagnosed and classified and the sentence made on the basis of this classification. It is clear that many of the traditional rules of evidence in criminal law would also have to be discarded, since the scientific evaluation of the criminal makes use of all available sources of information. The possibility for almost uncontrolled discretion, especially by the scientific evaluators, is very great. This is why, of course, it has never happened at the trial level. And in most modern situations at the corrections level, in Italy at least, a judge sits in conjunction with the diagnostic team in deciding subsequent disposition of the offender when sentenced. The extreme result, in the corrections sphere, of social defense by treatment of offenders was the famous Herstedvester Prison, whose director was a psychiatrist, not a prison administrator, and whose inmates were all placed on indeterminate sentences.

Conclusion

Each of the three approaches makes specific moral arguments, but it should be recognized that these arguments often rest on assumptions of fact. Can one punish an offender's criminal act, but truly leave the offender unscathed by the punishment, as the retributivists claim? Can punishment be shown to deter individual offenders? Is the general population actually deterred by the demonstration of criminal punishment? Can individuals be treated rather than punished? Although it is a controversial issue in the realm of ethics, I suggest that no moral theory, at least as far as punishment is concerned, is sufficient when stated in a vacuum. Its fact basis must also be demonstrated.

11

The Science of Punishment

The scientific study of punishment is embedded in the work of the great learning psychologists such as Watson, Guthrie, Thorndike, Mowrer, Skinner, and many others. Yet although punishments (most often electric shocks) as well as rewards were widely used by all these experimenters, few textbooks gave much attention to the process of punishment. In fact, it was not until 1964 that Professor R. L. Solomon,[1] in a now celebrated paper, subjected the research of the twentieth century to a balanced review, demonstrating that the findings of the effects of punishment had been ignored by most leading learning theorists. In fact, it was clear that B. F. Skinner had invented a legend that punishment "did not work," or if it did, the side effects it caused were too great to make it useful. In 1953, five years after he wrote his utopia *Walden Two* which depicted a society without punishment, Skinner announced: "In the long run punishment, unlike reinforcement, works to the disadvantage of both the punished organism and the punishing agency."[2] And up to 1961, he announced that punishment had only immediate and no lasting effects—unlike "positive reinforcement," rewards.[3] As Professor Solomon pointed out, Skinner's conclusion was hardly based on the research evidence. True, there had been many cases where the suppressive effects of punishment could not be demonstrated, but there were also a host of experiments where its effectiveness was unquestionable. Much of the disagreement had occurred because of a failure to take into account the variable effects of the kinds of punishments used, the subjects used, and many other factors that we will shortly discuss.

There is another set of studies of relevance to punishment in criminal justice, most of which have been conducted in the last decade. These are the econometric and statistical studies of the effects of deterrence. They analyze changes in crime rates in relation to variations in criminal punishments. Although most of these studies appear to have been conducted in ignorance of the established concepts of learning theory, we shall see that they have developed many of the same concepts.

How Punishment Works

There are probably as many different definitions or models of punishment as there are different schools of learning theory. When one reads the research, one is more and more impressed by the complexity of the concept, especially that it appears impossible to define punishment generally except operationally, in terms of the stimulus used and its direct effects on the behavior of the subject. Lest there should be any doubt that "punishment" is involved, the following is a description of a typical experiment in which a rat was punished by the famous psychologist, O. H. Mowrer:

> 1st trial: On insertion of food rod, rat dashed, quite as usual, to the rod and, taking it in his forepaws, started eating. Shock was applied. Rat dropped rod and "danced" around on the grill until shock went off.
> 2nd trial: After an interval of two minutes, food rod was again presented. Rat immediately ran to the rod, took it in forepaws, and started eating. When shock was applied, rat dropped rod, danced much as before, and squealed slightly.
> 3rd trial: This time rat ran toward rod and tried to grab the food off it, with teeth, without taking rod in forepaws. Probably got some food, but also got shocked. Danced and squealed.
> 4th trial: Very much like preceding trial.
> 5th trial: Rat would run toward food rod, then suddenly withdraw, pause a moment, and then repeat this performance. The "conflict" between hunger and fear of being shocked was thus very evident. After four or five successive advances toward and retreats from the food bar (without actually touching it), the rat came briefly to rest at some distance, and the experiment was discontinued.[4]

The single-minded, desired effect of punishment is to eliminate a particular behavior or sequence of behavior. Learning theory provides us with at least six ways in which this effect may be brought about.

FEAR: As in Mowrer's experiment described above, some have hypothesized that a noxious or painful stimulus, if presented at the same time as the undesirable behavior, will invoke fear in the subject, which will then be attached to the undesirable response. Thus, the response is eventually eliminated. The model here is generally that of Pavlovian conditioning (though Mowrer's is a slight variation). This process depends on the construct "fear" as the modifier of behavior. The punishment must evoke a fear response if it is to work, otherwise the undesirable behavior will only be eliminated temporarily by the pain from the noxious stimulus. For lasting effects, fear must be conditioned onto the unwanted behavior. However, some studies have reported that fear acted as a facilitator of responses,[5] which has led to an investigation of alternative hypotheses.

THE COMPETING RESPONSE HYPOTHESIS: E. R. Guthrie wrote that "punishment achieves its effects . . . by forcing the animal or the child to do something different."[6] Guthrie uses the example that if one wishes to stop a dog from jumping through a hoop, one will punish him in the front, not the rear. That is, the punishment is incompatible with the punished act, so the act will be suppressed. However, if one punishes the dog in the rear, he will jump through the hoop and instead of suppressing the act, punishment facilitates it.

THE ESCAPE HYPOTHESIS: Some would reinterpret Guthrie's example as being one of escape training. For example, we have a six-foot alleyway, with delineated goal and start boxes and an electrified grid floor. We place the rat in the start box and shock him immediately as the start box gate is raised. We persist in shocking him until he enters the goal box where there is no shock. The rat has escaped to the goal box. In subsequent trials, he quickly learns to make it to the goal. We have used punishment to teach him an alternate behavior.

THE DISCRIMINATION HYPOTHESIS: This approach is somewhat more "cognitive" in suggesting that subjects will discriminate between behaviors that are punished and rewarded. There have been many studies which presented rewards for alternate behaviors as well as punishments for unwanted behaviors,[7] with the result that extinction of unwanted behaviors occurred more rapidly. Similarly, for older children, elimination of unwanted behavior was achieved more easily by adding explanations of why the behavior had been punished, thus making it more clear under what conditions the behavior would be punished.[8]

THE SUPPRESSION HYPOTHESIS: E. L. Thorndike's original statement of the law of effect clearly described this effect of punishment: "When a modifiable connection between a situation and a response is made and accompanied or followed by an annoying state of affairs, its strength is decreased."[9] The assumption is that some form of inhibition is involved in suppressing the punished act.

THE AVOIDANCE HYPOTHESIS: If we return to our experiment of escape training and modify it slightly, it becomes one of avoidance training. Instead of shocking the rat in the start box, we give him five seconds to reach the goal box after the start gate has been raised. Only then do we shock him, and he usually learns to reach the goal box easily. He must, however, seek the goal, and so we call it active avoidance learning. Now, let us change the experiment once more. This time, we allow the rat to run the alley and reward him with food in the goal box. Then, after performance is well established, we shock him in the goal box, and eliminate the food (reward). Soon the rat stops running and stays in the start box. In this latter experiment (passive avoidance learning) we have taught the rat what not to do. In both escape training and active avoidance learning, we have taught the rat what to do. Punishment has been used in both experiments.

It is clear that punishment may be used both as a goad to action and as a suppressor of action. There is much research evidence to support both effects.[10] They are also sometimes termed, in the literature, "punishment training" and "avoidance training." Punishment training is the situation in which punishment is applied only after the unwanted act has been performed (the analogue of retribution). In avoidance training, punishment is applied before the unwanted act (the analogue of deterrence). We can see, however, that this terminology confuses things no end, since in the last experiment I described, punishment came after the unwanted behavior. It produced avoidance in the sense that the goal behavior had been previously built up by rewards, but when shocked, the rat learned to "avoid" the goal box. One might also just as easily say that he "suppressed" the behavior. The only way we can make any sense of this is to see punishment as a painful stimulus that occurs in a sequence of *events*. At least in the laboratory this is almost always the case (except in the rare examples of "one trial learning".). A punishment may be presented contiguously with one unconditioned response, but viewed within a sequence of trials, it is only truly "contiguous" in the first trial. It may be expected or anticipated more and more as the trials are repeated.

Differential Punishability of Behaviors

Can some kinds of behaviors be more easily eliminated than others? It would appear so. According to Professor Solomon, there are two kinds of behavior that have been shown in the laboratory to be easily inhibited by punishment. These are (1) "instrumental acts" or those acts that have previously been established by the experimenter by using a reward schedule, and (2) "consummatory acts" which are those concerned with the completion or satisfaction of basic consummatory behaviors, such as eating, drinking, sex. It has been shown time and again that if you punish instead of reward consummatory behavior, the animal (cat, dog, or monkey) will very quickly learn to starve itself, in some instances even to death.[11] There are, however, two kinds of behavior that are enhanced by punishment. One is a certain kind of instinctive behavior (imprinting) which appears to be facilitated by fear, and the other is behavior that has previously been established by punishment procedures.

Generalization

The process of generalization is also a well-established concept in learning theory. By this theorem, we should expect that the effects of punishment on particular kinds of behavior should generalize to other similar behaviors and situations. There is considerable research to suggest that this process indeed occurs.[12] We should expect therefore that the punishment of one criminal behavior (i.e., an offense) should generalize to other criminal behaviors which should be eliminated as a result of this punishment.

Crime and Punishment from the Laboratory Perspective

We can see that the role of punishment, even in the simplified laboratory setting is extremely complex. In some instances it has been found to be an effective suppressor of behavior, in others it is a stimulus to action.

Are we able to apply any of this knowledge to the problem of crime? Indeed we are. The most obvious immediate applications are to those kinds of "crimes" that are related to "consummatory behavior" such as drug use, alcoholism, deviant sexual behavior. A number of studies have been conducted in this area with mildly supportive results, both in the United States and in Britain. The standard procedure in Britain developed by H. J. Eysenck and his students, has been to show a homosexual, for example, pornographic pictures of homosexual situations and administer a painful stimulus (a shock, loud noise, etc.) and to reward pictures of heterosexual situations. Some success was achieved by these studies, although their lasting effects have yet to be ascertained.[13] Eysenck reports a number of successful cases, including the successful treatment of a man who had a fetish for ladies' handbags and baby carriages.

In the United States, Schwitzgebel[14] conducted a number of studies using drugs to create nausea (the painful stimulus). This was successful with a range of consummatory acts, especially the behavior of the alcoholic who is made nauseous when he goes to drink a glass of liquor. Schwitzgebel reports a number of cases of successful treatment of transvestism, sadism, homosexuality, and alcoholism by using a variety of punishment techniques such as nauseating drugs or electric shocks.

In the area of nonconsummatory behavior in criminal justice, I know of only one U.S. study of the effectiveness of the use of very painful stimuli that could be said to be in any way similar to the noxious stimuli of the laboratory. This is the study by R. Caldwell[15] of the effects on 1,302 offenders who were whipped between 1900 and 1942. Of the 320 prisoners who were whipped once, 61.9 percent were reconvicted. And of those who were whipped twice, 65 percent were again reconvicted. In England two government committees have thoroughly reviewed the effects of corporal punishment on offenders. In his recent book, *The Growth of Crime,* Sir Leon Radzinowicz reviewed these reports and concluded "that there was no evidence that offenders who were flogged as well as being sent to prison did any better than those who simply served terms of imprisonment or penal servitude."

Another area of direct application of the painful conditions of punishment is prison itself. I have already suggested that there may be an analogue between the prison and the experimental laboratory.

A number of studies have been conducted in prisons and juvenile institutions using a variety of behavior modification techniques. Most of these systems, however, are based on reinforcement schedules, using rewards and tokens, and do not rely completely on punishment training. Of course, in most total institutions, it is the combination of punishment with rewards (the most powerful modifier of social behavior according to established experimental research) that is used. The overall effectiveness of these systems has never been adequately evaluated. The advent of "A Clockwork Orange" did much to popularize the notion of modifying behavior through punishments and much to oversell the effectiveness of the technique. Whether or not these systems have worked, the feeling that prisoners are being "manipulated" by the scientific application of punishment is undoubtedly very high. The popular belief, however, grossly overrates the effectiveness of these techniques and usually substitutes science fiction for fact when criticizing it.[16]

These are, however, very limited applications. We must ask the bigger question: does punishment deter criminals or would-be criminals from future offenses?

INDIVIDUAL DETERRENCE: The work of Professor Daniel Glaser is most significant in this regard. His review of all research and statistics on the effectiveness of prison in preventing repeated offenses up until 1964 demonstrated a number of important points. In general, he concluded that approximately one-third of inmates are returned to prison some time after release, usually within two to five years.[17] More recent reviews of the effectiveness of prison as a reformative agent (or at least, if one does not like that term, as a deterrent) have all supported Glaser's conclusions, having found that roughly 40 percent of released prisoners were eventually returned to prison.[18]

These results were once used as evidence that prison is 60 percent effective in deterring future offenses. But such a conclusion cannot be simply drawn, since it is possible to predict with some degree of accuracy, on the basis of age, prior record, and type of offense, whether or not the offender will recidivate. These factors have nothing to do with what goes on in prison. No studies have been able to isolate prison as the effective agent that brings about the 60 percent rate of "reform."

It is nevertheless important to recognize that the studies of recommittal to prison necessarily deal with a sample with a double bias.

First, those who end up in prison for the first time usually have an extensive record of prior arrests or convictions. That is, it is very rare for a first offender to be sentenced to prison. We are, therefore, never dealing with "first offenders," or those one might expect to recidivate less. Second, the large institutions whose recidivism rates have been studied accumulate "hard core" offenders, since they receive longer prison terms. Thus, at any one time, a large prison will have a very high proportion of repeated offenders—much higher than in the general population. We should, therefore, expect a high recidivism rate for these institutions.

It has also been found that the length of prison term (i.e., severity of the punishment) has no demonstrable relationship to subsequent criminal behavior.[19] But again, such studies are confounded by the double bias of the sample, and there are some who insist that length of prison term *has* been shown to be an effective individual deterrent.[20]

Today, in the face of these conflicting interpretations of research findings, modern experts on the effectiveness of prison have nevertheless concluded that, "With few and isolated exceptions, the rehabilitative efforts [of corrections] that have been reported so far have had no appreciable effect on recidivism."[21] Why is this so when laboratory research suggests that punishment ought to work?

There are many answers to this question. One has total control over the punishment schedule in the lab. There is virtually no control in the criminal justice system. Prison as a punishment also lacks the specificity or "clarity" of the physical punishment so often employed in the laboratory. Though different persons no doubt have different pain thresholds, the variations are probably much less than individuals' perceptions of prison as painful. Furthermore, in the lab a series of short trials are performed in which a brief but effective punishment is used. On the contrary, in the criminal justice system, each "trial" (beginning with arrest through the end of prison term) is very, very long, by laboratory standards. Thus, the quality and duration of the punishment is much more complex in real life. Finally, we have seen that punishment may, under certain conditions, enhance unwanted behavior. It may be that behaviors learned in prison, perhaps "criminal behaviors" from other inmates, will be reinforced by the punishment of prison, since these behaviors have been established as a result of the punishment procedure.

GENERAL DETERRENCE AND MODELING: The "macro research" of punishment in criminology has concerned itself with general deterrence, not individual deterrence. Generally, the approach has been to compare variations in crime rates with variations in official criminal punishments and draw conclusions as to the effects of punishment on crime rates. The assumption here is that it is the general populace that is deterred by the punishment of an individual criminal. The scientific validity of the position requires that at least the psychological process of the general deterrence model be demonstrated. If it can be done in the laboratory, so much the better.

The general deterrence process has been clearly demonstrated to work in the laboratory by the long string of studies conducted to investigate the effects of modeling. In these experiments, models or actors are punished (varying the usual conditions of punishment and avoidance training, the status of the model, the subject, etc.), and the effects of these observed punishments upon the audience are assessed.[22] Much of the research in this area was conducted in relation to the learning of aggression from aggressive models and, incidentally, the complicating factor of punishers necessarily being perceived as aggressive. Although there is a wide variety of research findings in this area, it may safely be concluded that an audience (once again, usually children) learns response repertoires from watching models who are rewarded or punished and that many of the basic principles of direct learning also apply to learning from models. Modeling is the laboratory analogue of general deterrence. The general population is the audience, the various agents of the criminal justice systems are the model punishers, and the criminal the model for unwanted behavior which is punished. Of course, the audience's perceptions of the respective roles of these models and the relationship between the audience and the models are crucial to the outcome of the punishment, just as is the child's relationship to the punisher, usually a teacher or mother figure, in the lab experiments. The important point I wish to emphasize here is simply that the psychological process of general deterrence has been unequivocally demonstrated to work. Therefore, the macro studies of general deterrence are not founded on an arbitrary psychology, or even a simplistic psychology, as is often argued.

Now that we have established that fact, let us look at the research on the major parameters of punishment effectiveness in both the laboratory and the field. One should keep in mind that we will be continually jumping from the experiment where the individual is the direct observer of punishment to the collective level where an individual is part of a large audience to the punishment of role models. Indeed, at the macro level of research, we commonly lose sight of the individual who is one of that mysterious group who did *not* commit a crime. Those who *did* commit a crime are, of course, those for whom the general deterrence process did not work.

The Parameters of Punishment Effectiveness

THE SEVERITY OF PUNISHMENT: The early work of W. K. Estes and B. F. Skinner[23] led them to the conclusion that the suppressing effects of punishment were only temporary. They increased the severity of punishment (the intensity of the electric shock), but this had no effect on the rate of extinction (elimination) of the unwanted behavior. This conclusion stood unchallenged for twenty years. But, as we have seen, it was eventually proved superficial. The work of N. H. Azrin and W. C. Holz[24] and many others clearly demonstrated that "both non-rewarded and rewarded behavior can be quickly, completely, and permanently suppressed by punishment, provided it is severe enough."[25] Indeed, I have already reported the cases of animals "choosing" to starve to death rather than perform a food-rewarded but also punished behavior.

It is comparatively easy to gauge increments in the severity of punishment when one is using electric shock as punishment. What of other punishments and other subjects? Studies have not been conducted using very high intensities of punishment on human subjects because of ethical considerations. Thus, the findings for animals cannot be truly tested with humans. A number of studies have been conducted on children (the next best to animal subjects!) where intensity of punishment has been varied. The high intensity punishment used in these studies was typically a verbal rebuke, "No, that's for the other boy," combined with a loud noise (of around ninety decibels). It was found in these studies, with only a few exceptions, that "high-intensity physical punishment in most circumstances more effectively inhibits the punished behavior than does punishment that is less intense."[26] These researchers found that this principle applied even in the case of severe punishment for aggression in the home. Although severe punishment has been found to be characteristic of parents with aggressive children, their children's aggression occurs outside the home. Within the home, the aggressive behavior is effectively suppressed by severe punishment.[27]

The exception to this research has been the study by Aronfreed and Leff[28] who found that high intensity punishment did not always lead to better inhibition of behavior when children were placed in a temptation situation. These deviant results were explained by postulating that the punishment involved a high level of anxiety in the subjects which interfered with their ability to make the discriminations as to the appropriate behavior. In other words, it was argued that intense punishment creates an emotional level that interferes with the learning process. Other studies that have not supported the severity hypothesis have been those of field studies of child rearing, where parents have reported according to rating scales the degree, severity, and frequency of their punishment practices.[29]

We now turn to the criminological studies of general deterrence.[30] The pioneering works in this field were those which tried to demonstrate that the death penalty had no deterrent effect on homicide rates. The general approach of these studies, mostly conducted in the 1950s, was to compare the homicide rates of various states in the United States that had abolished the death penalty to those that retained it. The results of all of these studies have since been debated and reinterpreted to support either abolition or retention of the death penalty. However, the conclusions made at the time by these researchers themselves were generally that the death penalty could not be proved to have a deterrent effect.[31] Then, in a longitudinal study which examined homicide rates before and after abolition of the death penalty in particular states, Thorsten Sellin concluded, "there is no clear evidence in any of the figures we have examined that the abolition of capital punishment has led to an increase in the homicide rate, or that its reintroduction has led to its fall."[32] These results do not support the laboratory findings of the effectiveness of a severe punishment as an inhibitor.

However, there were many methodological flaws in these early studies, and consequently a new generation of deterrence research began in the late 1960s which used increasingly sophisticated statistical and methodological tools. This series of studies began with that by Professor Gibbs of the University of Arizona. For the first time, the parameters of severity and certainty of punishment were examined. Using the median number of months served in prison as the measure of severity of punishment, Gibbs examined homicides from 1959-61, using the rates provided by the FBI's *Uniform Crime Reports*. He found that as the homicide rate increased, the severity of punishments decreased. Using similar, though increasingly sophisticated measures, especially the inclusion of control variables, a long string of studies up until 1975 have generally supported this finding. Of twelve major studies during this period, eight found the same relationship between severity of punishment and homicide rates.[33] The relationship was more difficult to uphold for other crimes (the

FBI index crimes, which include homicide, rape, aggravated assault, larceny over $50, and auto theft, were most commonly examined). In fact, two of the studies, while finding support for the deterrence hypothesis for homicide rates, found the opposite for other crimes: crime rates for other index crimes, especially auto theft, *increased* as severity of punishment increased.[34] Thus, punishment may have facilitated the criminal behavior rather than suppressed it.

However, there were many uncontrolled variables in these studies, because we know that there are many factors that affect fluctuations in crime rates apart from punishment. The more important factors might be the level of activity of law enforcement, the number of personnel employed, changing social and economic factors. Few of these studies were able to control for such extraneous variables, but the more recent did to some extent. They also studied different time periods, although the bulk of supporting studies analyzed the same time period as Gibbs's original study. Only two of the discrepant studies were conducted for that period.

We may conclude, then, that although there are a few discrepant findings, on the whole macro studies of the relationship between the severity of punishment and the homicide rate provide general support for the deterrence hypothesis. These findings, taken together with the laboratory studies, allow us to conclude that very severe punishment should have a strong general deterrent effect.

THE DELAY OF PUNISHMENT: The experimental research conducted on animals, children, and adults is quite clear about this. The effectiveness of punishment in inhibiting undesirable behavior in animals decreases markedly as it is delayed from zero to five seconds after the undesirable act,[35] reaching a minimum of effectiveness after about thirty seconds. In a classic study of beagles, Solomon and his co-workers gave the dogs "taboo training" by providing them with ordinary dry dog chow in a dish beside another dish of very savory fresh canned horse meat. The dogs were trained to eat only the dry chow; each time a beagle tried to eat the delicious horse meat, the experimenter punished the dog by a sharp rap on the nose with a rolled up newspaper. The dogs were divided into three groups. Group one was punished as soon as it touched the forbidden meat with the mouth or tongue (no delay); group two was punished five seconds after eating the meat; and group three was punished after fifteen seconds. After the training period the experimenter left the room, and the behavior of the dogs was observed through a one-way mirror. "Resistance to temptation" to break the taboo and eat the forbidden meat was measured by the number of days it took each subject to break the taboo. Needless to say, the no-delay group resisted temptation for much longer than the other groups. But a striking finding was that the delayed punishment groups behaved during the testing period as though the experimenter were still there: "After eating the few dry chow pellets, they put their forepaws upon the experimenter's chair, or hid behind the chair . . . when they finally broke the taboo . . . they ate at brief intervals and ran away between bites." When the zero delay group finally broke the taboo, their mood changed abruptly and they happily ate the horse meat without any apparent "guilt."[36]

Similar experiments have been conducted with children, using a loud noise, sometimes accompanied by a verbal rebuke as the punishment for playing with forbidden toys. Once again, the longer the delay, the less effective the punishment.[37]

In criminological research there have been no formal studies on the effects of delayed punishment on deterrence of crime, although it is popularly believed that punishment has so little apparent individual deterrent effect because it is delayed so long in the criminal justice system. This is further exacerbated by the argument that most crimes provide the perpetrator with immediate rewards. Eysenck[38] has argued that an immediate reward will influence an organism much more than a delayed punishment, though there has been some disagreement since it has been shown that punishments can "reach back" further than rewards.[39]

There are a number of arguments against this interpretation of the lack of effectiveness of punishment in criminal justice because of delay. First, it may be argued (indeed, can be shown) that humans look ahead and can anticipate punishments more easily than animals, and therefore a delayed punishment acts almost immediately on the undesirable response. There are, in fact, ways of administering punishment to enhance this effect.[40] Second, there may be many secondary punishments attached to the forbidden act, such as the social stigma of getting caught. Again, the effects of "secondary reinforcers" have been well demonstrated in the laboratory.

It now becomes clear to us why the modern deterrence theorist has put more emphasis on the threat of punishment than the punishment itself. In this way, he is able to account for the obvious and unavoidable delay in actual punishment of the perpetrator. To the writer's knowledge, no experimental research has been conducted into the effects of threats of physical punishment versus actual physical punishment. In general, verbal rebukes have been found to be not as effective as physical punishments, but again these verbal punishments have usually been employed *after* the forbidden act. To test deterrence theory, the threats must obviously be made before—considerably before—the expected onset of the forbidden act.

Only one study has been conducted directly on this problem of threat, but threat of physical punishment was not used.[41] Using the usual "resistance to temptation" experiment, children were "punished" with severe and mild threats. For the mild threat, the child was told that the experimenter "would not be pleased" with him if he played with the forbidden toys. The severe threat added to this was that the toys would be taken away, the child would be "treated like a baby." Both threats were completely successful in inhibiting temptation to play with the forbidden toys. Since these threats may be considered rather mild as punishments go (as far as threats go for that matter!), these are rather striking findings. There is a great need to follow up this study with investigations into the effectiveness of different kinds of threats, such as withdrawal of love versus physical punishment, compared with other types of punishments and with reward—in fact, in relation to all the parameters of punishment that we are reviewing in this chapter.

It is worth noting that, as far as the criminal justice system is concerned, delay of punishment is not necessarily all that great. We tend to think of the punishment as being the sentence, if a fine, or the time served in prison. One could argue, however, that the process of punishment begins at the point of apprehension and the eventual sentence is simply the end of a punishment of very long duration.

The only way to increase the actual immediacy of punishment would be to allow for immediate and abrupt punishment such as was employed by the Romans for *furtum manifestum.* A thief caught in the act could be summarily dealt with on the spot. This is not possible with our current criminal laws, except in some instances of parking and traffic violations where a fine may be charged immediately upon apprehension. Even here, however, the immediacy of punishment depends entirely on detection of the crime. It is apparent that in criminal justice the delay or timing of punishments merges with the question of certainty of punishment. In practice, they are not always easily separable; but in the laboratory we can study them separately.

CERTAINTY OF PUNISHMENT: A common finding of two well-known field studies of delinquency was that the delinquents experienced inconsistent or erratic punishment at home.[42] The punishment practices to which they referred were those that mixed love-oriented techniques with laxity and punitiveness.

In a pioneering study by Fisher,[43] one group of pups was consistently rewarded by petting and fondling when they approached the experimenter. Another group received the same training except that they were occasionally shocked for making approaching responses. The pups who were both rewarded and shocked became much more dependent on the experimenter: their behavior had been strengthened rather than inhibited by the punishment. Similar results in pairing rewards with punishment have been found in a number of studies using animals, human adults, and children.[44] In fact, it has been found that children resist extinction of previously learned behavior when they have been both punished and rewarded for that behavior more than those who are rewarded only.

All of these studies have investigated only one aspect of inconsistency: the unpredictability of rewards or punishments. Other models of inconsistency could be employed, such as differing degrees of intensity of punishment—gradual increase or a sudden increase of punishment—or differing schedules of punishment administered by different experimenters in the roles of mother or father. And there are probably many other possible variations.

In the criminological field, since Beccaria and Jeremy Bentham, it is the certainty of punishment that has been the major object of inquiry. This concept can only be partly related to the experimental research on inconsistency since the concept of certainty reflects the basically rationalistic utilitarian model of psychology in which the incipient offender assesses his chances of "getting caught." To my knowledge, the experimental research on inconsistent punishment has not attended to this question, since it characteristically develops a schedule of random punishments which the subject could not learn to predict and therefore work out his chances of "getting caught."[45]

Fortunately, at the macro level of analysis, one never has to get down to those difficult questions of psychology, and previous researchers have contented themselves with constructing a statistical index of certainty. In his pioneering study, Gibbs constructed a "certainty index" simply by dividing the number of persons admitted to prison for homicide during the period he studied (1959-61) by the number of actual criminal homicide cases reported during that year. This way of arriving at a certainty index has been repeated in most subsequent studies.

Of the twelve studies conducted since Gibbs's in 1968, eight found very strong negative correlations between the crime rate and the certainty of punishment.[46] That is, they found that as the certainty of punishment decreased, the crime rate increased. The strength of the relationship was much stronger than that found between severity and crime rate. In fact, for those studies that previously had reported no relationship between severity and crime rate, at least a weak relationship was found for certainty in the expected direction. Only one study found no relationship at all.[47]

COGNITIVE STRUCTURE: All of the experimental research that I have so far described has to some degree relied upon the idea that some kind of internal state, such as fear or anxiety, is invoked by punishment and the subsequent inhibition of the undesired response is reinforced by the reduction in their emotional state. That is, the omission of the act is "rewarded" by a reduction in anxiety or fear. Similarly, we have seen that this emotionality is assumed by one aspect of deterrence theory which emphasizes the importance of the threat of punishment.

Other learning theorists have criticized this approach to punishment as being unduly biased toward behavior based on emotionality rather than "rationality" or "reason," usually termed "cognitive structure." As Professor Parke suggests, "an adequate theory of response inhibition in humans requires that both cognitive and emotional factors be taken into consideration."[48] By "cognitive structure" researchers have usually meant the degree to which reasoning and rationale are used by the punisher to "explain" the punishment. Field studies such as that by R. R. Sears[49] and his collaborators indicate that mothers who combined reasoning with physical punishment reported that punishment was effective more often than mothers who used physical punishment alone.

In the laboratory, experiments were designed more clearly to control the type of reasoning given the child and its effects on response inhibition. The design used was once again the "resistance to temptation" model, in which children were forbidden to touch or play with particular toys and were punished by a loud noise if they did so. Then the experimenter left the room, and the children were observed for their resistance to playing with the forbidden toys. The subjects were divided into groups, "with rationale" and "without rationale." All subjects were told, "Some of these toys you should not touch or play with," and for the rationale group was added: ". . . because I don't have any others like them. And if they were to get broken or worn out from boys playing with them, I wouldn't be able to use them anymore. So for that reason I don't want you to touch or play with some of these toys."[50] The provision of the rationale increased the effectiveness of the punishment to inhibit temptation to play with the forbidden toys. These findings have been repeated in many similar studies.[51] Other studies changed the type of rationale and still found it effective. In the study just described, the rationale was one explaining "objective" reasons for the rule (i.e., the toys will get worn out). In other studies, the rationale was one that emphasized the child's intentions: "*No, you should not have wanted to pick up that thing.*"[52]

Other research has shown that the generalization of response inhibition was not enhanced by the addition of a rationale to the punishment. However, two recent studies have shown that the addition of a rationale enhanced not only the effectiveness of punishment, but also the generalization of the inhibition to other forbidden acts.[53] The reason for this discrepancy may be that those studies demonstrating effectiveness of rationale in generalizing inhibition were conducted with adolescents, whereas most other studies were with younger children. The explanation advanced is that younger children respond to the immediacy of punishment and to each situation separately. In contrast, as the child grows older, he learns to discriminate the situation in which he is punished and develops general rules for his behavior. Thus, the cognitive structure of the punishment situation is more effective for the older child, because he is assisted in interpreting the situation by the rules he has learned and therefore is able also to generalize to other situations. Parke reports research that supports this hypothesis.[54]

The relevance of cognitive structure to criminological research on punishment is, of course, crucial. One of the broad assumptions of the criminal law is that the ordinary man knows what the law says and is thus able to adjust his behavior accordingly. The criminal law does not allow ignorance of the law as a defense, except in the rare cases of retroactive laws. Some apparently disturbing studies have been conducted in this area.

We saw in the last chapter how proponents of the utilitarian principles of punishment argue for the general preventive functions of the criminal law. People are not only deterred by the threat of punishment, but also learn as a result of the "moralizing educative and habituative" process of the criminal law. It follows, then, that law-abiding people should have a good knowledge of the criminal law, especially its punishments, and offenders should have a very poor knowledge.

The fact is, many studies have found that most people have precious little knowledge about the criminal law and its penalties.[55] In a well-known study, D. Miller[56] interviewed "criminals, potential criminals and law abiding citizens" and found that the general population had the least amount of knowledge concerning punishments for a variety of offenses, such as assault with a deadly weapon, rape, and check forgery. The sample of adult incarcerees was the most knowledgeable. Of course it is obvious that those who have been punished for crimes and mixed with others who have also been punished will naturally be more knowledgeable about punishment than the general population. One would therefore predict, according to the cognitive structure hypothesis, that this group would commit fewer crimes in the future. We know also that this is not the case. Miller's study cannot be used to disprove the general deterrence hypothesis, since one would need to survey those who have not yet committed an offense, but do subsequent to the survey, to be able to make a valid comparison with the general population's knowledge of the criminal law and its punishments. A further argument is often made that it is not so much specific knowledge of crimes and their punishments that is important, but a general disposition toward law-abiding behavior. But again, if one surveys the general population, according to their general perceptions of the seriousness of crime and punishment, and compares this with subsections of the population that display statistically higher rates of crime (e.g., poor black, lower social class), one finds generally no substantial differences.[57]

Perhaps what we should look at is not the knowledge of the punishments or the law per se, but the assessment that people make of the probability of being caught. It may well be that criminals or potential offenders, because they have more knowledge of the workings of the criminal justice process, are able to make more realistic assessments of the probability of getting caught and the likely severity of the punishment than the general population. Thus, they may assess the "pay-off" (reward) of committing a crime as well worth the expected probability of being punished at all or, if punished, the degree of its severity.[58] This would appear to be highly relevant to those crimes in which the reportability and/or clearance rates are very low (e.g., rape, burglary).

What I have suggested here is that the relationship between certainty and cognitive structure may be crucial to the effectiveness of punishment in the area of criminal justice. Indeed, the comparative importance and interaction among the parameters of punishment has been a major focus of experimental and, to some extent, criminal justice research.

INTERACTION AMONG THE PUNISHMENT PARAMETERS

Severity and Delay. In general, although there is some disagreement, laboratory research suggests that a severe punishment will effectively overcome the weakening effects of delay of punishment. This relationship is more clearly illustrated by Diagram 1.

DIAGRAM 1

*Relationship between Delay and Severity of Punishment
Found under Experimental Conditions*

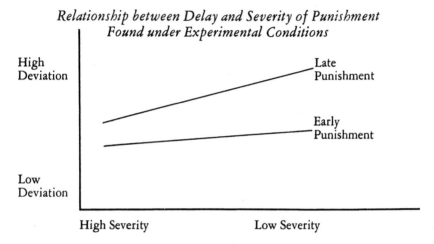

* This and diagrams 2, 3 and 4 are adapted from R. D. Parke, in *Early Experiences and the Process of Socialization,* ed. R. A. Hoppe et al. (New York: Academic Press, 1970), pp. 87–93.

Severity and Certainty. I have been unable to locate any experimental studies that have directly compared the effects of these two punishment parameters, although it would be reasonable to infer that a "sufficiently strong punishment will suppress behavior effectively even if it is only occasional."[59] There is little doubt that severity of punishment is the main or central parameter of punishment as far as the experimental studies are concerned.

Criminal justice research has focused almost entirely on the relationship between these two variables. These studies, where significant negative relationships with the crime rate have been found between certainty or severity, have almost all found certainty to be the more important variable.[60] It has been concluded by a number of these researchers that "severity only has a deterrent impact when the certainty level is high enough to make severity salient."[61] This postulated relationship is illustrated in Diagram 2.

DIAGRAM 2

Postulated Relationship between Certainty and Severity of Punishment Found in Criminal Justice Studies

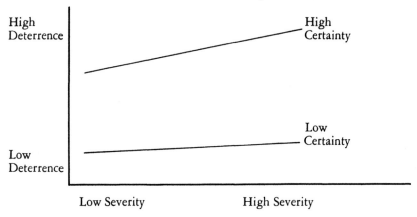

Cognitive Structure, Delay and Severity. As we saw above, high cognitive structure in the form of a rationale accompanying a punishment increased response inhibition. Parke reports a number of studies which have also shown that the provision of a rationale is sufficient to overcome the significant difference between early and late punishment. This relationship is clearly demonstrated in Diagram 3. The

DIAGRAM 3

Relationship between Cognitive Structure and Timing of Punishment

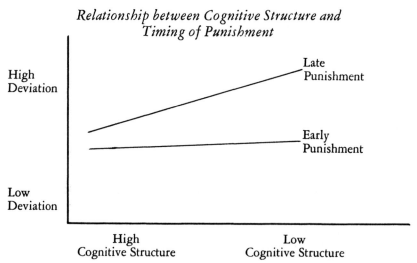

rationale was also able to make up for the loss of effectiveness of low intensity punishment, as we can see from Diagram 4 which displays essentially the same pattern as for delay and cognitive structure.

DIAGRAM 4
Relationship between Severity and Cognitive Structure

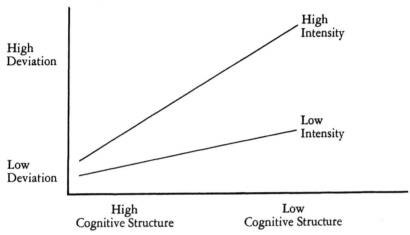

Another important finding has been that the provision of a rationale for the punishment considerably enhances the stability of response inhibition over time. In two studies,[62] it was found that subjects who were provided with a low cognitive structure during the punishment process, while resisting temptation at the initial five-minute testing period, were more likely to perform forbidden acts at later periods (three five-minute periods were used).

Varieties of Behaviors and Their Punishments

The research findings I have reported so far have been limited to a narrow range of punishments and behaviors. In the laboratory the punishments most commonly used have been those of electric shock, and the behaviors punished often have not been clearly specified, though usually they have been "instrumental" behavior—that is, behaviors that would lead the animal to a particular end in a sequence of behavior, such as running a maze where rewards were obtained at the end. For children, the kinds of behaviors punished have predominantly been those of touching or playing with attractive toys which the experimenter has forbidden the child to touch. The punishments most commonly employed here have been loud sounds and occasionally verbal rebukes. Other studies have also used aggression, again defined in a rather narrow setting, as the punishable behavior.

Because most of these experimental studies have been conducted in the laboratory, we must, of course, be wary of generalizing from them to field conditions. However, there is a line of studies, conducted in as close to "real life" conditions as possible, which have investigated the effects of social isolation ("time out") as a punishment on children in the classroom. Over the past ten years several studies have been conducted which have clearly demonstrated that time out is an effective punishment to suppress vocalization, aggression, and "out-of-sort" behavior.[63] The significance of this research is mainly the effects on children other than the child punished. These studies therefore provide the analogue of incapacitation as punishment. They have, however, been conducted predominantly with children of elementary-school age. It would be of special interest if such studies were conducted among adolescents (the upper end of which is the high crime-prone period) to see if incapacitation of delinquents also has desirable effects on other adolescents in contact with them. One suspects that research of this kind should have been conducted before it was decided to "divert" delinquents from the criminal justice system—back, one presumes, into the ordinary school.[64]

Criminal justice studies have mainly confined themselves either to homicide or the FBI index crimes, because statistics on these crimes are easily available. We have seen that deterrence has variable results according to the particular crime and it seems to have its most demonstrable effect on homicide. Two studies that examined other index crimes found that increases in severity and certainty of punishment were related to increases in these crimes, especially auto theft.[65]

A number of studies have been conducted in other areas, using different measures of certainty and severity and examining crimes other than the index crimes. Most of these studies have utilized the early methodology of the death penalty researchers, by taking advantage of changes in the severity and certainty of the law in relation to a particular crime, measuring the rate of that crime before and after the change. It has been found that a drastic increase in penalty and level of enforcement of parking fines on a university campus produced a 30 percent reduction in offenses;[66] but in another study various school offenses, such as violation of alcohol use rules, getting drunk, stealing or marking up library books, were not reduced by direct threats (this study used self-report methods rather than official records of offense rates).[67]

In a study of taxpayers, researchers tried various ways to stop taxpayers from cheating on their returns and found that appeals to conscience worked better than direct threats, although both were very effective.[68] The impact of harsher penalties for speeding was studied in Connecticut, and little support for deterrence was found.[69] Nor was the introduction of harsher penalties for rape found to have any effect on the rape rate in Philadelphia.[70] Finally, the effects of increases in severity and certainty of punishment for skyjacking were studied, using the reports of skyjacking in the *New York Times* as the measure of the "skyjacking rate." Increase in the certainty of punishment was found to have marked effects on reduction in the number of skyjackings, but the effects of severity appeared to be unsupportable.[71]

In general, our conclusions are that although there are some mixed results, deterrence has been shown to work for some crimes, especially if certainty of punishment is strong. The effects of increasing severity of punishment for crimes needs further study, but it appears as though severity is of lesser importance in suppressing unwanted behavior in the real-life situation of crime. This bears consideration since the majority of experimental studies have concluded that it is severity that is the dominant parameter of punishment.

Gaps and Shortcomings in Punishment Research

THE GAP BETWEEN THE EXPERIMENT AND REAL LIFE: For many obvious reasons that I have mentioned throughout this chapter, it is extremely risky to jump directly from the experiment to real-life situations. The laboratory resembles the perfect tyranny, and society has not yet achieved such a state of perfection. Thus, the results obtained with animals, children, and even adults although more definitive must be carefully researched in real life.

In fact, learning theorists have been accused of constructing a "mythology of childhood" that has nothing at all to do with real life.[72] But in defense of experimental studies, it must be said that they have led to a clear specification of the basic parameters of punishment and to a thorough analysis of the way punishment works. To bridge the gap to real life, naturalistic observations of the process of punishment would be of great benefit. Occasional surveys suggest to us that physical punishment, for example, is used by almost all parents.[73] Yet we know little of the situations in which they will use it, its effects, and the methods of its application. The more subtle verbal punishments used by both teachers and parents could also stand intensive naturalistic observations. Only in this way will we be able to make the bridge between the laboratory and real life.

SHORTCOMINGS OF CRIMINAL JUSTICE DETERRENCE RESEARCH: There are many, many criticisms made of these studies, so I will only mention the main ones here.[74]

All of the studies have relied on statistical measures of correlation from which one cannot easily make cause–effect conclusions. Thus, if we find that the crime rate during a particular period decreases when certainty increases, it does not follow that increased certainty caused the decrease. Statistically, one could just as well argue that the decrease in crime caused the increase in certainty. We do not make this conclusion because our prior knowledge of the effects of punishment tells us that this is not likely.

Further difficulty arises when one considers that there may be all sorts of other factors that affect the crime rate at the same time as the increase in certainty is operating. For example, there may be changes in official policy, economic conditions, urbanization, age structure of the population, and many other things, especially if the time period is a long one. However, it is true that later economic studies such as Ehrlich's managed to control for many of these factors, although some have argued that his selection of time periods was a crucial determinant of his results.[75]

There is also a "catch 22." To increase the certainty of punishment, one must necessarily increase the level of law enforcement. In so doing, one will necessarily increase the "crime rate" since one would expect the police to arrest more criminals. Thus the "crime rate" will go up rather than down, even though others may have been deterred.

Changes in sentencing policy or legislation may change the way crimes are "charged" and subsequently processed into a particular category. For example, reintroduction of the death penalty could result in more offenders pleading insanity as defense, thus possibly changing the categorization of their offense.

The majority of the sophisticated methodological studies have used imprisonment as their sole indicator of punishment. Investigation into a wide range of "punishments" concomitant to processing the offender from arrest to sentence ought to be considered, as we have seen that different punishments do have different effects.

Perhaps the most common argument against deterrence theory has been that it assumes a simplistic underlying psychology. It is surely quite clear that this criticism is unfounded. It was never applicable to Bentham's psychology, and is even less so to the psychology of punishment reviewed in this chapter, all of which may be construed as underpinning the assumptions of deterrence theory. There is the suggestion, though, that research and theory should be extended into the more cognitive aspects of punishment which both deterrence theory and punishment research have tended to ignore until very recently. But once we move into this area, I would argue that we are going beyond the meaning of the word "deterrence" and should substitute the word "prevention," which incorporates a much broader array of psychological, social, and political processes.

RESEARCH INTO GENERAL PREVENTION: If we were seriously interested in the prevention of crime by using punishment, we would go beyond the conventional punishing only after a crime is committed, and take seriously the writings of various authors concerning the moralizing, habituative, and educative effects of the criminal law. This expanded view of general prevention shows the great relevance of the research on the effects of punishment on children, since we know that, if habits or education are to be effective, starting early is a great advantage. The logical extension of this view, then, is that children should be educated from an early age concerning punishment and criminal laws that are both possible and dealt out. Research is therefore needed to investigate the process by which children learn not to commit crimes (i.e., socialization). Since most studies have shown that people are blissfully ignorant of the criminal law and its penalties, perhaps the crime rate is high because of this. A developmental approach seems to be more appropriate here.

PUBLICITY: A major point in Bentham's system was that the punishment of a crime should be widely and flamboyantly publicized. Up until the nineteenth century this aim was indeed achieved since, as we have seen, the public or community played a central part in the punishment—in many cases in actually administering the punishment, for example, the pillory. The popular belief appears to be that publicity of crimes, especially the fictional crimes of a TV series, *encour-*

ages the commission of more crimes.[76] Publicity is a central variable that has been left out of almost all deterrence studies, yet the communication of threats has been a central feature of advertising media in health and other propaganda campaigns. Considerable research evidence suggests that the use of threats of unpleasant consequences is most effective in changing behavior and attitudes.[77] The campaigns against smoking, overweight, toothpaste advertisements that emphasize "no cavities," and many others, make use of this long line of research. Once again, however, it has generally been found that milder threats appear to be more effective than severe threats. Research in the area of effectiveness of legal threats has been limited to the study mentioned earlier concerning tax statements, where it was found that threats were effective, but not as effective as "appeals to conscience." Another study sent threatening letters ("the records of the Department of Motor Vehicles show that you may be a negligent operator as defined by law") which mentioned the possibility of license suspension. Traffic convictions were substantially reduced by this threat.[78]

A recent study on the effects of publicity of punishment on the general deterrence of homicide has been conducted by Carol Trilling.[79] This study is noteworthy for the number of controls used, the elimination of spurious variables, and its use of individual homicide data.[80] Trilling found only minimal support for the general deterrent effects of actual punishment on the homicide rate, nor did she find any significant effects of the publicity of punishment as a deterrent. Bentham envisaged a day when the publicity of punishment would be enough in itself. So far, the empirical evidence does not favor his optimism.

Conclusions

What conclusions can we make from this bewildering array of research findings and interpretations? I have suggested that the retributivists must build a stronger case if it is shown that a single punishment may affect the whole person. We have seen from the laboratory research that punishments may be administered in such a degree and kind as to have an enormous effect on an individual, but may also eliminate specific behaviors and apparently leave the rest of the person's behavioral repertoire unaffected. The empirical evidence, therefore, is not damaging to the retributive argument, though it still remains for the retributivist to provide us with his list of retributive punishments and to spell out their effects, or lack of effects, on the individual.

The utilitarian is on much shakier ground. Although the laboratory experiments have shown that the models of both individual and general deterrence *should* work, empirical evidence from real life situations is inconclusive. The utilitarian, therefore, who supposedly sees punishment as inherently evil and must therefore demonstrate that the good it brings outweighs the bad (i.e., that punishment actually "deters" or "prevents" crime), finds himself in the position of having to admit that he is administering an evil even though there is no hard evidence that it is doing any good.

In the face of such uncertainty and doubt about its efficacy, why do we persist in its use? Throughout this book, I have given historical and cultural reasons in answer to this question. Perhaps the more obvious answer is that we are simply all sadists.

12

The Punishers
and the Punished

If the surveys of parental use of punishment are to be believed, the chances are that just about everyone has been physically punished; over 90 percent of persons surveyed in many studies since the 1930s report that they were spanked as children, and a similarly high proportion of parents admit to using corporal punishment with their children.[1] We also saw in Chapter 4 that corporal punishment of school children continues to be widespread. Therefore, the chances are that most people reading this book will not only have been corporally punished during their lives, but also will have found themselves in the role of punisher. To draw the distinction, therefore, between the punishers and the punished in terms of static characteristics such as personality traits appears highly artificial, since punishing and being punished are experiences common to us all. However, it may be that there are wide individual differences in responsiveness to punishment, either as the punisher or the punishee, so it is well to look at some of the research which postulates the existence of such differences and their personal and social correlates.

The Punished

Professor Eysenck[2] of the Maudsley Institute has advanced a number of propositions based on laboratory research of the kind that I have described in the previous chapter. Eysenck's basic propositions are:

1. The general population may be divided roughly into two broad personality or character types: introverts and extroverts. Cutting across this division is a continuum ranging from high to low neuroticism. These characteristics are defined and isolated according to pencil and paper tests developed by Eysenck.

2. There is a wide variation in susceptibility of individuals to punishment (conditioning) and these individual differences are distributed throughout the population normally just as height, weight, and intelligence. Furthermore, conditionability is an inherited biological disposition.

3. Generally, extroverts are less easily conditioned than introverts.

4. Although extroverts are less susceptible to physical punishments, they may be more susceptible to punishments that isolate them, such as prison, sensory deprivation, time out. Introverts are more susceptible to all types of punishment, especially physical punishment.[3]

This theory, while possibly plausible for some types of crimes, such as those built up through habit, cannot apply wholesale. It clearly conflicts with the most dominant crime causation theory in the United States, the theory of differential association, which argues that criminals learn crime from other criminals. They therefore must be good learners, not bad learners, to become criminals. Eysenck's theory, however, would apply if he could show that extroverts responded quickly to immediate rewards, but very slowly to punishments, since it has been suggested that most crimes provide the offender with immediate rewards.[4] When one overlays the neuroticism factor in Eysenck's model, this is in fact what he argues, since a factor of neuroticism is inability to delay gratification.

One could go on for many pages outlining a host of typologies of criminals and potential criminals and arguing for their greater or lesser responsiveness to punishment. However, it must be recognized that attempts to establish differences in personality and character traits and values between criminals and noncriminals have remained generally unconvincing. Although there are no doubt some specific types of personality "disorders" which are more likely than other types of behavior disorders to get a person caught up in the criminal justice system (e.g., the "psychopath" or "sociopath," the "dangerously violent person," the "kleptomaniac"—and the existence of these more extreme types is even strongly questioned by many), the majority of criminals cannot be distinguished by general personality characteristics from the noncriminal population, that is, of course, if one controls for social class, race, age, and sex.

It is a well-established fact that our prisons are populated predominantly by the lower socioeconomic classes, predominantly young, black males. While we cannot easily conclude that the first offenders of this specific group have offended because they were not susceptible to the threat of punishment, since there are a host of other reasons people commit crimes that may easily overwhelm the threat of punishment, it is a fact that the majority of repeat offenders are also from this specific group. Recognizing that the majority of the young, poor, black male population does not end up in prison, we are surely forced to conclude that there must be something special or peculiar to this group of repeaters. If, when we conduct our tests and cannot find essential differences between this offender group and the non-offender group, it makes a lot of sense to begin at the most obvious point: that the repeat offenders have not suppressed their criminal behaviors as a result of the punishment they have experienced. Therefore, either they are less susceptible to the effects of punishment as a suppressor or the process of punishment applied by the criminal justice system is having the opposite effect of facilitating the undesirable behavior. The most common circumstances in which this occurs, according to the experimental punishment research, are when one punishes behavior that has previously been established by punishment training or when rewards are used at the same time as punishment for the same behavior. Since research suggests that lower-class blacks punish with physical punishment[5] more than middle-class whites (who use guilt as the major mechanism of socialization), one might conclude that indeed much of black criminality has been established as a result of punishment training. For example, a juvenile gang member's misbehavior may bring him immediate rewards, such as status or "rep" with other gang members. If his parents find out, he may be severely physically chastised. Thus he is punished and rewarded, the net result being the strengthening of his mischievous gang behavior. According to punishment research, subsequent punishment will merely facilitate this undesirable behavior.

Psychoanalysts have argued that certain individuals have an overwhelming desire to be punished and commit crimes to satisfy this desire. Actually, as we saw in Chapter 2, the classical psychoanalyst would say that we all have an urge to be punished. Some psychoanalytical theorists have suggested that the middle class punishes much more behavior than the lower class, since the repression of sex is of major importance for the middle class. Perhaps this may have been so some years ago when these theories were invented, but it is certainly questionable today.[6] It would also lead to the hypothesis that middle-class individuals should be more criminal, since they need more punishment because they are more guilty. It turns out, however, that the middle class are more guilty about administering punishment, rather than receiving it, as we shall see.

Other psychoanalysts have pointed to the ability of certain individuals to play upon punishment to suit their own ends. Many of Professor Fritz Redl's aggressive delinquents tried all manners of trickery to provoke their group leaders into physically chastising them.[7] Punishment can be useful to the punished as a defense mechanism, especially if the punisher is full of guilt about administering punishment and it is physical punishment. We shall have more to say about this later, when we consider Professor Redl's punishment techniques.

To cover all the possibilities of behavioral types, their responsiveness to punishment, and their overlap with crime would take another book and would also take us beyond the boundaries of this brief survey. Suffice it to say that since we know that there are wide individual variations in height, weight, intelligence, response to pain, and many other attributes, it is reasonable to assume that there are wide variations in response to punishment. That such persons are distributed randomly throughout society's institutions is surely doubtful. Basketball players are, after all, abnormally tall. Why shouldn't repeat offenders be abnormally criminal?

One policy conclusion is inescapable. Since it would appear that, as a group, lower-class, young black males are currently least deterrable by criminal punishment, utilitarian doctrine leads us to recommend this group as a target group, for which special attempts should be made to increase the certainty of punishment, convey the threat of punishment, and publicize the application of punishment. Would this be discrimination? In the final chapter we will consider this problem in more detail, and hopefully resolve it.

The Punisher

We are all punishers. So long as there are children and animals in the world, there will always be someone readily available to punish. Parents, teachers, foremen, managers, and so on are called upon to punish those under them at some time or another. Among other things, the effective deployment of punishment makes them "good" or "bad" parents, teachers, or managers. Punishment is therefore very close to most of our hearts, and we find it very difficult to separate our thinking from our emotional attachment to it.

Most important, since we have all been on the receiving end of punishment, we find it very difficult to separate the process of punishment from the almost universal authoritarian nature of the situations in which it occurs. This point was most clearly demonstrated by the famous Milgram experiments.[8] In these studies, Milgram, using confederate subjects, tricked naïve experimenters into thinking that they were giving electric shocks to the subjects who were supposed to learn certain memory tasks. Whenever the subject gave a wrong answer (prearranged to be about three out of every four), the naïve experimenter was instructed to administer an electric shock to the "victim," who then responded increasingly with screams and kicking at the wall. The dial of the bogus generator ranged from "slight shock" to "Danger: Severe Shock." Of his forty subjects, only fourteen refused to obey the command to go beyond the level of extreme shock. Twenty-six shocked up to the extreme end of the dial, beyond the "Danger" point, even though they perceived that the shocks were very severe and heard the victims' screams.

Many different conclusions may be made from Milgram's studies. Milgram insists that the results obtained were most unexpected and that a group of college students surveyed as well as a number of Milgram's colleagues predicted that the majority of subjects would disobey much sooner. But from what we know of the cultural history of punishment of the Western world, these results are not at all surprising. It is perfectly natural for physical punishments, even severe punishments, to be administered to persons of lesser power on the commands of those of higher authority. Why should it be resisted when punishment is so much a part of the fabric of our way of life? The question not addressed by Milgram, therefore, was whether or not it was obedience that caused the naïve experimenters to punish the victims so mercilessly or the physical punishment itself. Would the naïve experimenters, for example, have obeyed commands to take off their clothes and copulate with the "victims"? Or would they have obeyed the commands if they had been allowed, say, half an hour to have a drink and get to know the "victim" first? The experiments leave many questions unanswered and have been criticized from many different points of view.[9] The popular conclusion drawn from these studies is that man is weak and obedient and, because of this, the situations of Nazi concentration camps arise. It should be said, however, that many of Milgram's naïve experimenters showed signs of deep stress and strain. Milgram describes one such person:

> I observed a mature and initially poised businessman enter the laboratory smiling and confident. Within 20 minutes he was reduced to a twitching, stuttering wreck, who was rapidly approaching a state of nervous collapse. He constantly pulled on his earlobe, and twisted his hands. At one point, he pushed his fist into his forehead and muttered: "Oh God, let's stop it." And yet he continued to respond to every word of the experimenter and obeyed to the end.[10]

The interpretation overlaid on these observations has been that the subjects did not really want to punish and only did so because they were told to, thus the considerable stress exhibited during the experiments. But we have seen throughout this book that we are deeply ambivalent about the use of punishment and have gone to all sorts of lengths to avoid directly administering it, or at least shouldering the responsibility for it. In the Milgram situation, it was not only perfectly clear who was doing the punishment, but it was also perfectly clear who was giving the commands or at least explicitly bearing the responsibility for administering the punishment. An alternative interpretation therefore may be that the subjects *wanted* to punish the victims and felt stress simply because of this desire. And since virtually all punishment in modern society is administered within an authoritarian setting, with the view to repressing undesirable behavior, the authoritarian setting provided in the experiment was a perfect one to enhance the subject's preparedness to punish.

The results are therefore not at all surprising, although they are significant, since the experiments do provide one analogue for the closed authoritarian situation of total institutions. Indeed, many of these findings were ratified by another famous experiment by Zimbardo,[11] who thrust college students into a "mock prison" and once again found that "ordinary" students suddenly developed harsh authoritarian and punitive attributes when forced to play the role of guards. Once again we should not be surprised at these findings. Punishment is embedded in the history of our culture and is deeply imprinted on our characters. Given the appropriate authoritarian conditions, it is only to be expected that "ordinary" persons will punish. This is especially true when the subjects, as in both experiments, are necessarily placed in a situation that is half real and half unreal so that they have no external cues to assist them in dealing with the deep psychological urges of culture that they are exposed to. It is likely that many were perceptually disoriented and unable to make firm judgments of what they were doing.

Authority, in our society, is inextricably and profoundly related to punishment. We have reached the stage, in fact, when one wonders whether either could exist without the other. Can one imagine punishment occurring between peers? This would be the experimental analogue of retributive punishment. Retribution has receded so far from our society that it has never been investigated in the same way as has utilitarian (authoritarian) punishment. This is, of course, understandable since our society depends upon authority for the maintenance of social order. Studies of retribution would necessarily turn to mutual bargaining over punishments.[12] The most insightful work in this area has been that conducted by the great Swiss psychologist, Jean Piaget in his study of the moral judgment of children. Piaget showed that blind obedience to authority, the parent, is the first justification of punishment learned by the young child, and this justification is later imputed to siblings and playmates who punish them. Piaget then argues that out of the basic structure of the social life of the child, a cooperative model of punishment ensues, where each child sees his punishment by another child as reciprocal or justified on the grounds of "mutual respect." In this way, children's games are played, and the rules abided by:

> The ethics of mutual respect, which is that of good (as opposed to duty), and of autonomy, leads, in the domain of justice, to the development of equity, which is the idea at the bottom of distributive justice and of reciprocity.[13]

Apart from the superficial assumptions of the nature of distributive justice, which I will discuss in more detail in the following chapter, Piaget also makes one very large assumption—that the structure of social relationships among children is made up of "equals." One doubts this very much since studies of gangs suggest that they can be highly structured in status. In this situation, "mutual respect" is more likely to mean respect for status or physical prowess. One might argue that, by definition, punishment between siblings should be dominated by the authority of each sibling over the other (i.e., the older or bigger over the smaller). However, since the parents have total control over the assignment of status in the family, they may easily cut across the "natural" pecking order and assign status according to other criteria, such as intelligence, success at school, beauty, etc. In this situation, it can be seen that the function of punishment among siblings would become a quest for status rather than mutual respect.

However, in the area of children's games, where children are "equalized" by the rules, Piaget did indeed show that punishment was justified by children on the grounds of reciprocity or mutual respect. His discovery of reciprocal punishment in children is of considerable importance to an evolutionary theory of punishment, as we shall see in the following chapter.

For the moment, we may conclude that probably all of us possess the desire to punish others of less power than ourselves, but we also suffer considerable guilt for wanting to do so. Moreover, there seems to be a third force (reciprocity) which demands that, in situations of wrongdoing, one *must* use punishment—and many feel guilty over that! In his treatment of aggressive children, for example, Professor Redl reports that even his trained clinicians who are, or were then, renowned for their nonpunitive approach, felt guilty if they did not use punishment techniques.[14] The conclusion is that perfect authoritarian conditions in which direct responsibility of the punisher is not clear provide the best possible situations for the ordinary man to turn into a torturer.

The experiments I have described were, after all, experiments of brief duration. What of situations in which these conditions pertain for long periods in real life? What do we know about prison guards, executioners, and torturers? Unhappily, very little, and what is known tends to be shrouded in myth and romance.

Executioners: The Hangmen of England

The history of and beliefs about the kinds of men who became executioners through British history make fascinating stories on their own, and certainly some of them were great characters in their own right.[15] In 1616, one Gregory Brandon succeeded the famous Derrick who executed the Lord of Essex, and through a practical joke, he was granted a coat of arms. From that day he was called "Esquire" and the honorific title has been attached to all executioners since. Brandon's son, Richard Brandon, "qualified for the post as a boy by beheading cats and dogs."[16] He was followed by one Lowen and then Edward Dun, who had the doubtful honor of exhuming Cromwell's body and hanging it.

On September 11, 1663, the most famous of all English hangmen, Jack Ketch, succeeded to the office and held it until 1686. During his "reign" he beheaded, hanged, and burnt many people, and bungled two famous executions—those of Lord Russell in 1683 and the Duke of Monmouth in 1685, in which he took several strokes to sever their heads. The belief is that he was a brutal, bloodthirsty fellow who was hated by the people. Since his name has ever since been used as a synonym for "hangman," one might say that he gave subsequent hangmen a bad name.

The next hangman of notoriety was John Price who hanged from 1714 to 1715. On taking the job, he began to live beyond his means and was eventually arrested for stealing seven shillings. This caused him to lose his job as hangman, and his life proceeded to go downhill. He became constantly drunk, was eventually accused and convicted of murdering Elizabeth White, and was sentenced to be hanged and gibbeted, a sentence that was carried out much to the delight of a vast crowd. The execution was accomplished on the spot where he was said to have committed the crime. His successor as executioner was William Marvell, a blacksmith. The strong Marvell was called upon to separate many pretenders to the throne from their heads, and it is reported that even though he received an extra three pounds for each execution of a peer, he found the demands of the job at Tower Hill too much for him and he eventually broke down and became dangerously ill. He turned to women and wine. A writ was eventually issued for his arrest, which was presented as he was on his way to Tyburn to perform an execution. The mob pounced on Marvell and he was unmercifully beaten. The execution could not be carried out, and a public furor broke out. He was turned out of office for neglect of his duties and so became progressively derelict. Finally, the unhappy Marvell stole ten silk handkerchiefs, was caught, and shipped off to the plantations of America.

Two more executioners, the "shadowy figures of Banks and Arnet,"[17] who followed were responsible for executing the most famous of English criminals, Jack Sheppard and Jonathan Wilde. Next came the laughing hangman, John Hooper (1728-35), "the ugliest being that could be imagined."[18] He was followed in 1735 by John Thrift, who held the office for seventeen years. Thrift was the "most polite hangman who had been born into the world." Unfortunately, his first execution, on March 11, 1735, required that he hang thirteen criminals at once, and in the excitement he forgot to pull down the caps over their faces—a serious oversight for which he was reprimanded. His next misfortune was when, after the hanging of Thomas Reynolds, the executed man thrust back the lid of his coffin and sat up! The methodical Thrift set to and hanged him again, only to be set upon by the mob and severely beaten. He was only doing his job!

The Jacobite rebellion of 1745 brought Thrift his most terrible tasks. On 30 July 1746, he was required to hang, draw, and quarter nine gentlemen. Nauseated, Thrift ploughed through his work, and even managed to bellow to the crowd at the end "God save King George." Gradually, Thrift began to lose his nerve, and in the execution of Lord Balmerino and Charles Radcliffe he made a terrible mess, unable to cleanly sever their heads. Every Jacobite in London now hated him. Eventually, in March 1750, at six o'clock in the evening as he was walking home from St. Gile's Church, he was chased by a mob shouting "Jack Ketch." He returned home for his cutlass, retaliated, and a man was killed in the open street. All onlookers insisted that Thrift had done it. He was convicted, but amid great suspense. He was eventually pardoned (he had only killed a Jacobite after all) and returned to office. It had all been too much for him, and he became dangerously ill and died. The mob even attacked his coffin.

Thomas Turlis, "the greatest of them all," took over in 1752. Turlis must indeed have been a strong man. He was constantly attacked, abused, covered with filth, but still he did his job. His was the very turbulent period, it will be remembered, in which Wilkes conducted his campaign against Parliament. It was Turlis who executed the mad Lord Ferrers, who caused a spectacle by giving money to the executioner's assistant instead of Turlis himself, as was the custom, causing a scuffle to break out between the two. An unseemly sight!

Next came Edward Dennis, whose "occasional stupidity prevented him from reaching the highest place in his profession."[19] It was Dennis to whom fell the job of executing the Reverend William Dodd, whose execution was made the biggest issue in the growing movement against public executions. The rumors were that Dennis was paid by Dodd's supporters to cut him down early and support his legs as he hung, so that he could later be revived. But all attempts failed. The Gordon riots also occurred during this time. Dennis happened to be passing a shop that was being pillaged by rioters and joined in. He was caught, found guilty, and sentenced to death. Dennis groveled before the judge and cried, "My will was innocent, my body was compelled."[20] Justice could never be so sweet: "He who has swung so many must at last swing himself!" it was said at the time. But he was granted a free pardon, "so that he could hang his fellow rioters." Once again we see that the justice of order reigned over the justice of reciprocity.

Dennis's assistant William Brunskill took over duties in 1786. This was not a good period for the executioner, since the number of executions was decreasing and many more were being sentenced to transportation. Next came Langley in 1814, followed by James Botting in 1817, whose *magnum opus* was the execution of the Cato Street gang on May 1, 1820.[21] Botting has been described as a ghoul, as was his successor James Foxen. It was reported that a city contractor who had done Foxen some favors asked him if he would have the heart to execute him should he be condemned to death. Replied Foxen: "Well Mister, somebody'd have to do it, so why not me, because I know how to do it more comfortably than anyone else."[22]

Then came Thomas Cheshire, of whom "everyone seems to have agreed that no finer specimen of humanity ever existed." He had a "basilish gleam of his eye" a "stealthy cat-like-clutch." Cheshire hobnobbed with "any scoundrel in the lowest tap-room." William Calcraft took over in 1829 and reigned until 1874—longer than any other hangman. In contrast to all other hangmen Calcraft was a "simple, kindly creature." However, although the "drop" had been introduced to the scaffold many years before, he insisted on a very short drop, so that his victims still suffered considerably from strangulation. Finally, after a long career, he died in 1879 and was immediately succeeded by William Marwood. The standard joke at that time was:

"If Pa killed Ma, who'd kill Pa?"

"Marwood."

Again, like Calcraft, Marwood (a "God-fearing man and a good husband"), appears to have attained a considerable measure of respect based on his ability to carry out his craft. He was indeed fond of saying of his predecessor, "He hanged them, I execute them."[23]

It was Marwood who devised the method of calculating the length of the drop so that death could be instantaneous from breaking the neck, rather than strangulation. Marwood was the last of the great hangmen, the man who modernized the craft.

Torturers

Dr. Frantz Fanon describes a number of cases of policemen or police inspectors suffering mental disorders as a result of administering torture to prisoners during the early stages of the Algerian revolution of independence against the French. The plight of the torturer is seen, by the torturer, as just as bad as or even worse than the tortured. A European police inspector (twenty-eight years old), who was severely depressed and had resorted to stuffing his ears with cotton wool to avoid hearing the screams he imagined during the night, complained:

> . . . they think they're going to be killed right away. But we're not interested in killing them. What we want is information. When we're dealing with those tough ones, the first thing we do is to make them squeal; and sooner or later we manage it. That's already a victory. Afterward we go in. Mind you, we'd like to avoid that. But they don't make things easy for us. Now I've come so as I hear their screams even when I'm at home. Especially the screams of the ones who died at the police headquarters. Doctor, I'm fed up with this job. And if you manage to cure me, I'll ask to be transferred to France. If they refuse, I'll resign. . . .
>
> . . . sometimes we almost wanted to tell them that if they had a bit of consideration for us they'd speak out without forcing us to spend hours tearing information word by word out of them. But you might as well talk to the wall. To all the questions we asked they'd only say "I don't know." Even when we asked them what their name was. If we asked them where they lived, they'd say "I don't know." So, of course, we have to go through with it. But they scream too much. At the beginning that made me laugh. But afterward I was a bit shaken. Nowadays as soon as I hear someone shouting I can tell you exactly at what stage of the questioning we've got to. The chap who's had two blows of the fist and a belt of the baton behind his ear has a certain way of speaking, of shouting, and of saying he's innocent. After he's been left two hours strung up by his wrists he has another kind of voice. After the bath, still another. And so on. But above all it's after the electricity that it becomes really too much. You'd say that the chap was going to die any minute. Of course there are some that don't scream; those are the tough ones.[24]

We see here shades of Milgram's experiment, when the punisher can stand it no more. Fanon reports another case of a European police inspector who made similar complaints about the inconsiderate, uncooperative nature of his victims:

> Our problem is as follows: are you able to make this fellow talk? It's a question of personal success. You see, you're competing with the others. In the end your fists are ruined . . . sometimes I torture people for ten hours at a stretch . . . you may not realize but it's very tiring.[25]

The problem that this man had was that he began to develop irresistible urges to settle every minor frustration with violent aggression. The incident that precipitated his appealing to Fanon (the psychiatrist) for help, was when he suddenly found himself tying up and beating his wife and children—yet before he had always been a mild and understanding father and husband. His plea to the psychiatrist was to help him go on torturing Algerians without any prickings of conscience. Fanon does not say how he responded to this bizarre but genuine request. He notes, however, that to assist in establishing such a state of calm would be simply to assist the development of a coherent, perfect sadism characterized by the popular image of the executioner who loves birds and the peace of listening to a symphony. That is, the executioner learns to separate his role as executioner from the rest of his personality.

The descriptions we have of Calcraft and Marwood perhaps suggest that this is what they were at last able to do in an increasingly sophisticated society in which the division of labor was becoming more and more evident. But prior to Calcraft, the descriptions we have of the hangmen are those of despicable persons, many of whom were unable to bear the psychological stress of their tasks, just as Fanon's patients. We can understand why a number of the executioners ended up on the other end of their rope!

Are we to conclude that those persons who devote their occupational lives to punishing others are sadists? Or, to be less extreme, are we to conclude that those who enter an occupation of punishment will become sadists as a result?

Are Prison Guards Sadists?

The small number of studies of prison guards, analyzed carefully, suggest that guards are no more sadistic or racist, either through their selection or after years on the job, than the rest of the population. Professor Hawkins in his excellent review of the prison literature concludes: "The truth . . . is simply that . . . guards . . . are for the most part ordinary human beings with ordinary failings and virtues."[26] It is true that they develop certain set ways of dealing with crises or of "explaining" inmate behavior.[27] These ways of behaving might be called rigid or stereotyped, but they are not sadistic. If this is so, if it is true that prison guards are basically no different from their counterparts in the "outside" population in character structure (assuming of course that social class, age, and sex are held constant), why do incidents such as Attica erupt with periodic frequency? The answer is that it is precisely because prison guards are "ordinary people" that they will indulge in violence—depending on the circumstance, either with or without provocation. Why? To answer this we must once again turn to the psychoanalysts and go back to the beginning of history.

In Chapter 2 I argued that the first truly cataclysmic act of violence was when the "father" of the primal horde was killed (and maybe even eaten). After that superhuman act of domination, men became extremely obedient, since they had killed. Death required that a great deal of time be spent transferring the rituals of obedience to the natural world and the world of social order. Man has since then developed visions of alternative social orders, and from time to time, he has risen up with super acts of domination (revolutions) only to fall back into almost slavish submission. Freud at first insisted that the basis of this aggression to kill the father was sexual, and thus he saw aggression and its characterological form of sadism as definitely sexual. But in his later work, *Civilization and Its Discontents,* the concepts of libido and aggression were almost cut loose from their biological roots in sexuality and became what I would call "cultural forces"—Eros, the life builder, and Thanatos, death the destroyer. Erich Fromm has extended this idea to describe the necrophiliac: the asexual sadist who kills and destroys for its own sake. Hitler, of course, is the archetype for this character. But to consider such extreme types leads us away from the majority of those who punish in real life, and that includes those under Hitler. Hitler destroyed out of a desire for total destruction. This is not to say that he did not use punishment in the traditional sense. Indeed he did so brilliantly by isolating a target group for the most severe punishment. But this was merely a means to mobilize the masses, to involve them directly in punishment.

It fell, as it always does, upon the obedient to administer punishment. It is now clear from the research of Fromm and Bettleheim[28] that those who were least able to resist these orders of destructive punishment were those who had not developed a clear and coherent set of convictions and values about the social order—usually, it seems, the middle-class Jews within the concentration camp, some of whom "identified" with the aggressors. Outside the concentration camp, it was the middle-class Protestant Germans who went over easily to Nazism, as Reich so brilliantly analyzed.[29] And it is entirely understandable. Because of the deep ambivalence toward dominance and submission we have felt since the beginning of history, the people in the middle—the middle-class man in society; the guard in prison; the teller in the bank; the teacher in the school; the ward supervisor in the mental institution; the policeman on the beat; the foreman in the factory—are the ones who face the greatest dilemmas in the use of punishment. They reflect our culture's ambivalence: they must punish and be punished; they must answer and be answered. When the social order places any of these "middle men" in an untenable position, such as police officers ordered to torture Algerians for ten hours a day or young and inexperienced prison guards from Upstate New York forced to supervise "bitter, angry, unintimidated aggressive inmates . . . many of whom regarded themselves as political prisoners"[30] (the situation during the Attica tragedy), it is little wonder that old cultural solutions will be relied on. Thus, Tannenbaum claimed that the "keynote to understanding the psychology of the prison keeper" was "the exercise of authority and the resulting enjoyment of brutality."[31] Tannenbaum is slightly inaccurate. Prison guards have only an ambiguous authority, as G. M. Sykes well demonstrated: "the custodians . . . far from being converted into brutal tyrants, are under strong pressure to compromise with their captives, for it is a paradox that they can ensure their dominance only by allowing it to be corrupted."[32] We have every reason to accept both observations as valid: given the deep ambivalence within all people concerning the use of punishment and its relationship to social order (i.e., the ongoing system of dominance and submission), a man could go either way depending on the condition of the prison and, most important, the conditions of the inmates he must confront. The deep interdependence between the dominant and the subordinate is, of course, a well-established fact in sociology.[33] It also applies to the relationship between the punisher and the punished, to which we may now turn.

The Punisher-Punishee Relationship

It is incredible that so little research has been devoted to this question in criminal justice. The only work I know of that has been directed to this question is that of Professor Fritz Redl, and it is stretching a point to place his work within the bounds of criminal justice.

Fritz Redl's work, entirely with children, puts punishment into proper perspective by arguing that punishment—"a painful attempt by the adult to influence either the behavior or the long range development of a child on a group of children, for their own benefit, by exposing them to an unpleasant experience"[34]—is only one of seventeen, and probably many more, ways of intervening or influencing children's behavior. In contrast to the torturer who is stuck with only one method, from which there is no escape for either him or the victim, a central feature of Redl's ego psychology is that in the use of punishment, escape hatches must always be available contingencies for both the punisher and punished.

The approach that Redl develops becomes a problem of analyzing carefully all situations in which punishment seems warranted (in terms of Redl's definition, not of the "principles of punishment") as a strategy for dealing with undesirable behavior. This requires that one have a detailed knowledge of the child in the psychoanalytical sense: a thorough case history, a deep understanding of his "mind"— that is, ego and superego function—based, for Redl at least, squarely on close observation of the child's ongoing behavior. In other words, it develops into a battle of wits.

For punishment to be successful, Redl recommends the following pointers:

1. Make sure the child actually experiences displeasure. As he points out, some children might like to be sent to their room, so they can masturbate!

2. The normal reaction to punishment is anger, so this should be taken into account when choosing and administering punishment, with due regard to the surrounding circumstances. Above all, one should not be surprised that the punishee gets angry when punished even though he may recognize that he "deserved" it.

3. The source of the child's displeasure (the adult who administers the punishment) and its real causes (his own misbehavior) must be made clear to the child.

4. If one is successful with (3), the child should get mad at himself for having misbehaved. This may lead to "regret" or "turning over a new leaf."

5. In a future temptation of similar kind, the child may make use of this experience, thus avoiding punishment.

Redl is also careful to point out that for some children—"children who hate," who are extremely aggressive—punishment in any form is completely useless, in fact plays into their hands. The process just described is a simple account of an extremely complex cognitive process, and it is in cognitive function that Redl has found the extremely aggressive child to be seriously disturbed. Such children are therefore unable, for example, to distinguish between the source of their predicament and its cause as described in (3). They are unable to use the experience to their advantage; in fact, they will often distort it completely in an effort to reinforce their view of the world as totally rejecting and discriminating against them. They will, if they can, maneuver the potential punisher into punishing harshly or even doing something that they can easily distort into "unjustified punishment."[35] For these children, "punishment is a marginal control technique" or a technique to be used for additional "reality rub-in" in later stages and not a technique for repair.[36]

A considerable amount of research has been conducted by learning theorists concerning the relationship between the punisher and the punished. Once again, this research has been with children. As a preliminary observation, we might note that there is, on the surface at least, a contradiction in their approach since, according to the principle of generalization, one would expect the punished child to reject or become fearful of the punishing agent. There is some evidence to support this,[37] but generally it appears not to be the case. In fact there are experiments that suggest the opposite, or at least that severe punishment may create excessive dependency on the punishing adult for the child.[38] Ethologists have found that punishment of young geese and other animals will increase the strength of "imprinting," the attachment of newly born chicks to an immediate object, such as the experimenter.

Most research, both experimental and field research, has suggested that the existence of a warm or "nurturant" relationship between parent and child enhances the effectiveness of all forms of punishment, since there are two negative reinforcers: the punishment itself, and the withdrawal of love.[39]

Our conclusion is that to those who are on the front line of punishment, such as guards, teachers, and parents, attempts to apply the "principles of punishment" in the heat of the moment may be fruitless. Punishment becomes rather a tool that is part of an arsenal of weapons the punisher and punishee may use in trying to control each other's behavior. To try to apply, for example, a retributive principle in a complicated setting, such as aggressive delinquents in an institution, without taking into account other social and psychological strategic factors in dealing with the delinquents would be to court disaster. The punishees would very quickly control the punishers. And that is not the way it is supposed to be!

The principles of punishment do not tell us how to be effective punishers. The science of punishment tells us that. Instead, the principles of punishment tell us how to use punishment morally, and the morality of these principles often rests on an assumed empirical base.

The Blood of the Murdered crying for Vengeance.

13

Conclusions: The Justice (and Grace) of Punishment

The Evolution of Punishment

Punishment has gradually evolved from a form displaying a wide range of horrendous punishments, as well as a wide range of more "acceptable" punishments, to a form today where the range of punishments is extremely narrow. The use of punishments involving bodily injury to the offender has been severely constricted; spectacular punishments of public ridicule are hardly ever resorted to; the death penalty, compared to even 100 years ago, is virtually nonexistent; the physical, and possibly psychological, conditions of prisons are far better today than at any other time in history.

Is this true progress or only an illusion? It is popularly argued that more punishment is dished out today, since there are more people in prisons. And what about psychological punishment? The answer is that it is by no means clear that there are more people in prisons, compared to previous periods in history, especially at the height of the Spanish Inquisition which used prison as its main punishment. And this is not even taking into account the thousands subjected to the galleys, slavery, and exile. Psychological punishment is also clearly far less common today. The punishments involving public ridicule, penance, and the psychological stress of the inquisitorial system were surely the most severe psychological punishments, verging on psychological torture.

Progress has been made. The problem is to assess its quality. For example, our rejection or, more accurately, our repression of harsh physical punishments is so absolute that we carry it to the point of injustice. It is no longer possible, indeed, it is unthinkable, to whip an offender as full punishment for an offense. Yet surely this might be more just than putting him in prison for a couple of years and thus indirectly punishing his family as well. In this instance, the justice of our preference for prison seems hard to defend. It is even more strange that we still allow people legally to beat children, yet we do not allow this for criminals. Is this just?

The answer to these questions depends upon three interrelated judgments. It requires an assessment of the nature of evolution, a judgment about the direction that civilization has taken, and finally a moral analysis of the fundamental concept of order. In what follows, I have undertaken to make these judgments, using a rather coarse psychoanalytic perspective. I have chosen psychoanalysis, aware as I am that the aspects of the theory upon which I depend are highly speculative and have been seriously criticized by many.[1] But it provides not so much an argument for the "true" origins of civilization, which after all nobody knows, as a graphic analogue within which to present a moral theory. Psychoanalysis, more than any other theory, highlights the paradoxical nature of the basis of our civilization. So when I speak of the primal crime, I am speaking of a myth, not a fact. And when I use the word "crime," I am using it in its broadest popular sense, not as a legal or even criminological term. I should add that many of the sociological conclusions that I arrive at, especially concerning the nature of order, may be reached using quite different perspectives.[2]

Obedience and the Origin of Order

Obedience has its beginnings in crime itself. This observation is one of the most profound insights that Freud had, yet it is also the most paradoxical. Perhaps I have repeated Freud's reconstruction of the primal crime too often. But I cannot emphasize it enough, since it was such a raw political act in the sense that it created both a political and a social order. It created political order by giving birth to the idea of authority, since the people recognized the right of the leader to enforce rules and thus became obedient rather than oppressed by the raw physical force that existed before the revolt. The paradoxical nature of this analysis must be clear, since it was revolt that created political order. It is small wonder that the maintenance of obedience has been the primary function of punishment in the major spheres of life: crime, family, slavery, military, religion. In fact, the most notable exception to this rule has been when political order broke down, as during the brief period of feuding in the middle ages.

The big question is, why constant punishment to maintain order? Freud's answer was the concept of repression, a word well chosen by Freud, the political connotations of which are often ignored by psychoanalysts. There are two important aspects of this concept in relation to punishment and political order. First, it is a way of dealing with guilt and, in the primitive reconstruction, of "burying" or "forgetting" the crime of having killed the father. We would prefer to forget that political order, a feature without which all complex societies would dissolve into chaos (for reasons that will become clear shortly), was created out of crime. The second feature of repression is that we, in fact, are never able to "forget" anything. Past misdeeds are repressed into the unconscious and remain there forever. All past deeds exist simultaneously. We have a picture of twentieth-century man sitting on top of a massive unconscious, full of guilt—guilt over his past deeds. Put all these men together, and you have a society of guilty, repressed people. Put these people together with their ancestors right back to the primal horde, and you have a whole culture of guilt, a culture built on repression.

But one may well ask, surely if everyone is filled with guilt, this will be enough to insure an almost voluntary or "psychologically determined" submission? Indeed, this is mostly true, but never certain. Authority cannot take chances, since we know that the urge to rise up is just below the surface. We rely on psychological repression to keep it there.

There is a further consideration that men, in comparison to animals, think beyond what they are or have and are therefore able to think beyond the given political order.[3] Mostly, this requires almost superhuman efforts of great thinkers, but we know from various revolutions in history that it can be done. It seems so "simple" and yet it's obviously so complex. Alan Paton, author of that great South African novel *Cry the Beloved Country*, on a CBS news interview[4] mentioned that the white minority in South Africa would be doomed to destruction on the day that the blacks simply said, "You can't do this to me, I won't stand for it anymore." In other words, obedience has been the black man's greatest oppressor. This is not to deny the economic basis to oppression, but only to show that the blacks, "if they wanted to," could rise up tomorrow and take over, or could have done so years ago. It would, of course, require *collective* action, and that is where political ideology becomes so important.

Now we can more clearly see the direct part that punishment plays in the maintenance of political order. Not only does it insure that more and more guilt is built up because of past misdeeds, but it also insures a differentiation between those in authority and subordinates. It is by punishment that authority shows itself. But this requires further clarification, because according to Freud before the crime occurred the primal horde was a raw tyranny, by which he meant that order was maintained by one tyrant using physical force or violence. The argument is that the crime which was committed created an order that was not based directly on physical force but on a certain degree of collective consent. Here is the crux of the matter. The raw tyranny prior to the primal crime was an order in which there was a mass of "equals," each one held individually in check by the leader. They were equals in the sense that they were differentiated only in one dimension: physical violence. Collective action overthrew that dimension of differentiation and introduced another; it decentralized the power structure into clans and family systems. Then, within families and clans, the tyranny of the leader (father) was reproduced, since he was physically the most powerful. Raw tyranny became no longer necessary within the family, since the father now had authority on his side; the people were obedient for reasons other than fear of physical reprisal. The social order was born.

Social Order and the Origins of Inequality

The social order was created out of the division of political spoils. It was, and is, a social order backed by authority, but it is also part of the definition of authority, since the order is social rather than physical (i.e., violence), as it was before the primal crime. Therefore, the social order created both social and political inequality, since its essential element is a social differentiation based on the unequal distribution of authority. The "pecking order" that was created by the primal crime was, in this sense, a "second order," an "artificial order" in contrast to the primal order of raw violence. Now we see what Jeremy Bentham meant when he referred to punishment as artificial. Now we see what he meant when he referred to the community as a fiction. The social order is a differentiation in the social structure of society created by men, first out of a raw act of collective violence, and then diversified out of the guilt of men's minds from having committed such a horrible crime. The great irony in this analysis of the origins of social order is that it was brought about by a collective action which sought equality. But it brought about even more inequality. Instead of a gulf between the leader and the rabble, it introduced a highly complex social organization to fill up that gulf. Thus, a structured inequality became the foundation of authority. Authority cannot exist without it unless we return to the most primitive form of order: tyranny. There have indeed been a number of "regressions" to this form of order in modern civilization—Hitler's Germany was one, where the gulf between the Fürher and the people became immense and the people were indeed equally the children of the fatherland.[5]

In sum, I have suggested that order was created by a criminal act, that order cannot exist without a structured inequality. Order and authority must be maintained by punishment, otherwise there would be even more revolutions and wars than we have had throughout history. The mechanism closely attached to the process of punishment that prevents people rising up and recommitting that original horrible crime over and over again is psychological repression.

It follows that, if crime created order, then the punishment that follows the crime must in some way reflect that crime and, by doing so, determine order. Therefore, to a large degree, we must accept that the distribution of punishment to individuals in society will naturally reflect the basically structured inequality of the social and political order. So, if we wish to show that the distribution of the punishment is unjust, we must show that structured inequality is unjust. And this, I suggest, is very difficult to do, unless one is prepared to either (1) relegate the maintenance of social order to a secondary position of importance, or (2) disagree with my basic postulate that the inequality of authority is essential for order. The arguments against the second point are those made by utopian anarchists and idealistic Marxists and may be dismissed as wishful thinking.[6]

Let us consider the first possibility of relegating the maintenance of the social order to a secondary position, for it turns out to be very relevant to arguments about punishment. Utilitarians, especially through the principles of deterrence, prevention, and social defense, see the maintenance of social order as their primary concern. It is therefore essential to them to demonstrate the morality of their primary justification of punishment: the social order. In contrast, the retributivists usually insist that their primary concern is with the morality of the punished act itself. This would seem to split off the question of morality from the question of the morality of the social order. Our task, then, is to examine two moralities: the morality of the social order assumed by the utilitarians and the morality of, for want of a better term, the moral order,[7] assumed by the retributivists.

The Morality of Social Order

Since I have suggested that the social order was created by a criminal act, it follows that the social order is necessarily immoral, since it is the fruit of crime. Of course, this argument does not stand close scrutiny, since one can think of many instances where the commission of a crime may have very "good" benefits (e.g., assisting a person who is in terrible pain because of terminal illness to commit suicide; murdering Adolf Hitler). In any case, it would seem that we must be able to show that the commission of the crime, a horrible crime at that, was worth the benefits that were gained. So far, I have shown that it produced a society of structured inequality. It is against this endogenous inequality that revolutions are fought, usually on the basis of some form of egalitarian ideology.

Yet, with the increased secularization of our society, social theorists have tended toward the view that what is good for society is good for man. Social order has been equated with moral order. This serious error was, perhaps, first most clearly committed by Emile Durkheim in his analysis of society and his approval of the mechanism of punishment reinforcing the moral indignation, the collective sentiment, and thus the morality of society. The pitfall into which one is led by this analysis is that it does not allow for the obvious facts that there are immoral social orders, such as, the USSR, Hitler's Germany, or Idi Amin's Uganda, or the USA—it all depends on one's morality—or does it?

On what grounds does one adjudge these societies "immoral"? There is only one way to tackle this question and that is to look to history, look to evolution, where we must try to make an assessment of the progress of civilization. In so doing, we must return to the concept of psychological repression. It is only through the use of this concept that any psychological progress in the human species can be shown to have taken place. And, if we went into the theory more fully, we could also see that "material" progress—man's science, technology, industry, and so on—even if it is a product of sublimation, as the Freudians say, is not automatically bad, simply because its products are sublimations. In fact it can only be shown to be "bad" if it can be shown that the process of repression, the precondition of sublimation, is "bad." It is popular today to argue that it is bad, or at least "nearly all bad."[8] But one can just as easily argue the other way. Especially as repression's major function throughout history has been to repress violence. The price we have paid for this, I admit, has been very high—the price of obedience. But the gains have been tremendous.

The major function that repression has served has been to enhance civilized man's capacity to substitute symbolic thought for actual behavior. This capacity is wonderfully illustrated by Eli Sagan in his fascinating analysis of cannibalism.[9] Professor Sagan documents the many and diverse cultures and early tribes of Western civilization that practiced cannibalism. In most cases human flesh was seen as the most delicate and delicious of all foods. There were many instances of individuals, indeed whole cultures, craving human flesh. In the face of such craving, why do we no longer eat it?

We have repressed the desire, and this repression is made the more possible by sublimating it into symbolic satisfaction. Thus, the Christian, when he partakes of the body and blood of Christ in the Eucharist, is obtaining symbolic satisfaction for concrete desires. But the ancient Aztec, who consumes the body of his god, is satisfying concrete desires by a concrete act. In his criticism of the anthropologist Murdock, who interpreted both these acts as identical, Professor Sagan notes:

> The Christian idea of the satisfaction of primitive aggressive needs is far removed from that of the Aztec. The cannibal activity of the Aztec is not a "rare spiritual experience"; it is a gross spiritual experience that is one of the least civilized aspects of Aztec society. It is true that the Aztec does literally what the Christian does symbolically, but it is precisely upon this capacity for symbolization and sublimation that culture is built and civilization erected. It is very important to point out the similarity of the psychological emotion in the Christian and the Aztec, but it is false to equate (psychologically and morally) a literal and a symbolic act.[10]

The morality of our civilization is surely abundantly clear from this example. This is not to say that our current civilization is absolutely moral, but it does affirm that we have progressed. Nor does this mean that, had civilization taken another direction, it might have turned out better. All it means is that, relative to yesterday, civiliza- ion is "moral." My view of morality therefore is one of pragmatic absolutism. I take the direction of civilization as a given beyond which we cannot go. Yet there is also a relative morality within this absolute in that the goodness of today can only be assessed in com- parison to the goodness of yesterday.

Using this framework, an assessment of the general morality of a social order depends on the extent to which that social order displays a development from the primitive to the civilized, which in my terms means (1) at the psychological level, the extent to which repression and sublimation have been successful in satisfying concrete desires, and (2) at the sociological level, the extent to which structured in- equality has replaced the gulf between the tyrant and the masses.

We can see that here is a moral scheme for assessing the compara- tive morality of social and political orders from an evolutionary point of view. There is a small problem with this argument, however, in that it still assumes morality began with society. It is apparent that Freud also made this assumption, since he consistently referred to the primal crime as a crime and in other places as a parricide. Of course, he most probably did not mean these terms in the strict legal sense. But he did mean that the primal crime was a terrible act, a wrongful act. It is as close to the popular image of crime as one can get.

The crucial question to which Freud did not address himself was, why were such acts wrong in a primitive society where one must assume there was no moral order? For Freud's analysis of the origin of repression to stand, one would have to argue that there was a moral order that preceded the primal crime; otherwise there would have been no reason at all for the "murderers" to feel guilty, since there would be no reason for them to feel that they had done anything wrong. We are forced, therefore, to look for a source of morality that transcends the social order. This is the morality of the retributiv- ists, and its source is the evolutionary law of reciprocity.

Reciprocity and Moral Order

In the second chapter of this book, I embarked upon a search for the "natural" origins of punishment. In that chapter, I argued that, because of the interrelationship of man with the harsh and unpredictable material world, pains that man experienced from dealing with that world were animated; he imputed responsibility to himself for disasters that occurred. It is clear that the potential for guilt existed before the social order was created. The connection between disasters (evil) and responsibility and the necessity to make amends for these evils were well established before the primal crime. Therefore, morality existed before crime and before political or social order.[11] More importantly, we can see that there is embedded in this schema, the notion of reciprocity, the idea that there was a give and take between Man and Nature. The nature of this reciprocity may be taken as psychobiological, because the necessity of this reciprocation arises from the interaction between the emerging biology of man and the emerging material conditions of nature, which in turn produces the developing psychology of human nature.[12] Reciprocity with the material world is absolutely necessary not only for survival, but also for development.

If we can accept this admittedly far-reaching speculation, it allows us to conceive of morality as *preceding* society, of having its origin somewhere deep in antiquity in the void between Man and Nature. This is the only way that I can see out of the blunt Freudian assertion that the primal crime was truly a crime. And now that we see it, we see its tremendous importance. It allows a morality that is not based on the social order.

It turns out, though, that reciprocity is also a mainstay of a particular type of social order: one that operates on the basis of free exchange among equals. Professor Lon Fuller, in his illuminating treatise *The Morality of Law,* argues that the idea of "duty" derives from the principle of reciprocity.[13] He describes three components of reciprocity which lead to duty:

1. Duty is "created" by the voluntary agreement of parties in reciprocal relationship.
2. ". . . the reciprocal performances of the parties must in some sense be equal in value."[14] What this means is that one does not exchange "a penny for a penny," because exchange requires that the same valuation be placed on two different commodities to be exchanged. Therefore, in the field of criminal punishment, one does not exchange a crime with a crime, but rather a crime with a punishment, and the attempt is made to insure that the punishment is equal in "value" to the crime. This is the moral basis of reflected punishment and of retribution.

3. ". . . the relationship within society must be sufficiently fluid so that the duty you owe me today, I may owe you tomorrow. . . ."[15] This last point is the most difficult, and probably utopian, since few, if any, societies are structured in this fluent fashion because of the necessity of structured inequality. Fuller notes that the only arena in which this principle is realized is an open market economy. Even there, these days, it is difficult to argue that the parties involved are of equal status when one considers the growth of multinational corporations. In the area of criminal, and all other punishment institutions for that matter, I have shown quite clearly throughout this book that reciprocity does not and cannot reach practical reality. Society is far too complex, the state has become too much the dominant punisher. It is clear from this analysis that in a socialistic society, where the obedience model of punishment (backed up by the state) plays a much more expansive role and inequality is structured much more formally into the political order at the expense of the social order, the principle of reciprocity has virtually no hope of surviving. Professor Fuller concludes—as he says, it is a "startling" conclusion —that it is only under a free market economy, capitalism, that the rule of reciprocity has any chance of survival. However, because of the growing power of the state, even in so-called capitalist societies, the possibilities of reciprocity holding sway in the area of criminal punishment are virtually nonexistent.

One can readily see that the more "equality" that can be generated, the more chance there may be for reciprocity. Therefore, the more one decentralizes authority the better. This is why a capitalist society is theoretically "more free" than a socialist society, since it diversifies political order into a greater area of social and economic orders, whereas the socialist system centralizes authority into one political order by attempting to do away with the social order.[16] Punishment under such conditions takes on its most oppressive form.

We can now see the tension between the two moralities of reciprocity and obedience that underlies all societies. All societies must have both to survive as moral societies; yet the two moralities are at bottom diametrically opposed to each other, since reciprocity requires the assumption of equality and obedience requires the assumption of inequality.

The principle of retribution as the punitive form of reciprocity affirms the moral order. The principle of obedience as the punitive expression of utilitarian theory affirms the social and political order.

Together they provide two different sources of moral justification of punishment. For example, the only unassailable justification of punishing a murderer is that it is an ancient crime, and ancient crimes have always been reciprocally punished. Therefore, not to punish him would be a negation of the moral basis of our culture. In contrast, if one justifies punishment of the murderer on the basis that it "upholds the social order" (and by implication political order), one is clearly open to the question: do you mean the social order that was created by murder? The hard answer, of course, is "yes," and one may extend this response to say that each punishment of a criminal "recreates" the social and political order. How else could it be, since there is no other alternative but a society structured on raw physical force?

In sum, it is important to recognize that crime creates the social and political need for punishment, not the other way around. On the other hand, it is a transcendent morality that makes it absolutely necessary that crimes be punished. We can see that the functions and origins of the obedience model of punishment are distasteful, given its murderous origin, and it is no wonder that they breed bitterness both in the punishers and the punished. It is clear that retributive morality is the purest and counterbalances the potential dangers of the obedience model. Finally, the comparative morality of the evolutionary perspective provides a point from which to evaluate a social order that might degenerate into immorality—that is, the ever-present possibility that the social order will dissolve into tyranny.

Inequality and the Distribution of Punishment

It is now apparent that one can only use "the defense of the social order" as a justification for punishment if it can be shown that the social order is just. Although some have argued that it does not follow that we should hold the distribution of punishment responsible for an immoral social order, we must see it as the expression of social order and therefore cannot avoid making a moral assessment of it.[17]

I have suggested that the social order created was one of structured inequality and this represented a decisive and desirable step in the development of civilization. The next question is, should punishment be distributed equally or in varying proportions according to each unequal status? It follows from my analysis that the punishment that would affirm the social order would also affirm unequal status. I know that this is a shocking thing to say these days, but it is the logical point to which my analysis has led me. However, the complexity of this conclusion is very great. Does it mean that the same punishment should be administered to everyone for the same crimes, which would simply and logically replicate the social order? It might be argued that if one really wished to affirm the social order, one should punish those of lesser status more than others. Furthermore, it is not clear what "same" means, since a $5 fine for a rich man may mean something much more to a poor man.

The clearest solution to equalizing punishments would be to use corporal punishments, which, although open to subjective differences in sensation of pain, are not open to the more widely perceived differences in "pain" such as prison, fines, probation, and the rest. Physical pain cuts much more across status differentials, so it is a more equalizing punishment. The analogy between this form of punishment—that is, violence as an equalizer or definition of "equality"—and that of "equality," based on violence, before society was established is too great to pass up. Corporal punishments are clearly primitive, because they satisfy a concrete desire with a concrete act, and therefore they are wrong. Yet by rejecting this form of punishment, we affirm inequality.

How, then, does one arrive at a just distribution of punishments? The only solutions that present themselves are to either affirm the justice of inequality or attempt to correct for the injustice of inequality by adjusting the punishment to make unequals equal. It is my view that the former solution is the only just and feasible solution and the latter is based on a false conception of the social and moral order. Since punishment is an expression of the social order, changing the distribution of punishment would merely change the exterior forms of social order and leave crime—the basis of social order—untouched. Thus, inequality would continue. Furthermore, the dimensions of inequality are far broader than simply punishment, especially its economic bases. To suggest that one could correct these economic inequalities by adjusting the punishments for crimes is clearly dangerous and immoral. It is immoral because it would mean punishing a rich man, say, with life imprisonment for murder, whereas a poor man for the same crime might receive only one year or even be excused altogether. This cuts across the notion of moral order that I have argued for previously: that ancient crimes must be reciprocally punished, therefore the punishment must reflect as closely as possible the offense. That is, it must be enough to make up for or correct the evil. I have shown throughout this book that the most common and primitive form of this principle was to reflect the crime, to try to reproduce the crime in the punishment. However, due to the constant progress we have made in our ability to substitute symbolic for actual satisfaction, we are able these days to be satisfied with a symbolic approximation of the punishment to the crime, usually in the form of prison or various fines.

It follows from this that the punishment, if it is to be moral, should be directly proportionate to the offense, if one is supporting a retributive view, and directly proportionate to the specific unequal status of the offender, under the obedience model. If we administer the "same" punishment to all offenders for the same crimes in direct proportion to the gravity of those crimes, we achieve both these aims. The principle of reciprocity is upheld, because the punishment is made to fit the crime. Since we do not allow the mitigating circumstances of unequal status to enter into the decision, this "same" punishment will be felt differently according to each one's unequal status. The punishments therefore are the same in their administration, but different in their significant effects.

The Justice of Effective Punishment

This conclusion leads us to our next question concerning the justice of punishment—is it just to use punishment, and its correlatives such as "treatment," psychosurgery, rehabilitation, to change offenders? We have seen in the previous two chapters that, if we really put our minds to it, we could make punishment quite effective in this regard. The popular view today is that it is unjust to change particular individuals (i.e., from disobedient to obedient) yet it is okay to use punishment as a general deterrent to make *everyone* obedient. This seems to me to be a contradiction. Viewed within my analytic framework, it is also unjust.

THE IMMORALITY OF GENERAL DETERRENCE: Although I have shown that both punishment which affirms the moral order (retribution) and punishment which affirms the social order are just, I have argued for the primacy of the former over the latter for two reasons. First, retribution affirms a moral order that transcends the social and political order. Second, the social and political order, though moral in the sense that they allow for the progress of civilization and the continuity of society, are nevertheless tainted by having been created by a criminal act. Furthermore, because of the "losing battle" that repression fights with violence, there is always the danger of the social order dissolving back into its primitive state. I showed, however, that it was the decentralization of authority from a situation of tyranny that represented the great step in civilization. This decentralization brought with it a structured inequality and broke up the mass nature of obedience. Therefore, any social order that reverts to a mass obedience is, by my analysis, immoral because it goes against the direction of civilization. It follows that any use of punishment designed for mass obedience is immoral, and since that is the explicit feature of general deterrence, it is immoral or at least potentially so.

The argument for the general preventive effects of criminal punishment also inflates the role of criminal punishment in maintaining obedience. I have shown clearly throughout this book that the bulk of punishment in the service of obedience is achieved in other social institutions, such as family, school, church, and military. Indeed, society has recognized this fact, which is why more severe physical punishments are permitted in schools and families than to criminals.[18]

There is no difficulty at all in concluding that, since general obedience is more than taken care of by other social institutions, any use of criminal punishment for reasons of general deterrence is never justifiable.

THE MORALITY OF INDIVIDUAL DETERRENCE: Individual deterrence is another matter. It seems to me that a system of punishment designed only to punish individuals who break laws has every right to make sure that the punishment is "felt." This means, therefore, that although the severity of the punishment should be kept closely in proportion to the offense, there is nothing wrong with getting what one can out of punishment, in the name of obedience, since we are not here concerned with mass obedience, but only disobedience of a few individuals. The only argument I can see against this is that, if every criminal were made obedient, we would have a whole society of conformists. But this presupposes that there is a fixed number of individuals who are likely to disobey, and once they are made obedient there will be no more criminals. The practical impossibility of this was clearly demonstrated by Enrico Ferri.[19] The idea is, of course, based on a false conception of the causes of crime and disobediences. The Freudian view is that we are all potentially disobedient—that the possibility for mass disobedience is always there. Therefore, one may change particular individual criminals, but there will always be plenty to take their place.

The carefully balanced justice of this approach I hope is now evident. Making sure that punishment changes individual transgressors into obedient persons is moral insofar as it affirms the social order. These criminals have every right to be changed into noncriminals. It is, after all, a stinking, rotten role to have to play, as Jean Genet has told us often enough.[20] There is no reason why they should be made to stay in that role, especially as there are plenty of others to take their place. The opponents of rehabilitation and its correlatives like to paint a science-fictional picture of the state doing its dirty work to these people. I cannot see that this is so, especially if the state is constrained by the retributive principle.

The particular practices of individual deterrence that have borne the brunt of criticism have been those of psychosurgery,[21] chemotherapy, and various forms of manipulative behavior therapy. Since these particular therapies, especially drugs and psychosurgery, can have a striking effect on behavior, there is every reason to encourage their refinement. Psychosurgery probably has the greatest potential, since it does not depend upon the individual's cooperation. The hysterical opposition to it, however, probably means that it will never be widely used, because it is a punishment that comes very close to physical injury— a form of punishment that civilization has rejected. We will therefore probably have to make do with the somewhat less effective methods of punishment outlined in Chapter 11. Thus, the celerity and certainty of punishment should be adjusted to have the greatest effect on the individual offender. Severity, of course, although a major factor in the effectiveness of punishment, must be tempered by the retributive principle. The factor of publicity of punishment, however, should not be used, since this is punishment in the service of general deterrence. This question is somewhat complicated and I will return to it again later.

THE AVOIDANCE OF PREDICTIVE PUNISHMENT: The question of predictive punishment is much more difficult to deal with. Suppose there is a man who has committed sixteen violent rapes, and you know he will commit another. Should he be put away for our protection before he has committed the next crime, indeed for the rest of his life, if necessary, until he is cured? It can be seen that this problem falls outside both the retributive and obedience models. The question is one of incapacitation: does society have the right to protect itself from potentially dangerous persons? It is a *defense* model and the answer, again, is a qualified "yes." Since I argue for the primacy of retribution, thence the unrelenting application of all our punitive technology to change the offender into a nonoffender, the problem of predictive punishment should hardly arise. Since those about whom we are concerned to predict punishment are usually those seen as "dangerous," their first offense is most likely to be a serious one, though not always. Thus, according to the retributive principle, the offender should not be "let off" or put on probation. He must be punished in proportion to the gravity of his offense. Therefore, there should be plenty of time to treat him in such a way as to change him, by psychosurgery, drugs, or whatever. The predictive punishment pattern only arises, it seems to me, because serious first offenders are not punished severely enough, nor are they given any treatment to insure that they do not repeat their offense.[22]

The criticism might be raised that this conclusion is entirely inconsistent with the conclusions reached on the lack of effectiveness of individual deterrence outlined in Chapter 11. The rejoinder is that we have never had the courage to change criminals because of the moral argument of the retributivists that it is somehow wrong to do so. This can be demonstrated very easily by the actual implementation of the treatment model applied to prisons in contrast to our academic belief in its dominance. During the late 1950s, a period when the treatment model for criminals held greatest sway in American textbooks on crime, for the 161,587 prisoners in America, there were no more than twenty-three full-time psychiatrists to treat them.[23] The supposed political tyranny that it is claimed underlies treatment of criminals is clearly a big bogey. It only becomes a tyranny when it is put to the service of general deterrence, as is the case in the USSR, with its phychiatric treatment of dissidents and its one-dimensional structure of inequality. It is even more ridiculous when the same people who criticize treatment as being tyrannical also claim that it is ineffective. Surely the least tyrannical treatment is that which has no effect?

We possess the technology to change people's behavior radically. It is admittedly a rough technology which, to eliminate violent behaviors, for example, also may eliminate other aspects of behavior such as certain emotions or cognitive skills. But, faced with the prospect of being sentenced to a life term in prison, might the costs of behavioral change be less to the offender? More importantly, adhering to the retributive model and facing the prospect of releasing a dangerous person after a fixed prison term, is it not worth the costs of sacrificing a few of one individual's behavioral patterns to protect us from his violence?

Epilogue: The Dangers of Reform

Since many of the views I have advanced in this chapter are ideal statements of principle, I know that there is not much chance of their being taken seriously to make specific reforms. I consider that to be indeed fortunate, since it would be a very dangerous undertaking to apply them, as it would any grand scheme. My reasons for taking this view are two: the nature of reform itself and the process of our unconscious that lies like a hungry leopard ready to pounce on any reform and devour it.

People in criminal justice know only too well that the best intentioned reforms often turn out to have unfortunate results. It has been apparent from my account of the reform in England in the eighteenth and nineteenth centuries that prices were paid for reforms, and it was by no means clear at the time whether these reforms would be beneficial. Systematic prison was one of the prices paid. Furthermore, it has been argued by a number of experts on the history of prison that it arose not out of any particular philosophy of punishment, but out of the bureaucratic and political conditions of the time. Some have termed this process the administrative solution to punishment, which adheres to three principles: custody, security, and control.[24] Others have even argued that the very inception of the American penal system was merely to satisfy administrative demands. Writing on the origin of the Walnut Street gaol, J. L. Gillin observes:

> Here we have the beginnings of the prison system in America . . . the model of prisons in the U. S. for the next 40 years. We should especially note that this system began not through the philosophy of any particular school, but through administrative and political demands of the time.[25]

As it turns out, the direction of reform from that period was commensurate with the direction of civilization: it helped in the repression of physical violence as a mode of punishment. The "price" of prison was a very logical outcome of this repression, since it insured, along with the move for secret as against public executions, that criminal punishment would be repressed into the unconscious of society, its prison fortresses. The secrecy and seclusion that prisons enjoy in modern society are quite phenomenal. Although there are some that are "open," most are separated from society by high walls, towers, bureaucracy, and often geography. It is argued by reformers that the public doesn't know what goes on "inside" and if only it knew, the move to improve conditions in them would be stronger.

Such a claim is naïve because it fails to understand the psychology of punishment in civilization. The isolation of criminals in confinement represents a great developmental step in the cultural progress of criminal punishment; it is another great achievement of repression. It should not be tampered with lightly. Those who press for abolition of prison do not understand the powder keg upon which prisons are built. To eradicate prisons would be to eradicate an important and valuable part of our culture—as seamy as it is, it is far less seamy than it might have been. We are capable of much worse, as the history of our exploits with criminals described in this book clearly demonstrates.

Reforms should affirm history rather than try to usurp it. Thus, for example, in the area of criminal sentencing, a popular area at present, practical moves to reform should be based soundly on the historical precedents of criminal law and not on grand schemes that will sweep all of what we have out the door. There have been many examples of grand schemes that looked great on paper, but by the time they had been transformed into legislation were utterly unrecognizable. It seems to follow from this that sentencing reform should not be achieved by new legislation, but by a close analysis and extrapolation from the already existing practice and theory of criminal law.[26]

Reforms in the forms of punishment should try to reaffirm the symbolic aspects of punishment, rather than the actual or "real" aspects of punishment. This idea is closely related with the question of publicity that I referred to earlier. Since I consider the use of publicity for the purposes of general deterrence dangerous, it is very difficult to affirm the desirability of reinforcing the symbolic aspects of punishment without also publicizing punishment itself. I must draw a fine distinction here between the publicity of actual punishments and the dramaturgical representation of punishments. It is the latter that should be emphasized, not the former. Thus, to televise an actual execution carried out inside a prison would not be a reform but rather a regressive step, since it would be a concrete representation of the punishment—not unlike the Aztecs actually eating their substitute sacrificial victim. The best way to enhance the symbolic satisfaction of punishment is to dramatize, through fiction, what might go on in prisons and in other criminal punishments. Fiction is surely the closest one can get to the symbolic substitution that I talked about in my example of cannibalism. It can be seen, also, that punishment in secret is likely to enhance the mystery and drama of criminal punishment, to stimulate the imagination.

Finally, we should never forget that crime creates the social order and not the other way around. Therefore, sweeping reforms in punishment are really up to the criminals. One is reminded of the French member of Parliament who was heard to mutter, upon the introduction of a bill to abolish the death penalty for murder, "Let the murderers make the first move."

Nor should we ever forget the psychological realities that underlie punishment of all kinds, especially criminal punishment. Reforms will be aborted unless they clearly recognize what they are up against. I have said much about this psychological reality throughout this book —much of it implicitly. Freud graphically portrays this "psychological truth," as he calls it, in his quotation of Heine:

> "Mine is a most peaceable disposition. My wishes are: a humble cottage with a thatched roof, but a good bed, good food, the freshest milk and butter, flowers before my window, and a few fine trees before my door; and if God wants to make my happiness complete, he will grant me the joy of seeing some six or seven of my enemies hanging from those trees. Before their death I shall, moved in my heart, forgive them all the wrong they did me in their lifetime. One must, it is true, forgive one's enemies—but not before they have been hanged."[27]

There is little grace in punishment. Only justice.

Footnotes

Chapter 1: Introduction: The Problem of Punishment

1. From Daniel Defoe, "A Hymn to the Pillory," in *The Earlier Life and Works of Daniel Defoe,* ed. H. Morley (London: Routledge & Kegan Paul, 1889).

2 A. Von Hirsch, *Doing Justice* (New York· Hill & Wang, 1976).

3. A. Flew, "The Justification of Punishment," *Philosophy* 29 (1954): 291-307.

4. H. L. A. Hart, *Punishment and Responsibility* (New York: Oxford University Press, 1968), pp. 4-5.

5. *Ibid.,* p. 4.

6. T. Szasz, *Pain and Pleasure* (New York: Basic Books, 1975), p. xiii.

7. Of course, the problem of pain does not end here. We know that there are people who find pain pleasurable. Indeed, Professor Szasz points out that life without pain, after all, would be a life close to death! We see, therefore, that pain is not the complete opposite of pleasure, nor is it inherently evil, since it is inherent in life itself—unless, of course, one believes that life itself is inherently evil, as was the case with the Calvanists and some puritan sects in the sixteenth and seventeenth centuries. A verse from one of Charles Wesley's hymns, often sung at the gallows, illustrates the strange worship of death in life, and again the profound relationship of punishment to religious feeling:

> *Ah, lovely Appearance of Death!*
> *No sight upon Earth is so fair*
> *Not all the gay Pageants that breathe*
> *Can with a dead body compare*

The relationship between these three concepts—pain as life, life as evil, death as life—and punishment as the mechanism combining all three, is examined in Chapter 7. It provides the cultural explanation of why the utilitarians so unquestioningly assumed pain to be intrinsically evil and the masses reacted to punishment so deliriously in the eighteenth century.

8. F. Kafka, "In the Penal Colony," in F. Kafka, *The Penal Colony,* trans. Willa and Edwin Muir (New York: Schocken, 1961).

9. The works of H. L. A. Hart are exemplary of this approach. The only legal theorist to defend with any vigor the idea of punishment as a moral reinforcer is Patrick Devlin. See: P. Devlin, *The Enforcement of Morality* (New York: Oxford University Press, 1968). It is true that Johannes Andenaes, the deterrence theorist, has advanced a "theory" of punishment as a "teacher of right and wrong." See: J. Andenaes, *Punishment and Deterrence* (Ann Arbor: University of Michigan Press, 1974). But this approach, along with other deterrence theorists (e.g., F. Zimring and G. Hawkins, *Deterrence* [Chicago: University of Chicago Press, 1973]) is more of a mechanistic approach to the function of punishment and morality in society. Devlin insists that it is morality that holds society together (and the analysis in Chapter 2 of the primitive origins of punishment supports this view) and therefore its enforcement by punishment is absolutely essential for the survival of society. Punishment may or may not teach right and wrong. The important fact is that it supports the morality of social order. We will return to a detailed discussion of this point in the final chapter.

Chapter 2: When Punishment Began

1. The affinity between Spencer's theory of intelligence and that of Piaget is quite striking. Although Piaget sees the physical environment as basically "punishing" for children in early life, he goes beyond this to show that children develop a deep sense of moral judgment as a result of punishment which occurs naturally in social life, especially among children We will consider Piaget's theory in more detail in the final chapter of this book. See: J. Piaget, *The Moral Judgment of the Child* (New York: The Free Press, 1965).

2. Freud pointed to other important *symbolic* aspects of man's relationship to the harsh environment. Man's mastery of fire, Freud saw as a significant psychological event The relationship of fire to the primitive urges of the libido, of course, he saw as almost direct. The supreme act of power for the primitive, Freud speculates, was the act of urinating on the fire to put it out: the control of one of nature's deadly tormentors (and, incidentally, a major tool of torture and punishment)! The early use of tools also has important psychological significance of power over the environment: man's quest for omnipotence. This has led many psychoanalysts to identify sexual inadequacy as a central trait of arsonists, and there is much case material to support this view. Man's quest for omnipotence might also be used to explain more recent historical events, such as the industrial revolution, or the uses of science. The psychological analysis of power at particular stages in history is especially important for the study of punishment, since it is important to discover whether or not there is an urge to punish, regardless of the other supposed justifications or necessities of punishment in society. We will have more to say about this in the final chapter.

3. Freud's construction of the primal horde and original crime has been severely criticized by a number of anthropologists. See, for example, A. L. Kroeber, *The Nature of Culture* (Chicago: University of Chicago Press, 1952). Kroeber at first dismissed Freud's theory as unscientific and historically inaccurate in his 1920 paper, "Totem and Taboo: An Ethnologic Psychoanalysis." Later, he reconsidered his criticisms, viewing Freud's theory as mythical and therefore of interest to the anthropologist, in his 1939 paper, "Totem and Taboo in Retrospect." Both these papers are reprinted in *The Nature of Culture.*

4. A. Montagu, *The Nature of Human Aggression* (New York: Oxford University Press, 1976). Also, A. Montagu, *Man and Aggression* (New York: Oxford University Press, 1968).

5. It should be made clear that in this discussion punishment is *not* synonymous with aggression. I am not arguing that man is naturally aggressive But I am argu-

ing, along with Montagu, that both cooperation and competition were necessary for aggression of an organized kind (such as wars and feuds) to arise. This is an extremely important point, as we will see later that feuds are a basic element in the history of punishment On primitive cooperation and competition, see: Montagu, *The Nature of Human Aggression* But it is difficult to go beyond Petr Kropotkin's classic *Mutual Aid* (Boston: Extending Horizon Books, 1914).

6. J. G. Frazer, *The New Golden Bough*, ed Theodor H. Gaster (New York: Criterion Books, 1959).

7. E. Durkheim, *The Elementary Forms of Religious Life* (New York: The Free Press, 1965). E. B. Tylor, *Primitive Culture* (London: J Murray, 1920), developed the original theory of animism.

8. I am not suggesting here that man sees himself as the center of the universe in the sense believed prior to Galileo. That was a period in which man had succeeded in completely separating himself from the natural order. In fact, nature was not seen to be ordered in the primitive sense (i.e., a "natural order") but rather, because of religion, nature was seen as a product of religion, and religion had taken on a character of its own, with a phantasmagorical stream of images and prohibitions centering on man This situation was to continue until Darwin once again demonstrated that man was very much a part of the whole species of life and was not recreated anew by God. Man had been, before Darwin, the object of religion rather than nature, which had, as we shall see shortly, a significant contiguity with a hitherto unmatched level of punishment.

9. Today our culture has evolved beyond this, to the point that we have great difficulty in seeing matter as animate, even in the face of scientific discoveries of the highly dynamic nature of matter. Matter, to the common man, is dead

10. Tylor, *Primitive Culture*, p. 481.

11. Freud has argued that prohibitions occur as a result of guilt—at the cultural level, guilt over the original crime of killing the father and eating him. Rituals or compulsions are necessary to guard against these repressed urges The individual develops a need for punishment to help reinforce the repression of his desire to kill.

12. Durkheim, *Elementary Forms of Religious Life*.

13. C. Levi-Strauss, *Totemism*, trans. Rodney Needham (Boston: Beacon Press, 1962).

14. S. Freud, *Totem and Taboo*, trans. A. A. Brill (New York: Random House, 1918), p. 185.

15. *Ibid.*, p. 183.

16. Levi-Strauss, *Totemism*, p. 89.

17. *Ibid.*, p. 70.

Chapter 3: The Sacred Forms of Punishment

1. J. Laurence, *A History of Capital Punishment* (New York: Citadel Press, 1960), p. 1.

2. E. Miraux, *Daily Life in the Time of Homer* (New York: Macmillan, 1965), p. 180.

3. *Ibid.*

4. *Ibid.*, p. 176.

5. F. Strom, *On the Sacral Origin of the Germanic Death Penalties* (Stockholm: Wahlstrom and Widstraud, 1942), p. 14.

6. Feuding is a particularly interesting form of "social justice," discussed in: G. Newman and C. Haft, "Feuding and Violence," unpublished paper, State University of New York at Albany, 1977.

7. H. Von Hentig, *Punishment: Its Origin, Purpose and Psychology* (Montclair, N. J.: Patterson-Smith, 1973), pp. 22-26. The English version is without documentation. I have therefore used the Italian translation: *La Pena* (Milano: Fratelli Bocca, 1942).

8. This is quite understandable to us in light of the argument presented in Chapter 2. The primitive mind views all accidents and injuries as intentional.
9. Von Hentig, *Punishment*, pp. 22-26.
10. These places of refuge are described in Moses, 2:21, 12; Moses 4:35; 6; Moses 5:19, 6-7: See, *La Pena*, p. 25. Von Hentig refers to several other methods used in a variety of primitive societies in limiting the pervasive or spiraling effects of the blood feud.
11. Even today, such killings and mutilations are reliably reported. As Von Hentig points out, many of these ritualistic practices are reverted to during times of war or terrorism. The mutilation of corpses during the Lebanese Civil War has often been reported in the popular press.
12. Livy 2, 5.
13. Bishop claims that the severing of the head with a single blow was the subject of great sport in the Colosseum during the final stages of the Roman Empire. He recounts in detail how gladiators were provided a series of beheadings, and a tally was kept as to which one used the fewest strokes to sever the heads of the unfortunate victims, a game not unlike golf. However, Bishop's work lacks any documentation, and in many places he clearly mixes imagination with fact. His description is suspect. On the other hand, there is little doubt that the severing of the head with one blow required great skill and practice, and many executioners were inadequate to the task—as we shall see. See: G. V. Bishop, *Executions: The Legal Ways of Death* (Los Angeles: Sherbourne Press, 1965).
14. Von Hentig, *Punishment*, p. 46; Strom, *Sacral Origin of the Germanic Death Penalties*, p. 14.
15. K. Von Amira, *Die Germanischen Todesstrafen. Untersuchungen zur Rechtsund Religionsgeschichte* (Munich: Abhandlungen d. Bayer. Akad. d. Wiss Philos-philol. u. hist. Kl. 31:3, 1922), p. 212.
16. T. Mommsen, *Romisches Strafecht* (Leipzig: Syst. Handbuch der deut. Rechtswiss. 1:4, 1899), p. 916.
17. A. Wuttke, *Der Deutsch Volksaberglaube der Gegenwart* (Berlin: Aufl. 3, 1900), p. 162.
18. There may, of course, have been other reasons for this practice in the Inquisition. See Chapter 5.
19. Strom, *Sacral Origin of the Germanic Death Penalties*, passim.
20. *Ibid.*, p. 171.
21. *Ibid.*, pp. 164f
22. *Ibid.*
23. *Ibid.*
24. *Ibid.*, pp. 101-02.
25. It is well known, of course, that Greek and Roman warriors preferred to die by the sword. Xenophon in the second book of Anabasis announces that beheading was the most honorable form of death.
26. Dante's *Inferno* is stark evidence of those deep, lasting fears.
27. See Bishop, *Executions*.
28. Holinshed's Chronicle of 1587 describes the Halifax Gibbet:

> There is, and has been, of ancient time, a law or rather custom, at Halifax, that whosoever doth commit any felony, and is taken with the same, or confesses the fact upon examination, if it be valued by four constables to amount to the sum of thirteenpense halfpenny, he is forthwith beheaded upon one of the next market days, or else upon the same day that he is convicted, if market be holden. The engine wherewith the execution is done is a square block of wood, of the length of four feet and a half, which doth ride up and down in a slot rabet or regall, of five yards in height. In the nether end of a sliding block is an axe, keyed or fastened with an iron into

the wood, which being drawn up to the top of the frame, is there fastened by a wooden pin (with a notch made in the same, after the manner of Samson's post), into the middest of which pin also there is a long rope fastened, that cometh down among the people, so that when the offender hath made his confession, and hath laid his neck over the nethermost block, every man there present doth either take hold of the rope (or putteth forth his arm so near to the same as he can get, in token that he is willing to see justice executed) and pulling out the pin in this manner, the head block wherein the axe is fastened doth fall down with such a violence, that if the neck of the transgressor were so big as that of a bull, it should be cut asunder at a stroke, and roll from the body by a huge distance. If it be so that the offender be apprehended for an ox, sheep, kine, horse or any such cattle, the self beast or other of its kind shall have the end of the rope tied somewhere unto them, so that they being driven, do draw out the pin, whereby the offender is executed. (Laurence, *History of Capital Punishment*, pp. 38-39).

29. The Earl of Morton, upon seeing the impressive performance of the Halifax Gibbet, ordered a similar machine to be constructed in Edinburgh, and it became fondly known as the Scottch Maiden. Some 120 people were decapitated by this extraordinary method, including the Earl of Morton himself on June 2, 1581. His head was exhibited for a year on a pinnacle on the Tollsworth (*ibid.*, pp 38-40). Its use was discontinued in 1710.

30. Bishop, *Executions*, also relates the instance of a botched execution in Utah. The case was that of Eliseo J. Mares, the son of a sheriff, sentenced to death for murder in 1951. None of the four bullets was fatal, having entered the wrong side of the chest. The condemned man bled to death.

31. Von Hentig, *Punishment*, p 79.

32. K. Von Kremer, *Studien zur Vergleichenden Kulturgeschichte*, Vol. III, p. 3. Reported in *ibid.*

33. Von Amira, *Die Germanischen Todesstrafen Untersuchungen.*

34. H. More, *The History of the Persecutions of the Church of Rome and Complete Protestant Martyrology* (n p., 1809), p 35

35. Strom, *Sacral Origin of the Germanic Death Penalties*, p. 102

36. *Ibid.*

37. A comprehensive catalogue of these laws of Moses are reported by Von Hentig in *La Pena*, passim.

38. E. R. Goodenough, *The Jurisprudence of the Jewish Courts in Egypt as Described by Philo Judaeus* (Amsterdam: Philo Press, 1968), p. 25.

39. Strom, *Sacral Origin of the Germanic Death Penalties*, p. 115.

40. Von Hentig, *Punishment*, p. 57.

41. J. A. St. John, *Manners and Customs of Ancient Greece* (New York: Kennikat Press, 1971), Vol. III, claims that hanging was very common in Sparta, whereas Von Hentig, *Punishment*, claims that it was almost never used.

42. From the *Haramal* reported by Frazer, *New Golden Bough*, p. 317. Frazer reports several instances of sacrifice by hanging, which appear to have been closely related to attempts to resurrect the image of kings and gods.

43. Strom, *Sacral Origin of the Germanic Death Penalties*, p. 153.

44. Frazer, *New Golden Bough*, pp. 316-19.

45 Von Amira, *Die Germanischen Todesstrafen Untersuchungen.* The hanging of animals as sacrifice alongside criminals should not be confused with the extensive practice during the middle ages of the hanging of animals *as* criminals—i.e., for criminal offenses. We shall look more closely at this practice in the following chapter.

46. Strom, *Sacral Origin of the Germanic Death Penalties*, pp. 128-30.

47. Von Hentig, *Punishment.*

48. Tacitus in his *Germania* observed that hanging was reserved specifically for robbery or theft and treason.
49. Strom, *Sacral Origin of the Germanic Death Penalties*, p. 149.
50. *Ibid.*, p. 159.
51. Frazer, *New Golden Bough.*
52. R. Bonner and G. Smith, *The Administration of Justice from Homer to Aristotle* (Chicago: University of Chicago Press, 1938).
53. G. R. Scott, *The History of Torture throughout the Ages* (London: Luxor Press, 1938), p. 181.
54. Von Hentig, *Punishment*, p. 50.
55. Scott, *Torture throughout the Ages*, p. 180.
56. *Ibid.*
57. Von Amira, *Die Germanischen Tadesstrafen Untersuchungen*, passim; Von Hentig, *Punishment*, pp. 48-50.
58. Strom, *Sacral Origin of the Germanic Death Penalties*, p. 222.
59. E. Mayer, *Die Entstehung der Germanischen Todesstrafe* (Der Gerichtssal, 1924), p. 388.
60. Von Hentig, *Punishment*, p. 61.
61. Strom, *Sacral Origin of the Germanic Death Penalties*, p. 223.
62. Jesus, of course, spoke from the cross. The Punic General Hamilcar, crucified for treason, harangued the Carthaginians for some time before dying, and there are many other instances. Crucifixion is not necessarily directly related to breaking on the wheel. Early forms simply tied the victim to a stake and left him to starve to death. Later the cross-board was introduced, and only later still was the practice of nailing to the cross introduced. The mythical origins of the cross, however, are scanty (Von Hentig, *Punishment*, p. 62)—that is, outside of the Christian portrayal of it. On the other hand, Von Hentig does report that the Jews requested Pilate to allow the legs of those on the cross to be broken, since it was considered that a man on the cross was "cursed in the sight of God." We therefore have evidence of a direct relationship between crucifixion and breaking. However, probably the more common affliction used with crucifixion was the scourging of the criminal either before or after crucifying him, with the view to cleansing him (Von Hentig, *Punishment*, p. 61). Whipping is, of course, a punishment unto itself, but I have reserved discussion of it until the following chapters, as I consider it more of an institutional punishment.
63. From Von Hentig, *Punishment*, p. 93.
64. *Ibid.*
65. The "crime" of giving birth to a dead child is indeed a fascinating one, for which there have always been serious punishments. Even in the English criminal law of the eighteenth century, it was the only crime for which the burden of proof lay with the defendant—that is, the mother with a dead baby was presumed guilty and she had to prove her innocence.
66. Strom, *Sacral Origin of the Germanic Death Penalties*, pp. 210f.
67. *Ibid.*, p. 174. Drowning often occurred as a result of ducking on the "cucking stool," but death was not the intended result of this punishment. This form of drowning is better treated as an institutional form, as is also the judicial practice known as "ordeal by water." We shall consider these in Chapters 5 and 6.
68. *Ibid.*
69. *Ibid.*
70. *Ibid.*, p. 208.
71. Von Hentig, *Punishment*, p. 96, reports, "When the castle of Vestenberg was built, the mason made a seat in the wall on which a child was put and walled up. The child wept, and to quieten it, it was given a nice red apple "
72. Strom, *Sacral Origin of the Germanic Death Penalties*, p. 208.

73. Mommsen, reported in Von Hentig, *La Pena*, p. 72.
74. Von Hentig, *Punishment*, p. 72, is misleading here when he goes on to include the wholesale drowning of a wide variety of animals—horses, oxen and carts, and so on—as sacrifices to various gods. These were sacrifices and not apotropaic practices. Again, in these examples, it was not criminals (either human or animal criminals) who were sacrificed, except one isolated example of the sacrifice of prisoners of war.
75. *Ibid.*, pp. 84-86.
76. Tacitus, *Annals* 15. 44
77. Von Hentig, *Punishment*, p. 84.
78. Scott, *Torture throughout the Ages*, p. 158. It is to be noted that Von Hentig, *Punishment*, p. 81, insists that the Jews did not use burning as a punishment, except as a "post-mortem ignominy."
79. W. Andrews, *Bygone Punishments* (London: William Andrews and Col, 1899), pp. 98-105.
80. Frazer, *New Golden Bough*, pp. 642-47.
81. Frazer says that the larger the number of criminals that were available, the more fertile was believed the land. If we applied this view today, we would develop a fascinating system of crime control, to say nothing of how modern social theories of crime causation would have to be changed!
82. Strom, *Sacral Origin of the Germanic Death Penalties*, pp. 90-97. However, he probably overstates his position; ". . . in no case can we document a direct connection between a penal act and a cult act," p. 97. The truth of this assertion depends on how one defines "penal act," which may be comparatively straightforward today, but certainly is not easy to do for the early stages of our history when criminal codes were not clearly formalized and religious and sacred proscriptions were an intrinsic part of penal law.
83. *Ibid.*, p. 197.
84. Von Hentig, *Punishment*, pp. 80-81.
85. H. Oldenberg, *Die Religion des Veda* (Stuttgart: J. G. Cotta, 1917), p. 573.
86. More, *Persecutions of the Church of Rome*, pp. 256-57.
87. Scott, *Torture throughout the Ages*, pp. 160-61.
88. Von Hentig, *Punishment*, p. 87.
89. *Ibid.*, p. 98; Scott, *Torture throughout the Ages*, p. 212.
90. Von Hentig, *Punishment*, p. 100.
91. J. Stow, *A Survey of London* (New York· Dutton, 1912).
92. Von Hentig, *Punishment*, p. 99.
93. *Ibid.*
94. Scott, *Torture throughout the Ages*, p. 211
95. *Ibid.*, p. 213.
96. Von Hentig, *Punishment*, p. 98.
97. *Ibid.*, pp. 98-99, is somewhat inconsistent here In a later passage he refers to the *burial* of entrails.
98. *Ibid.*, p. 98.

Chapter 4: Punishment and Obedience: Punishing Women, Children, Slaves, and Soldiers

1. This proposition was first stated by Gustav Radbruch in his *Elegantia Juris Criminalis* (Basel: Verlag fur Recht und Gesellschaft, 1950), in regard to the relationship between slavery and penal punishment It has been further supported by Professor Thorsten Sellin in his *Slavery and the Penal System* (New York: Elsevier, 1976).
2. See Chapters 5, 6, and 7.

3. There is, of course, a religious basis, as we saw in Chapter 3.

4. For example, the Texas criminal code allows for a greater degree of self-defense against attack than do most other codes.

5. P. Aries, *Centuries of Childhood* (New York: Alfred A. Knopf, 1962), p. 353.

6. W. W. Buckland, *A Textbook of Roman Law from Augustus to Justinian* (Cambridge: University of Cambridge Press, 1921, 1963).

7. L. Demause, "The Evolution of Childhood," *Journal of Psychohistory* 1, 4 (Spring 1974): 503-75.

8. Buckland, *Textbook of Roman Law*. We may note here the remains of the feudal tradition of dealing with criminal wrongs at the private level.

9. Von Hentig, *Punishment*, p. 34; *ibid.*, passim.

10. Demause, "The Evolution of Childhood," passim. Von Hentig, *Punishment*, p. 32. The exposure of "imperfect babies" also by the Spartans is, of course, well known. What is not often noted is that girls were easily the largest group put to death. One survey of 600 families of second-century inscriptions at Delphi showed that only 1 percent raised two daughters. See: J. Lindsay, *The Ancient World* (New York: Putnam, 1968), p. 168.

11. In Russia, the legal right of a husband to kill his wife for "disciplinary" purposes continued until the middle of the seventeenth century. See: W. Mandel, *Soviet Women* (Garden City, N.Y.: Anchor, 1975), p. 13. For a catalogue of other cruelties perpetrated upon women throughout history, see: E. G. Davis, *The First Sex* (New York: Putnam, 1971), pp. 254-55.

12. B. A. Hanawalt, "The Female Felon in Fourteenth-Century England," in *Women in Medieval Society*, ed. S. M. Stuard (Philadelphia: University of Pennsylvania Press, 1976), pp. 125-40. We may note that the common crime for which women were supposed to receive the dealth penalty in the middle ages was that of infanticide, as I mention in Chapter 6. However, the incidence of this crime on the records that Hannawalt studies was very low. Hannawalt suspects, however, that the community may have helped "cover up" such crimes, because of the commonly desperate economic conditions that prevailed at the time.

13. *Ibid.*

14. W. W. Fowler, *Social Life at Rome in the Age of Cicero* (New York: Macmillan, 1909), p. 177.

15. This law, obviously too severe and all-embracing, was later abolished as it was found unenforceable. W. W. Buckland, *The Roman Law of Slavery* (New York: AMS Press, 1969), p. 91.

16. St. John, *Manners and Customs of Ancient Greece*, Vol. III, p. 239.

17. Buckland, *Textbook of Roman Law*, passim.

18. G. R. Scott, *The History of Corporal Punishment* (London: T. Werner Lawrie, 1938), pp. 67-69.

19. Buckland, *Textbook of Roman Law*, p. 95.

20. Scott, *History of Corporal Punishment*, p. 69.

21. *Ibid.*, p. 72.

22. *Ibid.*, p. 76.

23. *Ibid.*, p. 77.

24. See Sellin, *Slavery and the Penal System*, for a review of all these forms of penal slavery. A major difference in the South from ancient Rome, however, was that slaves were not permitted by their Southern masters to learn to read or write.

25. Ingrahan v. Wright, 51 Led. 711 (1977).

26. Goodenough, *The Jurisprudence of the Jewish Courts in Egypt*, p. 68.

27. Demause, "The Evolution of Childhood," p. 527.

28. *Ibid.*, p. 535.

29. Aries, *Centuries of Childhood*, p. 128.

30. Demause, "The Evolution of Childhood," pp. 542f.

31. Aries, *Centuries of Childhood,* p. 128.
32. S. Painter, *William Marshall: Knight-Errant, Baron, and Regent of England* (Baltimore, Md.: Johns Hopkins Press, 1933), p. 14.
33. For an extensive list of such instances, see, Demause, "The Evolution of Childhood," p. 561, and C. Dunn, *The Natural History of the Child* (New York: John Lane, 1920).
34. Aries, *Centuries of Childhood,* p. 130. The practice of swaddling during this period was widespread, consisting of tightly binding up the infant so it virtually could not move. It is typical of Aries's very different interpretation from Demause's that Aries sees this stage as somewhat benign. Demause sees it as closely related to parental death wishes against their children and entirely punitive in nature (Demause, "The Evolution of Childhood," pp. 539-40).
35. L. Adamic, *Cradle of Life: The Story of One Man's Beginnings* (New York: Harper & Row, 1936), pp. 45-48.
36. Demause, "The Evolution of Childhood," p. 533.
37. Aries, *Centuries of Childhood,* p. 260.
38. See Chapter 9 for a detailed discussion of this.
39. Aries, *Centuries of Childhood,* p. 190.
40. For an historical review of the relationship between school violence and school discipline, see: J. Newman and G. R. Newman, "Crime and Punishment in the Schooling Process: An Historical Analysis," in *Theoretical Perspectives on School Crime,* ed. E. Wenk (Hackensack, N. J.: National Council on Crime and Delinquency, in press, 1977).
41. *Ibid.,* p. 190.
42. *Ibid.,* pp. 315-16.
43. *Ibid.,* p. 318.
44. R. C. Archer, *Secondary Education in the Nineteenth Century* (London: Cambridge University Press, 1921).
45. C. B. Freeman, "The Children's Petition," *British Journal of Educational Studies* 14 (May 1966): 216-23.
46. See P. Newell, *Last Report?* (London: Penguin, 1972).
47. *Ibid.*
48. *Ibid.,* p. 79.
49. *Ibid.,* p. 122.
50. *Ibid.,* p. 83. See also, for a comprehensive review of legal cases on corporal punishment in New York State, A. Faulkner, "The History of Legal Action in Corporal Punishment Cases in New York State, 1812 . . ." (Ed.D. diss., New York University, 1967).
51. C. H. Rovetta and L. Rovetta, *Teacher Spanks Johnny* (Stockton, Calif.: Willow House Publishers, 1968); L. Rovetta, *Corporal Punishment of Pupils* (Stockton, Calif.: Willow House Publishers, 1968).
52. The use of corporal punishment in America's schools has been extensively studied, and the evidence for its continuous widespread use is overwhelming. Easily the best book on this subject is that by A. Falk, *Corporal Punishment: A Social Interpretation of Its Theory and Practice in the Schools of the United States* (New York: Teachers College, Columbia University Press, 1941). See also: J. A. Mercurio, *Caning: Educational Rite and Tradition* (Syracuse, N. Y.: Syracuse University Press, 1972), where there are many reports of teacher opposition to attempts to abolish caning; Board of Education, City of New York, *Corporal Punishment in Schools,* 1908, being a survey of the use and rationale of corporal punishment in New York schools; and L. Y. Cobb, *The Evil Tendencies of Corporal Punishment* (New York: Mark H. Newman and Co., 1847), for the flavor of corporal punishment during that period.
53. Aries, *Centuries of Childhood,* p. 413.

54. From *Such, Such Were the Joys,* by George Orwell (New York: Harcourt, Brace and Jovanovich, 1947), p. 16.
55. C. E. Brand, *Roman Military Law* (Austin: University of Texas, 1968), p. xv.
56. There is some confusion over this point. It would appear that soldiers, while they had no right to appeal against their commander, could use a "provocatio" or an appeal to the people (*ibid.,* p. 65). It was out of these "appeals" that statutes were gradually formed. Later, these formed the basis of a criminal law system, using punishments favored by the people.
57. Livy 8. 7.
58. G. W. Currie, *The Military Discipline of the Romans from the Founding of the City to the Close of the Republic* (Bloomington: Graduate Council, Indiana University, 1928).
59. Brand, *Roman Military Law,* pp. 100-05.
60. *Ibid.,* p. 58.
61. S. Claver, *Under the Lash: A History of Corporal Punishment in the British Army* (London: Torchstream, 1954), p. 4.
62. *Ibid.,* p. 6.
63. *Ibid.*
64. A whip made of nine strands of thick cord or leather thongs two feet in length, with knots tied in each strand in three places.
65. The range and extent of punishments administered to American soldiers is clearly demonstrated by the following excerpts from the orderly books in the manuscript collection of the Fort Ticonderoga Library, Fort Ticonderoga, New York. I am indebted to Nicky Hahn for bringing this to my attention.

   Colonial Wars: 1758-59
   Ordinary theft: 500 lashes with cat-o-tails on bare back
   "Offering" to strike an officer: 400 lashes
   Desertion: 1,000 lashes
   Desertion to enemy: death
   Notorious offenders (theft): death
   Mutiny: death
   Neglect of duty: cashiered

   Revolutionary War
   Ordinary theft: 39 lashes
   Striking an officer and refusing duty: 39 lashes for each crime
   Desertion suspected: 39 lashes
   Desertion to enemy: 100 lashes and 12 months confinement
   Notorious offenders (theft): not listed for this period
   Mutiny: 39 lashes
   Neglect of duty: cashiered
   Drunk on post: 20 lashes
   Sleeping on post: 20 lashes

66. Claver, *Under the Lash,* p. 52.
67. *Ibid.,* p. xi.
68. S. L. Brodsky and N. E. Eggleston, eds., *The Military Prison* (Carbondale: Southern Illinois University Press, 1970), p. 25.
69. J. K. Taussig et al., *Military Law* (Annapolis, Md.: U. S. Naval Institute, 1963), p. 21.

Chapter 5: The Terror of Punishment

1. H. C. Lea, *The Inquisition of the Middle Ages* (New York: Harper & Row, 1969), originally published as Vol. I, *A History of the Inquisition of the Middle Ages,* 1887.

2. Scott, *Torture throughout the Ages*, p. 147.

3. *Ibid.*

4. Lea, *The Inquisition*, p. 133.

5. One might link this concept to that of "general deterrence" (see Chapters 10 and 13), because it is punishment designed to prevent the rest of the population from becoming heretics.

6. The structure of this organization of terror is strikingly similar to that described by A. Solzhenitzyn of Stalinist Russia. See *The Gulag Archipelago* (New York: Harper & Row, 1973), especially Vol. I.

7. Lea, *The Inquisition*, p. 168.

8. *Ibid.*, p. 250.

9. Professor Sellin also points out this fallacy in his *Slavery and the Penal System*.

10. Lea, *The Inquisition*, p. 307.

11. Scott, *Torture throughout the Ages*, p. 152.

12. We shall see in the following chapter how statistics on the death penalty in early English history have suffered a similar distortion.

13. H. C. Lea, *A History of the Spanish Inquisition* (New York: Macmillan, 1906), pp. 509-22.

14. *Ibid.*, p. 512.

15. A. Boileau, *History of the Flagellants, Otherwise of Religious Flagellations among Different Nations, Etc.* (London: Fielding and Walker, 1783).

16. Scott, *Torture throughout the Ages*, p. 117.

17. R. Krafft-Ebing, *Psychopathia Sexualis* (New York: F. J. Rebman, 1925), p. 36.

18. Scott, *Torture throughout the Ages*, p. 157.

19. Lea, *Spanish Inquisition*, p. 523.

20. V. Morais, *A Short History of Anti-Semitism* (New York: W. W. Norton & Co., 1976), p. 94.

21. The Jews have, of course, been persecuted periodically since time immemorial, and this has been thoroughly studied. We may note, however, that in England, they were not the objects of religious persecution, but rather were used for the financial betterment of the monarch—especially during the reign of Henry II. Usury (lending money on interest) was forbidden to Protestants, so the Jews did a roaring business, often lending at a rate of 40 percent or more. They were therefore hated by their debtors, and since they were a minority, the superstitions about their cannibalism of little boys were used by the king's office to extract money from them. They were required to pay a considerable amount of taxes, and especially harsh was Henry II's law that upon a Jew's death all his property went to the king; the Jew's family had to buy it back from the king. In this way, Henry financed many of his expensive ceremonies and feasts. His successors continued this practice, until Edward I made such financial demands on the Jews that they became penniless. Having outlived their usefulness, Edward had them expelled from England in 1290 (D. M. Stenton, *English Society in the Early Middle Ages* [London: Penguin, 1951], pp. 193-202).

22. H. Kramer and J. Sprenger, *Malleus Maleficarum*, trans. Montagu Summers (London: Hogarth Press, 1928), p. 44.

23. E. P. Evans, *The Criminal Prosecution and Capital Punishment of Animals* (London: Heinemann, 1906), pp. 18, 45-60.

24. Von Hentig, *Punishment*, pp. 112-16.

25. Evans, *Criminal Prosecution and Capital Punishment of Animals*, p. 173.

26. *Ibid.* Evans's methods of data collection are never stated, however, and one is not sure of the exhaustiveness of his search. He appears to have relied on the search of records in one or two provinces, with the rest of the cases collected from various secondary sources.

27. *Ibid.*, p. 140.

28. Demause, "The Evolution of Childhood," pp. 503-75.

29. Evans, *Criminal Prosecution and Capital Punishment of Animals.* The Christian justification for these terrible punishments was derived from Mosaic law, found in Exodus 22:19. It is a most disturbing irony that, as Evans notes, "the Christian law-givers should have adopted a Jewish code against sexual intercourse with beasts and then enlarged it so as to include the Jews themselves." In the fifteenth century, there were several serious legal cases concerning whether sexual intercourse with a Jew was equivalent to sodomy. One Jean Alard who kept a Jewess was convicted of sodomy and burned. The judgment was justified because ". . . coition with a Jewess is precisely the same as if a man should copulate with a dog."

30. *Ibid.,* pp. 98-102.

31. *Ibid.,* pp. 187f.

32 Sir W. Blackstone, *Commentaries on the Laws of England,* 17th ed., E. Christian (London: T. Tegg, 1830), Vol. 4.

33. G. Carson, *Men, Beasts and Gods* (New York: Charles Scribner's, 1972).

34. Evans, *Criminal Prosecution and Capital Punishment of Animals,* p. 139.

35. P. Singer, *Animal Liberation* (New York: New York Review, 1975); T. Regan and P. Singer, *Animal Rights and Human Obligations* (Englewood Cliffs, N. J.: Prentice-Hall, 1976).

36. Surely it is our "species" attitude to animals that at least works in favor of "endangered species." There are no longer court proceedings over individual animals. There are, however, many hearings conducted across the country which decide what species may or may not be killed, whether or not a particular species of animal (e.g., the coyote) is a "pest." These are trials, I suggest, not unlike those of the middle ages, except in this case the bogey is not demons, but ecology. Singer, *Animal Liberation,* also treats human retardates as equivalent to (and in some cases, lower than) animals. This seems to violate a clearly established fact: that humans *are* a species different from animals. A retarded human is a retarded human, with nothing at all in common with a chimp. Would Singer have us regard a retarded chimp as equivalent to a less intelligent species, such as a shark?

37. Although much of what today is called cruelty to animals is probably not punishment, strictly speaking, since it is often done for sport and other reasons and not because the animal has done something wrong, it is necessarily relevant to the history and practice of punishment. The reasons are two. First, it should be abundantly clear now that persons and objects are liable to a greater or lesser amount of punishment because of their particular status in relation to the institutions of social control. In other words, what a person or object is may be just as important as what the object has done in deciding the amount and type of punishment due. Second, what we do to animals, the way we treat them, may give us a further clue as to the complexion and general makeup of society at particular periods.

Animals were probably first used for sports of violence in the Roman Colosseum and have been used in various forms ever since. Most popular during the Tudor period in England was bull, bear, or horse baiting. The first bull-bait was held at Stamford, Lincolnshire, in 1209, and they were held regularly thereafter. Blaine's *Encyclopaedia of Rural Sports* (1840) provides us with a description of bull-baiting, from which the reader may decide for himself whether the sport is cruel or not.

> The animal is fastened to a stake driven into the ground for the purpose, and about seven or eight yards of rope left loose, so as to allow him sufficient liberty for the fight. In this situation a bull-dog is slipped at him, and endeavours to seize him by the nose; if the bull be well practised at the business, he will receive the dog on his horns, throw him off, and sometimes kill him; but, on the contrary, if the bull is not very dexterous, the dog will not only seize him by the nose, but will cling to his hold till the bull stands still; and this is termed *pinning the bull.* What are called good game bulls are very difficult to

be pinned: being constantly on their guard, and placing their noses close to the ground, they receive their antagonist on their horns; and it is astonishing to what distance they will sometimes throw them. It is not deemed fair to slip or let loose more than one dog at one and the same time.

This was no doubt a bloody sport, and we can conclude with some confidence that the people of the Tudor period were well used to the sight of blood. Again, one should not get too carried away with this observation: there are plenty of violent sports today. Cock fights and dog fights are still common in various parts of the United States, even though they have been outlawed. Legislation to prevent cruelty to animals has been somewhat more successful than that of trying to ban corporal punishment of children. The turning point in England came with the Martin Act in 1822, which specifically forbade cruelty to cattle. The "barbarous act" had to include malice toward the animal. Several revisions at later periods gradually expanded the act to cover wildlife and mental suffering. By 1911, all these acts were consolidated into one, so that cruelty was forbidden to all animals.

In the United States, similar laws were enacted in all states, and by 1910 there was "no state or territory lacking some general provision under which cruelty to animals may be prosecuted and punished." (R. C. McCrea, *The Humane Movement* [New York: Columbia University Press, 1910], p. 55). Today the situation is much the same, although there are a multiplicity of local laws to meet local conditions. In some places cock fights and dog fights are specifically forbidden. However, the master still has the right of life and death over his dog, as did the master over his slave in Roman times and the antebellum South. Dogs may be bought and sold, beaten privately, and one assumes no questions would be asked if one were seen burying one's dog in the backyard. And here again, the impracticality of Singer's arguments are clearly exposed. How could the individual treatment of domestic animals be controlled when the law prefers to keep hands off the family's treatment of its children? One could strangle his cat with impunity, since the life does not have to be accounted for. Would Singer require a death certificate to be signed?

38. S. Chandler, *The History of Persecution* (Hall: John Craggs, 1813), p. 315.
39. S. T. Bindoff, *Tudor England* (London. Penguin, 1969).
40. T. Gray, *Psalms and Slaughter* (London: Heinemann, 1972), p. 161.
41. Sir C. Firth, *Oliver Cromwell and the Rule of the Puritans in England* (London: Oxford University Press, 1956).
42. Chandler, *History of Persecution,* pp. 286-87.
43. *Ibid.,* p. 289.
44. *Ibid.,* pp. 300-07.
45. Andrews, *Bygone Punishments,* pp. 243-75. There is also considerable evidence of its frequent use in the records showing expenditure on repairs. The parish accounts of Worsborough, for example, show that repairs were made to the ducking stool every few years from 1703 to 1737.
46. A. M. Earle, *Curious Punishments of Bygone Days* (Rutland: Charles E. Tuttle, 1792).
47. J. W. Spargo, *Judicial Folklore in England Illustrated by the Cucking Stool* (Durham, N. C.: Duke University Press, 1944), p. 104.
48. *Ibid.,* p. 142.
49. Andrews, *Bygone Punishments,* p. 246.
50. *Ibid.,* p. 248.
51. Earle, *Curious Punishments.*
52. *Ibid.*
53. *Ibid.,* p. 280.
54. Andrews, *Bygone Punishments,* p. 280.
55. *Ibid.,* p. 281.

56. Earle, *Curious Punishments,* p. 102.
57. *Ibid.*
58. The following poem aptly captures the suffering of Jane Shore's penance which was ordered by Richard III's ecclesiastic court for witchery:

> *Submissiv., sad, and lonely was her look;*
> *A burning taper in her hand she bore;*
> *And on her shoulders, carelessly confused,*
> *With loose neglect her lovely tresses hung;*
> *Upon her cheek a faintish flush was spread;*
> *Feeble she seemed, and sorely smit with pain;*
> *While, barefoot as she trod the flinty pavement,*
> *Her footsteps all along were marked with blood.*
> *Yet silent still she passed, and unrepining;*
> *Her streaming eyes bent ever on the earth,*
> *Except when, in some bitter pang of sorrow,*
> *To heaven, she seemed, in fervent zeal to raise,*
> *And beg that mercy man denied her here.*
>
> (Andrews, *Bygone Punishments*)

59. Andrews, *Bygone Punishments,* pp. 239-42.
60. Earle, *Curious Punishments,* p. 109.
61. *Ibid.,* pp. 109-16.
62. *Ibid.,* pp. 117-18.

Chapter 6: Punishing Criminals

1. My reasons for selecting specifically English history are twofold. First, the history of English criminal law and punishment has an obviously close relationship to the history of the United States. Second, much of the socioeconomic history of European criminal punishment has been already covered in the excellent work of G. Rusche and O. Kirchheimer, *Punishment and Social Structure* (New York: Russell and Russell, 1968).
2. St. John, *Manners and Customs of Ancient Greece,* Vol. III, p. 230.
3. R. M. Geer, *Classical Civilization: Rome* (Englewood Cliffs, N. J.: Prentice-Hall, 1962), p. 68.
4. *Ibid.*
5. Bonner and Smith, *The Administration of Justice from Homer to Aristotle,* Vol. II, pp. 195f.
6. I do not want to suggest that capital punishment is therefore a function of dictatorial regimes. In feuding societies where there was no political "boss," the death penalty was still extracted through the process of vengeance.
7. Gortyn was the name of an ancient city of Crete. Two groups of inscriptions of local laws have been preserved, of the fifth and fourth centuries B. C., respectively. They consist of twelve columns of laws concerning debt, succession, marriage, and rights of slaves and are known as the Twelve Tables of Gortyn.
8. Bonner and Smith, *The Administration of Justice from Homer to Aristotle,* Vol. I, p. 78.
9. *Ibid.,* Vol. I, p. 282.
10. Often one-third of the fine was levied against the offender or one-half of the proceeds of confiscation of his property (*ibid.,* Vol. I, pp. 40-41).
11. Buckland, *Textbook of Roman Law.*
12. Confiscation occurred in Roman law as a part of *exilium,* or voluntary exile, applicable to Roman citizens. It is to be noted that economic sanctions were more appropriate to citizens, since they owned property. Slaves, in contrast, owned no property, so other forms of punishment were resorted to. There developed the

fourfold steps in penalties that could be applied to free men. These were called the *Relegatio,* or a popular decree denying the accused water, fire, or shelter.

1. Relegatio without loss of status, loss of life, or internment (usually to the stone and metal quarries—*ad metallum*).
2. Relegatio without loss of status or life, but internment.
3. Relegatio without internment, but loss of life.
4. Relegatio with internment, loss of life, citizenship, and confiscation (J. Goebel, *Felony and Misdemeanor* [Philadelphia: University of Pennsylvania Press, 1976]).

13. *Ibid.*
14. *Ibid.* See also G. Ives, *A History of Penal Methods* (Montclair, N. J : Patterson-Smith, 1970).
15. *Ibid.,* p. xiv.
16. The process of confiscation of property is considerably complicated by "feudal law" in which the serf or vassal is under contract to the lord. Goebel, *Felony and Misdemeanor,* pp. 244-45, describes the extensively complicated questions of inheritance under feudal law. There was no one simple principle operating.
17. The "Kings Peace" or "The Peace" and its variations has been seriously criticized by Goebel as a mythical construction of legal history. His criticism is that there is no record of any "crime" of breaking the Peace. The point to be understood is that the Peace was not a formal or even informal law that could be broken. Rather, Goebel tries to show that the Peace was a very strong social or psychological feeling on the part of the ordinary people to seek a way out of the unending violence of blood feud. It is more a "spirit for peace" which gained momentum throughout this period. Unfortunately, due to other forces in history—those of economics and religion—the quest for peace was to be shortlived, even aborted.
18. Goebel, *Felony and Misdemeanor,* p. 114.
19. Sellin, *Slavery and the Penal System.*
20. Goebel, *Felony and Misdemeanor,* p. 115.
21. *Ibid.,* p. 250.
22. J. Bellamy, *Crime and Public Order in England in the Later Middle Ages* (London. Routledge & Kegan Paul, 1973).
23. Bindoff, *Tudor England,* p. 38.
24. Here is a quaint comparison between these reports and the modern victim surveys which, we know, produce a measure of crimes by three and sometimes twenty times more than the officially reported rates. The quality of material used for this period is as follows: ". . . within a year [of 1461] Margaret Paston was able to write that there had never been so much robbery and manslaughter in her part of East Anglia" (Bellamy, *Crime and Public Order,* p. 9). One must depend upon individual anecdotes.
25. R. L. Storey, *The End of the House of Lancaster* (London: Stein and Day, 1966), pp. 86-87.
26. Bellamy, *Crime and Public Order.*
27. *Ibid.,* p. 192.
28. *Ibid.,* p. 197.
29. L. O. Pike, *A History of Crime in England* (London: Smith, Elder, 1873), pp. 110-11.
30. *Ibid.,* p. 2; Sir L. Radzinowicz, *A History of English Criminal Law* (London: Stevens, 1943), Vol. 1, p. 139.
31. Bindoff, *Tudor England,* p. 177.
32. W G. Calcutt, *The Common Law* (London: Heinemann, 1935), p. 171.
33 Lea, *The Inquisition,* p. 298; Bellamy, *Crime and Public Order,* pp. 139-40.
34. Bellamy, *Crime and Public Order,* pp. 180-82.
35. *Ibid.,* p. 183.
36. Earle, *Curious Punishments.*

37. Bellamy, *Crime and Public Order*, p. 182.
38. C. Stephenson and F. G. Marcham, *Sources of English Constitutional History* (New York: Harper & Row, 1937), p. 225.
39. Bellamy, *Crime and Public Order*, p. 182.
40. Andrews, *Bygone Punishments*.
41. *Ibid.*, p. 188.
42. This "drunk and disorderly" offense, as we would call it today, was dealt with in a variety of ways, depending on the locality. The "drunkard's cloak" is a popular "bygone punishment" which appears to have been confined solely to the Newcastle-on-Tyne area. This was a large wooden barrel into which was cut holes for the head and arms, and the drunkard was marched up and down the streets. Other punishments for drunkards were: hanging a heavy stone around his neck with "D" for drunkard stamped on it, small fines (five shillings), and ducking in cold water. Once again, all reported instances of the use of these punishments occurred during the seventeenth and eighteenth centuries (see: Andrews, *Bygone Punishments*, pp. 201-08; Earle, *Curious Punishments*).
43. Earle, *Curious Punishments*.
44. *Ibid.*
45. P. N. Walker, *Punishment: An Illustrated History* (New York: Arco, 1973), pp. 22-23.
46. Andrews, *Bygone Punishments*, pp. 143-58; Earle, *Curious Punishments*, pp 29-43
47. Scott, *Torture throughout the Ages*, p. 210.
48. Earle, *Curious Punishments*, p. 47.
49 Andrews, *Bygone Punishments*, p. 10.
50. Scott, *Torture throughout the Ages*, p. 235.
51. Andrews, *Bygone Punishments*, p. 149
52 Earle, *Curious Punishments*, p. 49.
53. *Ibid.*, p. 53.
54. Andrews, *Bygone Punishments*, p. 139.
55. *Ibid.*
56. *Ibid.*, p. 142.
57. Earle, *Curious Punishments*, p. 89.
58. One such example was the often quoted criminal sentence pronounced by the notorious Judge Jeffreys:

> "Hangman, I charge you to pay particular attention to this lady. Scourge her soundly, man: scourge her till her blood runs down! It is Christmas, a cold time for Madam to strip. See that you warm her shoulders thoroughly" (Scott, *Torture throughout the Ages*, p. 40).

59. Andrews, *Bygone Punishments*, p. 209.
60. R. Caldwell, *Red Hannah: Delaware's Whipping Post* (Philadelphia: University of Pennsylvania Press, 1947).
61. Caldwell claims that some kind of corporal punishment was used for almost all crimes (*ibid.*, p. 3) Barnes also says this (H. E. Barnes, *The Story of Punishment* [Boston: Stratford, 1930]). This is clearly a gross oversimplification There were many cases where fines only were levied, where serious penalties could be purchased off, and certainly a fine was almost automatic in addition to most corporal punishments, as we have seen.
62. I refer here to the very early criminal codes. Governor Andros proclaimed the laws of the Duke of York applicable to all settlements along the Delaware on September 25, 1676. These laws were first applied at Hempstead Long Island and came to be known as the Hempstead Code (Caldwell, *Red Hannah*, p. 4).
63. *Ibid.*, pp. 4-6.
64. Andrews, *Bygone Punishments*, p. 87.
65. For example, Barnes, *The Story of Punishment*.

Chapter 7: Death and Delirium:
Punishment Rears Its Ugly Head

1. See D. Hay et al., *Albion's Fatal Tree: Crime and Society in Eighteenth Century England* (London: Allen Lowe, 1975), p. 66, for a listing of these sayings and also a bibliography.
2. From *The Chronicles of Newgate* (1884), Vol. 1, p. 267. See also Radzinowicz, *English Criminal Law*, p. 176.
3. The procession is described countless times in most histories of criminal law and punishments concerned with the eighteenth century. This one is based on that provided by J. D. Potter, *The Fatal Gallows Tree* (London: Elek, 1965), pp. 36-38
4. This description, by Francis Place, has been quoted by Daniel Defoe, Henry Fielding, and others. (See Hay et al., *Albion's Fatal Tree*, p. 68.)
5. This letter is taken from Potter, *The Fatal Gallows Tree*, who does not state its original source. It is to be noted that this description corroborates that of Francis Place quoted above, but not that of Hay et al., who criticize the image conveyed by the frequent quotation of Place. The blatant ideological services to which Hay et al. attempt to reduce their accounts of eighteenth-century history of crime and punishment suggest that theirs is not to be taken as altogether accurate either.
6. G. T. Wilkinson, *The Newgate Calendar* (London: n.p., 1816), p. 252.
7. See Radzinowicz, *English Criminal Law*, p. 142; also Hay, *Albion's Fatal Tree*, for a brief discussion of these statistics. I will discuss them in more detail below.
8. Firth, *Oliver Cromwell and the Rule of the Puritans in England*.
9. M. Ashley, *England in the Seventeenth Century (1603-1714)* (London: Pelican, 1952), pp. 115-16.
10. J. Locke, *Second Treatise on Government* (Oxford: B. Blackwell, 1948), Secs 85 and 94.
11. I am inclined to think that this interpretation of Locke is both a little strained and inconsequential Locke defines property very broadly to include life and liberty. Certainly his was a philosophy of individualism. It was not, however, a class theory as others imply. See Hay, *Albion's Fatal Tree*, for this criticism of Locke.
12. The new East India Company raised £1,200,000 from the public in twelve days, and it loaned this money to the government (the first time we have used this word¹) at 8 percent interest. This, among other techniques, helped William to finance his war against the French. More importantly, the Bank of England was invested in heavily by Whig merchants who retained a majority in Parliament Eventually, the Tories also invested in the Bank, so that Parliament directly controlled the money— and thus the loans to the crown.
13. Potter, *The Fatal Gallows Tree*, p. 32.
14. Radzinowicz, *English Criminal Law*.
15. There has been some argument about this. Naturally, Hay et al. insist that there was no such approval. Radzinowicz cites the placid Parliament that made the laws as evidence of wide public approval, at least for the first part of the eighteenth century. This assumption might be reasonable, had the M. P s been elected by universal suffrage. Of course, they were not, so they could hardly be taken to represent the masses. Public "approval" may be inferred, not from the law, but from its ready participation in the hanging process. The public accepted it as part of the way of life, just as its ancestors had accepted whatever the king had pronounced.
16. J. H. Plumb, *England in the Eighteenth Century* (Baltimore, Md.: Penguin, 1963), p. 95.
17. Hay, *Albion's Fatal Tree*, p. 114. There were many cases of the condemned and their family and friends treating the execution as a wedding, complete with nuptial finery, white wands, and maidens dressed in white.
18 Charles Wesley, *The Journal* 1 (1849): 215.
19. For a further discussion of the psychology of the masses at the time and its rela-

tion to religion, see: G. R. Taylor, *The Angel Makers: A Study of the Psychological Origin of Social Change* (New York: Dutton, 1974). See also Chapter 9.

20. Radzinowicz, *English Criminal Law,* pp. 5-10.
21. *Ibid.,* p. 148.
22. Adapted from *ibid.,* pp. 151, 157.
23. *Ibid.,* p. 149.
24. H. Fielding, *An Inquiry into the Causes of the Late Increase in Robbers* (New York: AMS Press, 1751, 1975, rpt.).
25. Radzinowicz, *English Criminal Law,* p. 14.
26. Hay, *Albion's Fatal Tree,* pp. 65-117.
27. M. Foucault, *Birth of the Clinic: An Archeology of Medical Perception,* trans. Sheridan Smith (New York: Pantheon, 1973).
28. Potter, *The Fatal Gallows Tree,* p. 78.
29. W. McAdoo, *Procession to Tyburn* (New York: Boni and Liveright, 1927), pp. 272-88.
30. It is to be noted, though, that Penn had no compunction in introducing the Newcastle Code which called for brandings, floggings, and mutilations.
31. W. F. Poole, "Witchcraft in Boston," in J. Winsor, *The Memorial History of Boston* (Boston: J. R. Osgood and Co., 1881), Vol. II, p. 131.
32. N. Teeters, *Hang by the Neck* (Springfield, Ill.: Charles C Thomas, 1967), pp. 59f.
33. *Ibid.,* p. 76.
34. O. W. Burt, *American Murder Ballads and Their Stories* (New York: Oxford University Press, 1958), passim, stanzas from pp. 214-15.
35. *Ibid.,* p. 162.

Chapter 8: That Wonderful Utilitarian Punishment Scheme

1. Attributed to John Jay Chapman.
2. C. Phillipson, *Three Criminal Law Reformers* (Montclair, N. J.: Patterson-Smith, 1970), p. 57.
3. Abolished in England in 1834.
4. Phillipson, *Three Criminal Law Reformers,* p. 62.
5. See Radzinowicz, *English Criminal Law,* for a collection of foreigners' surprised observations of England's open trial system and minimal use of torture
6. *Ibid.,* p. 271.
7. Phillipson, *Three Criminal Law Reformers,* p. 62.
8. Fielding, *The Late Increase in Robbers.*
9. *Ibid.,* p. 118.
10. Radzinowicz, *English Criminal Law,* p. 255.
11. See Chapter 10.
12. Radzinowicz, *English Criminal Law,* passim.
13. Phillipson, *Three Criminal Law Reformers,* p. 59.
14. Fielding, *The Late Increase in Robbers,* p. 120.
15. *Ibid.,* p. 55.
16. C. B. Beccaria, *On Crimes and Punishments,* trans. Henry Paolucci (New York: Bass-Merrill, 1963).
17. *Ibid.,* p. 12.
18. *Ibid.,* p. 19.
19. *Ibid.,* p. 43.
20. *Ibid.,* p. 54.
21. Radzinowicz, *English Criminal Law,* p. 283.
22. Fielding, *The Late Increase in Robbers,* p. 64.
23. *Ibid.,* p. 21.
24. Phillipson, *Three Criminal Law Reformers,* p. 54.

25. Beccaria, *On Crimes and Punishments,* p. 99.

26. Bentham in M. P. Mack, ed., *A Bentham Reader* (New York: Pegasus, 1969), p. xv.

27. See, for example, H. Fingarette, *The Meaning of Criminal Insanity* (Berkeley: University of California Press, 1973); also G. R. Newman, "Clinical and Legal Perceptions of Deviance," *A. N. Z. Journal of Criminology* 9 (1976):37-47, for an assessment of similarities.

28. J. Bentham, *An Introduction to the Principles of Morals and Legislation,* in *Collected Works,* ed. J. H. Burns and H. L. A. Hart (London: Athlone Press, 1970), p. 13. Throughout the following exposition I have relied heavily on this work, which I consider to be his most basic and clearest.

29. *Ibid.,* p. 12.

30. *Ibid.*

31. *Ibid.,* p. 34.

32. *Ibid.,* p. 125.

33. *Ibid.,* p. 126.

34. *Ibid.,* pp. 172-73.

35. This is the solution of individualizing punishment put forward by D. Salleiles, *The Individualization of Punishment* (Boston: Little, Brown, 1911). Today, it is claimed that individualization does the opposite of achieving equity, since it suggests *different* punishments for the same crime—at least in the public's eyes. See: Von Hirsch, *Doing Justice,* p. 36, Chap. VII.

36. *Traites de Legislation Civile et Penale* published by Bentham's friend, Dumont, in 1802. This passage taken from chapter VII of C. M. Atkinson's translation (New York: Oxford University Press, 1914).

Chapter 9: The Reformation

1. E. P. Thompson, *The Making of the English Working Class* (New York: Vintage, 1966), pp. 370f.

2. *Ibid.,* p. 335.

3 *Ibid.;* also F. Engels, *The Condition of the Working Class in England,* trans. and ed. W. O. Henderson and W. H. Chaloner (Stanford, Calif.: Stanford University Press, 1958).

4. W. Reich, *The Mass Psychology of Fascism,* trans. V. R. Carfagno (New York: Reich Trust Fund, 1971).

5. Thompson, *The Making of the English Working Class,* p. 348.

6. *Ibid.,* p. 347.

7. M. Weber, *The Protestant Ethic and the Spirit of Capitalism* (New York: Charles Scribner's, 1958), p. 53.

8. Taylor, *The Angel Makers.*

9. *Ibid.*

10. Plumb, *England in the Eighteenth Century,* p. 121.

11. See Hay, *Albion's Fatal Tree,* for an extensive treatment of this question.

12. Bentham attended Wilkes's trials and was certainly not impressed by the bumbling, chaotic "technical system," as he called it.

13. See C. Hibbert, *King Mob* (Cleveland, Ohio: World Publishers, 1958); G. Rude, "The Gordon Riots," *Trans. Royal Historical Society* 5 (1956):6; J. P. De Castro, *The Gordon Riots* (Oxford: Oxford University Press, 1926); Thompson, *The Making of the English Working Class,* pp. 72-73. There is some argument as to whether a plot really existed and, if so, the extent to which there was a national underground organization. I have relied on Thompson's account, which seems the most balanced. There was a plot, its aims were vague, but the extent of the organization is unknown.

14. Plumb, *England in the Eighteenth Century.*

15. *Ibid.,* p. 200.

16. Radzinowicz, *English Criminal Law*, pp. 226-27.
17. Rev. T. Mozley, *Reminiscences, Chiefly of Oriel College and the Oxford Movement*, 2nd ed. (London: Longmans, Green, 1882), Vol. 1, pp. 191-92.
18. *Journals of the House of Commons* (1750-1754), Vol. 26, p. 190.
19. See Chapters 6 and 7.
20. This bill was, strangely, presented by Wilberforce, and it was connected also with a request to reduce burning to hanging for females convicted of high or petty treason. See Radzinowicz, *English Criminal Law*, pp. 476-78.
21. Mack, *A Bentham Reader*, p. 193.
22. J. Bowring, ed., *Collected Works of Jeremy Bentham* (New York: Russell and Russell, 1962), Vol. 9, p. 96.
23. See Mack, *A Bentham Reader*, p. 198.
24. Radzinowicz, *English Criminal Law*, p. 571.
25. J. B. Conacher, *Waterloo to the Common Market* (New York: Random House, 1975), p. 40.
26. See D. D. Cooper, *The Lesson of the Scaffold* (Athens: Ohio University Press, 1974); J. Jester, "The Abolition of Public Executions: A Case Study," *International Journal of Penology and Criminology* 4 (1976):25-32; P. Collins, *Dickens and Crime* (Bloomington: Indiana University Press, 1968).
27. D. J. Rothman, *Discovery of the Asylum* (Boston: Little, Brown, 1971), p. 82.

Chapter 10: The Principles of Punishment

1. I. Kant, *The Philosophy of Law, Part II*, trans. W. Hastil (Edinburgh: T. T. Clar, 1887), pp. 194-95. Throughout this discussion on retribution, I am concerned essentially to develop an analysis from the point of view of social theory. An excellent philosophical analysis may be found in J. Kleinig, *Punishment and Desert* (The Hague: Martinus Nijhoff, 1973), where a central thesis is that retribution is part of the definition of punishment.
2. Kant, *The Philosophy of Law*.
3. A. W. Gouldner, "The Norm of Reciprocity: A Preliminary Statement," *American Sociological Review* 25 (1960):161-78; B. Malinowski, *Crime and Custom in Savage Society* (Totowa, N. J.: Littlefield, Adams & Co., 1964).
4. P. M. Blau, *Exchange and Power in Social Life* (New York: John Wiley & Sons, 1964).
5. However, it does form the basis of my moral theory of punishment expounded in Chapter 13.
6. Of course, we should be careful not to confuse this with the many "crimes" against which punishments are never enforced. But to have been termed crimes in the first place, punishment has to be prescribed. Yet, some would even argue that in this case such acts are no longer crimes if they are never punished.
7. G. W. F. Hegel, *The Philosophy of Right*, trans T. M. Knox (London: Oxford University Press, 1969), Sec. 100.
8. Kant, *The Philosophy of Law*.
9. This is the position presently argued forcefully by Ernest van den Haag. See E. van den Haag, *Punishing Criminals* (New York: Basic Books, 1975).
10. An excellent example of this is the Roman Catholic doctrine of punishment which claims to be retributive but historically, at least since the Inquisition, has been plainly utilitarian in the sense that its aims were either to "reform" the religious deviant through punishment or to completely eradicate heresy by judicious use of torture and the death penalty. See, for example, Pope Pious XII, "Crime and Punishment," *Catholic Lawyer* 6 (1960):92.
11. See J. Hall, *General Principles of Criminal Law*, 2nd ed. (New York: Bobbs-Merrill, 1947).
12. See, for example, J. D. Mabbott, "Punishment," *Mind* 48 (1939):152-67.

13. This debasement of the retributive model is achieved by Von Hirsch, *Doing Justice.*
14. The modern approach to this question is to specify in great detail the gradation of sentences based on severity of the crime and the number of prior offenses. See A. M. Dershowitz, *Fair and Certain Punishment* (New York: McGraw-Hill, 1976).
15. For a more detailed discussion of this question, see van den Haag, *Punishing Criminals.* The answer to this problem lies in an assessment of the morality of inequality, which I discuss more fully in Chapter 13.
16. *Ibid.* See also E. van den Haag, "No Excuse for Crime," *Annals of the American Academy of Political and Social Science* 423 (1976):133-41.
17. Dershowitz, *Fair and Certain Punishment.*
18. Some research suggests that judges do not act in this way, so that we may infer, by and large, that they do not punish retributively (although they say they do). This is what one would expect, since I have shown that the retributive principle of punishment has all but disappeared from our criminal law, or at least has been heavily overshadowed by utilitarian principles. See J. Hogarth, *Sentencing as a Human Process* (Toronto: University of Toronto Press, 1971).
19. Phillipson, *Three Criminal Law Reformers*, p. 59.
20. Plato, *Laws* 11, 934.
21. We have an excellent example of a leading English criminal lawyer of this century embracing completely this idea by putting forward what he has shrewdly characterized as a "sophisticated" form of retribution: that the retributivist gives up both the notion that penal measures should be designed with an eye to atonement and that the severity of the punishment should be directly related to the severity of the offense. All the retributivist insists on is that no person be punished unless he has committed an offense This is an incredible evacuation of the basic principles of retribution and would allow for a utilitarian system such as that of the eighteenth and nineteenth centuries to be characterized as "refined retributivism." See N. Walker, *The Aims of the Penal System* (Edinburgh: Edinburgh University Press, 1966). This form of retributivism is sometimes called "retribution in distribution." See also Hart, *Punishment and Responsibility.*
22. Zimring and Hawkins, *Deterrence.*
23. J. Andenaes, "The General Preventive Effects of Punishment," *University of Pennsylvania Law Review* 114 (1966):949
24. G. Hawkins, "Punishment and Deterrence: The Educative, Moralizing and Habituative Effects," *Wisconsin Law Review* 2 (1969):550.
25. *Ibid.*
26. Freud and Nietzsche are usually credited with the discovery of the unconscious Of course, others using hypnosis, such as Freud's teacher Charcot, knew of behavior that was not "consciously" motivated, particularly under hypnosis, but it was Freud who gave the concept its substantive meaning and application
27. This school, very dominant at present, is known as "attribution theory." The assumption is that man is by nature teleological, and he seeks to perceive the "motives" of others using this schema. Thus, it is a psychology of cognition rather than behavior (as it has previously been understood by other psychologists), with the important implication that cognition is the central key to explaining behavior According to this model, intentions and "free will" become major theoretical categories, not as "objective" data, but as *perceived* data. That is, attribution theorists concern themselves with perceived freedom (of self and others) See, for example, E. E. Jones et al., *Attribution: Perceiving the Causes of Behavior* (Morristown, N. J.: General Learning Press, 1971).
28. See, for example, Phillipson, *Three Criminal Law Reformers*, who lists many acts of Parliament enacted as a direct result of Bentham's work.
29. Zimring and Hawkins, *Deterrence.* With the invasion of economists into the field of criminal justice, we may expect much more pressure on the criminal law to move in this direction. See, for example, I. Ehrlich, "The Deterrent Effect of Criminal

Law Enforcement," *Journal of Legal Studies* 2 (1972):259, a paper which had enormous publicity and probable political effects.

30. Bentham, *An Introduction to the Principles of Morals and Legislation*, pp. 159-60.
31. Salleilles, *The Individualization of Punishment.*
32. See, for example, H. Mayhew, *London Labor and London Poor* (New York: Dover, 1968), Vol. IV.
33. This is explicitly recognized by modern deterrence theorists, Hawkins, "Punishment and Deterrence," Zimring and Hawkins, *Deterrence.*
34. We should realize, however, that recommendations for pardons or commutation were the only form of discretion afforded to judges of the eighteenth and early nineteenth centuries. They were, in fact, hemmed in by an incredibly literal and stilted criminal law. The result was that the "slack" needed in any criminal law system to translate legislation into practice was deposited at the jury and prosecution level, where perhaps the first forms of "bargain justice" developed: prosecutor, defense, and jury bargained over the value of items stolen so as to charge the offender with misdemeanors instead of felonies. Also, on a very early use of plea bargaining: C. Cottù, *De l'administration de la justice criminelle en Angleterre* (Paris: G. Gaselin, 1820). Cottù provides a description of plea bargaining in dealing with the crime of using forged bank notes, where bargaining took place in front of the public, the judge, and the jury. I am grateful to David Thomas for his translation of Cottù.
35. M. Ancel, *Social Defense: A Modern Approach to Problems* (New York: Schocken, 1965).
36. E. Ferri, *Criminal Sociology* (New York: Appleton-Century Crofts, 1900).
37. Lady B. Wootton, *Crime and the Criminal Law* (London: Stevens and Sons, 1963).
38. Ancel, *Social Defense.*
39. *Ibid.*
40. Plato, *Gorgias* in *The Collected Dialogues of Plato*, ed. E. Hamilton and H. Cairus (Princeton, N. J.: Princeton University Press, 1961), pp. 262-63.
41. See, for example, A. J. R. Matthews, *Mental Disability and the Law* (Chicago: American Bar Foundation, 1970).
42. Wootton, *Crime and the Criminal Law.*
43. *Ibid.*, p. 108.
44. Ferri, *Criminal Sociology*, p. 185.
45. See, e.g., N. Morris and G. Hawkins, *The Honest Politician's Guide to Crime Control* (Chicago: University of Chicago Press, 1970).
46. E. Ferri, *Project for a Model Penal Code* (n.p., 1921), pp. 395-492.
47. E. g., Ancel, *Social Defense;* Wootton, *Crime and the Criminal Law.*
48. See Chapter 13 for a further discussion of this question.
49. Ferri, *Criminal Sociology*, p. 251.

Chapter 11: The Science of Punishment

1. R. L. Solomon, "Punishment," *American Psychologist* 19, 4 (1964):239-52.
2. B. F. Skinner, *Science and Human Behavior* (New York: Macmillan, 1953), p. 183.
3. B. F. Skinner, *Cumulative Record* (New York: Appleton-Century Croft, 1961).
4. O. H. Mowrer, *Learning Theory and Behavior* (New York: John Wiley & Sons, 1960), pp. 21-28.
5. R. M. Church, "The Varied Effects of Punishment on Behavior," *Psychological Review* 70, 5 (1963):372-80.
6. E. R. Guthrie, *The Psychology of Learning* (New York: Harper & Row, 1935), p. 158.
7. D. G. Perry and R. D. Parke, "Punishment and Alternative Response Training as Determinants of Response Inhibition in Children," *Genetic Psychology Monographs* 91, 2 (1975):257-79.

8. See J. C. Lavoie, "Aversive, Cognitive, and Parental Determinants of Punishment Generalization in Adolescent Males," *Journal of Genetic Psychology* 124, 1 (1974): 29-39.
9. E. L. Thorndike, *Educational Psychology*, Vol. 11, *The Psychology of Learning* (New York: Teacher's College, Columbia University, 1913), p. 4.
10. See Solomon, "Punishment"; also Church, "The Varied Effects of Punishment on Behavior," pp. 369-80.
11. Solomon, "Punishment," p. 64.
12. See, e.g., J. Deese and S. H. Hulse, *The Psychology of Learning* (New York: McGraw-Hill, 1967), Chap. 6.
13. H. J. Eysenck, *Crime and Personality* (Boston: Houghton Mifflin, 1964).
14. R. Schwitzgebel and R. Schwitzgebel, *Psychotechnology* (New York: Holt, Rinehart and Winston, 1973); R. Schwitzgebel and D. Kolb, *Changing Human Behavior: Principles of Planned Intervention* (New York: McGraw-Hill, 1974).
15. Caldwell, *Red Hannah*.
16. See, e.g., J. Mitford, *Cruel and Usual Punishment: The Prison Business* (New York: Alfred A. Knopf, 1973).
17. D. Glaser, *The Effectiveness of a Prison and Parole System* (New York: Bobbs-Merrill, 1969).
18. R. Martinson, "What Works? Questions and Answers about Prison Reform," *The Public Interest* 35 (1974):22-54; A. R. N. Cross, *Punishment, Prison and the Public: An Assessment of Penal Reform in Twentieth Century England by an Armchair Penologist* (London: Stevens and Sons, 1971); L. T. Wilkins, "Directions for Corrections," *Proceedings of the American Philosophical Society* 118 (1974):235-47; W. C. Bailey, "Correctional Outcome: An Evaluation of 100 Reports," *J. Criminal Law, Criminology and Police Science* 57 (1966):153-60; L. T. Wilkins, *The Evaluation of Penal Measures* (New York: Random House, 1969).
19. N. Morris and F. Zimring, "Deterrence and Corrections," *Annals of the American Academy of Political and Social Sciences* 381 (1969):137-46.
20. J. P. Gibbs, Paper presented to the School of Criminal Justice Colloquium on the Death Penalty, May 1977, State University of New York at Albany. See also, J P. Gibbs, *Punishment and Deterrence* (New York: Elsevier, 1975).
21. G. Hawkins, *The Prison* (Chicago: University of Chicago Press, 1976). Quote from Martinson, "What Works?," p. 47.
22. R. L. Solomon, L. H. Turner, and M. S. Lessac, "Some Effects of Delay of Punishment on Resistance to Punishment in Dogs," *Journal of Personality and Social Psychology* 8, 3 (1968):233-38.
23. W. K. Estes, "An Experimental Study of Punishment," *Psychological Monographs* 57, 3 (1944):263; Skinner, *Science and Human Behavior*.
24. N. H. Azrin and W. C. Holz, "Punishment," in *Operant Behavior: Areas of Research and Application*, ed. W. Honig (New York: Appleton-Century Crofts, 1966); also, Solomon, "Punishment."
25. B. F. Singer, "Psychological Studies of Punishment," *California Law Review* 58, 2 (March 1970):414.
26. R. D. Parke, "The Role of Punishment in the Socialization Process," in *Early Experiences and the Process of Socialization*, ed. R. A. Hoppe, F. C. Simmel, G. A. Milton (New York: Academic Press, 1970), p. 86. The other studies were: R. D. Parke, "Effectiveness of Punishment as an Interaction of Intensity, Timing Agent Nurturance and Cognitive Structuring," *Child Development* 40 (1969):213-35; J. Aronfreed and R. Leff, "The Effects of Intensity of Punishment and Complexity of Discrimination upon the Learnings of Internalized Inhibition" (unpub. manuscript, University of Pennsylvania, 1963); R. D. Parke and R. H. Walters, "Some Factors Determining the Efficacy of Punishment for Inducing Response Inhibition," *Monograph of the Soc. for Res. in Child Development* 32 (1967):109; J. A. Cheyne and R. H. Walters, "Intensity of Punishment, Timing of Punishment and

Cognitive Structure as Determinants of Response Inhibition," *J. Exp. Child Psychology* 7 (1969):231-44.

27. R. H. Walters and R. D. Parke, "The Influence of Punishment and Related Disciplinary Techniques on the Social Behavior of Children: Theory and Empirical Findings," in *Progress in Experimental Personality Research,* ed. B. A Maher (New York: Academic Press, 1967), Vol. 4, pp. 179-228. See also A. Bandura and R. H. Walters, *Adolescent Aggression* (New York: Ronald Press, 1959).

28. Aronfreed and Leff, "The Effects of Intensity of Punishment."

29. Walters and Parke, "The Influence of Punishment." See also H. S. Erlanger, "Social Class and Corporal Punishment in Child Rearing: A Reassessment," *American Sociological Review* 39 (1974):68-85, for a review of these studies.

30. I am indebted to Carol Trilling for her thorough and extensive review of the deterrence literature. See C. Trilling, "Publicity and Homicide: A View from the Deterrence Perspective" (Ph.D. diss., State University of New York at Albany, 1977).

31. T. Sellin, "Death and Imprisonment as Deterrents to Murder," and "Does the Death Penalty Protect Municipal Police," in *The Death Penalty in America,* ed. H. Bedau (Chicago: Aldine Publishing Co., 1967); K. Schuessler, "The Deterrent Influence of the Death Penalty," *Annals of the American Academy of Political and Social Science* 284 (1952):284; L. Savitz, "A Study of Capital Punishment," *J. Criminal Law, Criminology and Police Science* 49 (1958):338.

32. T. Sellin, "Capital Punishment," *Federal Probation* 25 (1961):70.

33. These were: J. P. Gibbs, "Crime, Punishment and Deterrence," *Social Science Quarterly* 48 (1968); L. N. Gray and J. D. Martin, "Punishment and Deterrence: Another Analysis of Gibbs' Data," *Social Science Quarterly* 50 (1969); C. Tittle, "Crime Rates and Legal Sanctions," *Social Problems* 16 (1969):109; F. D. Bean and R. G. Cushing, "Criminal Homicide, Punishment and Deterrence: Methodological and Substantive Reconsiderations," *Southwestern Social Science Journal* 52 (1971):277; W. C. Bailey and R. W. Smith, "Punishment: Its Severity and Certainty," *J. Criminal Law, Criminology and Police Science* 63 (1972):530; Ehrlich, "The Deterrent Effect of Criminal Law Enforcement"; W. C. Bailey, D. J. Martin, and L. N. Gray, "Crime and Deterrence: A Correlation Analysis," *J. Research in Crime and Delinquency* 11 (1974):124.

34. These were: Tittle, "Crime Rates and Legal Sanctions"; C. Logan, "General Deterrent Effects of Imprisonment," *Social Forces* 51 (1972):64.

35. See Singer, "Psychological Studies of Punishment," for a review of these studies; Solomon, Turner, and Lessac, "Some Effects of Delay of Punishment," pp. 233-38, Parke and Walters, "Some Factors Determining the Efficacy of Punishment."

36. Solomon, Turner, and Lessac, "Some Effects of Delay of Punishment "

37. Parke, "The Role of Punishment in the Socialization Process."

38. Eysenck, *Crime and Personality.*

39. K. E. Renner and L. Specht, "The Relative Desirability of Aversiveness of Immediate or Delayed Food and Shock," *J. Experimental Psychology* 75 (1967):568; also Singer, "Psychological Studies of Punishment."

40. Parke, "The Role of Punishment in the Socialization Process."

41. E. Aronson and J. M. Carlsmith, "Effect of Severity of Threat on the Devaluation of Forbidden Behavior," *J. Abnorm. Social Psychology* 66, 6 (1963):584-88.

42. S. Glueck and E. Glueck, *Unravelling Juvenile Delinquency* (Cambridge, Mass.: Harvard University Press, 1951); J. McCord, W. McCord, and I. Zola, *Origins of Crime* (New York: Columbia University Press, 1959).

43. A. E. Fisher, "The Effects of Differential Early Treatment on the Social and Exploratory Behavior of Puppies," reported by Parke, "The Role of Punishment in the Socialization Process."

44. *Ibid.*

45. This has been researched in the area of rewards, where varying schedules of reinforcement are often used according to a set pattern which the subject is able to "anticipate."
46. These were: Gibbs, "Crime, Punishment and Deterrence"; Gray and Martin, "Punishment and Deterrence"; Tittle, "Crime Rates and Legal Sanctions"; Bean and Cushing, "Criminal Homicide"; Ehrlich, "The Deterrent Effect of Criminal Law Enforcement"; Logan, "General Deterrence Effects of Imprisonment"; Bailey, Martin, and Gray, "Crime and Deterrence."
47. These were: T. G. Chiricos and G. P. Waldo, "Punishment and Crime: An Examination of Some Empirical Evidence," *Social Problems* 18 (1970-71):200; Bailey and Smith, "Punishment"; G. Antunes and L. Hunt, "The Impact of Certainty and Severity of Punishment on Levels of Crime in American States: An Extended Analysis," *J. Criminal Law and Criminology* 64 (1973):486. No relationship was found by Bailey, "Correctional Outcome." This study used data of 1967-68, whereas all other studies used data prior to this time, most for the same period as Gibbs's study. This might suggest that the effectiveness of punishment parameters varies considerably over long time periods, so that future studies should take this into account.
48. Parke, "The Role of Punishment in the Socialization Process," p. 91.
49. R. R. Sears, E. E. Maccoby, and H. Levin, *Patterns of Child Rearing* (New York: Harper & Row, 1957), pp. 325-47.
50. Parke, "The Role of Punishment in the Socialization Process."
51. Summarized in *ibid.*
52. Aronfreed, reported in *ibid.*
53. Lavoie, "Punishment Generalization in Adolescent Males."
54. Parke, "The Role of Punishment in the Socialization Process."
55. N. Walker and M. Argyle, "Does the Law Affect Moral Judgments?," *British Journal of Criminology* 4, 6 (1964):570. See also for a review of these studies: G. R. Newman, *Comparative Deviance* (New York: Elsevier, 1976), Chap. 3; and R. L. Henshel and R. A. Silverman, *Perception in Criminology* (New York: Columbia University Press, 1975).
56. D. Miller et al., "Public Knowledge of Criminal Penalties: A Research Report," in *Deterrent Effects of Criminal Sanctions*, Progress Report of California Assembly Committee on Criminal Procedure, California, 1968.
57. See, for example, Newman, *Comparative Deviance*, for a review of these studies. The pioneering study was: T. Sellin and M. E. Wolfgang, *The Measurement of Delinquency* (New York: John Wiley & Sons, 1963). An interesting recent study has linked the public perception of the seriousness of crimes inversely to crime rates. The authors of this study interpreted these findings as "against" the deterrence doctrine on the grounds that it was "extralegal" condemnation that was deterring, and not the law. But this is a narrow interpretation of the definition of deterrence, since one could easily argue that the findings lend support to the more general "educative, moralizing and habituative" effects of the criminal law. See: M L. Erickson, J. P. Gibbs, and G. F. Jensen, "The Deterrence Doctrine and the Perceived Certainty of Legal Punishments," *American Sociological Review* 42 (1977):305-17.
58. The work of Short and Stroedbeck used a similar model for the explanation of delinquent behavior. See J Short and F. Stroedbeck, *Group Process and Gang Delinquency* (Chicago: University of Chicago Press, 1965). Other studies dealing with the expected probability of getting caught are: D. Claster, "Comparisons of Risk Perception between Delinquents and Non-Delinquents," *J. Criminal Law and Criminology* 58, 80 (1967); J. Jensen, "Crime Doesn't Pay: Correlates of a Shared Misunderstanding," *Social Problems* 17 (1969); R. Meier and W. T. Johnson, "Deterrence as Social Control," *American Sociological Review* 42, 2 (1977):292-304.

59. Singer, "Psychological Studies of Punishment," p. 417.
60. At least this is the case with Gibbs; Tittle; Bean and Cushing; Bailey and Smith; Ehrlich; Logan; Bailey, Martin, and Gray.
61. Antunes and Hunt, "The Impact of Certainty and Severity of Punishment on Levels of Crime in American States," pp. 150-51. This finding was also supported by Logan, "General Deterrence Effects of Imprisonment."
62. R. H. Walters and J. A. Cheyne, *Punishment* (London: Penguin, 1972); Parke, "The Role of Punishment in the Socialization Process," p. 96.
63. For a summary of all these studies see R. Drabman and R. Spitalnik, "Social Isolation as a Punishment Procedure: A Controlled Study," *Journal of Experimental Child Psychology* 16, 2 (1973):236-49.
64. Much research has been conducted in this area on the effects of allowing mentally retarded and other handicapped in the normal classroom, the results of which generally suggest that the behavior of other children may be enhanced. See: G. R. Newman, "Deviance and Removal" (Ph.D. diss., University of Pennsylvania, 1972). None have been conducted on delinquents, to my knowledge.
65. Tittle, "Crime Rates and Legal Sanctions"; Bailey, Martin, and Gray, "Crime and Deterrence."
66. W. J. Chambliss, "The Deterrent Influence of Punishment," *Crime and Delinquency* 12 (1966):70-75.
67. R. Salem and W. J. Bowers, "Severity of Formal Sanctions as a Deterrent to Deviant Behavior," *Law and Society Review* 21 (August 1970).
68. R. D. Schwartz and S. Orleans, "On Legal Sanctions," *University of Chicago Law Review* 34 (Winter 1967):274-300.
69. D. T. Campbell and H. L. Ross, "The Connecticut Crackdown on Speeding: Time-Series Data in Quasi-Experimental Analysis," *Law and Society Review* 3 (1969).
70. B. Schwartz, "The Effect in Philadelphia of Pennsylvania's Increased Penalties for Rape and Attempted Rape," *J. Criminal Law, Criminology and Police Science* 59, 4 (1968):509.
71. R. Chauncey, "Deterrence: Certainty, Severity and Skyjacking," *Criminology* 12, 4 (1975):447.
72. A. C. Baldwin, *Theories of Child Development* (New York: John Wiley & Sons, 1967).
73. R. R. Sears, J. W. M. Whiting, V. Nowlis, and P. S. Sears, "Some Child Rearing Antecedents of Aggression and Dependency in Young Children," *Genetic Psychol. Monograph* 57 (1953):153-234. Also Erlanger, "Social Class and Corporal Punishment in Childrearing."
74. See Zimring and Hawkins, *Deterrence,* for a detailed analysis. Also: J. P. Gibbs, *Crime, Punishment and Deterrence* (New York: Elsevier, 1975).
75. P. Passel and J. B. Taylor, "The Deterrent Effect of Capital Punishment: Another View," Economics Workshop Discussion Paper 74-7509, Columbia University, 1975.
76. D. J. Abbott and J. M. Kalonico, "Black Men, White Women—The Maintenance of a Myth: Rape and the Press in New Orleans," in *Crime and Delinquency: Dimensions of Deviance,* ed. M. Riedel and T. Thornberry (New York: Praeger, 1974).
77. Singer, "Psychological Studies of Punishment"; S. Shah, "Treatment of Offenders: Some Behavioral Concepts, Principles and Approaches," *Federal Probation* 30 (1966):29.
78. An excellent review of the uses of "threat appeal" may be found in Zimring and Hawkins, *Deterrence,* pp. 141-71.
79. Trilling, "Publicity and Homicide." There have been a few studies on the relationship between crime and the media, but none of them have been formal pieces of research with any sound methodology, nor have they directed themselves to deterrence. The recent study by N. Shover, W. B. Bankston, and W. J. Gurley, "Responses of the Criminal Justice System to Legislation Providing More Severe

Threatened Sanctions," *Criminology* 14, 4 (1977):483-99, included publicity in its deterrence model, but did not attempt to assess its specific role in deterrence. The studies by Schwartz and Savitz in Philadelphia referred to in notes 70 and 31 above, found that publicity had little apparent effect on crime rate. But these studies were seriously lacking in controls. See, for example, T. A. Knopf, "Media Myths on Violence," *Columbia Journalism Review* 9 (1970-71).

80. The use of individual data was especially important since it avoided the serious methodological problem of previous studies which suffered from an "auto regressive effect." See Trilling, "Publicity and Homicide."

Chapter 12: The Punishers and the Punished

1. See Erlanger, "Social Class and Corporal Punishment in Child Rearing," for an excellent review of all these studies in relationship, especially, to postulated class differences. In general, Erlanger concludes that there are no significant class differences in use of corporal punishment. That is, as I have suggested earlier, punishment is universal.

2. Eysenck, *Crime and Personality.*

3. J. L. Parker, "Introversion/Extraversion and Children's Aversion to Social Isolation and Corporal Punishment: A Note on a Failure to Replicate Eysenck," *Australian Journal of Psychology* 24, 2 (1972):141-43, found no support for this hypothesis.

4. Singer, "Psychological Studies of Punishment"; Shah, "Treatment of Offenders."

5. Sears, Whiting, Nowlis, Sears, "Some Child Rearing Antecedents of Aggression." There is recent research which suggests that this difference is changing and the lower class is resorting less often to physical punishment. In fact, Erlanger, "Social Class and Corporal Punishment in Child Rearing," has questioned whether the difference has ever been present. Nevertheless, the distinction continues between the two classes in that the middle class uses reasoning, encouragement, and explanations much more, whereas the lower class is more negative in its approach. Erlanger does affirm that lower-class blacks do use more physical punishment.

6. See, for example, the works of Wilhelm Reich, *The Mass Psychology of Fascism,* who sees the lower middle class as the most susceptible to punishment and the most repressed. Once again, however, changes are clearly in progress. The lower class still abides by a conventional sexual morality, whereas the middle class has become considerably more liberal, with demands that sexual relationships be "meaningful," involve "love," and so on.

7. F. Redl, *Children Who Hate* (Glencoe, Ill.: The Free Press, 1951).

8. S. Milgram, "Behavioral Study of Obedience," *Journal of Abnormal and Social Psychology* 67, 4 (1963):371-78. Also, S. Milgram, *Obedience to Authority: An Experimental View* (New York: Harper & Row, 1974).

9. M. Wenglinsky, "Review Essay," *Contemporary Sociology* 4, 6 (November 1975): 613-17.

10. Milgram, "Behavioral Study of Obedience."

11. P. Zimbardo, "Pathology of Punishment," *Trans-Action* 9 (1972):4-8.

12. "Plea bargaining" would not be an analogue to retributive punishment, since it is not conducted between persons of equal power. It will be remembered that there was a period during the early middle ages when feuding parties bargained for reciprocal punishments. See Chapter 6.

13. J. Piaget, *Moral Judgment of the Child,* trans. Marjorie Gabain (New York: The Free Press, 1965), p. 324.

14. F. Redl, *The Aggressive Child* (New York: Basic Books, 1963), pp. 472-87.

15. See H. Bleackely, *The Hangmen of England* (London: Chapman and Hall, 1929).

16. *Ibid.,* p. 26.

17. *Ibid.,* p. 55.

18. *Ibid.*
19. *Ibid.,* p. 114.
20. *Ibid.,* p. 127.
21. *Ibid.,* p. 190.
22. *Ibid.,* p. 196.
23. *Ibid.,* p. 231.
24. F. Fanon, *The Wretched of the Earth* (New York: The Grove Press, 1968), p. 265.
25. *Ibid.*
26. Hawkins, *The Prison,* p. 106.
27. H. E. Barnes and N. Teeters, *New Horizons in Criminology* (Englewood Cliffs, N. J.: Prentice-Hall, 1943), have referred to one aspect of this as "lock psychosis."
28. E. Fromm, *The Anatomy of Human Destructiveness* (New York: Holt, Rinehart and Winston, 1973).
29. Reich, *The Mass Psychology of Fascism.*
30. Hawkins, *The Prison,* p. 95.
31. F. Tannenbaum, *Wall Shadows: A Study in American Prisons* (New York: Putnam, 1922).
32. G. M. Sykes, *The Society of Captives* (Princeton, N. J.: Princeton University Press, 1958).
33. M. Weber, *Theory of Social and Economic Organization,* ed. T. Parsons (Glencoe, Ill.: The Free Press, 1966); G. Simmel, *The Sociology of George Simmel,* trans. K. Wolff (Glencoe, Ill.: The Free Press, 1950).
34. F. Redl, "Framework for our Discussions on Punishment," unpublished paper, 1976, p. 12.
35. This ploy was used with great success by the Yippie movement in the 1960s. See J. Rubin, *Do It!* (New York: Simon & Schuster, 1970).
36. Redl, *Aggressive Child,* p. 475.
37. R. D. Parke, "Some Effects of Punishment on Children's Behavior," in *The Young Child,* ed. W. W. Hartup (Washington, D.C.: Nat. Assoc. for Educ. Young Child., 1972), Vol. II, p. 280.
38. *Ibid.*
39. Sears, Whiting, Nowlis, and Sears, "Some Child Rearing Antecedents of Aggression."

Chapter 13: Conclusions: The Justice (and Grace) of Punishment

1. I have reviewed these criticisms, made mostly by anthropologists, in Chapter 2. See especially footnotes 2, 3, 4, and 5 of that chapter.
2. Dahrendorf reaches virtually identical conclusions in his analysis of the justice of inequality and the social order, and his is a strictly sociological analysis. After concurring with Kant's famous rejoinder to Rousseau (that inequality is a "rich source of much that is evil, but also of everything that is good"), Dahrendorf argues that a perfectly egalitarian society would be a nonhistorical society: "The very existence of social inequality is an impetus toward liberty because it guarantees a society's ongoing dynamic, historical quality. . . ." See R. Dahrendorf, *Essays in the Theory of Society* (Stanford, Calif.: Stanford University Press, 1968), pp. 151-78.
3. See Chapter 2.
4. March 1977.
5. See Reich, *The Mass Psychology of Fascism;* and W. C. Langer, *Mind of Adolf Hitler* (New York: Basic Books, 1972).
6. See, for example, Kropotkin, *Mutual Aid;* Marquis de Sade, *The Complete Marquis De Sade,* trans. Paul Gillette (Los Angeles: Holloway House, 1966).
7. For distinctions between social, political, and moral order, see, N. G. Runciman,

Relative Deprivation and Social Justice (Boston: Routledge & Kegan Paul), pp. 36-52.

8. Some psychoanalytical thinkers, such as Norman Brown, assume that repression is somehow inherently bad. Brown argues that civilization has turned life into death by denying death through repression. It is my view that the morality of evolution requires the affirmation of life by the affirmation of repression. If it weren't for repression, the human race would have either wiped itself out or been wiped out by nature long ago.

9. E. Sagan, *Cannibalism: Human Aggression and Cultural Form* (New York: Harper & Row, 1974).

10. *Ibid.*

11. By adopting this view, we are saved from the threatening argument of such people as Genet, who taunt us with the claim that crime creates morality. This is a cheap trick on Genet's part, since he consistently equates social order with moral order. See especially his play, *The Balcony.*

12. See Piaget, *The Moral Judgment of the Child.* One will see here that I have adopted Piaget's interactionist view of psychological development. Piaget, it will be noted, developed his interactionist view of psychological development out of his early studies as a biologist, when he observed the constant reciprocation between animal organisms and their environment.

13. Indeed, Fuller's analysis of the functions of reciprocity are strikingly similar to Piaget's analysis of reciprocity among children. See *ibid.;* L. Fuller, *The Morality of Law* (New Haven, Conn.: Yale University Press, 1964).

14. *Ibid.*

15. *Ibid.*

16. Marxists would, of course, claim that it is the other way around—that when the state "withers away," all that will be left will be a social order and not a political order. The authoritarian basis of all Communist societies clearly demonstrates that the reality is the reverse of the Marxist doctrine.

17. van den Haag, *Punishing Criminals.*

18. I mean here offenders who are not in prison. The question as to whether severe physical punishment of prisoners is legally permissible is open. It probably is permissible, certainly in those situations of strictly confined institutions. The resort to physical punishment is much more likely, since the structure of authority is closer to one of tyranny, so a primitive social order will be upheld by primitive punishments.

19. Ferri, *Criminal Sociology.* He calculates that 1,000 born criminals would have to be exterminated every year.

20. J. Genet, *The Balcony* and other works.

21. See J. M. J. Delgado, *Physical Control of the Mind* (New York: Harper & Row, 1971).

22. The problem of "false positives" does not arise in this system, since it does not permit the predictive punishment of a dangerous person until after he has committed an offense. The social defense doctrine I advance here is that society has the right to protect itself from dangerous persons, but the right is delimited by the retributive principle. Nor do I address myself here to the repeating petty offender, who perhaps makes up the bulk of the work for criminal justice personnel. I do not consider such offenders a threat to society. In fact, their repeated punishment reinforces the social order for reasons that I have outlined throughout this chapter. However, should the occasion arise when such offenders were seen as dangerous, then the predictive model would apply.

23. A. C. Schur, "The New Penology: Fact or Fiction?" *J. Criminal Law and Criminology* 49 (1958):331-34.

24. M. Lopez-Rey and C. Germain, eds., *Studies in Penology* (The Hague: Martinus Nijhoff, 1964).

25. J. L. Gillin, *Criminology and Penology* (New York: Appleton-Century Crofts, 1945), p. 376.
26. In fact, this is the approach taken in the groundbreaking study conducted by Professor Jack Kress and his associates, where reform is being centered on the judiciary, which is involved in every step of the reformative research. See J. M. Kress, L. T. Wilkins, and D. M. Gottfredson, "Is the End of Judicial Sentencing in Sight?," *Judicature* 60, 5 (1970):216-22.
27. Quoted in S. Freud, *Civilization and Its Discontents,* trans. James Strachey (New York: W. W. Norton, 1961), p. 57.

Index